Smoking and the Workplace

Smoking and the Workplace

Editor: **Roger Blanpain**

Contributors

Gordon Anderson
Kadriye Bakirci
Roger Blanpain
Michele Colucci
Alvin L. Goldman
Carin Håkansta
Paulo Sergio João
Asbjørn Kjønstad
Yaraslau Kryvoi
Birgitta Nyström
Fumiko Obata
Michael Ohle
Antonio Ojeda Avilés
Marianne Thyssen
Gijsbert van Liemt
Yvonne Waterman

KLUWER LAW
INTERNATIONAL

A C.I.P. catalogue record for this book is available from the Library of Congress.

ISBN 90-411-2325-3

Published by:
Kluwer Law International
P.O. Box 85889
2508 CN The Hague
The Netherlands

Sold and distributed in North, Central and South America by:
Aspen Publishers, Inc.
7201 McKinney Circle
Frederick, MD 21704
USA

Sold and distributed in all other countries by:
Extenza-Turpin Distribution Services
Stratton Business Park
Pegasus Drive
Biggleswade
Bedfordshire SG18 8TQ
United Kingdom

Printed on acid-free paper

Printed in the Netherlands.

Table of Contents

CONTENTS

Introduction

Tobacco smoking is a subject of an ongoing and heated debate in quite a number of international organisations and countries. Not without reason.

First of all, tobacco continues to provide work to millions of farmers in the agricultural sectors and to many workers in the industrial and service sectors. Moreover, for many, especially developing countries, tobacco in its various forms, constitutes an important share of exports and an important part of tax revenues. Tobacco is a thriving, prosperous and money making sector.

At the same time hundreds of millions of people smoke. And here the real problem starts. Smoking is more than bad for your health. In the last century alone, world-wide, more than 100 million people died prematurely due to tobacco smoking. More than that, smoking is also bad for the health of non-smokers. Hundreds of thousands die yearly due to passive smoking (second-hand smoke).

These facts are undeniable. Smoking is now one of the main health targets of the world. The international community got its act together. The WHO concluded (2003) after years of tough negotiations, an agreement on combating tobacco. Member countries are called upon to push the consumption of tobacco back.

Smoking is, however, still a major problem in many enterprises, where yearly thousands of workers die prematurely for reasons of passive smoking.

The solution to that problem is very simple: enterprises should be smoke-free. Indeed, everyone, workers included, is entitled to "pure air" as health is a fundamental right of prime importance. Strong legislation is thus called for. But this is not so easy to obtain.

First of all, a considerable group of people, albeit the minority continues to smoke since they are addicted, though many of them would like to quit. Nicotine is a very strong drug. The younger people are when they start smoking, the more difficult it is to give up. Smokers resist initiatives to install smoke-free enterprises, as well as some managers, who continue to smoke.

The social partners, employers' associations and trade unions are caught in the middle. They have smoking as well as non-smoking members. Moreover, the trade unions of tobacco workers fight for their jobs and the tobacco industry for plenty of money. The industry is a very powerful pressure group and lobby.

So, in some countries, the trade unions want to leave it up to the workers themselves in the workplace to deal with the problem in a friendly way, so called respecting each other, forgetting, however, that smokers are addicts.

Especially in the hospitality industry conservative forces to keep "smoking as usual" are strong, saying that a prohibition of smoking would kill the industry.

In some countries, however, trade unions have crossed that bridge. In Ireland, Norway and Sweden, the trade unions do not any longer take it that hundreds of their members die every year due to second-hand smoke in bars and restaurants.

Difficult areas, besides the hospitality sector, are mental institutions and prisons. Lately, Governor Schwarzenegger took measures to regulate smoking in California prisons.

So, in many countries, the legislator and health groups are struggling to get enterprises smoke-free, the hospitality sector included. Some have succeeded, like Ireland, New York, Norway and New Zealand, just to give a few examples. In many other countries legislation is being elaborated.

So, it is an accurate time to have a book on smoking and the enterprise, on what is going on regarding smoking and the workplace.

One thing is sure. Employers have the responsibility to introduce a policy of non-smoking in the enterprises. And this for many reasons; especially since they are responsible for the health of their collaborators and liable for the damages caused to their health e.g. as a result of passive smoking on the premises.

This Bulletin addresses this and related issues as well at International and European levels by looking at what is happening in not less than 15 countries from around the globe, loyal to its comparative vocation.

Roger Blanpain
Honorary President of the International Society
for Labour and Social Security Law

List of Contributors

Gordon Anderson is Associate Dean at the School of Law of the Victoria University of Wellington, New Zealand.

Kadriye Bakirci is Assistant Professor of Employment Law and Social Security at the Management Faculty of Istanbul Technical University, Turkey.

Roger Blanpain is Professor of Labour Law at the Universities of Leuven and Limburg (Belgium) and Tilburg (The Netherlands), Past President of the International Industrial Relations Association, Honorary President of the International Society for Labour and Social Security Law and member of the Royal Flemish Academy of Belgium.

Michele Colucci is researcher at the University of Salerno (Italy) and agent of the Legal Service of the European Commission.

Alvin L. Goldman is a Professor at the University of Kentucky, USA.

Carin Håkansta is a researcher at the National Institute for Public Health, Sweden.

Paulo Sergio João is Professor of Labour Law at the Catholic University of São Paulo and at the School of Administration of the Foundation Getulio Vargas, São Paulo, Brazil

Asbjørn Kjønstad has since 1978 been Professor of Law at the University of Oslo, Norway. His main areas of work have been health, welfare, and tort law, including constitutional protection and the protection of human rights in these areas.

Yaraslau Kryvoi is a Lecturer at the Belarusian State University, Belarus. He is a graduate of St Petersburg State University (Russia) and holds Joint LL.M degree with honours from universities of Nottingham (United Kingdom) and Utrecht (the Netherlands).

Birgitta Nyström is a Professor of Private Law at the University of Lund, Sweden.

Fumiko Obata is a Professor at Kyoto University, Japan. She teaches on health and safety and environmental law.

Michael Ohle is a trainee solicitor in Whitney Moore and Keller Solicitors, Dublin, Ireland. He is a graduate of Trinity College Dublin where he received a Bachelor of Arts in Economics. He also holds a postgraduate diploma in Legal Studies from Dublin Institute of Technology.

Antonio Ojeda Avilés is a Professor of Labour Law and Social Security at the University of Seville, Spain (www.personal.us.es/aojeda).

Marianne Thyssen is a Member of the European Parliament and Vice-President of the Group of the European People's Party and European Democrats

Gijsbert van Liemt (gbvanliemt@compuserve.com) is a self-employed international economist based in the Netherlands.

Yvonne Waterman is a personal injury lawyer at SAP Advocaten in Amersfoort, the Netherlands, where she is presently engaged in the first Dutch court case against a Dutch tobacco firm. She is also finishing a Ph.D on the comparative employer's liability for occupational accidents and diseases. Comments and queries are welcomed at yvonnewaterman@hotmail.com.

List of Abbreviations

ABVV	the Belgian General Federation of Labour
ACLVB	the Federation of Liberal Trade Unions of Belgium
ACV	the Confederation of Christian Trade Unions
ADA	Americans with Disabilities Act
AIDS	Acquired Immunodeficiency Syndrome
ANA	All Nippon Airlines
AR	Annual Report
ARAB	*the General Regulation on Health and Safety at Work*
ASH	Action on Smoking and Health
BAT	British American Tobacco
BLQA	Brazilian Life Quality Association
CCOO	Spanish Trade Union Federation
CDC	Centres for Disease Control and Prevention
CIS	International Occupational Safety and Health Centre
CNTC	China National Tobacco Corporation
DFT	De Financiële Telegraaf
ECOSOC	Economic and Social Council
ENSP	European Network for Smoking Prevention
ETI	*Ente Tabachi Italiani*
ETS	Environmental Tobacco Smoke
EU	European Union
FAO	Food and Agriculture Organisation
FCLAA	Federal Cigarette Labelling and Advertising Act
FCTC	Framework Convention on Tobacco Control
FDA	Food and Drug Administration
FELA	Federal Employers' Liability Act
FSU	Former Soviet Union
FT	Financial Times
FTSE 100	the most widely used index for benchmarking UK shares (the name comes from the original joint venture between Financial Times and London Stock Exchange)
FUW	Finanz und Wirtschaft
GDP	Gross Deficiency Product
GSA	General Services Administration
HIV	Human Immunodeficiency Virus
IAA	International Affairs Assessor
IALI	International Association of Labour Inspectorates
IARC	International Agency for Research on Cancer
ICCPR	International Covenant on Civil and Political Rights
ILO	International Labour Organisation
IOHC	International Occupational Health Commission
IPCS	International Programme on Chemical Safety
IPT	Industrialized Products' Tax

ISSE-CE	Industry's Social Service of Ceará
JAL	Japan Airlines
JAS	Japan Air System
JTB	Japan Travel Bureau
JTI	Japan Tobacco
JTS	Japan Tobacco and Salt Public Corporation
MSA	Master Settlement Agreement
NCCIFTC	National Commission of Implementation of the Convention – International Frame for Tobacco Control
NGO	Non-governmental Organisation
NICA	National Institute of Cancer
NOHSC	National Occupational Health and Safety Commission
NSASA	National Sanitary Surveillance Agency
NTUC	National Trade Union Congress
OECD	Organisation of Economic Co-operation and Development
OSHA	Occupational Safety and Health Act
OTC	Office of Tobacco Control
PM	Philip Morris
PTT	Dutch Post Office
SAS	Andalusian Health Service
SLIC	Senior Labour Inspection Committee
STMA	China's State Tobacco Monopoly
TJI	Tobacco Journal International
TUC	Trades Union Congress
UN	United Nations
UNDCP	United Nations Drug Control Programme
US	United States
USDA	United States Department of Agriculture
USDA/ERS	United States Department of Agriculture Economic Research Service
USSR	United Socialist Soviet Republic
VBO	the Federation of Belgian Enterprises
VEV	the Flemish Employers' Association
WHB	Western Health Board
WHO	World Health Organisation
WTO	World Trade Organisation

International and European Reports

1. Unloved but Highly Profitable: The World Tobacco Industry in the Early 21st Century

Gijsbert van Liemt

The world tobacco industry is under attack from many sides. The September 2004 lawsuit brought by the US Federal Government is but one in a long series of lawsuits. The industry finds it increasingly difficult to advertise its products. Ever-increasing taxes push up the price and discourage demand for these products. Concern over the risks to public health has reduced the space where smoking is allowed. To target young people, the industry's most promising group of customers, is now seen as unethical. Yet the tobacco industry continues to be highly profitable. Year after year the leading tobacco companies report a steady stream of profits.

INTRODUCTION

There are basically two ways[1] of looking at the world tobacco industry. The first takes a country perspective; the second a company perspective. When, some twenty years ago, over half the world market was closed to imports, foreign investment or both, the second perspective was not all that meaningful. But now that Japan, the Republic of Korea, Eastern Europe, the former Soviet Union (and soon China) have liberalised their markets and many former state monopolies have been sold, the company perspective is becoming increasingly relevant. As tobacco factories close in Australia, China, France, Italy, Malaysia, Nicaragua, Papua New Guinea, Russia, Spain and the United States – to name but a few – the tobacco multinationals are redrawing the world production map taking into account their own long-term strategies in addition to local demand and installed capacity.

World demand for tobacco products appears to be past its peak. For decades, highly motivated anti-smoking activists (a.k.a. pro-health advocates) have been trying to convince the authorities and the public at large of the harmful consequences of smoking tobacco products and of the need to reduce demand. Success has come slowly. The adoption in 2003 of the WHO's Framework Convention on Tobacco Control (FCTC – *see* section 3.3) was a milestone. Their long battle has been good for the legal profession. As a result of the Master Settlement Agreement (MSA) alone (see section 2.3), the industry

---

[1] A third way would be to see how the industry is divided by product. But since by far the greatest share of world tobacco is used for making cigarettes we will concentrate on that product.

R. Blanpain (ed.), Smoking and the Workplace, 3–24
© 2005 *Gijsbert van Liemt. Printed in The Netherlands.*

will pay US lawyers US$ 500 million per year for 25 years. Governments are also receiving hefty sums. US states are guaranteed to receive over US$ 200,000 million as part of the MSA. In 2004, the European Union settled with *Philip Morris* for US$ 1,000 million the lawsuit it had brought against the major multinationals for their alleged role in cigarette smuggling. Yet the tobacco multinationals have been and continue to be highly profitable.

Their "secret" lies on the cost side. Every year brings new mergers and acquisitions (*see* section 2). The number of players active in the industry continues to go down. The remaining ones are getting bigger and bigger. Acquisitions enable them to realise economies of scale; rationalize distribution and marketing; concentrate production at fewer locations; rationalize the supplier base; and so continuously lower unit cost. And consolidation is far from over.

Litigation continues to be a threat, of course, especially in the United States. There is always the risk that a multi-billion dollar verdict will be upheld on appeal. But the companies argue that so far they have been able to manage the challenge of litigation (nonetheless, as a precaution they are separating their US operations from those in the rest of the world). Their confidence is not unrelated to the fact that governments now have a stake in the survival and the continued prosperity of the tobacco industry. The MSA foresees payments to American states over a period of 25 years. The 2004 settlement between *Philip Morris* and the European Union foresees payments spread over 12 years. These payments can only be made as long as the companies involved continue to be active.

This chapter is organized as follows. Section 1 looks at the world tobacco industry from a country perspective: where are the main markets and the main production locations, how does international trade flow? A subsection considers how China, where one-third of the world's cigarettes are being smoked, is preparing itself for the arrival of the multinationals following its accession to the World Trade Organisation (WTO). Section 2 takes a company perspective: how do the remaining large companies cope with stagnating world demand? A subsection deals with the threat of litigation. Section 3 discusses what governments do to limit the harm that smoking does to public health. Section 4 discusses how increases in productivity, concentration of production and stagnant demand together lead to a declining number of jobs in the industry.

1.   THE COUNTRY PERSPECTIVE: CONSUMPTION, PRODUCTION, AND INTERNATIONAL TRADE

1.1   The cigarette

Cigarettes are the most popular type of smoking tobacco. They are machine made, but an important (sub-market) segment consists of roll-your-own cigarettes. Other types of smoking tobacco are cigars and pipe tobacco, *bidis* (which are popular in India),[2] *cheroots*,[3] and *kreteks*[4] (popular in Indonesia). In India and Indonesia only a minority of smokers smokes (white) cigarettes. Until the

---

[2]   *Bidis* consist of a small amount of tobacco wrapped in *temburni* leaf and tied with a small string.
[3]   Small cigars made of heavy-bodied tobacco; they have no wrapper and contain a single binder.
[4]   Indigenous cheroots containing tobacco, cloves and cocoa.

1870s, cigarettes were rolled by hand, but since then, they are made by machines. Thanks to these machines, which can produce thousands of sticks per minute, cigarettes became an article of mass consumption. Today, over 80% of tobacco grown is used for cigarettes (FAO, 1990).

There are basically four types of cigarettes: Virginia; "American" blend; dark; and oriental cigarettes. The latter two, dark (traditionally popular in French, Spanish, and Portuguese speaking countries) and oriental (traditionally popular in the Eastern Mediterranean, Eastern Europe and the (former) USSR) are losing ground to the first two. Virginia (or "English") cigarettes are popular in the UK and in its former colonies. The American blend is currently the most popular type of cigarettes (FAO, 1990; Gale *et al.*, 2000)

1.2. Consumption

Until 1990 the world tobacco industry had been growing at a steady pace.[5] Between 1970 and 1990 world cigarette consumption increased by over 50%. After 1990, demand for cigarettes slowed down. OECD markets are in decline but non-OECD markets continue to grow. Opinions are divided as to whether or not growth in the latter group of countries outweighs decline in the former group (smuggling and the sale of counterfeit goods make it difficult to estimate world demand trends with precision). World cigarette production in 2001 was roughly at the same level as ten years earlier. "American Blend" cigarettes are gaining in market share.

Overall demand for cigarettes is determined by the number of smokers and by the number of cigarettes each of them smokes. In turn, these figures are influenced by the price of the product, real incomes, and government efforts to discourage consumption (*see* section 3). Retail price increases and declining real incomes have a negative effect on demand for tobacco products. This may, but need not lead to a reduction in the number of cigarettes consumed. People may simply buy cheaper cigarettes ("downtrading"). They buy local instead of imported cigarettes; popular instead of premium brands.

Structural and cultural factors also play a role. On the whole, the average cigarette smoker is likely to have a low rather than a high income, to have below average years of education, and to be male rather than female (but prevalence among women is on the increase). More cigarettes are consumed per capita in developed than in less developed countries (but the gap between the two groups of countries is narrowing).

In 2003, the Asia-Pacific region made up 53% of total world demand of 5,500 billion units (1990: 50%), with China alone taking up 30%; Eastern Europe stood at 14% in 2003 (1990: 12%), the Americas at 13% (1990: 18%), Western Europe at 12% (12%); and Africa and the Middle East at 8% (7%) (Altadis AR, 2003). The decline in the Americas is due above all to declining demand in the United States where per capita demand peaked around 1960, and total demand has been declining since the 1980s (FUW, 23.3.2002). Today some 8% of world demand originates in the US.

Marlboro is the world's leading brand. In 2003, 474 billion units of *Marlboro* cigarettes were sold. This represents 8% of the world market or 12·5%

---

[5]   For more elaborate data on production, consumption and trade *see* van Liemt, 2002.

of the world market outside China. The second most important brand (*Mild Seven*) has a more modest market share: it sells 120 billion units worldwide (JTI, AR 2003).

1.3   Production

Half the world's cigarette production originates in Asia. China alone produces 30% of the world total. Europe, the former USSR and North America produce 20, 12 and 10% of the world total respectively.[6] The United States has seen a sharp decline in output since the mid-1990s. In 2002 US cigarette output was 532 billion cigarettes, down from 755 bn in 1996. Declining domestic demand was a factor but the main cause was that exports halved from 244 bn pieces in 1996 to 120 bn in 2002 (USDA/ERS).

China plays a key role in the world tobacco industry. It accounts for 30% of world demand for cigarettes. Its share of world tobacco production is even higher. Domestic demand growth is slow; more and more anti-smoking laws are being introduced. But because of the huge size of the Chinese market (between 300 and 350 million people smoke cigarettes), foreign tobacco companies are more than keen to sell their products there.

1.3.1   Opening up the Chinese market

When China became a member of the World Trade Organization in 2001 it agreed to open up its domestic cigarette market. Tariffs on cigarette imports were scheduled to come down to 25% in 2004. Several joint ventures with foreign companies have been announced or are already in operation. Chinese manufacturers will have to compete at home with the multinationals and their superior financial resources; great marketing, production and distribution skills; well-known brand names; and long marketing experience. At first sight, this should not pose a problem; given its huge size, one might expect China to have a fairly well consolidated market with some highly efficient, well-known producers ready to take on the multinationals. But the Chinese market is highly fragmented. If the experience of previously closed markets such as Russia (where most cigarettes sold now come from the multinationals) or Poland (where these companies occupy 97% of the market) is anything to go by, there is reason to assume that the world's leading brands will soon be occupying a sizeable share of the Chinese market.

China's central government saw the need for domestic consolidation early on. Overcapacity is a big problem. At the end of 2002, China's cigarette manufacturing capacity was 3,060 billion pieces, while output was only 1,720 billion – over 40% of manufacturing capacity was left idle (Zhao, 2003). The tobacco trade and industry in China is controlled by a state monopoly (STMA) and run by the China National Tobacco Corporation (CNTC). In 2001, the STMA selected, through public appraisal, 36 cigarette brands from 29 manufactures as Nationally Known Brands. The Beijing authorities wanted these brands to be available throughout China (TJI 2/2002). In actual fact, however, the

---

[6]   Figures for 2001; source USDA-FAS, 2002.

Chinese market remains highly fragmented with hundreds of brands, few of which are known outside of their home province. This fragmentation has much to do with the financial contribution that cigarette factories make to provincial governments (*see* Box 1).

Box: 1 China's fragmented market facilitates the penetration by foreign brands

In anticipation of China's WTO accession, the Chinese central authorities wanted to have in place some highly efficient producers with nationally known brands selling high quality cigarettes capable of competing successfully with the foreign-owned multinationals. Provincial governments opposed these plans because they rely to a significant extent on the taxes contributed by "their" producers. In five provinces tax and profits generated by the tobacco industry account for over 20% of local government fiscal revenue. In eight provinces, they account for 10–20%.

China's State Tobacco Monopoly (STMA) has been trying to close or merge the small-scale manufacturers. In late 2002, there were 123 cigarette manufacturers in operation. One third of these produce fewer than five billion pieces per year. Only four produce over 50 billion pieces (the minimum economic scale is considered to be 15 billion pieces per year). There have been some mergers, but all of these were between manufacturers within the same province. Changing cigarette production quota is tantamount to reallocating fiscal revenues. Cigarette makers that did shut down saw their production quotas reallocated to other manufacturers within the same province (source: Zhao, 2003).

1.4   International trade

A sizeable share of world tobacco and cigarette production is traded internationally. Cigarette producers make intensive use of domestic tobaccos. Nonetheless, around 30% of world tobacco production (mainly high quality tobacco) is traded internationally. There are several reasons for this. First, some large tobacco growing countries (Malawi, Zimbabwe, Tanzania) manufacture few tobacco products of their own. In contrast, some important cigarette and cigar producing countries do not grow any tobacco domestically. The Netherlands (one of the world's top cigarette and cigar exporters) is a case in point. Others (e.g. Japan) do not produce enough to satisfy domestic demand. A third reason is that most cigarettes sold today are blended cigarettes, i.e. they contain a mixture of different types of tobacco. Few cigarette-producing countries grow all of these types.

The international cigarette trade displays a varied picture. The Chinese smoke almost exclusively domestically produced cigarettes. In other countries, domestic demand is also mainly satisfied by domestic production but, in addition, they are sizeable exporters. The United States is a good example. It exports one-fourth of its production. Yet other countries export most of their production. In 2001, UK production was 126 billion pieces out of which 100 billion pieces were exported. The Netherlands exported an even greater share of production: 104 billion pieces out of total production of 120 billion pieces.[7] A last category consists of countries that rely to a significant extent on imports to satisfy domestic demand. Examples are Japan (where imports make up 25% of domestic demand) and countries in the Middle East that do not have any production of their own. Russia was a main importer in the 1990s but has become virtually self sufficient in cigarettes since.

The analysis of world trade and production by country is but one way of looking at how the world tobacco industry develops. As a result of privatisation, consolidation, and the elimination of barriers to international trade and investments, the strategic considerations of a small group of multinational companies increasingly determine the location of production, and the volume and direction of international trade and investment flows. Section 2 discusses these strategies.

2. CORPORATE STRATEGIES

The OECD-based tobacco companies have reacted to stagnating demand in mature markets in basically three ways: consolidation, diversification, and increasing productivity. Consolidation and diversification is the subject of this section. Productivity is discussed in section 4.2.

2.1 Consolidation

Consolidation can make a critical contribution to profitability through the synergies and cost savings that can be achieved in marketing ("global" brands), manufacturing and distribution. Best practices are being applied across the group. Materials, products and packs are being standardised. The supplier base is being rationalized. Market power *vis-à-vis* suppliers and subcontractors increases.[8] The cost savings can be considerable. *Imperial Tobacco* calculated that its acquisition of *Reemstma* delivered 150 million GBP of synergy in 2003, its first year of consolidation, and that this would increase to 210 Million GBP in 2004. Expected synergies of the 2004 merger of *RJReynolds* and *Brown & Williamson* into *Reynolds American* is expected to build to US$ 550–600 by 2006 (FT, 16/9/04).

Consolidation in the tobacco industry had been taking place for quite some time, but it accelerated in the 1990s. Also, the size of the "deals" became steadily bigger. The most recent wave saw the take over of companies which

---

[7]   Source: USDA. In cigars, a comparable situation exists. The Netherlands is the second largest cigar manufacturer in the world behind the US. It exports close to 80% of production (TJI 6/2003).

[8]   Just like the cigarette manufacturers, their suppliers (the leaf dealers; the machinery and paper producers) must also cope with the consequences of stagnant demand for tobacco products. In reaction, they have rationalized production and raised productivity in an effort to maintain profitability. And they, too, have become involved in mergers and acquisitions. They want to become global players in their own right. This ties in neatly with the strategies of the tobacco multinationals. Similar to what is occurring in other industries (*see* e.g. van Liemt, 1998) the tobacco companies seek to do business with fewer suppliers but in the framework of long-term agreements.

themselves had already expanded outside of their home market. *British American Tobacco (BAT)* acquired *Rothmans* in 1999. That year also saw the merger of *Seita* of France and *Tabacalera* of Spain to become *Altadis*. *Austria Tabak* took over the cigarette activities of *Swedish Match* in 1999, and was then taken over by *Gallaher* in 2001. After an impressive shopping spree in Central and Eastern Europe, Germany's *Reemtsma*[9] was taken over by *Imperial Tobacco* in 2002. In 2003 *Philip Morris International* acquired Greece's *Papastratos Cigarette Company* (which also has operations in Romania). Many former state monopolies (such as Portugal's *Tabaquiera*) have come under the control of the multinationals. In the process, the degree of concentration of the industry continued to go up. In 2003, three companies *CNTC*[10] at 30%; *Philip Morris* at 17%, and *BAT*[11] at 15% controlled close to two-thirds of world cigarette production. They were followed by *Japan Tobacco (JTI)* with 8%, *Imperial* with 3.5%, and *Altadis, Gallaher* and *RJReynolds* (with around 2% each). Together these eight companies control around 80% of the world market.

In many countries the state monopoly was the exclusive producer and/or seller of tobacco products. One after the other these companies were privatised and absorbed by multinationals or would-be multinationals (Japan Tobacco is the exception; it became a major multinational in its own right – *see* Box 2). At first called in to supply farming advice, and manufacturing and marketing know-how, the multinationals would soon enter into joint ventures with or take an equity stake in the state-controlled companies. They often ended up taking over the whole company when local investors were unwilling or unable to finance the investments needed to reach the high levels of quality and productivity required to compete internationally.

For many of the privatised or soon to be privatised companies, collaboration with the large tobacco companies was essential for survival. The monopolies were usually far from "lean and mean". Trade liberalization often accompanied privatisation, forcing them to face two challenges simultaneously: they had to compete and do so in a more open environment. Collaboration helped them to modernise their production facilities; introduce modern distribution, management information and control systems; and provide training for their employees. The stronger financial position of the new parent company enabled them to invest in the replacement of assets, and in information technology. Lastly, the transfer of know-how helped them to reduce tobacco waste, achieve higher tobacco blend homogeneity, reduce cigarette weight variation, and lower energy consumption. Companies that did not modernise saw their market share decline, ran into financial problems, and risked cessation of business.

---

[9] As a result of a relentless internationalisation drive, Reemtsma saw its dependence on its German home market drop from two-thirds in 1991 to one-third in 1999. It purchased Tobacco Ljubljana in Slovenia in 1991; the Hungarian cigarette factory at Debreccenin in 1992; Slovak International Tabak in 1993; the Ukranian cigarette factories at Cherkassy and Kiew in 1994 and a majority in what became Reemtsma Polska in 1996. In 1998 it set up Central Asian market joint ventures in Kyrgyzstan and Kazakhstan, purchased a Russian factory in Volograd and the Macedonian Factory in Skopje; and in 1999 a majority in Cambodia«s Paradise Tobacco factory (TJI, 1/2002).

[10] Whether CNTC fully controls China's tobacco industry is a matter is a matter of dispute (*see* Box 1).

[11] i.e. before it spun-off of its US subsidiary *Brown and Williamson*.

Box 2: Japan Tobacco: From Government Bureau to major Multinational

Japan Tobacco was originally a government bureau. In 1949, it was incorporated as the Japan Tobacco and Salt Public Corporation (JTS) to act as the country's sole producer and supplier of tobacco and sole purchaser and supplier of salt products. In the 1970s, JTS came under pressure. On the one hand, demand for cigarettes slowed down. On the other, the US government exercised strong pressure on the Japanese government to open up the domestic market. JTS thus needed to become more efficient but it was handicapped by its status as a public corporation. Its operating budget and capital investments were approved by the government strictly on an annual basis (thus making long-term planning difficult). Diversification was prohibited. JTS was obliged to purchase all domestically grown tobacco, of which there was a substantial surplus and which was significantly more expensive than foreign-grown leaf tobacco.

A legal change enabled the establishment of Japan Tobacco Inc. that took over all of JTS' business and assets. The monopoly system for the sale of tobacco was abolished and the Japanese market was opened to foreign cigarettes. In the mid-1990s JT was listed on the stock exchange. The salt business was transferred to a separate entity. Since 1998, JT has been seeking to diversify. It made acquisitions in pharmaceuticals, vending machines, and food. In 1999, it acquired the non-US tobacco operations of *RJR Nabisco*. Even so, tobacco (with over 90% of sales), and especially domestic tobacco (with 77%) remain its main business. In 2002 the Japanese government reduced its part of JT's shares from two-thirds to one-half (source: Japan Tobacco, AR 2003)

2.2   Diversification

In addition to taking over competitors, the tobacco multinationals try to become less dependent on their traditional, stagnant markets through diversification. This has several dimensions: diversification (1) by market segment; (2) by target group; (3) by tobacco product; (4) by non-tobacco product; and (5) by geographical region. In part (and sometimes in large part) diversification has been achieved through mergers and acquisitions (*see* section 2.1 above).

(1) *Diversification by market segment*. Cigarettes are sold in different categories, from the premium, highly priced, high-margin category to the brandless ("generic"), low-margin type. The high margins of the premium cigarettes make them attractive to produce and sell. But by also offering cigarettes in the B- and C-category, companies reduce their vulnerability when customers "trade down", i.e. when they decide to buy cheaper rather than more expensive cigarettes.

(2) *Diversification by tobacco product*. Imperial Tobacco has targeted the roll-your-own market for expansion. It dominates both the supply of tobacco and that of cigarette paper for this market, and so benefits from smokers who shift to roll-your-own as a result of "downtrading". *Altadis* became the world's leader in premium cigars through a string of acquisitions.

(3) *Diversification by target group.* Women and young people are prime target groups. The proportion of smokers among women is lower than that among men. A manufacturer can raise its overall market share by successfully targeting women. Many women see smoking as a symbol of women's liberation. Manufacturers promote their cigarettes as a symbol of emancipation and independence. Some women believe that smoking keeps them slim. Manufacturers produce long, slim cigarettes especially for their female customers (Corrao *et al.*, 2000).

Young people are the other promising category of potential smokers from the companies' point of view. Most people start smoking when they are young. Nonetheless, while targeting young people makes good commercial sense, it has become highly controversial. The smoking habits of young people have moved to the centre of the debate on smoking and health. Teenagers are considered to be too young to properly assess the long-term consequences of smoking on health. Many of the actions aimed at discouraging demand for tobacco products (*see* section 3) target youth (no ads in youth magazines; no pictures of young people in ads; no TV ads early in the evening; retail access control and education programmes). The tobacco multinationals have stated publicly that they are sensitive to the debate surrounding young smokers. In many countries tobacco companies no longer advertise their products to a young audience. It is uncertain, however, to what extent young people pick up their more general adverts.

(4) *Diversification by non-tobacco product.* Food products are a favourite for tobacco companies seeking to diversify. *R.J. Reynolds* bought *Nabisco* (which, in turn, was later acquired by *Kraft*). *Philip Morris* (now: *Altria*) diversified into food (*Kraft*) and beer (*Miller*). *Japan Tobacco* derives a small part of its sales from food (frozen food, seasoning and bakery items). It has targeted pharmaceuticals as one of its future cash flow generators.

Logistics and wholesaling are other favourites. Through its purchase of *Austria Tabak, Gallaher* entered food distribution. Over 20% of *Altadis'* earnings originate in its logistics division. *Skandinavisk Tobakskompagni* owns the largest wholesaler of consumer goods in Denmark. With the takeover of Italy's *Ente Tabachi Italiani (ETI) BAT* became the owner of *ETINARA*, the subsidiary responsible for distributing *ETI*'s products (in 2004 *Etinara* was sold to *Altadis*). Diversification into food and other activities makes tobacco companies less dependent on the market for tobacco products. But producing and marketing cigarettes remain more profitable activities.

(5) *Diversification by geographical market.* After having "conquered" Latin America, Central and Eastern Europe, and the Central Asian republics in the 1990s, the focus of the OECD-based multinationals shifted to the Far East (and to a lesser extent Africa). *Altadis* now has a 12% market share in Cambodia; it became the dominant force in Morocco. *Austria Tabak* had a 67% market share in Guinea. *BAT* is building factories in Viet Nam and the Republic of Korea.

Thanks to diversification, the cost savings that follow from consolidation and their improved bargaining power *vis-à-vis* suppliers, the remaining companies continue to be profitable despite stagnating world demand. Few sectors have been as consistently profitable as tobacco processing. Over the period 1997–2003 *Imperial Tobacco* tripled its profits; compound earnings per share growth was 18% in that period (Imperial Tobacco, AR 2003). Among the 150 largest US companies, *Philip Morris* was the only one with average earnings growth per share of over 15% per year for the period 1960–99 and for each of the sub periods (1960–80; 1970–90; and 1980–99) (FUW 25/4/01). Shares in tobacco companies have proven to be excellent investments outperforming those of almost any other sector. Between 1998 and 2003, the value of a 100 GBP investment in *Gallaher Group* would have nearly doubled. The same hypothetical investment in the FTSE 100 (the most widely used index for benchmarking UK shares) would have resulted in a small loss. Over the same period, the total return of *Imperial Tobacco's* share was two-and-a-half times that of the FTSE 100.

2.3   Litigation

There is, however, one dark cloud on the horizon: litigation. Around the world, the tobacco industry is involved in hundreds of lawsuits.[12] Most of these take place in US courts. Most of the defendants are the large US companies. The compensatory and punitive damages claimed involve billions of US dollars, potentially threatening the very survival of the industry.[13] In the Engle case in Florida, the first collective ("class action") lawsuit to go to trial in the US, the claims for damages amounted to 144,000 million US dollars. The United States Federal government wants the US tobacco companies to forfeit US$ 280,000 million of past profits.

Tobacco litigation began in 1954. At first, plaintiffs had been individuals or groups of individuals suffering from smoking-related illnesses, or relatives of people who had died from such illnesses. In the late 1970s, plaintiff's lawyers began to seek discovery (mainly internal documents and employee testimony) from the defendants, to file multiple cases, and to cooperate among themselves. In the mid-1990s, provincial and state governments and health care insurance companies also started to sue the industry in an attempt to recover the costs of the treatment of smoking-related illnesses (Altria; Ciresi *et al.*, 1999). In 1999, the US Federal Government filed a lawsuit of its own against various cigarette manufacturers.[14]

Tobacco litigation is spreading to other countries but at a reduced scale. Its impact is less. Courts outside the US have been reluctant to hear this kind of case. "Class action" suits are not common in legal systems outside the US. Also, when compensatory damages are awarded they are typically well below US levels. In Europe, punitive damages are rarely awarded. This makes it less attractive for European lawyers than for US lawyers to start a lawsuit (US lawyers typically receive some 30% of the sum awarded). Also, the litigation

---

[12]   For an overview of the different types of suits, the arguments of the plaintiffs and the defence, as well as progress in the courts, visit the Altria website and *see* Philip Morris' Annual Reports/Notes to Consolidated Financial Settlements/Contingencies/Overviews of Tobacco-related Litigation.

[13]   To Keirse (2000), the tobacco industry's "never give in" strategy must be seen in the light of what happened to the US asbestos industry, where none of the main players survived. As of the end of 2002, 730,000 individuals had filed lawsuits against more than 8,400 defendants. Eighty-five corporations have filed for bankruptcy due to asbestos liabilities (White, 2004).

[14]   This case is going to trial in September 2004. It is not being brought as a product liability suit but under the 1970 Racketeer-Influenced and Corrupt Organisations (RICO) Act, designed to fight organised crime.

threshold in product liability cases is much higher in Europe, where unsuccessful plaintiffs may have to pay the defendants' legal costs as well as their own (Bergkamp and Hunter, 1996; White, 2004).

The companies consider that the threat of litigation is of manageable proportions.[15] The vast majority of the cases have been dismissed.[16] The verdict has gone against the tobacco companies in very few cases (these are being appealed). Some cases have been settled out of court (e.g. the 1997 US flight attendants case; the 2004 EU-Philip Morris settlement; and the MSA, *see* Box 3). But the perceived risk of litigation depresses the share price.[17] Litigation also gives the industry a poor image, a serious matter for companies that rely so much on the "feel good" factor in the marketing of their products. The tobacco companies want to be seen as good corporate citizens.[18]

Box 3. The US Master Settlement Agreement (MSA)

On 23 November 1998, the major US cigarette manufacturers signed an agreement with attorneys general representing 46 states, the District of Colombia, and the five US territories to settle all the state lawsuits seeking to recover the Medicaid costs of treating smokers. As part of this "Master Settlement", the cigarette manufacturers agreed to pay the states[19] US$ 206,000 million over 25 years to compensate them for the costs of treating smoking-related illnesses and to fund anti-smoking programmes. They also agreed to earmark US$ 1,450 million for anti-smoking campaigns; and US$ 250 million for setting up a national public health foundation to work towards deterring minors and youths from smoking. And they agreed to limitations on advertising and to limits on sporting event sponsorship. As part of the MSA, they are committed to work cooperatively with the tobacco growers' community to address concerns about the potential impact of the MSA on that community (Source: various).

---

[15] "We have demonstrated our ability to manage difficult litigation challenges ... the number of cases waiting to be heard in court today is the same or fewer than it was five years ago" comments William Ohlemeyer, vice-president and associate general counsel of Philip Morris (in TJI 3/2003 p. 31).

[16] Of the 3,000–4,000 lawsuits filed against *Philip Morris* fewer than 50 have gone to trial and the company has lost only six, plus the Engle case. An appeals court has, so far, never upheld a jury verdict against it (Buckley, 2002).

[17] It can be asked how justified this is. Through drastic price increases, the US tobacco companies were able to pass on to their customers the cost involved in the Master Settlement Agreement (Box 3). According to Gruber (2002), the price rise over 1997 and 1998 even exceeded the amount required to pay the costs of state settlements and, given the highly inelastic demand for cigarettes, may have actually increased the industry's profits (leading Gruber to wonder whether a 45 cents per pack tax on cigarettes would not have been better social policy).

[18] The industry has offered to lend support to the World Health Organization (WHO) in its fight to eradicate malaria and in AIDS prevention, and to finance International Labour Organization (ILO) projects to combat child labour.

[19] Earlier, the industry had settled with four states – Mississippi, Florida, Texas and Minnesota – for a total of more than US 40,000 million US dollars, payable over 25 years. The US Federal Government was not a party to the Master Settlement.

Despite the optimistic tone of their public statements on the threat of litigation in the US, the tobacco multinationals appear to be quietly preparing for the worst-case scenario. They are separating their US operations from their non-US operations. In 1999, *RJR International* was split off from *RJ Reynolds'* US activities and merged with *Japan Tobacco*. In 2003, *BAT* decided to merge its US subsidiary *Brown and Williamson* with *RJR* to become *Reynolds American*. Philip Morris *USA* and Philip Morris *International* are separate business units and, according to FUW (5/6/04), may well become independent companies soon.

3.   GOVERNMENTS AND TOBACCO

Governments face a dilemma. On the one hand, the growing, processing and sales of tobacco and tobacco products make a contribution (and sometimes a considerable contribution) to tax revenue, foreign exchange receipts and employment (discussed in the next section). On the other hand, governments have a duty to protect the health of their citizens. Smoking can be harmful to health. Treating people for smoking-related illnesses is expensive. Heated debates have taken place within the same government as different departments defend the interests they believe they should represent. How do governments cope with these conflicting pressures?

3.1.   Tax income, foreign exchange earnings and direct foreign investment

The economic importance of tobacco growing and processing differs from country to country. Cigarette (sales and import) tax can be a main source of government revenue. In Russia, cigarette tax revenue contributes around 8% to the state budget (TJI 6/99). At the sub-national level, this contribution can be even higher. In several Chinese provinces tobacco contributes over 20% to the budget (*see* Box 1).

  When the government owns the industry, it receives profits in addition to tax. That is a reason why, in several countries, State monopolies continue to control cigarette trade and production. In China, CNTC has been the Chinese State's top revenue generator for years. In 2001, the industry contributed 115 bn Yuan (US$ 13,900) in taxes (up from US$ 11,000 in 1999 – TJI 2/2003). Japan Tobacco earned over US$ 400 million for the Japanese State in the fiscal year ending March 2000 (BW, 28 May 2001). The monopolies can also play a social role. In Italy, several *ETI* factories were located in structurally weak areas.

  Then there is the balance of payments to consider: many low-income countries rely on the export of cash crops such as tobacco to pay for the service of their foreign debt. Tobacco exports make up close to 10% of Cuba's exports. For Tanzania this is 15%, and for Zimbabwe over 25%. In Malawi tobacco exports make up two-thirds of commodity exports.[20]

---

[20]   Figures for 1997–98. Source: UNCTAD, 2000.

People smoke, but whether they smoke domestically produced cigarettes using homegrown tobacco or use imported cigarettes and tobaccos can make a world of difference when foreign exchange is scarce. It is a reason why many countries were keen to limit the importation of cigarettes and encourage domestic producers to use local types of tobacco.

The tobacco companies have also been a prime source of investment in the formerly centrally planned countries of Central and Eastern Europe, and Central Asia. When others were reluctant to invest, they saw the possibilities offered by a combination of pent-up consumer demand, outdated production facilities and the association with "freedom" and "western style" living that so appealed to the people there. The companies have been successful in their lobbying to "open up" previously closed Asian markets such as Japan, the Republic of Korea and China.

3.2. Public health

Tobacco growing and tobacco processing may bring economic and social benefits, but the treatment of smoking-related illnesses is costly. Cigarette smoking causes cancer. It is addictive. The WHO estimates that tobacco products cause around three million deaths per year. Cigarette smoking is the major cause of preventable mortality in developed countries. Among men aged 35–69 years, more than one-third of all deaths are caused by smoking. The costs of treating all these people are enormous (WHO, 1997).

So far, smoking has not had the same impact on mortality among women and among people from developing countries. There is an approximate 30–40 year time lag between the onset of persistent smoking and deaths from smoking. The effects of the greater incidence of smoking among these two groups will thus be felt with a lag, but the impact is unlikely to differ fundamentally from the impact it is having on developed country males.

It can be argued that smokers willingly take a certain health risk when enjoying their smoke. They like the taste and the other things that they associate with smoking. But this does not apply to environmental tobacco smoke (ETS) or "second-hand tobacco smoke". Smoke gets in your eyes; in your clothes; and in your lungs. Non-smokers cannot escape from tobacco smoke in badly ventilated areas. This is both a nuisance and a health risk.

3.3. The way out of the dilemma

Faced with conflicting pressures, governments have tended to follow several strategies often simultaneously (making it difficult to assess the effectiveness of each). A recent strategy consists of seeking compensation for the costs of treating smoking-related illnesses (*see* section 2.3). Governments also set rules regarding the maximum content of hazardous substances in cigarettes. Most of all, however, governments try to discourage demand for what is, as the industry does not tire of telling us, essentially a legal product. Governments' rules on smoking are becoming ever more restrictive. Their efforts received a boost from the adoption on 21 May 2003 of the Framework Convention on Tobacco Control (*see* Box 4).

Box 4: The WHO's Framework Convention on Tobacco Control (FCTC)

The FCTC is the world's first public health treaty. It was unanimously adopted by the 192 member states of the World Health Organization (WHO) in May 2003. The Convention is a binding legal instrument (for the states that have ratified it). It will enter into force once it has been ratified by 40 countries.

The FCTC covers key areas of tobacco control including bans on advertising; the placement of health warning messages; prevention of youth smoking; protection from exposure to tobacco smoke in workplaces and public places; measures to combat smuggling; and increased tobacco taxes. The FCTC obliges contracting parties to develop and implement a national tobacco control strategy; to protect relevant public health policies from commercial and other vested interests of the tobacco industry; to afford each other legal assistance; to exchange research findings and other relevant information; and to promote economically viable alternatives for tobacco workers and growers.

Some of these provisions were already being implemented nationally before the adoption of the FCTC. But it was considered necessary to have an *international* treaty because of the international nature of the industry's main players, and because developing countries are widely seen as the most vulnerable when it comes to containing the marketing efforts of the multinationals. In addition, certain problems are typically transboundary in nature and need an international approach. These include marketing via satellite television and smuggling (source: various).

Governments discourage the use of tobacco products in several ways. They insist on:

- Limitations of the space where smoking is allowed to protect non-smokers from involuntary exposure to tobacco smoke. Smoking is being prohibited in public places (particularly health care and educational facilities), in mass transport and in workplaces. Legislation requires restaurants to reserve space for non-smokers (*see* e.g. Håkansta, 2004).
- Limitations by age group. It is prohibited to sell tobacco products to people under a certain age.
- Limitations on points of sale. The use of vending machines is being restricted when these cannot distinguish between young and adult customers.
- Health warnings stating that tobacco is harmful to health must be placed on packets and in ads, with the authorities prescribing the text and the minimum space allotted to the warning in the ad or on the packet (*see* e.g. Box 5).
- Education. Governments sponsor education and public information programmes on smoking and health.
- Advertising bans. Restrictions concern the location of ads, the media used (no billboards, no ads in the printed media or in cinemas), the images presented (no young people, no cigarette packets), and the time when broadcasting is allowed (not during hours when children watch television).

Box 5: Canada Health Warning Messages

In Canada, the 2000 Tobacco Products Information Regulations require that tobacco products display prescribed health warning and information messages. Slide and shell packages are common in Canada. The slide must be used for a health information message. These messages entice people to quit smoking ("Consider talking to a health care professional"), encourage them to persist ("Each time you try, you can learn more about how to succeed"), or explode popular myths ("You can quit without a lot of weight gain").

Fully 50% of the exterior shell of the cigarette package must be used for a health-warning message. The warnings draw attention to the danger of lung cancer ("85% of lung cancers are caused by smoking. 80% of lung cancer victims die within three years"), other lung diseases (with photos of affected lungs), and enhanced risk of heart attacks. They stress the dangers of second-hand smoke ("You are not the only one smoking this cigarette"), particularly the harm done to children ("Don't poison us"!). They warn smokers that tobacco smoke contains hydrogen cyanide (which causes headaches); that tobacco use can make them impotent; and that tobacco can be harder to quit than heroine and cocaine.

Understandably, the manufacturers do not like these measures that intend to contain demand. The ban on advertising is particularly controversial. As a group, the manufacturers argue that such a ban has little or no effect on smoking (*see* on this also Saffer, 2000), but that it does harm the value of their prime asset, the brand name (Box 6). On the other hand, existing manufacturers are thought to benefit because a ban discourages new entrants (it takes millions to introduce a new brand but this makes little commercial sense when you cannot even advertise its name).

Box 6. The ban on advertising and the value of the brand name

Restrictions on advertising are meant to discourage demand for cigarettes. Above all, they are expected to discourage young people from starting to smoke. Tobacco companies contest such bans. To them, advertising is a key means for maintaining loyalty to the brand and for persuading existing smokers to switch brands; advertising does not increase overall consumption or cause anybody to start smoking.

Advertising is the key to the image of glamour, sophistication, freedom, and healthy outdoor living, that the tobacco companies want their product to be associated with. It is an essential tool for establishing new brands. The success of a tobacco company is driven by the power of its brand portfolio. As in other consumer goods industries, brands are often a company's most valuable asset. *BAT* describes itself as "one of the world's largest trade mark owners". *Philip Morris* attributes its success to the power of its "global brand portfolio".[21] The value of *Marlboro*, Philip Morris' most valuable and the world's leading cigarette brand, has been put at US$ 21,000 million.

---

[21]   *See* the 1999 BAT and Philip Morris Annual Reports.

The tobacco companies have adopted different strategies to compensate for the effects of the advertising bans (but it is becoming steadily more difficult to do so). These strategies range from quickly introducing a new brand before a ban comes into effect; to "brand stretching" or "trademark diversification",[22] and "borrowing" an existing brand name that was not previously associated with cigarettes.[23] The sponsorship of sports and cultural events has become popular (source: various).

3.3.1   Taxation

Raising the tax on tobacco products is a component of virtually every government's tobacco policy. On the surface, it is an attractive component because it raises the price of tobacco products (and thus discourages demand) *and* it raises government revenue (and keeps the treasurer happy). In actual practice, the situation can be more complicated (*see* e.g. the studies in Jha and Chaloupka, 2000). First, overall demand for cigarettes may decline so steeply that the lower sales volume outweighs increased revenue through the higher tax per packet. Second, a flat tax per packet acts as a regressive tax as it weighs more heavily on people with a low income.

A third constraining factor is that, as a result of the tax increases, prices become so high compared to those of surrounding countries that legally sold cigarettes are being substituted for smuggled ones. In 1993, smuggled cigarettes made up 60% of the Quebec market, forcing the Canadian Government to cut back taxation. In Brazil, in 2003 around one-third of all cigarettes consumed were either smuggled or faked.[24] Within the EU, the governments of the "old" members are placing considerable pressure on the new, low-income member states to raise their cigarette taxes.

Box 7. Smuggling

Smuggling, the illegal import of cigarettes, is a major headache for many governments. Smuggled cigarettes have made up over a quarter of the local market in e.g. Estonia, the Philippines, Ukraine, and the UK. Loss of tax revenue in the country of destination is but one effect of smuggling. It also undermines government efforts to discourage the consumption of cigarettes through higher prices; leads to the corruption of public officials and agencies; paves the way for other, more serious forms of smuggling (drugs, people) and is said to help foment terrorist activities.

The higher the price difference with the neighbours the more attractive a country becomes as a destination for smugglers. Smuggling cigarettes can be a hugely profitable business (earnings are estimated to be in the range of US$ 600,000 per truckload destined for the British Isles – CGE, March 2000).

---

[22]   Such as "Marlboro country" or "Camel Adventures".

[23]   Reemtsma sells BOSS and DAVIDOFF cigarettes and Altadis "Omar Sharif" and "Alain Delon" cigarettes.

[24]   Up from only 5% in 1991, most of these come from Paraguay. Whilst in Brazil cigarette taxes make up 70% of the retail price in Paraguay this is only 13%. The number of cigarette factories in Paraguay went up from two in 1998 to 29 in the course of 2001 (TJI, 4/2002 and 3/2003).

The tobacco companies benefit from the sales of smuggled products origi-nating in their factories just as they do from any other sales. Smuggling also helps establish their brand name in the country of destination, which can be useful when the brand is not (yet) legally available there. But the position of companies that sell through "normal channels" is different. They lose market share and so become the government's allies: both have an interest in combating illegal imports.

Whether smuggling takes place with the knowledge or the collaboration of the tobacco companies is a moot point. The companies claim that they neither control nor have any influence over smuggled products. However, certain governments are not convinced of their innocence and have taken them to court over this. The Canadian Government successfully sued one of the US tobacco companies, which it accused of aiding smugglers who redirected exported Canadian cigarettes back into Canada (TJI/1/99; TJI 1/00). In 2004, *Philip Morris* chose to settle with the European Union over a lawsuit to recover customs revenues lost through smuggling (TJI/5/00) (source: various).

4. EMPLOYMENT AND PRODUCTIVITY

4.1 Employment

Employment is at the centre of the debate on the effects of tobacco control.[25] The tobacco industry likes to emphasize that many jobs are at risk, and that many people depend on the continued prosperity of the tobacco industry. Studies sponsored by the World Bank and the WHO on the other hand typically emphasize that many farmers are only part-time farmers, that retailers would find other products to sell, and that in any case the money previously spent on tobacco would create jobs in other consumer industries.

The number of people employed is going down due to a combination of stagnating demand, consolidation, and productivity growth. Currently, around one million people are employed in the world tobacco processing industry (but the vast majority of these are active in just three countries: China, India and Indonesia). Tobacco *growing* is a more labour-intensive activity. It continues to give work to millions of people.

Table 1 gives employment trends in tobacco processing for OECD coun-tries for which sufficiently long time series are available. Following considerable job losses in the 1980s, (in the US one-third and in UK, two-thirds of all employed lost their job in that decade), these data show that in the 1990s employment in the tobacco industry declined in all countries. Job losses of 30% are no exception. In Australia and Korea the number dropped by more than 50%. The data given are for the tobacco industry as a whole, encompassing also other tobacco products than cigarettes (although the latter is its main compo-nent). Comparisons with only cigarette production volumes are therefore not entirely meaningful. Nonetheless, cigarette production decreased much slower than employment and appears to have been only a minor factor in explaining

---

[25]   Van Liemt 2002 gives a more elaborate discussion of the employment dimension.

Table 1. Number of employed persons in the tobacco industry (ISIC 314 or 16); selected OECD countries (1990 to 2000)

	Employment	
	1990	**2000**
Australia	2,900[4]	1,100[6]
Denmark	1,550	1,370
Germany	19,300[1]	13,000
Hungary	3,400	2,100
Ireland	1,310	940[7]
Netherlands	5,900[3]	5,300[7]
New Zealand	600[2]	500[6]
Poland	11,000[3]	9,400
Rep. of Korea	7,200	3,100
Spain	10,600[5]	7,500
Turkey	32,100	18,900
United Kingdom	9,000[5]	6,400
United States	41,000	28,000[7]

1. 1991; 2. 1991–92; 3.1992; 4. 1992–93; 5. 1993; 6. 1999–00; 7. 1999.
Source: OECD (various years).

job loss. Higher productivity and rationalisation in production and distribution have been the main causes.

The downward trend in employment continued after 2000 (the latest year for which OECD data are available). Demand in the OECD area is going down. Consolidation of the industry is accelerating (section 2). Production, distribution and research and development are being concentrated at fewer locations. Capacity utilization is reaching higher levels thanks to benchmarking and standardization. In 1999, following its acquisition of *Rothmans, BAT* announced the closure of factories in Australia, Malaysia, Nicaragua, Papua New Guinea, Singapore, South Africa, Spain, Suriname, Switzerland, and the UK (BAT AR, 1999). In 2000, *Altadis* announced the closure of eight of its 14 Spanish factories (and the construction of two new plants). Out of a total of 7,000, 2,000 jobs would be lost. On the French side, 1,400 jobs, or one-third of the workforce, would be shed (FT, 21/12/00). In 2003, the company announced that it would reduce its total work force by a further 17% (TJI 4/03). *Imperial* announced the closure of facilities in Germany, the Netherlands, Cambodia and the UK (Imperial, AR 2003). In 2002, *JTI* announced that it would reduce its number of production plants from 25 to 17 with a loss of 4,000 jobs (JT AR 03). A year later, the company announced the closure of another six plants in Japan by 2005 (TJI 5/2003). In 2003, *RJ Reynolds* announced that it would cut 2,600 jobs (or 40% of the total of 6,500) (DFT, 17/9/03). In China, up to one hundred thousand jobs (or one-third of the total) may be at risk in the medium term.

4.2.1. Productivity

The cigarette industry has experienced major productivity improvements. The production capacity of the latest cigarette machines increased from 250 cigarettes per minute (cpm) to 16,000 cpm in less than a century (Box 8). But such

high-speed machines alone cannot ensure high productivity. It is equally important to get the logistics around the machine right. The layout of the plant needs
to be such that high volumes can actually be achieved.

Box 8. Productivity increases in the tobacco processing industry

Until the 1870s, all cigarettes were rolled by hand. Particularly dexterous
(women) workers could roll four cigarettes per minute. The first cigarette
machine, introduced in 1867, could produce 60 cigarettes a minute. It
caused a sensation and had two effects. First, fewer people were needed to
make the same number of cigarettes. Second, cigarettes could now be produced on a large scale, thus paving the way for them to be marketed to a
broad customer base. In subsequent years these two effects (high productivity and mass marketing) continued to reinforce each other.

The capacity of cigarette machines did not stop increasing: 250 cigarettes
per minute (cpm) in 1910; 1,000 cpm in 1921; 1,300 cpm by 1930; 1,500 cpm
by 1955; 1,750 cpm by 1965. After 1965 a handful of competitors managed
to come up with ever-faster machines. Production of cigarettes per minute
increased to 4,000 by 1968; 5,000 in 1976; 7,200 in 1982; and 10,000 in 1988.
Still, there proved room for greater speed and by 1999 the fastest machines
could produce 16,000 cigarettes per minute (source: based on TJI).

Around the world, production is being concentrated in fewer, bigger and more
efficient plants. *Philip Morris(PM)'s* new cigarette manufacturing plant in
Tanauan, Batangas, Philipines, the company's single biggest investment in the
ASEAN region, has a capacity of 40 billion pieces per year. Production will
initially be exported to Thailand and later also to other countries in the region
(TJI 3/2003). *BAT's Souza Cruz* plant in Cachoeirinha (Rio Grande do Sul), the
most modern tobacco production facility in Latin America, can produce up to
45 billion cigarettes per year (TJI 3/2003). *PM*'s Izhora facility (near St
Petersburg) has a capacity of 70 billion pieces. *PM's* modern facility at Bergen
op Zoom in the Netherlands produces 90 billion cigarettes annually (or 1·7% of
the world total) with just 1,900 people. Employment in the world tobacco
processing industry can only go down further when such high levels of productivity become the norm.

4.3   Employment in tobacco growing

Tobacco is a labour-intensive crop that provides work and income to millions
of people and is mostly grown in developing countries. The share of these
countries in world production and exports is growing, but it is a slow process.
For one, there are limits to the possibilities of changing one tobacco for another
in existing blends. For another, many governments consider tobacco growing a
strategic activity and are reluctant to see it disappear. As is the case with other
types of agricultural activity, governments support tobacco growing for financial (contribution to government revenue), social (it provides employment),
strategic (no need to import in times of war or crisis) and political (tobacco

farmers may be located in sensitive border areas) reasons. Not infrequently, a combination of these factors is at work.

Governments support tobacco growing in various ways. Some subsidise production. Others oblige cigarette manufacturers to use a certain percentage of homegrown tobacco (or provide manufacturers with financial incentives to do so). Yet others oblige the state monopoly to buy up all (or all unsold) domestically grown tobacco (sometimes at high prices). In short, in many cases either the taxpayer or the smokers are asked to subsidise domestic tobacco production.

Tobacco growing will continue to occupy many people but their number will go down (unless demand picks up on a significant scale). Just where this will occur is hard to predict. Logically, people involved in the production of high quality tobaccos at competitive cost of the type for which demand prospects are good should be in a more favourable position than others. But, and as is the case in other agricultural sectors, subsidies, import barriers and the availability of low-cost irregular migrants may prove to be equally important in determining where production will remain and where it will disappear.

CONCLUSION

The world tobacco industry is increasingly dominated by a small number of multinational companies. These large players are thriving. Worldwide demand for cigarettes may be stagnating but their sales volumes continue to increase thanks to a steady stream of acquisitions. Taking over less efficient competitors provides them with opportunities for cost savings, synergy and scale economies. They can produce and sell high volumes, have the resources to invest in the latest technologies and the know-how to organise production in and around the plant in accordance with global best practice.

Litigation continues to be a threat, particularly for companies operating in the United States. The claims for damages are so high that US companies may not survive a verdict against them. The US tobacco majors argue that they have successfully managed the risks of litigation in the past. When an industry-wide settlement was unavoidable (as in the MSA) its costs were simply passed on to consumers. But as a precaution, they are insulating their US tobacco activities from their non-US tobacco activities. It is ironical that just when ever-lower trade barriers are about to create a truly integrated world cigarette market, the need to cope with the special legal and institutional regime in the US is leading to a new geographic segmentation of that market.

A key question is whether youth smoking can be contained. The WHO's FCTC is expected to act as a catalyst in translating expert concerns regarding the effects of smoking on health into government action to reduce tobacco consumption and combat second-hand smoke. The tobacco companies have publicly declared that they support measures to prevent youth smoking. Based on past experiences, the pro-health lobby is sceptical of these statements. The industry insists that it has changed.

Employment in the industry will continue to go down. The world is awash with abandoned cigarette factories. Privatisation, consolidation, together with trade and capital liberalization provide the multinationals with the free-dom to select the locations where they can produce large volumes for domestic and export markets. This being a capital-intensive industry, low labour cost are probably less important for their choice of location than political stability, a predictable legal framework and efficient logistics. In China, which is suffering from considerable overcapacity, up to 100,000 jobs may disappear (unless the country were to become a major export platform).

Normally, the scale economies achieved in a competitive, open trading environment lead to fewer jobs (per unit of production) but also to lower costs, lower prices and thus to enhanced purchasing power for consumers. However, in tobacco this consolation escapes redundant workers. Scale economies have indeed led to fewer jobs and to lower unit costs but, due to higher taxes, not to lower prices. Thus far, profitability does not appear to have suffered though.

BIBLIOGRAPHY

AR. (Tobacco) Company Annual Reports. Various companies, various years.

Bergkamp, L; Hunter, R. 1996. *Product liability litigation in the US and Europe: Diverging procedure and damage awards*, in *Maastricht Journal of European and Comparative Law*, pp. 399–418.

Buckley, N. 2002 *A growing fire around Big Tobacco* in FT 4 November.

Business Week (BW).

Ciresi, M; Walburn, R.; Sutton, T. 1999. *Decades of deceit. Document discovery in the Minnesota tobacco litigation*, in *William Mitchell Law Review*, Vol. 25, No. 2.

Consumer Goods Europe (CGE) various countries, various issues.

Corrao, M.A.; Guindon, G.E.; Sharma, N.; Shokoohi, D.F. (eds.). 2000. *Tobacco Control Country Profiles*, American Cancer Society, Atlanta, GA.

De Financiële Telegraaf (DFT).

Finanz und Wirtschaft (FUW).

Financial Times (FT).

FAO. 1990. *Tobacco: Supply, demand and trade projections, 1995 and 2000* (Food and Agriculture Organization of the United Nations, Rome).

Gale, F.; Foreman, L.; Capehart, T. 2000. *Tobacco and the economy: Farms, jobs, and communities* (Economic Research Service, US Department of Agriculture, Agricultural Economic Report, No. 789, Washington DC).

Gruber, J. 2002 *Regulating Tobacco in the United States: the Government and the Courtroom* in: *World Economics* Vol. 3 No. 3 July-September

Hammond, R. 1998. *Addicted to profit: Big Tobaccos expanding global reach* (Essential Action, Washington, DC, and at www.essentialaction.org/addicted/addicted.html).

Håkansta, C. 2004 *Workplace smoking: a review of national and local Practical and regulatory Measures* (ILO SafeWork Working paper, ILO, Geneva, mimeo) and at: www.ilo.org/public/ english/protection/ safework/tobacco/tobacco_report.pdf.

Jha, P.; Chaloupka, F. (eds.). 2000. *Tobacco control in developing countries*, Oxford, Oxford University Press.

Keirse, A.L.M. 2000 "Rokers hebben er tabak van! Over schadeclaims tegen de tabaksindustrie in de Verenigde Staten, Frankrijk en Nederland" In: *Ars Aequi* april 2000 pp. 252–259.

Van Liemt, G. 1998. *Applying global best practice: Workers and the "new" methods of production organization* (ILO, Employment and Training Papers, No. 15, Geneva), and at: www.ilo.org/public/ english/employment/strat/publ/etp15.htm

Van Liemt, G. 2002 *The World Tobacco Industry: Trends and Prospects* (ILO Industrial Activities Department, Geneva, 2002, mimeo) and at: www.ilo.org/public/english/dialogue/sector/papers /tobacco/wp179.pdf

OECD. *Industrial Structure Statistics*, (various years) OECD, Paris.

Saffer, H. 2000 *Tobacco advertising and promotion* in Jha and Chaloupka.

Tannenbaum, D.; Weissman, R. 1998. *The Tobacco Papers*, in *Multinational Monitor*, Vol. 19, Nos.

7 and 8, July/August, and at: http://members.nbci.com/_XMCM/que_merda/ transgenicos/ perolas/y-1/monitor.htm

Tobacco Journal International (TJI).

UNCTAD. 2000. *Handbook of Statistics.*

United States Department of Agriculture Economic Research Service (USDA/ERS): *Tobacco Situation and Outlook* (USDA, Washington DC). Various issues.

United States Department of Agriculture, Foreign Agricultural Service (USDA/FAS): *Tobacco: World Markets and Trade* (USDA, Washington DC). Various issues.

White, M. 2004 *Asbestos and the future of mass torts* in: *Journal of Economic Perspectives* Vol. 18, no. 2 spring 2004, pp. 183–204.

World Health Organization (WHO) 1997 *Tobacco or Health: A Global Status Report* WHO, Geneva).

Zhao, Jiancheng 2003 *Combating Protectionism* in: *TJI* 4/2003.

2. The ILO and Workplace Smoking

Carin Håkansta

The International Labour Organization is the UN organization dealing with all matters concerning work. It has a longer history than the UN itself and a different structure than the rest of the UN Family: the governing body of the ILO does not only consist of representatives of the member country governments, but also of representatives from employers' and workers' organizations in all the member countries. The backbone of this tripartite organization is a number of conventions, recommendations and guidelines that have been negotiated and accepted by the three social parties. Since the beginning of ILO's existence in 1919, occupational health and safety has been high on the agenda. A large share of ILO's conventions and recommendations set world standards for health and safety precautions at work. However, no ILO instrument (yet) deals with workplace smoking.

This chapter is an attempt to capture the reasons why the ILO is (and should be) involved in the question of workplace smoking, what has been done so far, and what the future may hold.

Does health promotion make sense?

Health promotion, i.e. the science and art of helping people change their lifestyle to move toward a state of optimal health, should make sense in a world where non-communicable diseases linked to lifestyle factors are on the rapid increase. In middle and high income countries, obesity, stress, alcohol, and tobacco related illnesses are causing huge costs to the governments. However, health promotion is seldom getting the attention it should and one reason is probably the cost crisis of many health systems today. Ministries of health are faced with the impossible equation of financing increasingly sophisticated and expensive health care systems for an ageing population from a shrinking tax base.

Health promotion is not only needed in the rich countries. As incomes increase and low income countries increasingly adopt the consumerist lifestyle of the "North", non communicable diseases are slowly but surely adding to the "traditional" communicable diseases in the countries. With a narrow tax base and pressure from their lending banks to cut back public expenditures, it is very difficult for governments to find resources for health promotion. This is especially the case in countries that are hard hit by the HIV/AIDS pandemic or where emigrating health care staff cause shortages of trained personnel.

WHO's Commission on Macroeconomics and Health, a think tank of prominent health economists and policy makers, presented a report in 2001 that is well known in the health circles. The report stressed the urgency of this "double burden of disease" in low and middle income countries, where the

R. Blanpain (ed.), Smoking and the Workplace, 25–41
© 2005 *Kluwer Law International. Printed in The Netherlands.*

burden of non-communicable diseases could become as heavy as the one of communicable diseases. To reverse this trend, the report suggested more invest-ments in health promotion in order to prevent these new diseases. Tobacco was mentioned as one of the main preventable risk factors. The OECD similarly singled out smoking as one of the main threats to the health and economies of the developing world. The report, Poverty and Health, explained the causal relationship between tobacco and poverty (OECD, 2003). OECD's three-year health project *Towards High-Performing Health Systems* reached the conclusion that a balance must be found between preventive and curative health care in order to benefit the health of the people (OECD, 2004).

Does workplace health promotion make sense?

Health promotion in the workplace should make excellent sense to employers and governments who compete for market shares in the increasingly competitive global economy. When it is important to produce at a low cost and workers are expected to be ever more efficient and better qualified, the logical conclusion should be that workers need to be strong and healthy enough to keep up with the increasing demands.

In fact, it should be in the interest of governments, employers as well as trade unions to promote workers' health, but it is not always evident. As already mentioned, ministries of health are often under tough pressure to keep together the health system, but ministries of labour are seldom in an easier position. Apart from often being weak ministries with limited resources, health promo-tion is seldom at the top of the priorities. One problem is the difficulty to measure positive effects of health promotion. Workers saved from deadly acci-dents make immediate impact in the occupational death records, while the prevention of stress-related illnesses or cancer has a long latency between expo-sure and effect, and for most of the time, will never show in the statistics of work related deaths and illnesses. Another problem is the competition from other labour issues. For instance, in a country where unemployment is a big problem, employers and trade unions may prefer less decent working conditions, such as longer working hours for a lower salary, rather than the loss of jobs. Similarly, in a country where mine accidents kill hundreds of people every year, or HIV/AIDS take thousands of lives, it may not be surprising that promotion of a healthier lifestyle (with the exception of preventing HIV/AIDS) receives little attention from trade unions, employers or government.

What does the ILO do about smoking?

Although most governments and a substantial number of employers and trade unions acknowledge the usefulness of workplace health promotion, opinions are thus divided regarding how high a priority it should be given. That is probably the reason why there is no official ILO programme on smoking today. However, there are exceptions. There has been a successful programme to pre-vent drugs and alcohol at the workplace, in collaboration with the United Nations Drug Control Programme (UNDCP). A more recent initiative, SOLVE, is a training programme at the enterprise level with the objective to prevent psychosocial problems (including tobacco) at work. The logic behind these programmes is that the workplace is an excellent entry point for health promotion since most people spend the brunt of their time awake at their workplace. Furthermore, it should be an economic incitement for employers to promote workers health and longevity and in workers' organisations' interest to promote better health care for their members.

When Dr. Brundtland took over as the Director General of the WHO, she made smoking one of her priority issues. A new department was set up, the Tobacco Free Initiative, and it was decided that WHO's first ever convention would be developed: the Framework Convention on Tobacco Control (FCTC). For the ILO, this decision meant a new focus on tobacco for two reasons. On the one hand, there was great worry among employers' and workers' organisations in tobacco growing and tobacco production; would this new instrument mean a similar decline in tobacco use in the developing countries as occurred in Europe and North America the previous ten years? On the other hand, prevention of workplace smoking had a prominent place in the text of the convention, and WHO made it clear that this was the main responsibility of the ILO, not the WHO.

The ILO deals with two aspects of tobacco. One of these aspects is employment in the tobacco sector. ILO's Sectoral Activities Department carries out research on the financial and employment prospects for the tobacco industry, especially in view of the effects of the FCTC (e.g. van Liemt, 2002). Some of this research led to a report called *Employment trends in the tobacco sector: Challenges and prospects* (2003), and was followed by a tripartite meeting in Geneva in February 2003. During this meeting representatives from the large tobacco companies, joined by representatives from trade unions in the tobacco growing industry, declared that the FCTC was a threat to employment in the sector. However, the ILO report concluded that the relocation of companies and technical innovations were also important reasons behind the loss of employment in the tobacco sector (ILO, 2003).

Parallel to the activities in ILO's Sectoral Activities Department, the occupational health aspects are dealt with by ILO's InFocus Programme on Safety and Health at Work and the Environment (SafeWork). Representatives from both departments have been active as observers to the negotiations of the FCTC (1999–2003), and as active participants in the Ad Hoc Inter-Agency Task Force on Tobacco Control, which was set up by the WHO in 1998 after a decision by the UN Secretary General. This task force regularly brings together representatives from a large number of UN organisations and reports the latest progress to the Economic and Social Council (ECOSOC).

ILO SafeWork activities

The three most important areas of work for ILO SafeWork in relation to workplace smoking are prevention, regulation and enforcement. Prevention because exposure to second-hand tobacco smoke is at par with other hazardous exposures, and thus, should not be allowed at the workplace. Regulation because an increasing number of countries are currently introducing partial or total smoking bans in all or some of their workplaces. Enforcement because labour administrations are under pressure to implement and enforce these new rules.

In order to gain more knowledge about the reality and needs of countries, with regard to workplace smoking, ILO SafeWork carried out a survey in 2003 to the members of the International Association of Labour Inspectorates (IALI),[1] the collaboration centres of the International Occupational Safety and Health Centre (CIS)[2] and to a number of trade unions. The information gathered from the 72 responses to the survey provided the base for a working paper published in 2004: *Workplace Smoking. Working Paper: A Review of National and Local Practical and Regulatory Measures*, from now on called "the ILO Review" (Håkansta, 2004). The aim of the publication was to provide information and stir a debate, but also to come up with guidelines for future ILO action. The ILO Review could serve as a background document for a tripartite discussion and lead to a set of guidelines or a code of practice on workplace smoking.

The ILO Review has four parts: a definition of the problem; legislative aspects of the problem; examples of good practices; and important elements for achieving smoke-free workplaces. The following sections will provide some highlights from the publication.

The ILO Review: Problems with workplace smoking

From an occupational health and safety view, the crux of workplace smoking is not that workers have adopted an unhealthy habit. It is the exposure of second-hand tobacco smoke to the smoker as well as his or her co-workers.

Problems related to workplace smoking:

- Illness, including different types of cancer, heart disease and respiratory disorders.
- Accidents due to fires, explosions, lack of concentration, reduced vision.
- Bad working morale due to conflicts between smokers and non-smokers, or discrimination related to smoking.
- Higher costs due to increased sick absence, higher maintenance costs, higher insurance costs.

Causes of problems related to workplace smoking:

- None or inadequate legal framework to support the creation of workplace policies.
- Low awareness levels of the health, safety and financial implications of workplace smoking.
- Lack of knowledge among the social partners about how to take action

---

[1] The International Association of Labour Inspectors (IALI) is a worldwide association of over 90 members from more than 70 different countries, established to provide mutual support to labour inspection bodies mainly through conferences and other events and through networking.

[2] The International Occupational Safety and Health Information Centre (CIS) collects and disseminates information on the prevention of occupational accidents and diseases. It collaborates with 120 national institutions around the world.

Non-smokers inhaling second-hand tobacco smoke risk contracting the same illnesses as smokers are liable to contract, such as cancer, heart or lung disease. The problems become more acute if the worker is, for example, asthmatic or pregnant.

If workers are exposed to tobacco smoke and other dangerous substances at the same time, the risk factor is much higher. For example, a non-smoking worker exposed to asbestos runs a five-time higher risk of dying from lung cancer than a worker not exposed to asbestos. The same risk among smokers, which is 11 times higher than non-smokers not exposed to asbestos, multiplies 50–80 fold when combined with asbestos (Woitowitz, 2003:38). There is also a negative synergistic effect between smoking and alcohol consumption, which could increase risks of cancer of the oral cavity, pharynx, larynx and oesophagus. These occupational risks have been documented by the International Agency for Research on Cancer (IARC)[3] and the International Programme on Chemical Safety (IPCS)[4] (IARC, 2002; IPCS, 1999).

In addition to being a health problem, smoking is a safety hazard that each year leads to deadly explosions and fires. Lack of concentration during smoking and the potential source of conflict between smokers and non-smokers are other reasons for dealing with the phenomenon seriously.

The economic aspects to smoking at work are also important arguments for smoke-free workplaces. First of all, smoking is a financial burden for everyone, but in particular in the low-income population groups – where smoking is generally more prevalent. Secondly, employers and the society as a whole gain from smoke-free workplaces because cleaner air leads to increased productivity, lower maintenance costs, and lower health costs (Håkansta, 2004; Mackay, 2002)).

An important element in the work of labour inspectors is to be able to measure the tobacco smoke in the air. If the results from air measurement find high levels of pollutants, this can be used as an argument for proponents of regulations, or as a tool by the ones who evaluate and control smoking regulations. The most commonly used method is to survey the perceptions of workers, which does not always produce an accurate result, but more reliable measuring methods are often time consuming and costly. The most extensive measurement of workplace air quality was the European CAREX report of 1998, which used proxy values to compare exposure to second-hand tobacco smoke and other carcinogenic substances at the workplace. It was a first attempt to arrive at a more systematic international measurement of workplace exposures to carcinogens, and showed that smoking was the second largest source of carcinogenic exposure at work in Europe after UV radiation.

---

[3] The International Agency for Research on Cancer (IARC) is an arm of the World Health Organization. IARC's mission is to coordinate and conduct research on the causes of human cancer, the mechanisms of carcinogenesis, and to develop scientific strategies for cancer control. The Agency is involved in both epidemiological and laboratory research and disseminates scientific information through publications, meetings, courses, and fellowships.

[4] The International Programme on Chemical Safety (IPCS) is a UN programme with two main roles: to establish the scientific health and environmental risk assessment basis for safe use of chemicals and to strengthen national capabilities for chemical safety. Within the programme, three UN organizations cooperate: ILO, WHO and UNEP.

The ILO Review: Legislative aspects

Is a law necessary to create smoke-free workplaces? Experiences from many countries suggest that a legislative framework is important in many respects. First, a law is one of many measures that can "normalise" non-smoking at work as it places obligations on workers to change their smoking behaviour. This forced change of behaviour can eventually change attitudes towards smoking so that it becomes "normal" to go elsewhere when smoking. Secondly, a law institutionalises the rule of non-smoking and facilitates enforcement. Thirdly, a law may be the only efficient means of achieving change in sectors such as the hospitality industry and smaller enterprises, which are more difficult to persuade through non-legislative measures.

Legislation protecting workers against exposure to second-hand tobacco smoke exists to an increasing extent at the national or sub-national level. At the international level, the FCTC includes important passages that place obligations on States Parties to develop more smoke-free work environments.

Article eight of the FCTC, Protection from Exposure to Tobacco Smoke, addresses the question of smoke-free workplaces:

(...)2. Each Party shall adopt and implement in areas of existing national jurisdiction as determined by national law and actively promote at other jurisdictional levels the adoption and implementation of effective legislative, executive, administrative and/or other measures, providing for protection from exposure to tobacco smoke in indoor workplaces, public transport, indoor public places and, as appropriate, other public places.(...)

Apart from leading to a legal instrument, the four years of negotiations increased awareness and inspired many nations to start and intensify their tobacco prevention work.

National laws regulating smoking exist in various forms. The ILO Review showed that most countries introduce laws according to a step-by-step development that usually start with laws that ban or restrict smoking in public places. The intention of these laws is primarily to protect the general public, but since these places are also the workplace of many, they also serve to protect workers from being exposed at their workplace. A common second step, and laws that are also quite common today, are laws that regulate smoking in public sector workplaces. The more difficult areas to regulate are private sector workplaces and the hospitality industry. It is not uncommon that larger companies set a trend of smoking policies even before a law covering private enterprises is in place, but it remains difficult to implement laws banning smoking in smaller enterprises. The most controversial area is the hospitality industry, where some states in the United States took the lead in the 1990s and where Australia, Canada and Europe are following suit in the 21st century amid a lively public and political debate. In 2004, New Zealand, Ireland and Norway were the only countries with national smoking bans in all workplaces, including restaurants and bars. Sweden will follow suit in 2005.

Many countries have followed a similar step-by-step development of legislation, evolving from smoking bans in public places, to eventually include public sector workplaces, private sector workplaces and, in time, the hospitality industry. However, for this gradual evolution to be successful, it is important to support the implementation of laws with awareness campaigns and various incentives for people to stop or reduce their smoking, such as stop smoking initiatives and cigarette taxes. It is also important that the legislative framework clearly states who is responsible for the enforcement of the law. The importance of collaboration within governments and treating exposure to second-hand tobacco smoke as an occupational safety and health issue cannot be understated.

Creating a law is not enough. There must also be an enforcement mechanism in place, and in that respect the role of labour inspectors cannot be understated. The emerging needs of labour inspectors to enforce smoking bans were discussed at a meeting organised by the Senior Labour Inspection Committee (SLIC)[5] in Dublin in May 2004. The theme was "Environmental Tobacco Smoke (ETS) at the workplace". Labour inspectors from all EU Member and Accession States were invited to discuss the duties and responsibilities of the different sectors involved and the role of the labour inspectorate in raising awareness and securing compliance. One issue of particular interest to labour inspectors is ventilation. The stance taken by SLIC is: "If smoking is not banned, then risks need to be evaluated and preventive and protective measures implemented, but it is also important to note that no tolerable level of ETS exposure has been suggested or recommended". SLIC recognised that some countries may not be able to introduce a smoking ban through legislation or workplace policy, especially in areas such as the hospitality and prison sectors, at least not in the short term (SLIC, 2004).

The ILO Review: Good practices

The survey ILO SafeWork carried out in 2003, asked the participants to send information about national or local laws or regulations regarding smoking at work and examples of work done in promoting smoke-free workplaces. Many responses contained interesting and innovative initiatives, some of which were recounted in the ILO Review. A few examples of initiatives taken by governments, employers and workers from the ILO document have been selected here to illustrate good practices from different parts of the world.

Strong **government** support is important because of the positive signal it gives to workers and employers to take the matter seriously. Considered a health matter by many governments, smoking tends to be a question for the ministry responsible for health. In the promotion of smoke-free workplaces, the involvement of the ministry responsible for labour is also desirable, as well as other ministries, for example education, social affairs, and finance. Government action is most effective when there is an interdepartmental response to smoking, such as in the case of Thailand (*see* Box 1 below).

National campaigns for smoke-free workplaces also benefit from a more structured and far-sighted non-smoking effort, which can be observed in countries that have national action plans and/or inter-departmental tobacco control offices.

---

[5]   The SLIC Committee is a forum for discussion between the European Commission and the representatives of the national authorities who are, among other things, responsible for monitoring the enforcement of secondary Community law and who are consequently in direct contact with the social partners. It is also a forum for the national authorities to compare experiences of the structure, methods and instruments of labour inspection.

Box 1: The Government of Thailand: An interdepartmental response

Thailand's National Committee for Control of Tobacco Use was created in 1989. Chaired by the Minister of Public Health, it also includes the National Legislative Assembly's Committee on Health and the Environment, the Ministries of Health, Finance and Education, members of media, and experts from NGOs. The involvement of the Ministry of Finance is important because of its control over production and sales of tobacco products. Complementing the work of the National Committee for Control of Tobacco Use, the Thai Health Promotion Fund, established in 2001, carries out promotion of smoke-free workplaces. There are also programmes established for departments under the Ministry of Public Health, e.g. the Departments of Medical Services and Health. One of these programmes is specifically concerned with smoking at work and workers' health promotion. It is implemented throughout the country at national, regional, local and enterprise level. (Håkansta, 2004)

Workers' organizations can also play an active role in the promotion of smoke-free workplaces. Although some still maintain that smoking bans are intrusive on the smokers' privacy, most unions are now supportive of bans to protect workers' health. Workers' organisations can support workers who want a smoke-free workplace and inform their members about existing laws and possible access to legal assistance. They can also be instrumental in awareness raising activities, which would lead to better understanding of new regulation as well as less tension between smokers and non-smokers and avoid discrimination related to smoking. Box 2 below illustrates the role a trade union can play:

Box 2: Committed Singaporean trade union: NTUC

Within the framework of a National Smoking Control Programme, the Health Promotion Board works closely with the National Trade Union Congress (NTUC) and various workplace health facilitators to implement education and cessation programmes at workplaces.

Examples of specific activities carried out by NTUC:

- Helps the Health Promotion Board disseminate free consultation and education to workplaces wishing to carry out anti-smoking educational or cessation programmes.
- A Quit Smoking Support Group website with frequently asked questions on smoking; the benefits and methods of quitting smoking; normal reactions after quitting; how to deal with the urge to smoke; and personal testimonies from union leaders on how they have successfully quit smoking.
- Motivational talks and cessation counselling workshops coordinated jointly with the Health Promotion Board to help union leaders and members quit smoking (Håkansta, 2004).

Employers also have a responsibility to protect their workers from exposure to second-hand tobacco smoke. It is in their interest to make the transition from smoking to non-smoking working environments as painless as possible for everyone involved. One way of doing this is to involve workers in the development process of the policy. Another way is to offer support to workers who want to stop smoking. In Box 3 the Swedish communication equipment producer Ericsson is presented to illustrate how an employer can assist.

Box 3 Committed Swedish employer: Ericsson

To integrate the smoking policy into the organization, Ericsson went through the following measures:

1. Created a steering committee for the planning, monitoring and evaluation of the policy composed of the human resources department, the managing director, union leaders, media and smoking workers
2. Adopted a public, written policy that was approved by the management board
3. Distributed advance information to all involved sectors, such as unions and management
4. The managing director wrote a personally signed letter to all employees and managers

Specific activities related to the policy included: a baseline survey measuring attitudes to smoking; a competition; "Stop smoking groups" with assistance from the occupational health services; articles on smoking in the company newsletter; policy guidelines and information about passive smoking developed for managers; designated smoking areas (ENSP, 2001: 113).

The ILO Review: Key elements for achieving smoke-free workplaces

There are many important aspects of a successful transition to smoke-free workplaces, and much depends on surrounding circumstances, such as the smoking prevalence among the workers; existence of other workplace health promotion activities; legislation in place; available occupational health services; and a functional labour inspection system. The ILO Review selected the following six key elements in how to create smoke-free workplaces.

1. The first element is innovative partnerships, or coalitions between different sectors in a country. What these coalitions look like will depend on the particularities of the country. In countries where religion plays a central role in society, such as Bhutan and Cambodia, it makes sense to involve religious authorities (in these cases monks) in smoke-free campaigns. In other places anti-smoking NGOs may team up with trade unions to demand better protection for workers against the exposure to second-hand tobacco smoke. Another unusual coalition was the lobby behind the Californian smoke-free workplace law, in which representatives from the trade unions and from the employers fought together for a law that was to become the first smoke-free workplace legislation in the world.
2. The second element is the importance of dealing with workplace smoking as

an occupational health and safety issue. Finland illustrates this point in several respects: Finnish national safety and health institutions are active in promoting smoke-free workplaces; the government has declared passive smoking an occupational health risk; and smoking regulation is part of occupational safety and health legislation. Australia (Box 4) is another example of strong government support and dealing with smoking as a labour issue.

Box 4 Australia: National Occupational Health and Safety Commission

- 1994: The National Occupational Health and Safety Commission (NOHSC) endorses a Guidance Note on Passive Smoking in the Workplace, drawn up to assist employers to carry out their duties. The note was the result of a joint project set up by the government with trade union and employer representatives.
- 2002: The NOHSC calls for a voluntary ban on environmental tobacco smoke in all Australian workplaces as soon as possible. It says that the move was justified because World Health Organization guidelines and medical and government reports in Australia had confirmed that passive smoking could increase cancer, heart disease and asthma risks.
- 2003: NOHSC releases a revised guidance note that replaces the one from 1994. It is stricter and holds employers responsible for eliminating all smoking from workplaces. (NOHSC, 2002; Håkansta, 2004).

---

3. The third element is knowledge. Spreading information and raising awareness about the health risks of smoking as well as exposure to second-hand tobacco smoke in a systematic manner, preferably through national all-encompassing programmes. Another important aspect is to inform employers and workers about their rights and duties under the existing legislation. Employers and trade unions, in their turn, have an important responsibility to inform and educate workers.
4. The fourth selected element is clear guidelines. The survey showed that a number of guidelines, handbooks and leaflets already exist for the purpose of guiding the promotion of smoke-free workplaces. Table 1 below shows a summary of the analysis of 18 guidelines collected during the preparatory work of the working paper. Table 2 provides more information about the publishers of the guidelines.

The main conclusion from the analysis of the guidelines was that there was a similar pattern, although the target groups were different. Six out of the eighteen guidelines target employers only and two only target workers. The others target various groups or have not defined their audience.

Almost all guidelines provide background information including comprehensive scientific and legal information regarding the effects of workplace smoking. More than half also found it valuable to stress the cost implications of workplace smoking and the potential conflicts that can arise because of smoking at work.

The third category in the table, elements in guidance to workplace policy, is the main theme of a majority of the guidelines. Some guidelines even provide examples of a worker questionnaire, a model policy, and examples of best

Table 1. Analysis of guidelines to smoke-free workplaces

Variables	World Bank	US Government, CDC	UK ASH/TUC/ WHO	UK HSC	Sweden Tobacco Centre	Spain C.C.O.O.	Philippines Government	Norway Dir. of Health	Netherlands STIVORO	Japan Min. of Labour	Europe EU/TUC	Europe ENSP	Europe WHO	Hong Kong/ World Bank	Germany Bund Verlag	Germany Min. of Health	Canada (BC). WorkSafe	Australia NOHSC
1 Target Group(s)																		
Workers			×	×											×			×
Employers		×	×	×	×	×		×	×				×		×		×	×
OSH professionals				×			×											×
Government	×						×				×							
Not specified												×		×		×		
2 Background Information																		
Occupational safety and health effects	×	×	×	×	×	×		×	×	×	×	×	×	×	×	×	×	×
Cost effects	×	×	×	×	×				×			×	×	×	×	×	×	
Conflicts	×	×	×		×	×	×	×	×	×		×	×	×	×	×	×	
Legal information		×	×	×	×	×		×	×	×	×		×			×	×	×
3 Elements in Guidance to Workplace Policy																		
Management commitment	×	×			×	×	×	×	×	×	×		×					
Assessment	×	×		×	×			×	×	×	×		×			×	×	
Consultation/Working Group		×		×	×			×	×	×	×		×	×		×		×
Information/ Awareness raising	×	×			×	×	×	×	×	×	×	X**	×	×		×	×	×
Formulation	×	×			×	×		×	×	×	×	X**	×	×		×	×	×
Non-discrimination		×	×			×		×		×			×				×	×
Logistical action*		×		×	×		×	×	×				×		×		×	×
Disciplinary actions			×	×	×		×	×	×				×	×			×	×
Monitoring/evaluation	×	×	×	×	×		×	×			×		×				×	×
Integrated in overall health plan	×		×	×	×						×			×				×

Table 1.　Continued

Variables	World Bank	US Government, CDC	UK ASH/TUC/WHO	UK HSC	Sweden Tobacco Centre	Spain C.C.O.O.	Philippines Government	Norway Dir. of Health	Netherlands STIVORO	Japan Min. of Labour	Europe EU/TUC	Europe ENSP	Europe WHO	Hong Kong/World Bank	Germany Bund Verlag	Germany Min. of Health	Canada (BC). WorkSafe	Australia NOHSC
4 References to Workers' Assistance																		
Cessation aid	X	X	X	X		X	X	X	X		X	X**	X	X		X		X
Legal aid		X	X								X	X**			X			
5 Examples																		
Model policy		X						X			X		X	X	X			X
Model questionnaire					X			X					X	X		X		
Good practice		X	X					X	X		X		X		X			
6 Location of Smoking Areas																		
Complete indoor ban	X			X		X	X	X	X		X	X**	X		X	X	X	X
In designated smoking areas	X	X	X	X	X	X	X											
In workspace if consent/ in separated work areas										X								
Not specified														X				

*Eliminate tobacco vending machines, create safe and healthy indoor and outdoor designated smoking areas, remove ashtrays, site no-smoking signs.
**This is a call to the European Governments to implement laws that oblige employers to provide smoke-free workplaces.

(Håkansta, 2004)

Table 2.   Presentation of origin of guidelines

	Country/Region	Publisher
1	Australia	National Occupational Health and Safety Commission (NOHSC)
2	Canada (British Columbia)	WorkSafe. Workers' Compensation Board
3	Germany	Bundesministerium für Gesundheit (Ministry of Health), Bundeszentrale für gesundheitliche Aufklärung
4	Germany	Bund Verlag. Author: Joachim Heilmann
5	Hong Kong/World	World Bank Web Site: www.worldbank.org/hnp Author: Judith Mackay
6	Europe	World Health Organization, Europe
7	Europe	European Network for Smoking Prevention (ENSP)
8	Europe	Funding: the European Union. Organizer: Trades Union Congress (YUC), United Kingdom.
9	Japan	Ministry of Labour
10	Netherlands	STIVORO for the Dutch Government
11	Norway	Directorate of Health and Social Affairs
12	Philippines	Civil Service Commission
13	Spain	C.C.O.O (Spanish Trade Union Federation) Castilla-La Mancha/ Junta de Comunidades Castilla -La Mancha (Regional government of Castilla-La Mancha)
14	Sweden	Centrum för Tobaksprevention (Centre for Tobacco Prevention)
15	United Kingdom	Health and Safety Commission
16	United Kingdom	Action on Smoking and Health (ASH), National Asthma Campaign, Trades Union Congress (TUC), WHO Europe Partnership Project
17	United States	US Department of Health and Human Services. Centers for Disease Control and Prevention (CDC)
18	World	World Bank

practices (as indicated in category five of the table). Elements such as social dialogue, assessment and monitoring are in practically all the guidelines. Other elements, such as management commitment and non-discrimination, are in only half of the guidelines, perhaps because those are less clear-cut issues. The issue of discrimination, for example, is dealt with quite differently by different guidelines, although many suggest that the general approach should be to concentrate on banning the *smoke* and not the *smokers*. Examples of guidelines stressing the importance of preventing discrimination against or stigmatisation of workers on the basis of their tobacco habit are: the Spanish trade union C.C.O.O., the European trade union project and the Australian Guidance Note. A passage from the Australian document reads:

"No programme to eliminate ETS from the workplace should involve discrimination against or stigmatisation of workers based on their dependency on tobacco. Nor should stigmatisation of workers involved in the implementation of a smoke-free workplace be tolerated. The promotion of "Quit" smoking programmes has an important place in workplace smoking policies. These programmes should be offered and delivered in a supportive way and in accordance with best practice in the management of addiction and dependency." (NOHSC 2003, p. 4)

Other guidelines, such as the ones from ASH and WHO Europe, are supportive of non-smokers' rights but not as open to the argument of smokers rights. They argue that the right to health is more important, i.e. to work in an environment free from second-hand tobacco smoke, than the individual rights of smokers to pursue their habit at the workplace.

Disciplinary action is also dealt with quite differently by the various guidelines. The Swedish "Toolbox" for instance, takes a soft approach suggesting that breaking the smoking rules should be corrected through one-to-one dialogue. Other examples, including the ones from Australia, the Philippines and the Netherlands are stricter and refer to legislation that stipulates fines or imprisonment for breaking the non-smoking rule in workplaces.

The fourth category refers to workers' assistance. A majority of the guidelines suggest the provision of aid to workers who want to quit smoking. Several guidelines provide legal information and aid to workers who want to take legal measures against their employers. Many of these provide examples of court cases featuring workers against employers, explanations of legal texts and contact details of available legal aid. Guidelines targeting employers on the other hand tend to suggest how disputes can be avoided or solved more easily: through a participative process, a clear policy and a mechanism for conflict solving.

The last category, the position on smoking areas, was difficult to determine because of the various nuances in the position of the guidelines. The categorisation of the variable is therefore not precise but an approximation. The differences in position are partly explained by recent research showing that it is expensive and difficult to achieve the necessary air ventilation in an indoor designated smoking area without the tobacco smoke drifting into other sections of the building. The 2003 Guidance Note from Australia and the employers' guide from Norway have taken note of these theories, and take a position against indoor designated smoking areas. For this same reason, the Australian guidance note does not endorse the Australian Standard *The Use of Ventilation and Air-conditioning in Buildings, Part 2: Ventilation Design for Indoor Air Contaminant Control*, but suggests the creation of safe outdoor designated smoking areas. A number of other guidelines suggest that total smoking ban is the ideal solution but in workplaces where this is not feasible, designated smoking areas will have to be created. The World Bank represents this view, recommending that designated smoking areas are considered a transitional arrangement before a total ban can be introduced. Other guidelines are more flexible, allowing smoking if all workers agree, if the creation of designated smoking areas is too difficult, or if ventilation systems are installed. The centre of attention of guidelines with a more flexible attitude is often on mutual respect and a reduction of conflicts between smokers and non-smokers.

Some of the differences in contents and tone of language in the guidelines are due to the rapid change in governments' position *vis-à-vis* workplace smoking during the past five to ten years, which have rendered parts of some guidelines obsolete. Examples of this process are the two German guidelines from

1995, eight years before the introduction of the current German legislation, which holds employers responsible for the provision of smoke-free work areas. The emphasis of these guidelines is on peaceful solutions to conflicts related to smoking and the use of existing related legislation rather than guidelines to employers regarding their rights and duties, as would probably be the case in an updated version of the guidelines.

5. The fifth element is access to workplace assistance for workers wishing to quit smoking. Depending on the ambition and amount of resources, these activities can range from full fledged programmes with therapies and remedies, to simple self-help groups. The advantage of such activities is that they give a positive signal from the management to the workers and to the surrounding community that they care about workers' health and safety. They can have a positive effect on the transition to a smoke-free workplace, making it as painless and friction-free as possible.
6. The sixth element is a participative process of developing smoking policies and a holistic view of health and safety policies. It was suggested that a workplace policy should be developed in a democratic way, involving all the relevant departments of an enterprise or organization and as many workers as possible. It was furthermore suggested to see the policy in a holistic way, taking into consideration the other workplace policies in place and other occupational health issues that need to be addressed. To keep up the quality of the policy, it should also go through regular cycles of evaluation and adjustments.

ILO's future involvement

Workplace smoking has attained a higher profile in the last five-ten years, notably because of WHO's stepped up action but also because of media attention linked to anti-tobacco activism and high profile court cases against the tobacco companies. The majority of law suits by workers against employers or tobacco companies have taken place in the US, but some are also taking place in Canada, Europe and Australia. However, other countries are following suit. Japan recently reported the first law suit where an employee of a ward in Tokyo received damages for having been exposed to second-hand tobacco smoke. This is quite a feat in a country where 30% of the population smokes and the Ministry of Finance owns 50% of Japan Tobacco, the world's third largest cigarette manufacturer (Sanchanta, 2004). The scientific community have added to this attention by publishing a large number of articles about tobacco use.

This publicity, coupled with the action taken by the WHO (Article eight of the Framework Convention on Tobacco Control), has to some extent paved the way for ILO to work more with the issue of smoke-free workplaces. ILO is the international organisation with the best position to reach out to workers and employers, and matters of creating and enforcing labour law are within the mandate of the organisation. An active ILO would therefore be of great value in future developments.

As already mentioned, information and raising awareness are essential elements for countries that are in the transition to smoke-free workplaces. However, smoking is a habit that stirs many emotions, and can become a very controversial question if handled the wrong way. Smoking is not just any hazardous exposure that can be removed from workplaces if that is what the law stipulates. The habit is an important part of many people's lifestyle, a way of relaxing and socialising, and seen as something deeply personal and private. In addition, to quit smoking can be extremely difficult and painful. That is why information and raising awareness at the workplace is so important, and why the ILO is in a unique position with its tripartite structure and long history of workplace norm setting. The message should be crystal clear: The issue is not whether you smoke or not; the issue is that second-hand tobacco smoke kills, and every worker has the right to a safe and healthy workplace. Therefore, you cannot smoke where your colleagues work.

Lessons learned from nations that have been active in promoting and creating smoke-free workplaces for many years, such as the Scandinavian countries, Australia and parts of Northern America could and should be transmitted to other countries so that mistakes already made are not repeated. The ILO could play an important role in transmitting this knowledge.

Most labour administrations and inspectorates are already overloaded, under funded and under staffed. With the additional burden of enforcing workplace bans on smoking, support will be needed in terms of training and guidelines. This is also an ILO mandate.

When smoking bans enter workplaces, trade unions may need training in how to support workers who are discriminated against because of their smoking habit. Or they may on the contrary be asked to assist workers who want a smoke-free working environment against the will of the employer. This is also an area in which the ILO could be instrumental.

To conclude: Is there a chance that the ILO will continue to be active in the areas listed above? It is difficult to say and will depend on several factors. One factor is the long-term effect of the FCTC on tobacco consumption and legislation in the world. If many governments decide to make workplaces smoke-free, there will be more reason for the ILO to get involved. On the other hand, there is also a question of demand: Will employers and trade unions in the tobacco sector want ILO's involvement in promoting smoke-free workplaces if sales go down and jobs disappear? And lastly, how will the ILO prioritise between different occupational health and safety issues? Will smoking be able to "compete" with other health problems?

REFERENCES

CAREX/Finnish Institute of Occupational Health: *Occupational Exposure to Carcinogens in the European Union in 1990–93* (1998).

ENSP (European Network for Smoking Prevention): *Smoke Free Workplaces Improving the health and well-being of people at work* (2001).

Håkansta, Carin: *Workplace Smoking Working Paper: A Review of National and Local Practical Measures*, ILO SafeWork (2004).

IARC (International Agency for Research on Cancer): *Monographs* Volume 83 (2002).

ILO (International Labour Organization): *Employment trends in the tobacco sector: Challenges and prospects. Report for discussion at the Tripartite Meeting on the Future of Employment in the Tobacco Sector.* ILO (2003).

IPCS (International Programme on Chemical Safety): *Environmental Health Criteria 211 Health Effects of Interactions between Tobacco Use and Exposure to other Agents* (1999).

Mackay, Judith; Eriksen, Michael: *The Tobacco Atlas*. WHO (2002).

NOHSC (National Occupational Health and Safety Commission): *Guidance Note on Elimination of Environmental Tobacco Smoke in the Workplac*e (2003).

OECD (Organisation for Economic Co-operation and Development): *Poverty and Health* (2003).

OECD: *Towards High-Performing Health Systems* (2004).

Sanchanta, Mariko: "Japanese workplace safety. Landmark passive smoking ruling" in *Financial Times*, 14 July 2004.

SLIC (Senior Labour Inspectors Committee) Plenary, Dublin 19–21 May 2004: *Outline Thematic Day 20 May: Environmental Tobacco Smoke (ETS) at the Workplace.*

Van Liemt, Gijsbert: *The world tobacco industry: Trends and prospects*, ILO Sectoral Activities working paper, 2002.

WHO: *Macroeconomics and Health: Investing in Health for Economic Development. Report of the Commission on Macroeconomics and Health* (2001).

WHO (World Health Organization): Text of the *Framework Convention on Tobacco Control* (2003). http://www.who.int/tobacco/areas/framework/final_text/en/.

Woitowitz H.J. "Wirkungen von Asbest auf den Menschen" in Albracht, G; O.A. Schwerdtfeger: *Herausforderung Asbest*, 2003.

3. The European Union, Tobacco and Health

Marianne Thyssen

I. INTRODUCTION

In recent years, the European Union (EU) has taken a number of important steps in the fight against tobacco and illnesses related to its consumption. Within its areas of competence, the EU has developed a series of preventive measures designed to discourage tobacco use, and acted as a co-ordinating platform for public health officials from the EU Member States to share best practices and develop common strategies. While many obstacles remain, the EU has thus established itself as a leading force in what is becoming a globally ever more acute concern.

The challenges in Europe accurately reflect the nature of the problem. In Europe, 39% are smokers, a figure that has remained relatively constant over the last 20 years. In fact, between 1995 and 2002, not only did the percentage of European smokers increase, their average consumption also went up, from 16·11 cigarettes/day to 16·5. Furthermore, there are strong indications of an increase in smoking among adolescents and people with less education, two of the socio-demographic groups least likely to stop smoking. Over half a million Europeans die of tobacco-related illnesses each year and, on present trends, this number is set to increase.[1]

There is however cautious cause for optimism. Europeans are not only among the best informed on the health risks associated with smoking, they are also generally in favour of regulating tobacco use, advertising and pricing more heavily. This ought to make them responsive to the kind of regulatory action the EU and the Member States have recently been intensifying their efforts in, for instance banning tobacco advertising, increasing the size of health warnings on tobacco products and restricting smoking in public places. While many are sceptical about whether these measures will ultimately help, the EU and the Member States are only at the very early stages of implementing them and conclusive results will take time to materialise.

II. THE DEVELOPMENT OF EU COMPETENCE IN TOBACCO CONTROL

Nearly all tobacco control measures presently in place in the Member States have an EU-dimension. In the late 1980s when the European Community (EC)

---

[1]   Special EuroBarometer 183/Wave 58.2"Smoking and the Environment: Actions and Attitudes" – European Commission, November 2003.

R. Blanpain (ed.), Smoking and the Workplace, 43–58
© 2005 *Kluwer Law International. Printed in The Netherlands.*

began to acquire competence to address health determinants through legislation, only Italy and Portugal had banned tobacco advertising (1963 and 1982, respectively), and only Ireland required strong health warnings to be printed on cigarette packets. Finland and Sweden, who joined the EU in 1995, also had various measures in place prior to the build-up of EU legislation in the field. Today, both tobacco advertising and labelling are subject to strict, uniform rules across the EU, and other restrictions, such as laws following the example set by Belgium in 1987 prohibiting smoking in public places, have also been incorporated into EU policy. The Union has therefore played a central role in the development of tighter laws against tobacco in the Member States.

The first concrete EC measures against tobacco came in the context of a political initiative, launched by the 1984 European Council in Fontainebleau, for concerted Community action to prevent cancer. The three Europe Against Cancer (EAC) programmes ran from 1987 to 2002, consisting of a committee of cancer experts from the Member States assisting the work of a Commission task force assembled for the purpose, and a specialised agency, the European Bureau for Action on Smoking Prevention (BASP, until 1995), set up to co-ordinate national anti-smoking campaigns and to disseminate information. Under the third action programme (1996–2002) two new organisations were financed: the European Network for Smoking Prevention (ENSP) and the European Network on Young People and Tobacco (ENYPAT). From the beginning, tobacco was high on the list of EAC's priorities and in much of the legislation currently in force across the EU, from upwards harmonisation of taxes on tobacco products to harmonised labelling requirements, can be traced to proposals made in EAC's early action plans.

Simultaneously with the EAC programmes early activism, the Community acquired legislative authority in certain areas relating to public health through the 1986 Single European Act (SEA). The 1957 Treaty of Rome had left all responsibility in the health-domain to Member States, and the SEA did not set out to fundamentally alter this balance. However, in order to fulfil its aim of completing the Single Market, the SEA granted the Community the right to "issue directives for the approximation of such laws, regulations or administrative provisions of the Member States as directly affect the establishment or functioning of the common market",[2] taking into account a "high level" of health protection.[3] The SEA moreover brought an end to national vetoes in most areas of EC decision-making, in place since 1966 and the so-called Luxembourg compromise. This enabled the tabling of legislation which previously would not have stood a chance of passing if one Member State was known to be against it. Together, these developments opened the door for significant EU action in the fight against tobacco, albeit on relatively narrow, and as will be explored below, ultimately highly contested grounds.

Successive revisions of the EC Treaty, in Maastricht in 1992, Amsterdam in 1997, and Nice in 2000, have added to the legal base upon which the EU can act in order to tackle tobacco. Therefore, in addition to Article 95 EC and its aim to ensure the smooth functioning of the Single Market, actual and potential legal bases for conducting EU-wide tobacco policy now include Articles 93 EC

---

[2] Article 94, Treaty establishing the European Community (consolidated text), *Official Journal C 325 of 24.12.2002.*

[3] Article 95(3), *ibid.*

(taxation), 137 EC (worker protection), 152 EC (public health, although this article excludes harmonisation) and 153 EC (consumer protection). However, while most of these empower the EU to take legislative action, in practice they contain very little room for manoeuvre as they limit such action to measures that complement the efforts of Member States.

Nonetheless, as a result of these developments, the EU has achieved a number of successes in the fight against tobacco. While it is arguably hamstrung by the lack of a clear, unequivocal mandate to pursue an EU-wide policy in the health domain, it has often found a way to make the most of its limited competences. Before looking in detail at what has been achieved however, a brief overview of the EU decision-making procedure and its main limitations for the pursuit of an ambitious anti-tobacco policy are helpful.

III. THE EU LEGISLATIVE PROCESS AND SOME INHERENT LIMITATIONS

1. The EU legislative system: procedures, legal instruments, main players

The EU produces legislation through a series of detailed procedures, characterised by different levels of involvement by the Commission and the European Parliament. In the case of anti-tobacco legislation, the two main procedures to consider involve action based on Article 95 EC and action based on Article 152 EC. In the case of the former, the European Parliament and Council work in co-decision and are authorised to issue directives for the harmonisation of national laws. The co-decision procedure is an innovation of the Maastricht Treaty, and has since been extended to more policy areas.

Anti-tobacco measures based on the public health provisions of Article 152 EC on the other hand, involve the European Parliament only when they consist of so called "incentive measures" which preclude any harmonisation. Alternatively, Article 152 EC authorises the Council to adopt non-binding recommendations in matters relating to public health which can imply the need for harmonisation. In such action, the Parliament is not formally involved.

EU legislative acts come in four main forms. *Regulations* are the most powerful in the sense that they are directly applicable in all Member States without needing to be transposed into national law. *Directives* on the other hand set out binding targets and timetables but require Member States to enact national legislation or other measures to bring these about. Member States are obligated to inform the Commission of what action they are taking and are answerable to it for delays and shortcomings. *Decisions* are also binding, but usually involve specific instructions aimed at one or more Member States, at EU institutions and their internal administrative programmes or even individuals. Finally, *recommendations and opinions* are non-binding acts often adopted in areas in which EU competence is limited.

In the campaign against tobacco, the EU's main legislative instruments have thus come to consist of directives issued by the European Parliament and the Council through co-decision, with Article 95 EC acting as the legal base. Other legislative measures have come in the shape of regulations (e.g. for the management of the Community Tobacco Fund, a research and information programme), decisions (e.g. on a programme for Community Action in the field of public health to complement national efforts), and various recommendations urging Member States to tighten their tobacco controls. Together, these are designed to constitute mutually reinforcing measures with which the EU, within its competence, conducts its anti-tobacco policy.

There have traditionally been four main players in the adoption of EU legislation concerning tobacco. The Commission's relevant department, charged with the task of preparing directives and recommendations for consideration by the European Parliament and the Council, is the Directorate-General for Health and Consumer Protection. In the Parliament, the committees responsible for preparing legislation in anti-tobacco matters have varied depending on the main points of debate and the reorganisation of committee responsibilities. For our purposes, the two committees that have been most involved in the matter are Environment, Public Health and Consumer Policy, and Legal Affairs and Internal Market. In the sixth session of the directly elected Parliament (2004–2009), the competences have once again been modified. The relevant committees today are the Committee on the Internal Market and Consumer Protection and the Committee for the Environment, Public Health and Food Safety. The responsibilities of Parliamentary committees are important as they do the preparatory work for the plenary session. Furthermore, although uncommon, it is not excluded for them to take very different positions on the same policy-issue. This was for example the case in 2002 with the directive on banning tobacco advertising, as will be studied below. Finally, in the Council the appropriate configuration consists of Ministers of Health meeting approximately four times a year in the Employment, Social Policy, Health and Consumer Affairs Council (EPSCO).

2.   Some structural obstacles to stronger EU tobacco regulation

The European Community can act only within the fields and for the purposes mentioned in the European Treaty. This fundamental rule on the allocation of powers, also known as the principle of attributed powers or competences, is clearly expressed by Article five EC. In areas which do not fall within its exclusive competence the Community can only take action, respecting the principles of subsidiary[4] and proportionality.[5]

As touched briefly upon above, directives issued on the basis of Article 95 EC aim to harmonise national laws as they have an impact, at present or with likelihood in the future, on the functioning of the Single Market. However, in order to ensure the "high level" of health protection demanded by paragraph three of Article 95 EC, this cannot be construed, in the case of tobacco or other health determinants, as a simple reregulatory provision.

In other words, it does not allow for the option of basing the free movement of tobacco products on the level of regulation of the Member State where it is lowest. On the contrary, it requires "upwards" harmonisation, or "reregulation".

---

[4]   This means that the Community can only act if and in so far as the objectives of the proposed action cannot be sufficiently achieved by the Member States and can therefore, by reason of the scale or effects of the proposed action, be better achieved by the Community.

[5]   No Community action can go beyond what is necessary to achieve the objectives of the European Treaty.

The problems here are essentially two-fold. First, the EU needs to demonstrate that differing national regulations indeed constitute obstacles to the free movement of goods, and cigarette manufacturers as well as some Member States have contested this to be the case for the tobacco sector. Second, and more consequentially, the EU needs to ensure that the intended level of "reregulation" does not violate the cornerstone principle of proportionality, which states that EU measures should do no more than strictly necessary for the fulfilment of their objectives. This is an especially acute concern in a field like public health, traditionally a high national priority in European welfare states.

Without entering into a discussion on complicated constitutional questions such as increasing EU competence in public health and the relative powers of the EU institutions, suffice to say that the status quo presents obstacles to the pursuit of stronger EU-wide tobacco regulation. Nor does the situation appear set for major change under a future European Constitution, as will be described in section VI. For now however, the European Court of Justice has ruled in favour of the use of Article 95 EC as the legal basis for EU-level anti-tobacco legislation – including reregulation – when justified carefully and correctly.[6]

IV.   MAIN EU LEGISLATION IN FORCE

As discussed, EU legislation in the field of tobacco exists in the shape of regulations, directives, decisions and recommendations, arrived at via a number of different procedures. Many of these have since been amended, replaced or superseded by legislation taking into account more up-to-date scientific evidence or otherwise reflecting the changing political will of EU citizens and Member States. This section will therefore cover only the main legislation in force in the EU today.

1.   The Labelling Directive[7]

The objective of the latest labelling directive, proposed by the Commission in November 1999 and finally adopted by the European Parliament and Council in June 2001, was to recast three previous directives on labelling and tar yields from 1989 to 1992.[8] As the evidence on the harmful effects of smoking mounted during the 1990s, it became necessary to adjust the previous warnings and yields accordingly.

Since the 1992 directive, cigarette packets were required to carry the general warning "Tobacco seriously damages health" plus a more specific warning chosen from a list. Together the warnings had to cover a total area of 48% of the packet, in addition to which tar and nicotine yields had to be indicated. However, the directive only stated that the warnings had to be legible and

---

[6]   Judgement of the Court of Justice of 10 December 2002 in Case C-491/01, for a preliminary ruling on Directive 2001/37/EC – Manufacture, presentation and sale of tobacco products.

[7]   Directive 2001/37/EC of the European Parliament and of the Council of 5 June on the approximation of laws, regulations and administrative provisions of the Member States concerning the manufacture, presentation and sale of tobacco products, *Official Journal L194 of 18.7. 2001.*

[8]   Directive 89/622/EEC, and Directive 92/41EEC on labelling; Directive 90/239/EEC on tar yields.

against a contrasting background, an ambiguity which led to 68% of cigarette manufacturers indicating the warnings in gold-coloured lettering – a reflective colour varying with the light which made the text indistinguishable from certain angles.

Of the current EU Member States, only Poland, Sweden and Finland had, at one time or another, implemented larger compulsory warnings than the prevailing EU standard. However, these all dated from before their respective accessions to the EU. The entry into force of the new standard in January 2004 pursuant to the new directive therefore represented a substantial upwards revision of labelling regulation in all Member States.

The labelling directive went through the entire length of the co-decision procedure, from Commission proposal through two readings in both the European Parliament and the Council to the convening of the Conciliation Committee. The drawn-out procedure was largely due to disagreement on first, the sizes of the new compulsory warnings and second, on whether to allow a temporary derogation for cigarettes manufactured for export outside the EU. The Council first favoured warnings of 25% of the surface area of the packet and no derogation for exports. The Parliament on the other hand opted for areas of between 40 and 50% depending on the number of official languages in a Member State, and a three-year transition period for exports to allow for the negotiation of international standards so as not to immediately disadvantage European exporters outside the Single Market.

In the end, the Parliament's proposals largely constituted the backbone of the final directive. Health warnings were to consist of a rotating general warning (either "Smoking kills/Smoking can kill/Smoking seriously harms you and others around you") covering between 30 and 35% of the packet depending on the number of official languages, as well as one additional warning chosen from a list (e.g. "Smokers die younger/Your doctor or your pharmacist can help you stop smoking/Smoking can cause a slow and painful death") to cover between 40 and 50% of the back. Similar proportions were established for tobacco products other than cigarettes. Furthermore, the warnings had to be in uniform black bold print against a white background framed with black borders.

Other provisions of Directive 2001/37/EC include:

- Maximum yields, per cigarette, of 10mg of tar, one mg of nicotine and ten mg of carbon monoxide, to be indicated in a similar white box as the warnings and covering between ten and 15% of the side of the packet;
- Prohibition of misleading descriptors such as "light", "mild" and "low tar",
- A derogation for exports until 2007;
- Tobacco manufacturers must submit to Member States a list of all ingredients used in their products, which will then be communicated to the Commission. By the end of 2004, the Commission would then propose a directive for a common list of authorised ingredients in the further interests of public health and the internal market.

There were various additional suggestions during the legislative process, for example on mandatory and commensurate warnings on vending machines, but they were felt to exceed the legal basis of Article 95 EC. In this respect, the institutions were guided by the October 2000 decision of the Court of Justice to annul the 1998 directive banning tobacco advertising on the grounds that it had, among other things, wrongly applied Article 95 EC in extending the ban to indirect advertising such as that found on vending machines and other "static advertising media".[9]

The labelling directive itself was also soon contested in front of the Court of Justice by tobacco companies from around the world. Their arguments revolved mainly around, again, the validity of Article 95 EC as the legal basis and the directive's adherence to the principle of proportionality (they had lobbied hard for a 10% packet compromise). In its ruling of 10 December 2002, the Court however ruled that the directive had solid legal grounds in Article 95 EC, and that the high level of reregulation was consistent with proportionality (in that anything less would have amounted to a failure to ensure a "high level" of health protection). The Court also ruled that the prohibition of descriptors such as "light" and "low tar" did not apply to cigarettes manufactured for export outside the EU.[10]

The labelling directive is, in many ways, a good example of deft EU legislation based on a significant convergence of opinions in the Parliament and Council, and one in which the Parliament was able to show its strength. Both institutions largely agreed that Article 95 EC could and should be used to produce upwards harmonisation, despite the fact that it entailed considerable adjustments in every Member State (in the final Council vote however, Germany, Austria and Luxembourg abstained). Agreement on a common EU labelling standard in 2001 also facilitated its introduction as the *de facto* global standard in negotiations leading up to the 2003 World Health Organisation Framework Convention on Tobacco Control (FCTC), a one-of-a-kind international health treaty between some 170 countries. The labelling provisions of the FCTC are set to be implemented evenly across the globe from 2006 onwards, depending on when a country ratifies the Convention, thereby alleviating the impact for European exporters of having to comply with the EU standard by 2007.[11]

2.   Commission Decision on visual health warnings on the effects of smoking[12]

Throughout the discussions on the labelling directive, the European Parliament was in favour of making visual warnings compulsory alongside the rotating text warnings. On this matter however, the Council opinion prevailed. A majority of Member States argued that this would be a step too far, and that for the new text warnings to have maximum effect there should be a period during which they remained unchanged. It was therefore agreed in the labelling Directive that

---

[9]   Judgement of the Court of Justice of 5 October 2000 in case C-376/98, Germany v. European Parliament and Council, on Directive 98/43/EC – Advertising and sponsorship of tobacco products.

[10]   *See* footnote 49 above.

[11]   The FCTC also includes binding provisions on advertising, sponsorship, and smoking in public places.

[12]   2003/641/EC: Commission Decision of 5 September 2003 on the use of colour photographs or other illustrations as health warnings on tobacco packages, *OJ L226 of 10.9.2003.*

Member States could use photographs if they so chose, in accordance with the Commission's guidelines.

The Commission produced these guidelines in September 2003. By 30 September 2004, it would draw up a list of acceptable photographs and other visual images from which Member States could choose ones suitable for their purposes. They could oblige manufacturers to start applying them from October 2004 on the side of the additional health warning, in a manner which does not obstruct the text itself or the "graphical integrity" of the image.

Anti-smoking groups across Europe have been campaigning hard for Member States to move quickly on this issue. They often cite the example of Canada, which replaced traditional text warnings with colour images already in 2001. Graphic colour pictures of, for example, lung tumours, diseased hearts, a premature baby on a life support system and rotting teeth printed on the top half of cigarette packets sold in Canada led to a 3% decrease in the number of smokers in two years, with 44% saying they have been encouraged to give up.[13] By way of contrast, only 15% of Europeans questioned for a November 2003 EuroBarometer on Smoking and the Environment felt that text warnings alone would alter smokers' behaviour. The percentage rose dramatically to 38% in the case of colour images, corresponding roughly to the Canadian experience.[14] Furthermore, it is noteworthy that the Canadian health warning is on the top half of the packet, as opposed to the bottom half as in the EU, thereby making it more difficult to cover with the kind of special pouches tailored for the purpose that have recently gone on sale in Europe.

3. The advertising directive[15]

Few pieces of recent EU legislation, especially relating to health, have aroused as much controversy as the directive banning the advertising and sponsorship of tobacco products. In essence, this controversy has little to do with actual health concerns, but revolves mainly around the sponsorship-part of the directive, and most notably its effect on Formula 1 motor-racing. Despite pledging initially to introduce a comprehensive tobacco sponsorship-ban for the sport by 2002, the promoters of Formula 1 have instead begun to move races away from Europe in anticipation of the ban's entry into force in July 2005 to parts of Asia where tobacco-laws are looser and numbers of tobacco-consumers are rapidly increasing.

The Commission tried on two previous occasions to bring about a directive regulating tobacco advertising. The first time, in April 1989, it merely sought to harmonise national laws to include a compulsory warning within the space occupied by the advertisement. In March 1990, the European Parliament voted to extend the scope of the proposed directive to any "advertising medium and sponsored activities",[16] thereby introducing the idea of a comprehensive

---

[13] "Shocking images on packets help smokers quit," *Daily Telegraph,* 10 January 2002.

[14] *See* footnote 44 above.

[15] Directive 2003/33/EC of the European Parliament and of the Council of 26 May 2003 on the approximation of laws, regulations and administrative provisions of the Member States relating to the advertising and sponsorship of tobacco products, *OJ L152 of 20.6.2003.*

[16] *OJ C 96 of 17.4.1990.*

ban on direct and indirect advertising, including sponsorship. For lack of Council support, the Commission withdrew its proposal and presented a second one in June 1991 covering essentially all forms of direct and indirect advertising. In February 1992, the Parliament again supplemented the proposal with provisions banning the sponsorship of tobacco products. The directive coincided with the 1991 entry into force of a directive adopted in 1989 banning all forms tobacco advertising on television in the EU.[17]

It was not until December 1997 that the Council reached agreement on the proposed directive. With strong opposition from Germany and Austria, and abstentions from Denmark and Spain, it was only after the UK obtained an extended transition period for the ban on tobacco sponsorship of international events (essentially Formula 1), that a qualified majority was reached. The Council confirmed the ban on sponsorship and most forms of direct and indirect advertising, so that Parliament could approve the proposal, in May 1998, as the best available compromise.

The October 2000 annulment by the Court of Justice of Directive 98/43/EC was a severe blow. Germany, bringing the case to the Court, argued that not only was the use of Article 95 EC (then Article 100a EC) not possible where the "centre of gravity of a measure is focused not on promoting the internal market but on protecting public health", but also that the measures themselves were disproportionate especially considering the insignificant volume of cross-border trade in indirect advertising media (e.g. vending machine fronts, parasols, ashtrays, etc.). The Court accepted these arguments but stated that "a directive prohibiting certain forms of advertising and sponsorship of tobacco products could have been adopted" on the basis of Article 95 EC if it was clearly intended to restrict advertising with an impact on the Single Market. It could not be used to ban all forms of advertising, which would be tantamount to the EU being able indiscriminately to decide on the general conditions of market entry and regulation in Member States.[18]

The Commission tabled a new proposal, in May 2001, taking into account the judgement of the Court. This time, the advertising ban was limited to the press, radio and Internet, and the sponsorship ban to events "taking place in several Member States or otherwise having cross-border effects". In Parliament, the Committee on Legal Affairs and the Internal Market tabled 25 amendments with the aim of making the directive "legally watertight", restricting the scope of the sponsorship and radio advertising ban to transmissions of "substantial" cross-border effect, and allowing Member States more freedom in the implementation of the ban.[19] In plenary however, the Parliament rejected most of the amendments proposed, siding with the opinion of the Committee on the Environment, Public Health and Consumer Policy that the proposed directive already strayed far from the more ambitious and comprehensive objectives of Directive 98/43/EC and that it was legally valid as it stood. In December 2002, the Council concurred, albeit after somewhat unexpected votes in favour from Austria, Luxembourg and Sweden (hesitant due to its unique

---

[17] Directive 89/552/EEC, amended by Directive 97/36/EC, on the coordination of certain provisions laid down in law, regulation or administrative action in member states concerning the pursuit of television broadcasting activities ("Television without frontiers" – directive).

[18] *See* footnote 52 above.

[19] Report Medina Ortega – A5/0344/2002.

culture of oral tobacco and related advertising), which left Germany and the UK as the only Member States against.

The main provisions of Directive 2003/33/EC thereby came to include:

– A ban on tobacco advertising in printed media, radio and the Internet on the basis of Article 95 EC;
– Advertising in the printed media is limited to publications intended exclusively for professionals in the tobacco trade and to those published in third countries which are not destined primarily for the EU;
– A sponsorship ban on radio broadcasts and events of cross-border effect (with no exception for Formula 1);
– The free distribution of tobacco products in the context of national sponsored events is prohibited;
– Indirect and "static advertising media", which use the logos and designs of tobacco brands but don't mention their names, are not covered by the directive;
– Member States must bring into force laws and enforcement mechanisms that comply with the directive by 31 July 2005.

Therefore, four years later than originally provided for by Directive 98/43/EC, the EU-wide ban will enter into effect. To date however, 18 of the 25 Member States have implemented such bans and the "reregulatory" effect of the current advertising directive will therefore be smaller than in the case of the labelling directive. Furthermore, the final fate of the advertising ban is still undecided as Germany has once again challenged it in the Court of Justice.

Nonetheless, the EU ban does achieve a number of notable objectives. Because of the disproportionate media attention surrounding the fate of Formula 1 in the context of the sponsorship provisions of the new directive, they have simply gone somewhat unnoticed. The fact is that the directive's advertising provisions pull the rug out from under the tobacco industry by removing their access to a platform they have come to rely on to a great extent. Adolescents are known to pick up smoking as part of seeking self-assurance, independence and peer-acceptance, images and perceptions which tobacco advertising has traditionally tried to associate with their products. With tobacco advertising set to be banned, not only in the EU but on a global scale in accordance with the WHO FCTC, this is now hopefully set to change.

4.   Council Recommendation 2003/54/ EC of 2 December 2002 on the prevention of smoking and on initiatives to improve tobacco control[20]

Prohibited from deciding on more comprehensive anti-tobacco legislation on the basis of Article 95 EC, the EU has initiated a number of action plans and programmes on the basis of Article 152 EC. In accordance with the article's aim for a "high level of human health protection in the definition and implementation of all Community policies and activities", including in encouraging Member States to intensify their cooperation in domains that fall within "the

---

[20]   OJ L22 of 25.01.2003.

fight against the major health scourges" facing the EU, a series of policy recommendations have been issued by the Council.

In the tobacco field, the most recent one dates from December 2002, adopted at the same Council meeting at which agreement on the advertising ban was reached among Member States. It is therefore no coincidence that Council Recommendation 2003/54/EC contains many of the tobacco control measures that had to be left out of the advertising directive for the legal reasons detailed above. Member States are urged to adopt measures aimed at prohibiting the following forms of advertising and promotion:

– The use of tobacco brand names on non-tobacco products or services;
– The use of promotional items (ashtrays, lighters, parasols, etc) and tobacco samples;
– The use and communication of sales promotions, such as discounts, free gifts, premiums or opportunities to participate in promotional contests or games;
– The use of billboards, posters and other indoor or outdoor advertising techniques (such as advertising on cigarette vending machines);
– The use of advertising in cinemas.

Other items in the Recommendation regroup and prioritise various options identified for possible EU action in a 1996 Council Resolution on the reduction of smoking in the European Community.[21] Four sets of measures are specifically recommended. First, in order to limit the access of children and adolescents to tobacco products, Member States are encouraged to require vendors to verify the age of buyers when in doubt, remove tobacco products from self-service displays and to restrict access to vending machines and distance sales, e.g. via the Internet. Second, they are urged to target the effects of second-hand smoke by implementing legislation protecting non-smokers at workplaces, on public transport and in other enclosed public places. Educational establishments and healthcare facilities should especially be targeted.

Third, Member States should impose stricter regulation on tobacco companies notably by requiring them to declare the expenditure they incur on advertising, marketing, sponsorship and promotional campaigns. Such information would be valuable when deciding, perhaps sometime in the future, to require tobacco companies to contribute to research on tobacco-related health problems or alternative crops for tobacco growers. Finally, the Recommendation calls on Member States to strengthen programmes aimed at both discouraging the initial use of tobacco products and overcoming tobacco addiction. They are also urged to continue using fiscal measures to contribute to price increases.[22]

The first review of measures undertaken by Member States in response

---

[21] *OJ C 374 of 11.12.1996.*

[22] The taxation of tobacco products is predominantly the responsibility of the Member States. However, Article 93 EC provides for the harmonisation of excise duties to promote the smooth functioning of the internal market. Successive EU directives have therefore aligned the structure and rates of excise duties, the most recent dating from February 2002.

to the Recommendation is scheduled for 2006. It will be up to the Commission to identify shortcomings and to suggest further measures in relevant areas.

V.   OTHER EU ANTI-TOBACCO ACTIVITIES

1.   Programme for Community action in the field of public health (2003–2008)[23]

Deriving its legitimacy from the same Article 152 EC as the 2002 Council Recommendation, the programme for Community action is an ambitious exercise placing the EU at the centre of health policy coordination and improvement in the coming years. It regroups and recasts the achievements of ten earlier action programmes implemented since 1993, from the Europe Against Cancer programme through AIDS prevention to fighting drug addiction, into one comprehensive EU public health programme. It is predicated on intensive cooperation, networking and sharing of best-practices among Europe's top experts in each of its respective fields, with the aim not of supplanting national health strategies, but of complementing them insofar as the health problems cannot be effectively addressed at purely national level.

The general objectives of the EUR 312 million programme are threefold: to improve information and knowledge with a view to developing public health and health systems, to enhance the capacity to respond rapidly and in a coordinated fashion to health threats, and to prevent diseases through addressing health determinants. The common actions developed under each of these headings consist, for example, of integrating more closely the health information and reaction systems in Europe and of preparing new EU legislation that takes an inter-sectoral approach and puts health concerns at the centre of EU policies.

As far as the fight against tobacco is concerned, the priority thus given to public health concerns at EU level, even in the absence of a dedicated legal base warranting centrally-led regulation, is promising. After all, tobacco is the biggest avoidable cause of death in the EU today, something which will surely not escape the attention of EU health professionals when deciding on common priorities.

2.   Community Tobacco Fund[24]

Besides its legislative instruments and policy coordination channels, the EU has its own resource in the fight against tobacco in the shape of the Community Tobacco Fund. It was set up in 1992 in response to criticism that the EU heavily subsidized tobacco production through the Common Agricultural Policy (CAP)

---

[23]   Decision 1786/2002/EC of the European Parliament and of the Council of 23 September 2002, adopting a programme of Community action in the field of public health (2003–2008), *OJ L 271, 9.10.2002.*

[24]   Commission Regulation (EC) No 2182/2002 of 6 December 2002, laying down detailed rules for the application of Council Regulation 2075/92 with regard to the Community Tobacco Fund, *OJ L331 of 7.12.2002.*

but did not give enough support to health initiatives.[25] Therefore, as part of the overall reform of CAP expenditure, deductions from the premiums granted to tobacco producers were channelled into the Fund. The Agriculture and Fisheries Council reached a political agreement during its meeting of 22 April 2004 to phase out production-related tobacco subsidies to European Union tobacco farmers by 2010, a decision which undoubtedly reinforces the Community's tobacco control credibility.

Prior to 2002, the Tobacco Fund was used to finance agricultural research into less harmful tobacco varieties and production methods, as well as information actions to improve public understanding of the harmful effects of tobacco consumption. As from 2003, the research strand was replaced by studies and action to enable tobacco producers to switch to other crops or economic activities, and the information strand was expanded. To this effect, the Commission invites natural and legal persons established in the Community with proven expertise in health and tobacco issues to present proposals for the funding of information campaigns aiming to:

– raise public awareness of the harmful effects of tobacco consumption, including passive smoking;
– improve the effectiveness of messages and communication methods concerning the harmful effects of tobacco;
– prevent and stop people from smoking;
– disseminate the results achieved in the above areas to the widest possible number of competent national authorities and relevant sectors.

Some of the most noteworthy campaigns financed by the Tobacco Fund include the 2001–2003 *Feel free to say No* campaign aimed at 12–18 year-olds, and a 2003 study into the use of colour photographs on cigarette packets. Disappointingly however, between 1993 and 2001, EUR 31 million of the total EUR 42 million allocated for health projects went unused due to insufficient calls for tender and rigidities in the management of the Fund. Furthermore, the amounts spent, on for example the EUR 18 million *Feel free to say No* campaign, were deemed to be insufficient for the high media profile required for the projects' success. In 2004, it was announced that the Fund would be discontinued in 2008, but that available funds for health projects would increase in the remaining years.[26]

3. Smoking at the workplace

Passive smoking is undoubtedly a major issue which needs particular attention. As mentioned above the Council recommendation of 2 December 2002 on the prevention of smoking and on initiatives to improve tobacco control therefore

---

[25] Because of its labour-intensity and low producer price, tobacco farming in the EU is almost entirely dependent on subsidies it receives from the CAP.

[26] Council regulation nr 864/2004 of 29 April 2004 amending regulation no 1782/2003 establishing common rules for direct support schemes under the common agricultural policy and establishing certain support schemes for farmers, and adapting it by reason of the accession of the Czech Republic, Estonia, Cyprus, Latvia, Lithuania, Hungary, Malta, Poland, Slovenia and Slovakia to the European Union.

calls upon Member States to implement legislation and/or other effective measures to provide protection from exposure to environmental tobacco smoke in indoor workplaces, enclosed public places and public transport. Some Member States, such as Ireland, Malta and Sweden, already moved in this direction, by introducing smoking bans in workplaces and, more broadly, in all public places.[27]

Smoking at the workplace is also indirectly restricted through EU legislation by Directive 89/654/EEC, which states that employers have a responsibility to ensure sufficient ventilation and fresh air at workplaces, and Directive 92/95/EEC which states that pregnant and breastfeeding employees may not be exposed to cigarette smoke.

The European Commissioner for Health and Consumer Protection, David Byrne, announced at a tobacco conference in Helsinki[28] in August 2003 that he and his colleague responsible for Employment and Social Affairs, at the time Anna Diamontopoulou, were also working to introduce Europe-wide legislation to ban smoking at work. On several occasions Commissioner Byrne reconfirmed that he would like to see the toxic influence of tobacco smoke in the workplace tackled.[29] Unfortunately, until now no Commission proposal of that kind has been tabled.

Nevertheless there exists promising indications that the 2004–2009 Commission will place renewed emphasis on the campaign against tobacco. Besides urging, among other things, ever stronger action by Member States to prevent smoking among adolescents, it has identified tackling smoking at the workplace along with other public places as a priority.

This became clear days before the parliamentary hearing of the Commissioner-designate for Health and Consumer Protection, Mr Markos Kyprianou.[30] Answering to a written questionnaire drawn up by the Committee on the Internal Market and Consumer Protection and the Committee for the Environment, Public Health and Food Safety, he announced that his personal aim would be to ensure that the Irish, Maltese and Swedish example would be followed throughout the European Union by the end of his mandate (October 2009), thanks to cooperation at EU as well as national level.

VI.   EU ANTI-TOBACCO ACTION UNDER A FUTURE CONSTITUTION

The Convention on the Future of Europe was convened in February 2002 in order to make the EU more transparent, effective and democratic. Among its tasks was to propose "a better division and definition of competence in the

---

[27]   Belgium already prohibited smoking in public places in 1987.

[28]   'EU Tobacco Control Policy', 12th World Conference on Tobacco or Health, Helsinki, Finland, 3–8 august 2003.

[29]   'Driving Public Health in Europe' – The role of Workplace Health Promotion, 4 European Conference on Promoting Workplace Health, Dublin, 14 June 2004; 'Changes in the air', Tobacco Control Conference Limerick, 17–18 June 2004.

[30]   The European Parliament's specialised parliamentary committees have conducted a series of hearings with the 24 Commissioners designate in preparation of Parliament's vote of approval on the new College of Commissioners as a whole. The hearing of Mr Kyprianou took place in Brussels on 8 October 2004.

European Union".[31] Few expected a radical reworking of the division of competence set out in the Treaties, with primary attention focussed on institutional
questions.

With regard to public health, the division remains more or less the same.
The internal market and "common safety concerns in public health matters" are
categorized as shared competences, with "protection and improvement of
human health" categorised as an area where the Union may take supporting,
coordinating or complementary action.[32] Their current *ad hoc* relationship is
therefore more or less preserved. The Convention working group on
"Complementary Competences" clearly did struggle with the issue however,
stating in its final report that, "in order to clarify the legal situation, it should be
specified in the Treaty that measures to harmonise legislation based on Treaty
provisions on the internal market may apply only with respect to areas of public
health if the principal objectives, contents and intended effects of such measures
relate to Treaty Articles on the internal market".[33]

On paper therefore, the fight against tobacco under the proposed
Constitution would be conducted via roughly the same institutional interplay
as today. The relevant Articles in the new Constitution correspond in most
respects to Articles 95 EC and 152 EC.[34] The Union's coordinative functions in
the public health domain are also set to remain relatively similar.

VII. CONCLUSIONS

The contribution of the EU in the fight against tobacco is undeniable. In
addition to its multi-layered and complementary anti-smoking initiatives, it has
adopted a substantial body of law, even with only a secondary legal basis to
regulate in the public health domain. These laws are among the strictest in the
world, and they have helped drive a global anti-tobacco campaign in the World
Health Organisation. Much legislation has of course been held back by the
absence of a more robust legal basis, for example regarding indirect tobacco
advertising, but in the end the EU legislative system is, in the health domain as
in all policy areas, only as competent as the Treaties allow it to be.

The draft Treaty establishing a Constitution for Europe, to which
Member States have given their consent and which now await ratification,
appear mainly to seek to clarify the legal basis upon which the EU acts. The
Union is still invited to propose health legislation within its sphere of competence and to act as the motor for analysing and developing common health
strategies, but it remains to be seen whether the Constitution will indeed constitute a more unequivocal legal base for action.

As health-care costs related to smoking continue to mount in Europe, the

---

[31] Laeken Declaration, 15 December 2001.
http://europa.eu.int/futurum/documents/offtext/doc151201_en.htm.
[32] Articles I-13(2) and I-16(2), Draft treaty establishing a Constitution for Europe – OJ C 169,
of 18.7.2003.
[33] Final report of Working Group V on Complementary competences, p. 12. http://register.
consilium.eu.int/pdf/en/02/cv00/00375-r1en2.pdf.
[34] Articles III-64, III-65, III-179, Draft treaty establishing a Constitution for Europe.

EU may well continue to act as a pivotal forum and source of impetus for anti-tobacco measures.

4.   Is it a Human Right to Smoke Tobacco?

Asbjørn Kjønstad

The author examines the European Convention for the Protection of Human Rights and Fundamental Freedoms, Article 8 on the right to respect for private life and its relationship to other basic principles. He maintains that it is not a human right to smoke tobacco, and, if at all, it is a weak right, which would not have significance in respect to the employer's rights to the use of his own property.

1.   A BRIEF BACKGROUND[1]

The general opinion is that the wish to smoke is a private matter, though not in all places. However, this has not always been so.

Smoking has been known of since the time the American Indians smoked peace pipes. The tobacco plant was brought to Europe with Columbus approximately 500 years ago.

At the time of the turn of the previous century, chewing and sniffing tobacco were the dominant forms of tobacco usage in Norway. It was possible to work whilst chewing tobacco and the chewing of tobacco did not pollute the air. Eventually regulations were established in respect to the permission of spitting tobacco.

At the time, the smoking of cigars, pipes, and cigarettes was not particularly widespread. This kind of activity generally took place in special smoking rooms, the men normally wearing so-called smoking jackets. The Norwegian writer Bjørnstjerne Bjørnson referred to his smoking room as the "pigsty", and it would have been beyond the wildest imagination of the then major authority of Norwegian contemporary society and intellectual life that it should be considered a human right to smoke.

The early cigarette machines appeared in Norway approximately one hundred years ago. After a decade or two of mass production of cigarettes, widespread smoking emerged. Following World War II, home-rolled cigarettes became quite common.[2] Gradually, it became common for people in Norway to smoke anytime and anywhere. The major reasons for this were the idols created by the film industry and the aggressive advertising of the tobacco industry sweeping across the country, particularly extensive between the wars and from

---

[1]   I wish to thank Professor Kirsten Ketscher, doctoral candidate Njål Høstmælingen, and student Børge Alsvik who have read drafts to this article and provided constructive suggestions.

[2]   Karl Erik Lund *Samfunnsskapte endringer i tobakksbruk i Norge i det 20. århundre* (1996).

R. Blanpain (ed.), Smoking and the Workplace, 59–66
© 2005 *Kluwer Law International. Printed in The Netherlands.*

about 1950 until 1975, when the tobacco advertising ban entered into force.[3] This development scarcely represented the condoning of the right to smoke on working premises and in public places, but rather of behaviour to be tolerated (*precario*).

With the so-called "Smoking Act" of 1988, smoking in public places and on working premises where two or more people were gathered together was prohibited. The Act was introduced as a "liberty law"; the right to breathe smoke-free air being the major issue. From 1 June 2004, legal protection against passive smoking was extended to also include indoor restaurants.[4]

2.   PROBLEMS

The so-called Smoking Act of 1988 and the new Act of 2004 represent radical changes to the regulations controlling smoking activities in Norway. Nobody has claimed that the new legal situation is in conflict with international conventions on human rights, which from 1999 onwards are part of, and supersede, Norwegian law.[5]

But what if an airline, a hospital, a school, a sports organiser, or others having the right to determine the use of vessels, buildings, or designated areas, decide on the total prohibition of smoking? The Smoking Act of 1988 does not contain a prohibition against smoking at the entrance to a building or in the office of an employee not sharing office space with others.[6] Would one, by establishing a total prohibition against smoking, intrude too closely into the private sphere of those who wish to and/or have to be present in these places?

By its decision of 3 December 2003 establishing its working premises as a smoke-free area, the municipality of Levanger in Norway went even further than the Smoking Act: "It is not permitted for employees to smoke during working hours in municipal buildings and their adjacent properties".

This regulation is relevant both in respect to time and place, which are generally, but not always, concurrent matters. The legal basis for the regulation in respect to the employees' activities during working hours is the employer's right to decide. Regarding municipal buildings, areas, and means of transportation, the right of use also concerns adjacent property.

The county commissioner of Nord-Trøndelag made a check on the legal authority to the Levanger regulation, basing it on the Local Government Act section 59. The regulation was subsequently abolished as the country commissioner found that it was in conflict with the European Convention for the Protection of Human Rights and Fundamental Freedoms, Article 8, which, *inter alia*, protects the right to private life. In a decision of 13 April 2004, the county commissioner noted: "The right to smoke must basically be considered part of

---

[3]   Tove Nielsen "Tobakk og reklame mellom krigene" in Sejersted and Svendsen *Blader av tobakkens historie* (Published on the occasion of the Tiedemann's tobacco company anniversary) (1978) p. 348; Lund *op.cit.*, particularly pp. 191–2005; and Joner and Joner *Det store bedraget* (2002), particularly pp. 39–50 and 196–209.

[4]   *See* Asbjørn Kjønstad "Røyekefrie serveringssteder", *Lov og Rett* 2004 p. 211.

[5]   *See* Act of 21 May 1999 No. 30 relating to the strengthening of the status of human rights in Norwegian law (The Human Rights Act).

[6]   National Council on Tobacco and Health (Statens tobakkskaderåd) *Lufta er for alle! Retten til å puste i røykfri luft* (1985) pp. 127–128; and Ot.prp. No. 27 (1987–1988) p. 25.

the right to private life, and a prohibition against smoking is an encroachment on this right".

I shall refrain here from further examination of the municipal regulation and the county commissioner's review of the regulation. It is merely mentioned as an example of a more general situation which might actually become relevant to other municipalities and institutions, both in Norway and abroad.[7]

My main intention with this article is to examine the area between the individual freedom to smoke and the decision-making power allocated larger groups to prohibit smoking. In sections 3, 4, and 5, I shall discuss whether it is a human right to smoke tobacco, and, if so, the force of such a right. In section 6, I shall focus on the question of whether limitations could be placed on such a right. Although I particularly wish to emphasize international decisions in respect to human rights, I shall also discuss the significance of some Norwegian regulations reflecting similar regulations in many other countries, a key issue being the degree of emphasis allocated to the various principles and regulations.

3. HUMAN RIGHTS

Human rights have profound historical roots, from Greek philosophy, through the Christian religion, Roman law, the Magna Carta Libertatum of 1215, the American Declaration of Independence of 1776, the French Revolution of 1789, and the Norwegian Constitution of 1814. It is often stated that human rights are "universal, eternal, and inviolable".[8] This concerns norms which were "common to all peoples, regardless of time, place, and status, and above the norms created by mankind".[9]

The term "human rights" engenders a large number of associations, such as: "Prison torture, demonstrations, liberation movements; courageous people participating in uprisings against a superior force; election observers in the field; heated debates at the UN General Assembly and solemn judges at the European Court of Human Rights in Strasbourg".[10]

During the post-war years, a number of human rights have been implemented in international conventions. Among the basic rights and freedoms are: The right to life, liberty, and security; freedom from torture and ill-treatment; prohibition of slavery and forced labour; the freedom to test one's rights before a court; fair trial; prohibition against discrimination; the right to respect for private life and family, one's home and correspondence; the freedom to think, believe, and express opinions; to meet, organize and form unions; the right to take part in government; and economic, social and cultural rights.

Smoking is not an inborn need of man such as eating, drinking, sleeping, moving about, voicing one's opinion, etc. When considering smoking, we are thus clearly outside the core of human rights.

A possible right to smoke has not been mentioned in any of the international conventions, and hence could scarcely belong among the more basic

---

[7] In Denmark, there are similar situations, where some lawyers refer to the smoking of tobacco as a human right, see the Internet edition of the newspaper Jyllands-Posten, 13 May 2004.

[8] Torkel Opsahl *Internasjonale menneskerettigheter* (1996) p. 1.

[9] Njål Høstmælingen *Internasjonale menneskerettigheter* (2003) p. 29.

[10] Høstmælingen *op. cit* p. 27.

rights. If a right at all, it would need to be examined by an interpretation of the various regulations in respect of human rights.

4. THE RIGHT TO RESPECT FOR PRIVATE LIFE

The European Convention for the Protection of Human Rights and Fundamental Freedoms Article 8 No. 1 states, *inter alia*: "Anyone has the right to respect for his private life".

This is a regulation which may contain a number of diverse freedoms. Njål Høstmælingen claims that this has to do with a general regulation, "a safety measure, a kind of collection of other civil rights not otherwise specified in the conventions". The regulation gives "individuals the right to dispose of themselves and what is theirs, without external interference". One might speak of a "private sphere", a "peaceful private life", and "privacy". It is important that individual people choose their own "lifestyle", develop their "personality", and "live their personal life as they choose".[11]

Such an individual belief does not cause problems as long as the decisions by one person do not have negative consequences for others. Jack and Jill still have to make their own decisions in respect to whether they should eat fish or meat, drink coffee or tea, read the Times or the Daily Mail. Should this also be the case in respect to smoking and drinking?

However, the smoking of marihuana and hashish is prohibited in Norway, and this is also the case with other narcotic substances.[12] Even those who are severely dependent on such substances could be charged with possession and use. Nobody has ever claimed that it is a human right to use such narcotic substances and that Norwegian legislation is in conflict with international conventions on human rights.

Also, with respect to legalized intoxicating substances, such as alcoholic beverages, there are important restrictions in Norwegian law. Drinking on work premises and/or during working hours is fair reason for the termination of employment or for giving notice. Health personnel, professional chauffeurs, and others are not permitted to drink alcohol or use other intoxicating substances during working hours.[13] Exceptions are not made in respect of alcoholics and others dependent on these intoxicating substances. Nobody has claimed it is a human right to use intoxicating substances during working hours or in the workplace.

There is also reason to mention the Social Services Act, section 6-2 which states that users of intoxicating substances can be placed in institutions, by force, for three-months duration. Section 6-2a states that pregnant women using intoxicating substances can, by force, be placed in an hospital to undergo treatment; the concern for the foetus is placed above the individual freedom of the mother. In The European Convention for the Protection of Human Rights

---

[11] Høstmælingen *op. cit* pp. 215–217, cf. Opsahl *op. cit.* p. 20.

[12] *See* Act relating to medicines etc. of 4 December 1992 No. 132 section 24, as amended of 19 December 2003 No. 123.; and the General Civil Penal Code of 22 May 1902 No. 10 section 162.

[13] *See* Act of 2 July 1999 No. 64 relating to health personnel etc. (the Health Personnel Act); and the Act of 16 July 1936 No. 2 respecting obligatory abstinence from indulgence in alcoholic liquors or other intoxicating or tranquillising substances for persons in certain positions.

and Fundamental Freedoms, article 5 on the right to individual freedom, derogations are made in the first sentence, regarding the deprivation of freedom in respect to alcoholics and drug users.

According to this, there is both in Norwegian legislation and international conventions a very strict regulation on the use and abuse of narcotics and alcohol. With this in mind, it would seem particularly inconsistent if there were actually a right to smoke and if this were considered a human right. This is particularly relevant with respect to smoking during working hours and/or on the work premises.

5. HUMAN RIGHTS VERSUS PERMISSION TO SMOKE

In the assessment of whether smoking is a human right, and, if so, the possible significance of this right, it is important to look at such a possible right in conjunction with other human rights.

First, in this respect, I would like to mention that the right to respect for private life does not only comprise the right of choosing one's own lifestyle, but also the right of not being exposed to pollution. The European Court of Human Rights (ECHR) has applied Article 8 for protection against noise from airplanes, and against noxious odours and polluting gases stemming from industrial waste sites.[14] In my opinion, tobacco smoke, which contains a number of cancer-causing substances and many other substances of a more or less injurious nature could be equated with noise, smells, and other types of pollution.

Second, the right to good health is protected according to the International Covenant on Economic, Social, and Cultural Rights, which is now also incorporated in Norwegian law and supersedes it. According to Article 12, the States Parties to this Covenant recognize the "right of everyone to the enjoyment of the highest attainable standard of physical and mental health".[15] The right to good health is one of the most basic rights, and the smoking of tobacco among the most detrimental aspects to good health in our country. It is assumed that, on an annual basis, approximately 7,500 Norwegians die from active smoking, while approximately 500 die from passive smoking.[16]

Third, the right to a safe work environment is an important human right, cf. the Covenant Article 7 sentence b, on the right to "safe and healthy working conditions". This corresponds to the Norwegian Working Environment Act sections 7, 8, and 14 on the employers' obligation to ensure that the premises are of such a nature that the work environment is completely secure. Further, it is important that employers, according to the Act of 16 June 1989 No. 65, are obliged to obtain industrial injury insurance, ensuring the employees the right to compensation on absolute grounds in the event of industrial injuries and illnesses. In the so-called passive smoking case from the Norwegian Supreme Court (Rt. 2000 p. 1614), a female bartender who smoked and was also exposed to passive smoking in a discotheque where she was working, obtained the right

---

[14] Høstmælingen *opcit.* p. 228.

[15] *See* Torkel Opsahl "Pasientens menneskerettigheter" in *Statsmakt og menneskerett* vol. 2 (1995) p. 207; and Brigit Toebes "The Right to Health" in Eide, Krause, and Rosas *Economic, Social and Cultural Rights* (2001) p. 169.

[16] *See* NOU 2000: 16 *Tobakksindustriens erstatningsansvar* pp. 78–79.

to full compensation from the industrial injury insurance. This means that employers through their insurance premiums are liable for illnesses caused by a combination of the employees' smoking and the passive smoking taking place on the work premises. It is not in agreement with legal principles to consider tobacco smoking a human right, which employees in the public sector cannot dispute.

Fourth, the right to make decisions regarding private possessions is a human right. According to Article 1 to Protocol No. 1 to the Convention: "Every natural or legal person is entitled to the peaceful enjoyment of his possessions".[17] This regulation is also part of, and supersedes, Norwegian law. Hence, a municipality may decide on the use of its property. This applies to transportation, buildings, and sites. The no-smoking rule outside the entrance to municipal buildings should be within the decision-making authority of the municipality as the lawful owner of the property.

Protection against pollution, the right to good health, the right to a proper work environment, and the right to make decisions regarding private possessions, all contribute to the weakening of a possible right to smoke. This particularly relates to smoking during working hours or on the work premises. If smoking is considered a part of the right to respect for private life, this has to be in one's leisure time and at places which one owns or where one is granted permission to smoke.

Nevertheless, it is rather unclear as to whether it is possible to derive from international conventions a principle that the smoking of tobacco is a human right. This implies that a possible right of this nature would be very weak when Norwegian legal sources are considered.[18]

In my opinion, it is not possible to establish a general principle in respect of tobacco smoking being a human right. This also means that employers should have the right to prohibit smoking during working hours, including breaks for which the employees are paid a salary. Further, this means that owners of transportation means, buildings, and sites must be allowed to prohibit smoking on their premises.

If smoking is considered a human right, it is indeed a weak right. This implies that the right to smoke would have to yield to contrary-minded opinions, even not very strong ones.

6.   THE PROPORTIONALITY PRINCIPLE

The European Convention for the Protection of Human Rights and Fundamental Freedoms Article 8, No. 1, on the respect for private life, is not absolute. According to the Convention Article 8, No. 2, public authorities may intervene with this right when this is "in accordance with the law and is necessary in a democratic society in the interests of national security, public safety and the economic well-being of the country, for the prevention of disorder or

---

[17]   *See* Catarina Krause "The Right to Property" in Eide, Krause and Rosas *Economic, Social and Cultural Rights* (2001) p. 191.

[18]   *See* the Norwegian Supreme Court plenary decision in Rt. 2000 pp. 1006–1007; Jørgen Aall "EMK- og EØS-plenumsdommens bidrag til avklaring av folkerettens stilling i norsk rett" *Jussens Venner* 2001 p. 73 at pp. 83–86.

crime, for the protection of health and morals, or for the protection of the rights and freedom of others".

The background for this can be found in the employer's right to make decisions and/or the owner's right of use. In the case of smoking, this concerns the protection of health, and in the case of passive smoking, it concerns people's right to breathe unpolluted air. The key issue is therefore what is "necessary"; there should be a relationship between the significance of the decision and what can be achieved by it.

The right to respect for private life is not only stated in the European Convention for the Protection of Human Rights and Fundamental Freedoms, Article 8, but also in the UN International Covenant on Civil and Political Rights of 16 December 1976 (ICCPR), Article 17. These regulations are both incorporated in, and superseded Norwegian law.

Exceptions are expressed in different ways: Whereas the European Convention Article 8, No. 2, bases exceptions on "what is necessary in a democratic society", the UN Covenant Article 17 states that "no one shall be subjected to arbitrary or unlawful interference of his privacy, family, home or correspondence, no unlawful attacks on his honour or reputation".

Both conventions show that there must be strong grounds for a legal decision to be set aside. In order for a municipal decision to be regarded as arbitrary and disproportionate, it must, in my opinion, be obviously unreasonable or unfair. This kind of wording was used by the Norwegian Supreme Court when it set the legal standard for the decisions taken in plenary session in respect to the constitutional protection of social security law.[19]

A complete smoking prohibition comprising an entire working day of seven-eight hours could be extremely difficult to endure for people with nicotine dependency. Nicotine dependency is as severe a dependency as cocaine, heroin, and alcohol.[20] The degree of dependency varies from one smoker to another, but most smokers show abstinence symptoms if they have not smoked for a few hours. With a smoking prohibition, those most dependent would either have to try to quit smoking, to use nicotine flavoured chewing gum or nicotine plaster, or to seek to obtain one or two non-paid smoking breaks per day, which are spent outside the employer's property. It is necessary not to underestimate the burden of this for some people, but considerable demands are put on the employer when the issue concerns intoxicating substances. At any rate, most people can cope with no-smoking air travel lasting for 10–12 hours.

What could be achieved by a total smoking prohibition will vary. In this respect, it is important that the major tasks of hospitals and the municipalities to be those of serving patients and clients, and that this is financed by tax revenue. An employee has to endure restrictions on personal freedom during the period he or she receives payment for making his or her skills available to the employer. A day with six smoking breaks of ten minutes each, results in the loss of one full working hour. Smoking on the work premises pollutes the air for

---

[19] *See* Asbjørn Kjønstad "Trygderettigheter, Grunnloven og Høyesterett" *Lov og Rett* 1997 p. 243 at pp. 260–263.

[20] *See* Erik Dybing and Tore Sanner "Nikotinavhengighet – medisinsk-biologiske forhold" *Tidsskrift for Den norske lægeforening* (Journal, the Norwegian Medical Association) 122, 2002, pp. 302–305.

other employees and for the users of municipal services, leading to increased ventilation and cleaning expenses, etc.

The European Convention for the Protection of Human Rights and Fundamental Freedoms Article 8 No. 2 explains clearly what is "necessary in a democratic society". Based on this, the democratic opinion of the local community is of great importance. Municipal government has been a foundation of Norwegian life since the introduction of the laws on municipal government of 1837; it is a major principle of the Local Government Act of 25 September 1992 No. 107; and the principle constitutes the foundation for the European Charter on Local Government, ratified by Norway 26 May 1989.[21]

The importance of measures taken against smoking is also apparent in the extensive efforts against smoking taken by the World Health Organization (WHO) in recent years, particularly during the leadership of the then Secretary General, Gro Harlem Brundtland. The main principles are now implemented in the WHO Framework Convention on Tobacco Control, ratified by 40 countries in November 2003 and will come into force in March 2005. In the Preamble, it is stated that "the spread of the tobacco epidemic is a global problem with serious consequences for public health that calls for the widest possible international cooperation and the participation of all countries in an effective, appropriate and comprehensive international response". Article 8 deals with protection against passive smoking. Each country is to ensure "protection from exposure to tobacco smoke in indoor workplaces, public transport, indoor public places and, as appropriate, other public places".

It is also necessary to put some emphasis on the symbolic value of smoking prohibition, particularly in respect to smoke-free schools, hospitals, and municipal health and welfare services.

Finally, there is reason to consider the legal technical aspects. Total prohibition or an inflexible regulation is normally simpler to enforce than regulations consisting of one main rule and a number of more or less arbitrary derogations applying to situations where smoking prohibition is of no great significance.

---

[21]   Eivind Smith: Grunnlovfesting av kommunalt selvstyre" *Lov og Rett* 2003 p. 3 at pp. 8–12.

National Reports

5. Belarus

Yaraslau Kryvoi

1. SMOKING IN BELARUS AND FORMER SOVIET UNION

Belarus is a country in Eastern Europe, with population about 10·5 million, which was a Soviet Union republic before 1990s. Occupying less then 1% of the territory of the former USSR, it produced more then 4% of its GDP and had one of the highest standards of living in the Soviet Bloc. Following independence in 1991, gross domestic product declined rapidly. Belarus has retained many of the Soviet era structures and western influence has been considerably less than in neighbouring Baltic States or Russia.

The Soviet Union had a wide range of anti-smoking policies. Although advertising was unnecessary and nonexistent, tobacco advertising was banned, smoking was forbidden in many public places including subways, buses and restaurants, cigarette packages carried health warnings, and anti-smoking campaigns were televised.[1] In spite of that, male smoking rates in the former Soviet Union are now among the highest in the world with rates over 50% seen in all FSU countries except Moldova and reaching 60% or more in Armenia, Kazakhstan and Russia.[2] Worldwide less than 20 countries are reported as having rates over 60%.

Marketing and advertising efforts of international tobacco companies resulted in the rapid increase of smoking among young females in Belarus and other countries of the former Soviet Union. It made it much more complicated to control the consumption of tobacco among women aged between 28 and 29 years of age. In females aged older than 60 this indicator is nine times lower.

In Belarus rates in men have been hovering around 52% to 55% for some time, while rates in women have climbed steadily from under 5% in the mid 1990s to a maximum of 12% in early 2000s. Today rates of current smokers in Belarus imply that initiation of smoking has increased rapidly between generations and especially in the younger age group. The results of several studies suggest that there are about 53% of male smokers and 19·7% of female smokers.[3]

The percentage of those smoking from time to time is almost the same among women and men. The analyses of data for current tobacco users indicate that the following trends exist:

---

[1]   Gilmore A., Pomerleau *et al.* Prevalence of smoking in eight countries of the former Soviet Union: results from the living conditions, lifestyles and health study. European Centre on Health of Societies in Transition. London, 2003.

[2]   Date according to: Gilmore A, McKee M, Rose R. Smoking in Belarus: evidence from a household survey. European Journal of Epidemiology 2001;17:245–53.

[3]   *Ibid.*

R. Blanpain (ed.), Smoking and the Workplace, 69–74
© 2005 *Kluwer Law International. Printed in The Netherlands.*

- the highest percentage of those who occasionally smoke are in the period between 15 and 29 years old;
- the highest level of daily smoking is among those aged between 25 and 39 years old;
- there is a steady decline of those who smoke occasionally or regularly over 40 years of age.

It is important to indicate that the level of smoking in the group aged 15–19 is 43·6% and more than a half of them (73%) have tried smoking or smoked regularly by the age of 17, i.e. while in secondary school.

There is an unusual tendency of Belarusians to smoke in public venues: 65% do it at work and 28% when travelling. 73% of Belarusians explain their smoking as a habit, and one third say that they fight against nervous irritation. Females living in urban areas have a tendency to smoke 13 times more than those living in rural areas.[4] The highest percentage of smokers is among young, unskilled, unemployed persons.

The level of smoking in Belarus as compared with other European countries is relatively high. It is determined by the fact that in other European countries there are effective measures to reduce tobacco use while in Belarus policies and activities aimed towards tobacco reduction are still at their early stages.

2.   PERCEPTION OF SMOKING

The majority of Belarusians realise that smoking harms not only health of smokers, but also health of others, i.e. of passive smokers. 87% of non-smokers compared with only 48% of smokers believe it is definitely bad for health. Ninety-one percent of non-smokers compared with 72% of smokers believe that passive smoking is definitely bad for health. Most of the people support the idea of banning smoking in public places, with only 11·2% against it.[5]

3.   MEASURES TO REDUCE TOBACCO USE

According to Article 46 of the Constitution of Belarus everybody is entitled to healthy environment and to compensation if this right is violated. However, there is no comprehensive legislative act that regulates all aspects of smoking and in particular passive smoking. Rationales such as fire safety play a much more important role in reducing tobacco use rather than health of those exposed to passive smoking.

Administrative Code of Belarus provides for a number of sanctions against those who smoke in venues, where it is not allowed to do so. There are fines administered for smoking on trams, trolleybuses, public buses (Article 110–2 of Administrative Code), on ships (Article 110–1 of Administrative Code), on suburban trains and in non-designated areas of long-distance trains.

Another justification of prohibiting smoking in public places could be

---

[4]   Bulletin "Tobacco and Health" No. 5, dated May 8–14. Kyiv, 2004.
[5]   Tobacco control resource centre: http://contact.tobinfo.org.

based upon rules of consumer protection. One of rationales of consumer protection legislation is to provide consumers with healthy environment. Article one of the Consumer Protection Act defines safety of service as safety for life, health property of consumer and environment in the process of rendering a service. This norm can be construed in a way that health and environment includes air free from tobacco smoke, because the latter is indeed very harmful for one's health. However, there has been no legislation, so far, whereby the courts interpreted consumer protection legislation in this way.

3.1. Age restrictions on sale

The Presidential Decree 'On state regulation of production, circulation, advertisement and consumption of tobacco, raw materials and products' forbids the sale of tobacco products to those aged under 18 years old. It is prohibited to distribute tobacco products as gifts or lottery prices or in any other forms free of charge to persons younger than 18 years old. Recently there have been new attempts to prevent youths from starting smoking, with introduction of new provisions such as prohibition on the sale of small quantities of tobacco products and a ban on advertising in close proximity to educational establishments. All sales outlets should have clear labels on cigarettes about prohibition of sales to those younger than 18 years old. This resulted in the decline in self-purchase of cigarettes by underage persons.

3.2. Price and tax measures

Although there are tax measures, which significantly increases price of cigarettes, it is much lower than in EU countries. It can be partially explained by modest level of income of the majority of population. The cost of a pack of cigarettes is on average less than US$ 1 which makes cigarettes easily affordable to everybody. The government, however, intends to significantly increase the price of cigarettes in the near future.

3.3. Advertising

Multinational tobacco enterprises have started to develop new markets, which were closed before early 1990s. As a part of rapid and large scale privatisation of state assets, most of the former Soviet Union countries privatised their tobacco industries and the international tobacco companies established a local manufacturing presence. It is estimated that between 1991 and the end of 2000, the international tobacco companies invested over US$ 2·7 billion in ten countries of the former Soviet Union and tripled cigarette production capacity in their newly acquired factories.[6]

The importance of the international tobacco companies' advertising in Belarus illustrated the fact that, despite its small official market share, British

---

6   Gilmore A, McKee M. Tobacco and transition: an overview of industry investments, impact and influence in the former Soviet Union. (submitted) Tobacco Control.

American Tobacco and Philip Morris had in 2001 the highest outdoor expenditure and the ninth and the tenth highest television advertising expenditures of all companies in Belarus.[7] Production of tobacco remains a state owned monopoly in Belarus. However, the state manufacturer has only a 40% market share, with the rest made up largely of illegal imports.

The government undertook measures to control tobacco advertising by imposing a number of restrictions, though not introducing a general ban on tobacco advertising. It is not allowed to place tobacco advertising on television and radio from seven a.m. until ten p.m., on the front and last pages of printed media or in mass media designated for youth. There are also some other restrictions on outdoor advertising – it is not allowed to place advertising on any means of transportation, in close proximity (less than 100 meters) to the premises of healthcare, culture, education and sport.

According to the Presidential Decree tobacco advertising should not imply that smoking promotes success or makes physical or psychological condition better. It is also obligatory to include warnings about the consequences of smoking for health. However, effective implementation of tobacco advertising is not always in place. For instance, most of advertising hoards display tobacco trademarks and young people with shiny smiles, bright flowers and expensive cars.

3.4. Packaging and labelling of tobacco products

Belarusian legislation provides for certain information to be included on packaging of tobacco products in Belarusian or Russian languages, including warning about harmful consequences of smoking for health and prohibition to sell tobacco products to those aged under 18 years old. Normally such warning consists of the worn-out phrase "Smoking is harmful for your health", which have been used for decades. There are proposals to oblige tobacco producing companies to include more sophisticated warnings, such as "Smoking kills" or "Smoking causes cancer", but these proposals have not been realised by the government yet.

3.5. Other measures

Other measures taken by the government include adoption of various programmes aimed at promotion of healthy lifestyle and refusal from smoking,[8] which however have proved to be of very limited effectiveness. There are not enough measures taken to inform students and youths about harmful consequences of smoking, and especially of passive smoking.

4. SMOKING IN PUBLIC PLACES

There is no general prohibition on smoking in public places in Belarus. Instead there is a list of places where smoking is not permitted which includes the following:

---

[7]   ERC Group plc. World Cigarettes 2001 (volume 1). Newmarket: ERC Group, 2001.
[8]   Minsk City Council: Plan of measures to promote healthy lifestyle of Minsk residents for 2002–2006.

- organisations of healthcare, culture, education, sport, or trade and consumer services premises;
- in hospitality venues, except for those which sell tobacco products and have designated areas for consumers with ventilation systems;
- on premises of public (state) service, local executive bodies;
- at all types of railway stations, in airports, underground pedestrian crossings, in metro stations;
- on all kinds of public transportation, trains, ships, planes, except for long-distance trains, ships and planes with specially designated areas for smoking.

In all of these places it is necessary to designate special separated areas for smokers. The requirements for equipment of specially designated places are stipulated in a special Resolution of Ministry of Health of 22 April 2003, where it is indicated that smoking rooms should be separated from all other places and constructed of fireproof materials. However, the main rationale for issuing such instructions was fire safety, rather than protection of health of passive smokers.

5. SMOKING AT THE WORKPLACE

Every employee according to Article 22 of the Labour Code has the right to a working place which corresponds to the rules of safety of labour, protected from the effects of dangerous and (or) harmful industrial factors. According to the Labour Code it is possible for an employee to refuse to work if there is an eminent threat to his or her life or health and to those who surround the employee. However, there have been so far no cases reported when employees have refused from working on the basis of their exposure to passive smoking.

There is a general rule in Article 410 of the Labour Code that an employer is liable for the deterioration of an employee's health resulting from fulfilment of employer's duties. Employers' liability for harm inflicted to employees' health according to Article 411 of the Labour Code depends on employer's guilt (negligence). The employer is guilty if the rules of safety have not been observed. These rules of safety at work are adopted in accordance with guidelines of Ministry of Labour and Social Protection. Guidelines of the Ministry of Labour "On the procedure of drafting, consultation and approval of instructions on safety at work" dated 14 July 1994 include a requirement to warn employees about inadmissibility of smoking in non-designated areas, but do not elaborate any further and leave the right to establish non-smoking areas to the discretion of employers. Therefore, the problem of smoking and passive smoking in work place is normally tackled by employers themselves in the rules of work.

Thus there are no obligatory guidelines or rules regarding second-hand smoking at the workplace. Legislative acts usually prohibit or limit smoking in the workplace on the basis of fire safety.[9] At the same time many employers take effective measures to combat smoking at workplace to protect the health of their employees, and even adopt special provisions in the form of codes of ethics to prevent others from second-hand smoking, a good example of that is the Code of Professional Ethics of the National Bank adopted in 2004. However,

---

[9] *See*: Rules of safety at work for automobile transport adopted on 01.03.2002.

measures taken by employers are normally of a voluntary nature and therefore cannot be enforced in the courts.

6. CONCLUSION

There is still a long way to go to change legislator's perception towards both passive and active smoking at the workplace. Until now there is no general legislative prohibition on smoking at the workplace in Belarus, though smoking is normally not allowed at the workplace by the rules of work adopted by employers. However, general prohibition is likely to appear soon, as Belarus signed in 2004 the WHO Framework Convention on Tobacco Control. According to Article 8 of the Convention the government undertook obligation to adopt measures for protection from exposure to tobacco smoke in indoor workplaces, which will have to be implemented in the national legislation of Belarus.

REFERENCES

Gilmore A, McKee M, Rose R. Smoking in Belarus: evidence from a household survey. European Journal of Epidemiology 2001; 17.

Gilmore A., McKee M. Tobacco and transition: an overview of industry investments, impact and influence in the former Soviet Union. Tobacco Control 2004; 13: 136–142.

Gilmore A., Pomerleau et al. Prevalence of smoking in eight countries of the former Soviet Union: results from the living conditions, lifestyles and health study. European Centre on Health of Societies in Transition. London, 2003.

Bulletin "Tobacco and Health" No. 5, dated May 8–14. Kyiv, 2004.

Tobacco control resource centre: http://contact.tobinfo.org.

Ministry of Health of Belarus: http://www.minzdrav.by.

Minsk City Council: Plan of measures to promote healthy lifestyle of Minsk residents for 2002–2006.

'A tactical market'/Interview with Denis Gourinovich, corporate relations manager at British American Tobacco in Belarus. Tobacco Journal International, 2003–02–13.

6. Belgium

Roger Blanpain[1]

I. STATEMENT OF THE PROBLEM

Complaints at work about the nuisance and annoyance caused by tobacco smoke are all too common. They involve serious complaints connected with damage to health, stress, harassment, etc. which sometimes end in victims, after years of pressing for a smoke-free atmosphere, being forced to hand in their notice and so lose their job.

Just listen:

SOME PERSONAL TESTIMONIES

1. Resigned her job ...

Dear Professor,

I should like to thank you warmly for being the person who is campaigning within the University and also in the media for a general ban on smoking.

For myself, personally, it is now too late; in February 2003 I resigned from my job after having worked at the University for almost ten years. What regrettably made me do this was the fact that I was powerless to enforce my rights as regards the ban on smoking in my work environment.

...

I am mildly asthmatic and have very sensitive airways (on entering the building in the mornings I was confronted by "bad air" and was able to tell that one of my colleagues who was a smoker had arrived before me, which immediately put a damper on my working day).

I was fortunate in having an office to myself but was surrounded by offices in which people smoked (and I could smell it); people also smoked in the corridors and in places where clear no-smoking signs were displayed. The smokers ignored the ban and nobody else dared say anything. In the long run, however pleasantly I attempted to draw attention to the ban I became the complaining bore who was always droning on about it.

For years I tried everything, including approaching the Health and Safety Service and consulting Idewe, but the message was always that the University's policy was to allow smoking in offices (not public areas???!!!) and not much could be done about it, and that I should just raise the matter with my departmental head. The departmental head refused to listen, and my own courteous

---

[1] Translated by Rita Inston.

R. Blanpain (ed.), Smoking and the Workplace, 75–102
© 2005 *Kluwer Law International. Printed in The Netherlands.*

requests and even a jocular New Year's appeal directly to my smoking colleagues proved useless. I even considered taking legal action to enforce my rights, but that would also have made it impossible for me to continue working at the University.

In my letter of resignation I expressed my regret that the University was unable to guarantee its staff a healthy work environment but have never received any response to this at all.

In my view, in fact, its personnel policy still leaves a lot to be desired.

But the real purpose of this note is simply to thank you, because people like you are needed in order to bring about a basic change in attitudes. Belgians could learn a lot from the Anglo-Saxon countries in this respect. For example, my husband works for an American company and the problem is non-existent there – it is standard practice to have a general ban on smoking and it is properly observed. And he found it difficult to believe the problems I experienced at the University and how powerless I was.

Yours sincerely

M.

2.   Made ill by her colleagues' smoking and dismissed ...

...

"It may interest you to know that in 1994, after a career of some 15 years as a director's secretary, I was dismissed because I became ill as a result of my colleagues' smoking. I complained no end about the smoking but was just seen as a moaning bore.

Yet when the technical staff pointed out that the smoke was causing damage to the computers a ban on smoking was quickly introduced. They're prepared to do more for computers than for people!

I consulted a lawyer, but he was unable to do anything.

Since I am a single parent with four children, three of whom were still studying at the time, you can well imagine what a tragedy this caused. (I am not entitled to a widow's pension because my husband never lived in Belgium – I mention this to draw attention to certain mediaeval conditions.)

A few years ago my youngest daughter had a very serious accident which meant that she had to interrupt her studies, etc., etc. and entailed heavy expenses that have been difficult (or impossible) to meet.

I am not seeking to attract pity but to underline the fact that smoking can have very serious consequences.

My children have now left home and the three eldest have jobs. The youngest has resumed her studies and is in her second year, and fortunately is entitled to exemption from social security means-testing.

At present I am living in an unfurnished attic room and share a bathroom with the other tenants here. Although there was perhaps no need to tell you my story, I hope that it can be passed on to somebody in a position of responsibility."

C.

3. Stand up for your rights ... it can work ...

Dear Professor,

...

"Every day I am seriously troubled by having to endure passive smoking at work. Two thirds of the employees here are forced to put up with the reign of terror imposed by smokers, from seven o'clock in the morning to five o'clock in the evening (for four days a week). The rooms where people smoke are small and cannot be ventilated. The windows cannot be opened and there is no air-extraction system.

My protests are dismissed by the boss as "Don't talk rubbish" or "Grow up".

I am very concerned about my own health and that of my colleagues and don't know who I should turn to with any reasonable chance of successfully solving this problem.

...

I should be most grateful if you would be kind enough to give me your advice.

Yours faithfully,

P.

Dear Professor,

Thank you so much for your support. With the aid of your documentation I have in the meantime succeeded in having measures taken and the ban on smoking is now observed. I now, of course, find that I am treated with great hostility by those of my colleagues who are smokers. I hesitated for a long time because I feared just such a reaction. But in the end somebody has to decide to make a stand once and for all. And I see health as my highest priority.

Once again, my heartfelt thanks,"

P.

4. A hopeless situation ...

"I am one, among many others, who for many years has been putting up with my colleagues' smoking. I have reached the point where I am absolutely sick and tired of it.

Thanks to "Make a stand against cancer" on passive smoking, I have decided to stand up for my health.

I read your book with considerable interest and gleaned a great deal of useful information from it.

Allow me to give you just a brief outline of my situation: I am employed at ...

I work there alongside two colleagues who are both heavy smokers (a cigarette every 10–15 minutes). After a week in this reeking smoke (it has a harmful effect on my breathing, makes my eyes sting and irritates my throat) my clothes smell and even my skin smells.

Whenever I open a window (which actually doesn't bring much relief) it is closed again because there is a draught. In summer, everything has to be kept shut tight anyway because the air conditioning is on. If we had to keep everything shut tight for safety reasons, I could understand it.

I am also tired of arguing with smokers, because it's no use. More than once I've been given the stupid answer "But you're also smoking, just for free".

Yesterday at my annual medical check-up I made a complaint to the doctor, who sympathized with my situation. But when he began to go on about launching campaigns to get them to stop smoking my immediate response was "You know yourself that it won't work".

We are now going to discuss the matter on Tuesday with those responsible on the health and safety committee.

Going to the union for help also gets you nowhere: a week ago I attended a meeting (of the 15 people present, only three were non-smokers), you just start up an argument.

Some 75% of the management are smokers, but you have to start somewhere.

All I intend to ask for is to be transferred to a team in which my colleagues don't smoke.

All this will give you an idea of how difficult the situation is. I should be glad to keep you posted on how my case develops and also hope for your support. Meanwhile thank you for your time, and hoping to hear from you (it would give me great encouragement in launching off on this hopeless case).

Best wishes,"

P.

5. A passive-smoking postman ...

"As a confirmed non-smoking postman I am the victim, like so many other people, of passive smoking. For me passive smoking means that because smokers expose me to their poisonous and deadly tobacco smoke I am wantonly being condemned to die by inches. This is because every day I am still wantonly exposed in society to the dangers of passive smoking. I have hyper-reactive airways and thus fall into the high-risk category of those who become victims of tobacco as a result of passive smoking ..."

6. And the baby?

"Although I am not yet pregnant at the moment I am certainly thinking about it.

The problem is that I work in a school where a great deal of smoking goes on. The fact that this takes place during breaks in the staff common-room gives me no problem. I believe that smokers are entitled to a room where smoking is allowed. If I can't stand it, I stay away.

What I do have a problem with is the following. At our school fund-raising activities are organized on a regular basis. Some of these activities take place during school hours, where children are therefore present and where people may smoke as they wish. Other activities take place at the weekend in our "functions room" (which also serves as a gymnasium for the pupils) where there is also no ban at all on smoking. Result: the non-smokers are subjected to passive smoking, often unwittingly. The headmaster (himself a smoker) maintains that he can't make such activities non-smoking events because then almost nobody comes to them and as a result no money is raised.

Up till now I have on each occasion dutifully said nothing and on each occasion dutifully endured passive smoking; on each occasion I have dutifully come home with my clothes smelling, etc.

But once I am pregnant the health of myself and my child comes first and I plan to refuse to participate in activities where smoking is permitted.

Possibly with the result that my colleagues are not going to thank me for it and that my headmaster is going to 'harass' me.

So what I am asking is this. Am I in the right? Am I entitled to refuse to do these things? Can my headmaster dismiss me on these grounds? Are there any legal texts that I can cite for this specific case, or who can I turn to for help"?

X.

II.   RIGHT TO A SMOKE-FREE WORKPLACE

The starting principle is clear: the right to health is a fundamental right enshrined in the Belgian Constitution (Article 23). The Constitution also provides for the right to a healthy environment. This fundamental right obviously also applies within enterprises. Employees have the right to a healthy environment, and this means the right to a "non-smoking" workplace.

Accordingly, one of the employer's obligations consists in:

"taking all reasonable care to ensure that work is performed in decent conditions with regard to the safety and health of the employee ..." (Article 20.2 of the Contracts of Employment Act).[2] As already stated, "health" is a fundamental right. This fundamental right must be respected within enterprises like everywhere else.

An enterprise is any place where work is performed by employees and thus includes the hotel and catering sector, restaurants and bars, hospitals, schools, universities, exhibition centres and so on.[3]

---

[2]   Act of 3 July 1978. *See* also Article 4 § 1.2 of the Welfare Act (Act of 4 August 1996 on employees' welfare in the performance of their work): "Welfare shall be pursued through measures relating to:

   2: the protection of employees' health at work".

[3]   There is a twofold ban on smoking in these cases, since the Royal Decree of 15 May 1990 banning smoking in certain public places is applicable to such areas that are enclosed.

III.   THE COURTESY STRATEGY

For decades the tobacco industry has been promoting a courtesy strategy whereby, under the slogan "we work it out together", it is proposed that smokers and non-smokers should come to an agreement on the matter and that both parties "must adopt a considerate and tolerant attitude". "We set the rules between ourselves", so it goes.

The Belgian government also sticks to this model.

The General Regulations on Health and Safety at Work (ARAB) are in fact very lax on the subject. The relevant provision (Article 148 decies 2 bis) as introduced by Miet Smet, the Minister for Employment and Labour, via Royal Decree of 31 March 1993[4] reads as follows:

> "The employer shall take such measures as are necessary to ensure that smoking behaviour during work and during breaks and mealtimes is adapted to accommodate the mutual expectations of smokers and non-smokers. These arrangements shall be based on mutual tolerance, respect for freedom of the individual and courtesy.

The employer shall, where necessary, take physical measures to eliminate nuisance attributable to environmental tobacco smoke".

Thus, policy on smoking within enterprises must be shaped by:

– the mutual expectations of smokers and non-smokers,
– tolerance,
– respect for freedom of the individual, and
– courtesy.

The possible installation of an extraction system is also hinted at.

In introducing this provision the government is playing along with the wishes of the unions, who are unable to take up any particular stand on the matter because a substantial minority of their members and officials are active smokers. Consequently, the unions prefer to let the problem of smoking at work drift and the tobacco industry's strategy of "it has to be settled at enterprise level" is perpetuated. In practice smokers do not find the unions unsympathetic, as is clear *inter alia* from the case of Jean Leeman, who paid for his legal action himself at a cost of no less than 5000 euros.

The Belgian government persists in its folly. At a workshop on "An active policy on smoking in the workplace" held by FOD Employment on 21 October 2003 certain senior public officials expressed the view that a ban on smoking in the workplace would be going too far; that non-smokers are actually too aggressive and that smokers should not be socially isolated. In other words, that the courtesy strategy should be adhered to. Appropriate arrangements must be agreed on locally, so the view went. A special area must, in any event, be set aside for smokers. The State Secretary for Welfare's representative was, nevertheless, supportive of the right to a smoke-free workplace.

The senior public officials in question are clearly again going along with the attitude of ABVV (the Belgian General Federation of Labour) and ACV (the

---

[4]   *B.S.* 5 June 1993.

Confederation of Christian Trade Unions), who are unwilling to offend the smokers – albeit a minority – among their leaders and members and in addition want to exempt the hotel and catering sector, where the most deaths occur, from the possibility of a right to a smoke-free workplace and a ban on smoking.

All this means that in Belgium the argument is becoming ever more circular. The law is not being observed in places where there is already a partial ban on smoking, such as restaurants, bars and so on, and for enterprises in general a ban on smoking is as yet a non-starter.

In practice, the result is a policy of tolerance which in most enterprises adds up to the fact that non-smokers are required to be courteous and to put up with passive smoking with all its attendant damage to health.

The fact is that smokers are addicted and constantly in need of an injection of nicotine. For many of them, as indeed the personal testimonies cited earlier demonstrate, there is little room left for courtesy towards non-smokers.

The courtesy strategy has failed. The law needs to be made tougher in some other way.

IV. THE ROLE OF THE COURTS

In the last resort, certain employees have taken their fate into their own hands and gone to court to assert their right to a smoke-free workplace.

A. The martyrdom of a police officer: Jean Leeman

This case, which was contested before the Brussels Labour Court,[5] illustrates only too harrowingly how trivially the dangers of passive smoking are treated by certain employers. Jean LEEMAN is and assistant police officer who worked in the Brussels police district. He was an unacknowledged victim of passive smoking.

1. The facts: request for a smoke-free room

On 2 July 1990 Jean joined the Brussels police force, where he is employed in the traffic division. He is assigned to outdoor duties, such as directing traffic and supervising the observance of traffic regulations.

Jean has to perform his administrative tasks, such as processing his reports on offences, in the briefing room. Since there is no canteen, meal breaks are also spent in this room. On average, he spends some three hours every working day in the briefing room.

Jean submitted a request to his divisional superintendent, the labour inspectorate and the health and safety medical adviser that a "non-smoking" work area should be allocated to him for these hours spent indoors.

2. Medical certificates

Jean backed up his request with medical certificates. The certificates he submitted were as follows:

---

[5]   Judgment of 4 October 2002. Unpublished.

*certificate dated 4 July 2002 from the physician treating him, Dr P. Van Breusegem, who attests that he "has established that Jean, who is one of his patients, suffers from a disorder that is worsened the more he is exposed to the presence of cigarette smoke (passive smoking). Every day that he is exposed to cigarette smoke increases the risk of health-threatening complications, with potentially serious repercussions on the vital prognosis";

*certificate dated 12th August 2002 from Dr P. Coussement, a cardiologist, in which the latter confirms "that the inhalation of tobacco smoke, whether active (through smoking) or passive (through spending time in a smoky environment) is damaging to health. More particularly in the case of the above-mentioned patient with known atherosclerotic coronary artery disease, inhalation of cigarette smoke is absolutely contra-indicated";

*certificate dated 29 August 2002 from Dr P. Van Breusegem specifying that Jean "suffers from a chronic disease which does not render him unfit to work but which means that any exposure to cigarette smoke poses a threat to his health. The mechanism that creates this threat is not comparable with that of air pollution but is specific to the combustion of tobacco products.

Such exposure must be regarded as harmful irrespective of its duration, most certainly in the case of repeated exposure whose effects are cumulative over time";

*certificate dated 10 September 2002 from Dr P. Coussement stating that "the long-term harmful effects of exposure to tobacco smoke on the human body, especially the cardiovascular system, are well-known. The risk of cardiac and vascular diseases in the event of exposure to tobacco smoke is present continuously from the start of exposure and increases with the duration of exposure. Since Mr Jean Leeman already suffers from an atherosclerotic coronary artery disease and as a result of this had a heart attack in April 2001, exposure to tobacco smoke can imminently cause serious damage to his state of health";

*certificate dated 5 September 2002 from Dr Bouchlis, a member of Dr Van Breusegem's practice, who attests that Jean "underwent surgery five (5) years ago for clogging of the arteries in the context of cardiac arrhythmia. Investigation has revealed that a lateral branch of one coronary artery is still blocked and cannot be blown open by a balloon operation or the insertion of a stent.

Given the tendency of coronary arteries to narrow, in his case it is crucially important for him to avoid cardiovascular risks such as smoking, both active and passive. In his case exposure to smoke can have harmful effects with unknown consequences".

It could not be clearer.

3. Ban on smoking: not observed

The employer arranged for a "no smoking" sticker to be put up in the briefing room and introduced a complete ban on smoking. However, the ban was not observed.

In point of fact the total ban on smoking that was issued remained, in practice, a dead letter.

4. The struggle through the courts

a. The Labour Tribunal: inhuman

In the end, Jean took his case to the Brussels Labour Tribunal under the summary proceedings system. This means that an application is made for the court to take peremptory measures. However, Jean was sent packing because in the court's view there was no strong case for urgency. Jean was left to fight his own cause.

b. The Labour Court: a sound decision

So, he lodged an appeal with the Brussels Labour Court. Here again, Jean was asking for a smoke-free room in which to work.

In contrast to the Labour Tribunal, the Labour Court took the view that "*the applicant's precarious state of health justifies taking necessary interim measures in a case of strong urgency*".

The Court found in Jean's favour and ordered the police authorities "**to take urgent measures to ensure that the briefing room is effectively made totally free of tobacco smoke in view of the precarious state of health**" of Jean.

The Court based its judgment on the grounds of the legislation in force, as follows:

> "*Article 148 decies 2 bis of ARAB (the General Regulation on Health and Safety at Work) stipulates, under the heading*

'**Control of nuisance attributable to environmental tobacco smoke**',

that '*the employer shall take such measures as are necessary to ensure that smoking behaviour during work and during breaks and mealtimes is adapted to accommodate the mutual expectations of smokers and non-smokers. These arrangements shall be based on mutual tolerance, respect for freedom of the individual and courtesy.*

The employer shall, where necessary, take physical measures to eliminate nuisance attributable to environmental tobacco smoke'.

In addition, Article 20.2 of the Contracts of Employment Act of 3 July 1978 provides that the employer is under an obligation 'to take all reasonable care to ensure that work is performed in decent conditions with regard to the safety and **health** *of the employee'.*

Health protection is, furthermore, guaranteed by Article 23 of the Belgian Constitution, while Article five of the European Convention on human Rights provides that everyone has the right to security of person;

In so far as the situation *in casu* could possibly be seen as a form of harassment with respect to the appellant reference should be made to the Act on Protection Against Violence, Harassment and Sexual Harassment at Work, which prescribes that in the performance of their work employers and employees must refrain from harassment at work, a concept that is defined more precisely as unjust and persistent conduct, outside or within the workplace, that may find expression in particular in forms of behaviour and actions aimed at or having the effect of impairing the personality, dignity or physical or mental well-being of an employee in the performance of their work or creating an offensive, humiliating or hurtful environment".

The Labour Court also based its decision on the fact that the employing police division had issued a ban on smoking and that the police authorities were consequently under an obligation:

"to take every care to ensure the strict and effective application of the rules issued by themselves on the basis of the legislation on the matter that is in force and known to them".

In short, the briefing room had to be rendered completely smoke-free in the immediate interests of Jean's precarious state of health.

B.   The Adriana Nooijen case[6]

On 25 April 2000 the Breda District Court ordered PTT (the Post Office) to implement a total ban on smoking in its Breda branch,[7] on application from a Mrs Nooijen who was requesting a ban on smoking in the room (sorting area) where she works, the corridors in the building and the canteen that is provided for members of staff.

The Court ruled on the matter as follows:

"*That smoking is damaging to health and that non-smokers are also caused harmful health effects or nuisance by others smoking around them, especially if they suffer from disorders of the respiratory passages, is a generally accepted presumption and also the basis for the legislation on the protection of non-smokers in the 1989 Tobacco Act.*

...

The right to protection of physical well-being, or health, is a fundamental right enshrined in the Constitution. It naturally also takes effect in labour law. Article 7:658, paragraph one of the Belgian Civil Code imposes an obligation on employers to arrange areas in which work is performed on their behalf in such a manner as to, and to take all such measures and issue all such instructions as are reasonably necessary in order to, prevent employees from suffering injury in the performance of their work duties. Article three of the Working Conditions Act imposes an obligation on employers to organize the work in a manner, and arrange workstations in a manner, such that there is no resultant harmful influence on the health of the employee.

Article 4.9 of the Decree on Working Conditions prescribes that effective

---

6   *See* Appendix II.
7   Except for a designated smokers' room that causes no nuisance to non-smokers.

measures must be taken to prevent employees from being exposed to sub-stances in the course of their work to a degree such that damage may be caused to their health or nuisance may be caused to employees. Paragraphs two and three of this Article lay down detailed rules on the order of priority according to which employers must take measures. They must begin with, inter alia, organizational measures that eliminate the danger at source. Only if this is not effective can other possible measures, such as the extraction of polluted air, be considered.

Given the above-mentioned hazard to health posed by tobacco smoke these statutory provisions mean that employers are under an obligation to ensure that both while they are working and during their breaks non-smoking employees are in an environment that is totally free from tobacco smoke. This is because there is no safe lower limit. The danger must, in the first instance, be tackled at source by means of an organizational measure. A total ban on smoking is appropriate to this purpose and is generally indicated inside office buildings. Employers cannot counter this by invoking the wishes of other employees who want to smoke, since it is incumbent on these smokers to respect the health of non-smokers.

PTT is not fulfilling this obligation in its Slingerweg mail-sorting centre. Nooijen's workstation in the large sorting area is not really partitioned off from her smoking colleagues who work in the same area. The argument that the ventilation system removes the risk of her being exposed to others' tobacco smoke does not release PTT from its obligation, and is in any case implausi-ble. No technical reports to prove it have been submitted by PTT. Lastly, Nooijen is also exposed to colleagues' tobacco smoke in virtually all the other rooms in the sorting centre for virtually all the time.

Health protection is an issue that is by its very nature of urgent importance. This is true for everyone in general. In Nooijen's case there is the additional consideration that, on the basis of the statements produced, it is sufficiently likely that she belongs to the extra-vulnerable category of people who experi-ence unusual health disorders and nuisance as a result of tobacco smoke. This case is therefore one in which the need for an arrangement to enforce the employer's obligation is a matter of urgency".

Judgment in summary proceedings

The President of the Court

"orders the defendant to introduce, within fourteen (14) days of the pro-nouncement of this decision, a total ban on smoking in the defendant's prem-ises at Slingerweg seven in Breda, except for a designated smokers' room that causes no nuisance to non-smokers;

prescribes that the defendant shall pay the plaintiff a penalty payment of 1000 Belgian francs for each day of failure by the defendant to comply with this Order, subject to the payment of a maximum total penalty payment of 100 000 Belgian francs;

prescribes that the penalty payment specified in this Order is susceptible to subsequent adjustment by the court hearing the main proceedings in so far as it is found unacceptable by the standards of reasonableness and fairness to uphold the penalty payment chosen for the purpose, in view of the extent to which the obligation has been fulfilled, the gravity of the infringement and the degree of culpability of the infringement;

awards legal costs against the defendant and orders the latter to pay the costs incurred by the plaintiff estimated to date at 2022.56 Belgian francs; pronounces this Order immediately enforceable".

V. LIABILITY

A. Sources of law

It is clear from the Leeman and Nooijen cases that the employee has the right to a smoke-free workplace.

To marshal the arguments once again:

1. health is a fundamental right;
2. that right also applies within the enterprise: the employee has the right to a healthy work environment, i.e. a smoke-free workplace;
3. such a right is created by, *inter alia:*
   - *Article 20.2 of the Contracts of Employment Act, as indicated above;*
   - *The Act of 11 June 2002 on Protection against Violence, Harassment, etc.;*
   - *National Collective Agreement No 72 of 30 March 1999 on the prevention of work-related stress;*
   - *the Welfare Act of 4 August 1996, and more specifically the Royal Decree of 28 May 2003.*

Let us scrutinize these sources closely.

1. Harassment at work

a. Active smoking = harassment

It is beyond all doubt that smoking at work amounts to a form of (prohibited) harassment of non-smokers, given on the one hand the smell and on the other hand the enormous damaging consequences for the health, both physical and mental, of the non-smokers there.

In point of fact the Act of 11 June 2002 on Protection Against Violence, Harassment and Sexual Harassment at Work[8] prescribes that "employers and employees ... shall be under an obligation to refrain from harassment" (Article 32 bis).
For the purposes of the Act harassment means:

"any form of unjust and persistent conduct, outside or within the enterprise or establishment, which may find expression in particular in *forms of behaviour*, words, threats, *actions*, gestures and biased written communications and which are aimed at or have the effect of impairing the personality, dignity or *physical or mental well-being of an employee or other person*

---

[8]   *B.S.* 22 June 2002.

in the performance of their work, jeopardizing their employment or creating a threatening, hostile, offensive, *humiliating* or hurtful *environment*" (Article 32 ter,2).

Smoking by others impairs the physical and mental well-being of the non-smoker.

Some employees have resigned from their jobs because they could no longer cope with the smoke at work.

b. Possibility of lodging a complaint

An important role is played here by the health and safety medical adviser, who is an expert in the psycho-social aspects of work and violence, harassment and sexual harassment at work, and possibly the union representative who may assist this medical adviser.

Any employee who feels that he/she is the victim of violence, harassment or sexual harassment at work can turn either to the health and safety medical adviser or the union representatives who assist this adviser or to the public officials responsible for supervising enforcement of the Act, in order to lodge a formal complaint.

c. Legal action

In cases where acts of harassment at work are brought to the attention of the employer, the latter must take appropriate measures. If the employer fails to take the necessary measures the health and safety medical adviser, in consultation with the victim, can apply to the public officials responsible for ensuring enforcement of the Act.

Legal proceedings to defend the interests of passive smokers can be instituted by:

(1) trade-union and employers' organizations classed as having representative status, such as ABVV (the Belgian General Federation of Labour), ACV (the Confederation of Christian Trade Unions), ACLVB (the Federation of Liberal Trade Unions of Belgium), VBO (the Federation of Belgian Enterprises) and VEV (the Flemish Employers' Association);
(2) a non-profit organization such as VZW Rookvrij, the anti-smoking lobby in Belgium.

d. Sanctions

Persistent forms of harassment are punishable by either a sentence of eight days' to one month's imprisonment or a fine of 26–500 euros, or both.

2. *Stress*

Existing rules on stress prevention also apply to passive smoking in the workplace and its detrimental effects.

In this case we are dealing with the application of National Collective

Agreement No 72 of 30 March 1999, concluded within the Nation Labour Council, regarding policy on the prevention of work-related stress.[9]

For the purposes of this National Collective Agreement, stress means:

> "a state of affairs which is perceived as negative by a group of employees and accompanied by complaints or dysfunctioning from a *physical, mental and/or social point of view* and which is a result of the fact that employees are rendered incapable of meeting the requirements and expectations demanded of them in the context of their employment".

By virtue of the Welfare Act and its implementing Decrees, employers are under an obligation to pursue a policy aimed at the collective prevention and/or rectification of work-related stress.
Such a policy entails, more specifically:

...

"the planning of prevention and implementation of policy regarding employees' well-being in the performance of their work with a view to a systematic approach encompassing, *inter alia*, the following elements: techniques, organization of work, *working conditions*, social relations and *environmental factors* at work".

It is beyond all doubt that passive smoking causes stress among the non-smokers group and in some cases leads to depression.

For these reasons also, employers should introduce a ban on smoking and ensure its observance. The trade unions should co-operate in overseeing the observance of this Agreement. A National Collective Agreement that has been pronounced generally applicable is, in fact, binding on pain of criminal sanctions.

3. *Royal Decree on the supervision of employees' health*[10]

This Royal Decree of 28 May 2003, which has been issued in implementation of the above-mentioned Welfare Act (Act of 4 August 1996 on employees' welfare in the performance of their work), has the objective of "promoting and maintaining employees' health by means of risk prevention" (Article three). This takes place through the introduction of preventive measures by means of which the health and safety medical adviser must take steps to, *inter alia*, ensure that the employee is not exposed to a "chemical agent" (Article 2.3a).

There is not the slightest doubt that smoke, both primary and secondary, constitutes a chemical agent. We need only repeat what Professor Johan Vansteenkiste says on the subject: "Environmental smoke contains thousands of chemical substances, at least 40 of which are known to be carcinogenic".[11]

---

[9]   Pronounced generally applicable by Royal Decree of 21 June 1999 (*B.S.* 9 July 1999).
[10] *B.S.* 16 June 2003. Let's indicate that the pregnant workers enjoys special protection against chemical agentia, like benzene, caused by smoking.
[11] *See* Chapter I, § 2.

The health and safety medical adviser must consequently propose to the employer all such appropriate individual and collective protective measures as are indicated.

Information on these measures must be provided to the health and safety committee at the workplace concerned (Article 34).

This Decree, which with a view to the protection of employees' health should be interpreted broadly, consequently imposes an obligation on the health and safety medical adviser to propose a ban on smoking; a proposal that the employer should comply with.

4. *Other Royal Decrees related to smoking*

The following provisions should also be noted:

- in *rest areas* in the extraction industries in opencast or underground workings "the necessary measures must be taken to protect non-smokers against nuisance caused by tobacco smoke";[12]
- in *living quarters* on board fishing vessels "appropriate measures" must, "as far as is possible, be taken to protect non-smokers against nuisance caused by tobacco smoke";[13]
- likewise in *recreation rooms* and *shelters* on temporary or mobile construction sites the necessary measures must be taken to protect non-smokers against nuisance caused by tobacco smoke;[14]
- The General Regulations on protection of the population, employees and the environment against the hazard of ionizing radiation stipulates that smoking is prohibited within any controlled zone where there is a *danger of contamination*. It is also prohibited to bring tobacco into such zones;[15]
- under the rules on the protection of employees' health and safety against the risks of *chemical agents* at work the health and safety medical adviser must, in determining carboxyhaemoglobin levels, take account of non-work-related causes such as tobacco.[16]

B. Rights and obligations of the employer

1. *Ban on smoking*

As stated, the employer – and this applies both in the private and in the public sector – has a duty to issue a ban on smoking and to uphold it.

He also has the right to do so. The employer possesses specific authority within the enterprise. He is legally entitled to regulate the organization of work within the enterprise in accordance with the interests of the enterprise and its workforce. This managerial prerogative obviously gives him the right

---

[12] Royal Decree of 6 January 1997, *B.S.* 12 March 1997.
[13] Royal Decree of 13 July 1998, *B.S.* 31 July 1998.
[14] Royal Decree of 25 January 2001, *B.S.* 7 February 2001.
[15] Royal Decree of 20 July 2001, *B.S.* 30 August 2001.
[16] Royal Decree of 11 March 2002, *B.S.* 14 March 2002.

to regulate, and hence ban, the right to smoke within the domain of the enterprise.

2. Recruitment and smoking

The employer also has the right, when hiring new employees, to make it a condition that they undertake not to smoke at work.

3. Imposition of disciplinary penalties for unlawful smoking

If an employee nevertheless persists in smoking, the employer is entitled and possibly under an obligation to impose disciplinary penalties. These must be included in the company's works rules as set out in the staff handbook, and depending on the circumstances in any given case can range from a reprimand, fine or temporary suspension to dismissal for just cause.

4. Liability of the enterprise and its responsible managers

The enterprise is also liable for damage caused to employees or other workers as a result of passive smoking in the event of negligence on the part of the employer where there is a causal connection between such negligence and the damage suffered by the employee.

In cases where there is no ban on or effective regulation of smoking and an employee has suffered damage as a result, i.e. because of passive smoking, the enterprise can be ordered to pay compensation.

5. The role of employee representatives

It goes without saying that employee representatives, i.e. the workplace health and safety committee and where applicable the union delegation, should collaborate in supervising health in the workplace and the provision of a smoke-free environment for employees to work in.

Up till now they have failed to do so, or not done so adequately. The unions are also at fault here.

This cannot continue. Smoke contains medically harmful elements against which employees, in accordance with the above-mentioned Royal Decree of 28 May 2003 on the supervision of employees' health, must be protected. Employee representatives, and particularly the unions, should live up to their responsibility in this respect.

Furthermore, the unions and their legal services are well-placed to assist any of their members who are victims of passive smoking at work in formulating and instituting possible legal claims for damages.

It must not, incidentally, be forgotten that employers' organizations and trade unions are themselves also employers and should impose a ban on smoking within their own organizations, including the meetings that they organize and hence also their members, certainly when employees of the organization are taking part.

6. The role of other groups

Other associations such as VZW Rookvrij (the anti-smoking lobby in Belgium) or Liga tegen Kanker (the Anti-Cancer League) can also assist victims of passive smoking in any legal actions they may wish to bring regarding damage suffered, by financing (part of) the costs of these legal actions or on the basis of the opportunities offered by the legislation on harassment at work[17] and stress. In addition there is the obligation on the employer to ensure that there is healthy air in the workplace, and the appropriate Labour Tribunal can, if so requested, compel its enforcement.

VI.   DE LEGE FERENDA

A.   Tightening up the ban

The existing legislation provides a basis for employees to assert their right to a smoke-free workplace.

It is in any event already a fact that an employer who has his employees working in unhealthy conditions carries both civil and criminal liability for damage to health. The prospect of being held liable in this way is prompting a great many employers to establish an active policy on smoking within the enterprise and to introduce a ban. More needs to be done, however. The government has a duty to issue clear rules on the matter and safeguard the lives of thousands of fellow-Belgians.

Many non-smokers dare not voice their objections, because their boss smokes and they fear for their job. The 1990 Decree banning smoking in restaurants and other places is not observed and the major unions prefer to let things drift in the hotel and catering sector.

The Ministers for Public Health and for Employment should therefore shoulder their responsibility and issue the appropriate Decrees to put into effect a strict ban on smoking within the workplace and in all public places. They possess the powers to do so and need only follow the examples set by other countries in line with the urgings of the World Health Organization and the European Union.

B.   International and European legislation

At international level the issue of tobacco control is very high on the agenda: on 21 May 2003 a *Convention on Tobacco Control* was adopted within the framework of the **World Health Organization (WHO)**.

The Convention was supported by all WHO Member States. Including Belgium.

---

[17]   *See* Chapter III, § 3, B.

As at 11 October 2004 a total of 168 countries, including the European Union, had already signed the Convention.

Belgium, like all other signatories, is committed to incorporating the Convention's provisions into its national legislation.

The Convention provides an international framework for the control of tobacco use and contains provisions on tobacco advertising, sponsorship, tax policies, pricing, labelling, illegal trade in tobacco products and also passive smoking.

It prescribes that WHO Member States, i.e. including Belgium, shall adopt and implement effective measures in connection with, *inter alia*, passive smoking.

Its Article eight is in fact specifically devoted to protection against exposure to tobacco smoke, i.e. passive smoking, and reads as follows:

1. "Parties recognize that scientific evidence has unequivocally established that exposure to tobacco smoke causes death, disease and disability.
2. Each Party shall adopt and implement ... effective ... measures providing for protection from exposure to tobacco smoke in indoor workplaces, public transport, indoor public places and, as appropriate, other public places".

Article 12 requires Parties to the Convention to institute public awareness campaigns against issues such as passive smoking.

In addition, Article 19 requires Parties to the Convention to take all necessary measures as regards civil and criminal liability resulting from tobacco use, including the payment of compensation.

On 2 December 2002[18] the **Council of the European Union** adopted a Recommendation on the prevention of smoking and on initiatives to improve tobacco control.

Point four of this Recommendation recommends that Member States, i.e. including Belgium, "*implement ... effective measures ... that provide protection from exposure to environmental tobacco smoke in indoor workplaces, enclosed public spaces and public transport. Priority consideration should be given to, inter alia, educational establishments, health care facilities and places providing services to children*".

Member States are also asked to "*implement all necessary and appropriate pro-cedures to verify compliance with the measures set out in this Recommendation*" (point 8). Member States must "*inform the Commission every two years of action taken in response to this Recommendation*" (point 9).

CONCLUSIONS

Health is a fundamental right. Every employee has the right to a smoke-free workplace. Employees should stand up for their right. The government must help them to do this, since many employees are afraid of losing their job, particularly in cases where their boss is a smoker.

In any event it is already a fact that employers who have their employees

---

[18]   Council Recommendation 2003/54/EC [2003] OJ L022/0031.

working in unhealthy conditions carry both civil and criminal liability for any damage to health. The prospect of such legal action is prompting a great many employers to establish an active policy on smoking within the enterprise and to introduce a ban on smoking. More needs to be done, however.

The government must face up to its responsibility: by introducing a ban on smoking in all workplaces, as in Ireland, the Netherlands, Norway and many other countries, opt unequivocally in favour of employees' health and make the ban on smoking really effective. It must be done. A Royal Decree containing a smoking ban is expected to be in force by 1 January 2006, excluding, however, the hospitality sector.

APPENDIX: THE JEAN LEEMAN CASE

Summary Proceedings No 250

LABOUR COURT, BRUSSELS

JUDGMENT

OPEN-COURT SESSION OF
FOURTH OF OCTOBER TWO THOUSAND AND TWO

Summary proceedings
Contested action
Final.

In the case
LEEMAN Jean, assistant police officer, resident at 1000 Brussels, Pijlstraat, 7/26;

appellant, defendant in a counterclaim, appearing in person, assisted by J. Vanneste, barrister of 1000 Brussels, Verenigingstraat, 28;

v

BRUSSELS CITY POLICE – ELSENE, represented by its police authority with offices at 1000 Brussels, Kolenmarkt, 30, defendant, appellant in a counterclaim, represented by A. Swinnen *loco* W. Muls, barrister of 1000 Brussels, A Dansaertstraat, 92;

After due deliberation the Labour Court, Brussels pronounces judgment as follows:

Having regard to the procedural documents, more particularly:

- the application for an injunction dated 19 July 2002;
- the certified copy of the decision of the officiating President of the Labour Tribunal, Brussels dated 26 August 2002 rejecting the application;
- the petition for appeal received at the Court registry on 2 September 2002;
- the submissions of the parties;

Having heard the pleas and assertions of the parties at the special open-court session of 27 September, whereafter the proceedings were closed;

The appeal was lodged in due time and in the proper manner and is therefore admissible;

It is lodged against the decision dated 26 August 2002 delivered by the officiating President of the Labour Tribunal, Brussels, in summary proceedings, whereby the application of 19 July 2002 made by the present appellant for an injunction ordering the present defendant immediately to take all such measures as are appropriate to enable the appellant to spend the hours during which he works indoors in a tobacco-free environment, if necessary by allocating him a separate work room free from environmental tobacco smoke during these indoors working hours, on pain of a penalty payment of 1000 euros for each day or part of a day that the appellant continues to be employed in a situation of exposure to environmental tobacco smoke, and ordering the defendant to pay the costs, including court fees, is pronounced admissible but unfounded for lack of urgency, and the appellant has his application dismissed and is ordered to pay the costs of the proceedings;

The subject-matter of the appeal is a request to the Court:

"Without prejudice and not acknowledging anything pronounced against the appellant

Consequently to set aside the contested judgment and in delivering judgment anew do what the first-instance court should have done, namely: to order the defendant immediately to take all such measures as are appropriate to enable the appellant to spend the hours during which he works indoors in a tobacco-free environment, if necessary by allocating the appellant a separate work room free from tobacco smoke during his indoor working hours, on pain of a penalty payment of 1000 euros per working day for which the appellant continues to be employed in a situation of exposure to environmental tobacco smoke and has to spend his indoor working hours in a room containing environmental tobacco smoke;

Also to order the defendant to pay the appellant 1000 euros for making a provocative and reckless defence;

Award the costs of the proceedings against the defendant, including the court fees";

The defendant asks the Court in submissions:

"To pronounce the appeal inadmissible and not allowable, or at least unfounded;

To dismiss the appellant's petition and order him to pay the costs for both the first-instance proceedings and the appeal proceedings, including court fees;

To order him, in addition, to pay a sum of 1500 euros to the defendant for instituting provocative and reckless legal proceedings".

THE MAIN CLAIM

Urgency

The defendant disputes the urgency of the claim, given that:

- the appellant did not make his first complaint about environmental tobacco smoke until one year after his heart attack, i.e. on 13 March 2002, and subsequent to that date did nothing for four months before suddenly applying for an injunction;
- the medical certificates deposited with the court by the appellant suggest no urgency and, furthermore, it would appear from the certificate issued by Dr Bouchlis that his heart problems should be attributed to other causes;
- to date, the appellant has not as yet actually instituted main legal proceedings on the matter against the defendant;

Under Article 584, second paragraph, of the Belgian Judicial Code the President of the Labour Tribunal delivers an interim injunction in cases he considers urgent, in circumstances that fall within the jurisdiction of the Labour Tribunal, which jurisdiction is not disputed by the defendant;

In accordance with case-law and legal doctrine urgency exists wherever the fear of substantial damage or serious hardship make it desirable to have a ruling that cannot be obtained immediately or in time from the court that is to hear the main proceedings (Court of Cassation 11 May 1990, *T. B. H.* 1990, 774; Court of Cassation 21 May 1987, *Arr. Cass.* 198687, 1287; *Pas.* 1987, 1, 1160; *R. W.* 1987–88, 1425; Neufchâteau Court of First Instance (summary proceedings) 30 November 1988, *J. T.* 1989, 602; Brussels Court of First Instance 17 September 1985, *R. W.* 1985–86, 2581; Turnhout Canton Court (summary proceedings) 30 November 1988, *Turnh. Rechtsl.* 1989, 9; Ghent Canton Court (summary proceedings) 10 November 1982, *R. W.* 14584–85, 1094; Bergen 2 February 1989, *Pas.* 1989, II, 189; Luik 27 June 1984, *Jur. Liège* 1984, 415; Brussels 31 August 1983, *R.P.S.* 1983, note by F. Kint and 1984, 213; Brussels Canton Court (summary proceedings) 8 December 1981. *R. W.* 1982–83, 1139, note by P. Temmens; Brussels 19 May 1980, *R. W.* 1983–84, 367; G. De Leval, "L'Examen du fond des affaires par le juge des référés", *J. T.* 1982, 421, No 5; G. Closset-Marchal, "Le référé aujourd'hui", *Ann. Dr. Fac. Liège* 1986, 312; G. De Leval and J. Van Compernolle, "L'évolution du référé: mutation ou renouveau"?, *J. T.* 1985 (517), No 6; J. Van Compernolle, "Actualité du référé", *Ann. Fac. Dr. Louvain* 1989, 145);

The circumstances determine the urgent nature of the measure. A serious threat to a right entails urgency and justifies an application for an injunction. In assessing the legitimacy of the application the judge conducting the summary proceedings must take the interests and rights of both parties into consideration. The urgency is greater, the more closely the legal position is connected with our cultural values and the general interest and the higher the hierarchical ranking therefore occupied by the rules that govern it (G. Rommel, "Bevoegdheid, urgentie en voorlopigheid in het sociaal kortgeding: tendensen en perspectieven", *J.T.T.* 1982, 69);

The defendant's assertion that the appellant did nothing for four months as from 13 March 2002 is not really tenable, given that his letter on the subject dated 13 March 2002 was addressed to his divisional superintendent and that during the period at issue he informed or consulted both the labour inspectorate and the health and safety medical adviser about this problem, as is apparent from the letter dated 28 May 2002 written by Dr D. Van Duffel, medical labour inspector, and the communication of 3 July 2002 from Dr P. Vermeiren, health and safety medical adviser, addressed to Mr Thielemans, Mayor of Brussels and Mr Vanreusel, Chief Commissioner of Police (documents two and six submitted by the appellant);

Furthermore, the position is that a possible omission on the part of a litigant does not in itself preclude urgency (*cf.* Kortrijk Canton Court (summary proceedings) 29 April 1996, *T.B.H.* 1996, 10–10); not every delay in bringing the dispute before the summary proceedings judge may cause the application for an injunction to be dismissed (*cf.* Brussels 1 February 1996, *T.B.H.* 1997, 427) and as well as the fact that urgency must exist at the time of the application for an injunction this must be assessed at the time of the ruling (*cf.* Court of Cassation 4 November 1996. *R.W.* 1976–77, 2146; D. Lindemans, *Kort geding*, Kluwer 1985, p. 86);

The defendant is also wrong in asserting that the urgent nature of the case cannot be inferred from the medical certificates and reports deposited in the case file by the appellant;

The urgency of the case is in fact explicitly apparent from the content of the following medical certificates regarding the appellant's state of health:

*certificate dated 4 July 2002 from the physician treating him, Dr P. Van Breusegem, who attests that he *"has established that the appellant, who is one of his patients, suffers from a disorder that is worsened the more he is exposed to the presence of cigarette smoke (passive smoking). Every day that he is exposed to cigarette smoke increases the risk of health-threatening complications, with potentially serious repercussions on the vital prognosis";*

*certificate dated 12th August 2002 from Dr P. Coussement, a cardiologist, in which the latter confirms *"that the inhalation of tobacco smoke, whether active (through smoking) or passive (through spending time in a smoky environment) is damaging to health. More particularly in the case of the above-mentioned patient with known atherosclerotic coronary artery disease, inhalation of cigarette smoke is absolutely contra-indicated";*

*certificate dated 29 August 2002 from Dr P. Van Breusegem specifying that the appellant *"suffers from a chronic disease which does not render him unfit to work but which means that any exposure to cigarette smoke poses a threat to his health.*

The mechanism that creates this threat is not comparable with that of air pollution but is specific to the combustion of tobacco products.

Such exposure must be regarded as harmful irrespective of its duration, most certainly in the case of repeated exposure whose effects are cumulative over time";

* certificate dated 10 September 2002 from Dr P. Coussement stating that *"the long-term harmful effects of exposure to tobacco smoke on the human body, especially the cardiovascular system, are well-known. The risk of cardiac and vascular diseases in the event of exposure to tobacco smoke is present continuously from the start of exposure and increases with the duration of exposure. Since Mr Jean Leeman already suffers from an atherosclerotic coronary artery disease and as a result of this had a heart attack in April 2001, exposure to tobacco smoke can imminently cause serious damage to his state of health";*

* certificate dated 5 September 2002 from Dr Bouchlis, a member of Dr Van Breusegem's practice, who attests that the appellant *"underwent surgery five (5) years ago for clogging of the arteries in the context of cardiac arrhythmia. Investigation has revealed that a lateral branch of one coronary artery is still blocked and cannot be blown open by a balloon operation or the insertion of a stent.*

Given the tendency of coronary arteries to narrow, in his case it is crucially important for him to avoid cardiovascular risks such as smoking, both active and passive. In his case exposure to smoke can have harmful effects with unknown consequences";

Contrary to what the defendant maintains, it cannot seriously be inferred from the aforementioned certificate provided by Dr Bouchlis that a different issue is involved here, notably that the heart problems cited by the appellant have another cause for which the defendant cannot be held responsible, such as personal eating, drinking, smoking and exercise habits, or in other words that the cause lies with the appellant himself, absolutely no proof of which is supplied by the defendant;

Nor can the urgent nature of a case depend on whether or not main legal proceedings have been initiated, a precondition which is nowhere stipulated in law;

On the basis of what is stated above and in accordance with the aforementioned case-law and legal doctrine it must be concluded that the appellant's precarious state of health justifies taking necessary interim measures in a case of urgency;

As to the decision on an application for an injunction

The defendant alleges that the appellant before the court ruling in summary proceedings is in actuality seeking not an immediate injunction but a judgment on the substance of the case;

A court rules in summary proceedings on an application for an injunction (Article 584, first paragraph, of the Belgian Judicial Code) without causing prejudice to the case itself (Article 1039 of the Judicial Code);

The fact that a judgment delivered in summary proceedings is without prejudice to the case itself means that the decision is not binding in any way on the court hearing the main proceedings. The latter remains free to exercise its discretion and can adjust, change or supplement the decision delivered in summary proceedings (E. Leboucq and W. Van Eeckhoutte, "Het sociaalrechterlijk kort geding", *R.W.* 1982–83, 1094);

The fact that the decision is immediately enforceable does not mean that it has to incorporate a time-limit or that it is necessarily of a temporary nature. The provisional nature of the decision does not preclude the possibility of a judgment delivered in summary proceedings causing damage in certain cases and of that damage sometimes being irreparable. The decision is provisional only with respect to the assessment of the case by the court subsequently hearing the main proceedings, not as regards its *de facto* consequences (Court of Cassation 6 February 1930, *Pas.* 11.930, I 87);

In ruling in summary proceedings the court is at liberty to adopt such measures as it sees fit, in so far as the circumstances require that the measure in question be adopted immediately;

It assesses the expediency of taking action in the light of the urgent necessity involved and, within the limits of what is being claimed, chooses from the range of possible measures on the basis of what the circumstances call for by way of a provisional measure to be adopted. The circumstances which the court ruling in summary proceedings takes into account can be of various kinds: any damaging effects of the measure it orders, and if so the fact that they may be irreparable (Brussels Canton Court (summary proceedings) 31 December 1978, *T.B.H.* 1978, 645); a high degree of certainty regarding the predicted outcome of the main proceedings (Brussels Canton Court (summary proceedings) 29 March 1983, *T.B.H.* 1983 680; Brussels Canton Court (summary proceedings) 9 June 1978, *T.B.H.* 1978, 361; I. Verougstraete, "Het kort geding. Recente trends", *T.P.R.* 1980, 262); the financial, moral and physical state of the parties (Brussels Canton Court (summary proceedings) 15 March 1983, *T.B.H.* 1984, 86); and the interests of the parties (Brussels Canton Court 15 March 1983, *T.B.H.* 1983, 678; Brussels 6 October 1983, *J.T.* 1984, 134, note by L. Van Bunnen);

It should, however, be noted that the task incumbent on the President of the court of delivering an immediate judgment no longer implies that an assessment of the substance of the case lies outside his jurisdiction. The Court of Causation ruled to this effect in a judgment of 9 September 1982, declaring: "that the fact that Article 1039 of the Belgian Judicial Code states that rulings on applications for an injunction delivered in summary proceedings may not cause prejudice to the case itself *does not preclude* an investigation by the court of the rights of the parties, provided it does not issue any order whereby those rights are definitively and irrevocably infringed" (Court of Cassation 9 September 1982, *Arr. Cass.* 1982–83, 277; *R.W.* 1983–84, 1338, note by Laenens. This viewpoint has been repeatedly confirmed by case-law and legal doctrine (for example, Court of Cassation 29 September 1983, *Arr. Cass.* 1983–84, 85; Court of Cassation 22 February 1991, *Arr. Cass.* 1990–91, 683; Court of Cassation 25 April 1996, *R.W.* 1996–97, 432 and 1289, with conclusions by G. Dubrulle; G. Closset-Marchal, "Le référé aujourd'hui", *Ann. Dr.* 1986, 310; De Leval and Van Compernolle, "L'évolution du référé: mutation ou renouveau"?, *J.T.* 1985, 518);

Nevertheless, it has to be established that in his application and submissions the appellant is claiming only immediate measures such as are rendered necessary and urgent by his state of health with respect to environmental tobacco smoke, and that the Labour Court is not in actuality being asked to deliver a judgment on the substance of the case regarding the possible effect of environmental tobacco smoke on his heart disorder, as is wrongfully maintained by the defendant;

The provisional measures

The appellant is requesting that the defendant be ordered immediately to take any such measures as are appropriate to enable him to spend the hours during which he works indoors in a tobacco-free environment, if necessary by allocating him a separate non-smoking work room during these indoor working hours;

On 2 July 1990 the appellant was recruited as an assistant police officer into the Brussels police force, legal head of the Brussels City-Elsene police district, where he is employed in the traffic division and principally assigned to outdoor duties such as directing traffic and supervising the observance of traffic regulations;

The defendant infers from this that the appellant only exceptionally needs to spend time indoors in the premises of the police force;

The facts of the matter are, however, that the appellant has to perform his administration tasks, such as processing his reports, in the briefing room, where he also has to wait to be given each day's assignments, and that meal breaks are also spent in this room since there is no canteen;

For example, his three last time-sheets dated seventh, ninth and 16 September 2002 (patrol reports, appellant's documents 12a to 12c) show that on average he spends some three hours every day in the briefing room;

Article 148 decies 2 bis of ARAB (the General Regulation on Health and Safety at Work – Royal Decree of 31 March 1993) stipulates, under the heading

"Control of nuisance attributable to environmental smoke",

that: "the employer shall take such measures as are necessary to ensure that *smoking behaviour* during work *and* during breaks and mealtimes is adapted to accommodate the mutual expectations of smokers and non-smokers. These arrangements shall be based on mutual tolerance, respect for freedom of the *individual* and courtesy.

The employer shall, where necessary, take physical measures to eliminate nuisance attributable to environmental tobacco smoke".

In addition, Article 20.2 of the Contracts of Employment Act of 3 July 1978 provides that the employer is under an obligation "to take all reasonable care to ensure that work is performed in decent conditions with regard to the safety and health of the employee".

Health protection is, furthermore, guaranteed by Article 23 of the Belgian Constitution, while Article five of the European Convention on Human Rights provides that everyone has the right to security of person;

In so far as the situation *in casu* could possibly be seen as a form of harassment with respect to the appellant reference should be made to the Act on Protection Against Violence, Harassment and Sexual Harassment at Work of 11 June 2002 (*B.S.* 22 June 2002), which in its Article 32 bis prescribes, in summary, that in the performance of their work employers and employees must refrain from harassment at work, a concept that in Article 32 ter, 2 is defined more precisely as unjust and persistent conduct, outside or within the workplace, that may find expression in particular in forms of behaviour and actions aimed at or having the effect of impairing the personality, dignity or physical or mental well-being of an employee in the performance of their work and creating an offensive, humiliating or hurtful environment;

That the defendant is sympathetic towards the relevant legislation in force, given the issue that has arisen, can be inferred from the question on the matter put by Mr Vanreusel, Chief of Police-Superintendent, to the health and safety medical adviser Dr B. Vermeiren as evidenced by the latter's reply as well as his letter of 3 July 2002 addressed to the Mayor (documents two and three deposited by the appellant), and from the fact that the defendant subsequently arranged for a "no smoking" sticker to be displayed (document four deposited by the defendant) so that a total ban on smoking was then introduced in the briefing room;

However, the reality is that both in his submissions and in the open-court session the appellant expressly declares that the total ban on smoking that has been issued is not being observed at all but remains a completely dead letter, which fact is not seriously disputed by the defendant;

The defendant consequently has a duty to take every care to ensure the strict and effective application of the rules issued by itself on the basis of the legislation on the matter that is in force and known to it;

In view of the identity of the defendant the Court does not consider it necessary to make the fulfilment of this duty subject to a penalty payment;

The defendant must accordingly take urgent action to see to it and ensure that the briefing room is effectively made completely free of tobacco smoke in the immediate interests of the appellant's precarious state of health;

The main claim is for these reasons admissible and well-founded;

The counterclaims of the two parties

The appellant is claiming the payment of 1000 euros for a provocative and reckless defence since the defendant is blaming him for the media publicity received by the case through his agency, while the defendant is claiming compensation of 1500 euros for the initiation of a provocative and reckless legal action given that the appellant has not produced any new evidence on appeal, that he has not as yet initiated main legal proceedings and that his appeal "was lodged purely in order to attract renewed attention to himself in the media";

Given the content of the present judgment, however, the fact that there is nowhere in the law any provision stipulating that main legal proceedings must also be initiated, and that the defendant produces no proof whatever that the appellant's purpose in lodging the appeal is solely to attract media attention to the case and himself, the counterclaim made by the defendant is unfounded; and the same is also true of the appellant's counterclaim, given that he fails to furnish proof of abuse of the rights of defence on the part of the defendant as concerns the latter's last-mentioned allegation and that widespread media attention is an inevitable attendant circumstance of judicial proceedings (*cf.* X. De Riemaecker and G. Londers, *Statuut en deontologie van de Magistraat*, Die Keure 2000, p. 316), something which can only be to the benefit of democracy provided, of course, that the coverage and reporting are objective and accurate;

The counterclaims are thereby unfounded;

ON THOSE GROUNDS:

THE LABOUR COURT,

Having regard to the Act of 15 June 1935 on language use in legal proceedings as amended to date, more particularly its Article 24;

Ruling *inter partes* and in summary proceedings,

Declares the appeal admissible and well-founded;

Sets aside the contested decision of 26 August 2002;

Pronouncing judgment anew;

Declares the main claim admissible and well-founded, as follows:

Confirms the total ban on smoking in its briefing room issued by the defendant, effective and strict observance of which, without exceptions, must be ensured and enforced with the utmost rigour by the defendant as a matter of urgency;

Declares the respective counterclaims of the appellant and defendant admissible but unfounded;

Orders the defendant to pay the costs;

These costs are estimated for the two parties at:

for the appellant:

- 59.70 euros application costs,
- 100.40 euros court fees first instance (after conversion),
- 133.86 euros court fees appeal (after conversion),

for the defendant:

- 100.40 euros court fees first instance (after conversion),
- 133.86 euros court fees appeal (after conversion);

Pronounced and delivered in open-court session of the First Chamber of the Labour Court, Brussels, on 4 October 2002.

7. Brazil

Paulo Sergio João[1]

1. BRAZIL AND TOBACCO SMOKING

This report focuses on Brazilian federal legislation. It does not consider the State or municipal laws.

Throughout many decades, smoking was considered in Brazil as an alternative life-style. However, nowadays, it is recognized by science as a disease caused by the dependence on a drug.

In Brazil, one out of every seven deaths is due to the use of tobacco.

This is related to the internationalisation of the commerce of tobacco products.

Globalization allows the major international conglomerates of tobacco to expand in countries with low production cost and high consumer potential.

Such a process caused a great expansion of the tobacco market in Latin America. Nowadays, the worldwide scenario indicates that, even though cigarette consumption decreased in most of the developed countries, the global consumption increased with 50% from 1975, due to the increase in cigarette consumption in developing countries.

The recognition of the fact that the expansion of the tobacco consumption is a global problem led to the conclusion in the framework of the World Health Organisation of the Framework Convention on Tobacco Control (2003).

2. ABOUT THE BRAZILIAN LEGISLATION, ON SMOKING RELATED AFFAIRS

Beyond the confirmation of the Frame – Convention, mentioned above, Brazil has been adopting, systematically, legal measures to combat smoking. Among these, the following measures are mentioned:

(a) Those related to exposure risks of the environmental smoking pollution:
   – Inter-ministerial Administrative Rule no. 3.257 of 22 September 1988,

---

[1]   This report was coordinated by Dr. Paulo Sergio João, professor of Law School in Pontifical Catholic University of São Paulo and Business School Escola de Administração EASP, were part of the team: Jorge Gonzaga Matsumoto, attorney and Juliana P.Hansen, Vanessa C.Galera, Manoela B. Alcântara, Priscila M.B.Lenza e Marina G. Butkeraitis, students of the Pontifical Catholic University of São Paulo.

R. Blanpain (ed.), Smoking and the Workplace, 103–112
© 2005 *Kluwer Law International. Printed in The Netherlands.*

which establishes restrictive procedures applied to smoking in the working environment, and for example, provides for smoking areas which are adequately isolated and ventilated.

- Law no. 9.294 from 15 July 1996, which forbids using cigarettes, cigars, pipes, or any other product derived from tobacco, in collective places, private or public, such as, public sections, hospitals, class rooms, libraries, working places, theatres and cinemas, except in specially designed smoking areas.
- Ordinance no. 2.018 of 1 October 1996, which implements Law no. 9.294/96, defining the concepts of collective places and properly isolated areas, destined exclusively for smoking.
- Health Ministry Administrative Rule no. 2.818 from 28 May 1998, which forbids tobacco smoking within the Health Ministry dependencies in the Federal District, States and Municipalities.
- Law no. 10.167 of 27 December 2000, which modifies Law no. 9.294/96, forbidding the use of smoking products derived from tobacco in aircrafts and other collective transport vehicles.
- Inter-Ministerial Administrative Rule no. 1.498 of 22 August 2002, which recommends that health and educational institutions install programmes to develop areas which are free from environmental tobacco exposure.

(b) Related to traffic accidents, through the Law no. 9.503 of 23 September 1997, which forbids driving under the influence of any substance that is sedative or that causes physical or psychological dependence, or driving a vehicle with only one hand, except when the person must do the standard driving signals with the arms, shift gears, or activate the vehicle's accessory equipments.

(c) Related to the access to tobacco derived products:
- Law no. 10.167 of 27 December 2000, which altered Law no. 9.294/96, forbidding sales via postal channel, sample distributions or prizes and the commercialisation in educational or health care establishments.
- Resolution of the National Sanitary Surveillance Agency no. 15 of 17 January 2003, that forbids selling tobacco derived products via internet.
- Law no. 10.702 of 14 July 2003 that alters the Law no. 9.294/96, forbidding the sale of tobacco products in the buildings of the Public Administration.

(d) Related to youth protection:
- Law no. 8.069, of 13 July 1990, regarding the Children's and Teenager's Statute forbidding the selling, supplying or delivering to children or teenagers of products which have components that may cause physical or psychological dependence.
- Law no. 10.167 of 27 December 2000, altering Law no. 9.294/96, forbidding the participation of children and teenagers in publicity for tobacco derived products.
- Labour Ministry Rule no. 06 of 5 February 2001, that forbids youths under 18 from working in the harvesting of tobacco or the making of tobacco products.
- Resolution of the National Sanitary Surveillance Agency no. 304 of 7 November 2002, that forbids production, importation, commercialisation, marketing and distribution of food in the form of cigarettes, cigars, or any

other smoking products, that are derived or not from tobacco, and also the usage of food packages that simulate or imitate cigarette packages, or even names of trade marks that belong to smoking products, derived or not from tobacco.

- Resolution of the National Sanitary Surveillance Agency no. 14 (17 January 2003) which altered the Ordinance no. 104/01, imposing the printing of the following sentence on the packages of tobacco derived products: "Sales forbidden to those younger than 18 – Law 8069/1990 and Law 10.702/2003" imposes the use of sentences like "For adults, only" and "Product for those older than 18".
- Law no. 10.702 of 14 July 2003, altering Law no. 9.294/96, forbidding the sale of tobacco derived smoking products to persons, younger than 18.

(e) Related to aid to smokers established by the Health Ministry Administrative Rule no. 1.575 of 29 August 2002, which consolidated the National Smoking Control Programme.

(f) Related to publicity and funding of tobacco derived products:
- Constitution of Brazil's Federative Republic of 5 October 1988, which determines that the tobacco publicity is subjected to legal restrictions and will contain a warning about the harms caused by its use.
- Law no. 8.078 of 11 September 1990, Customer's Protection and Defence Code that forbids abusive and deceiving publicity.
- Inter-ministerial Administrative Rule no. 477 of 24 March 1995 which recommends the television broadcasts to avoid the transmission of images of VIP's, who are smoking, as well as the refusal of the sponsoring of public health campaigns by the tobacco industry.
- Law no. 10.167 of 27 December 2000, altering Law no. 9.294/96, which restricts the publicity for tobacco derived products by way of posters, panels and signs in shops, in magazines, newspapers, television, radio and outdoors, as well as advertising via electronic channels, including internet. Equally forbidden is indirect publicity, also known as merchandising as well as the advertisements in stadiums or similar places and also the funding of national and cultural sportive events.
- Resolution of the National Sanitary Surveillance Agency no. 15 of 17 January 2003, that specifies the concepts of advertising for tobacco products and of the selling places.
- Law no. 10.702 of 14 July 2003, altering Law no. 9.294/96, forbidding the funding of international sportive events by cigarettes makers, starting on 30 September 2005 and imposing the publication of warnings of the harmful health effects of tobacco at the opening and ending, and during the transmission of international sport events, in intervals of 15 minutes, allowing the Health Ministry to provide advertisements about the harmful effect of tobacco.

(g) Related to the information of the public:
- Law no. 7.488 of 11 June 1986, which established the National Day against Smoking (29 August) to be organised all over the country.
- Inter-ministerial Administrative Rule no. 3.257 of 2 September 1988, which provides for rewarding certificates to the companies which introduced anti-smoking programmes.
- Resolution from the National Sanitary Surveillance Agency no. 46 of 28

March 2001, which determined that the following information has to be printed on the pack of cigarettes: "This product contains more than 4.700 toxic substances, and nicotine which causes physical or psychological dependence. There are no safe levels for the consumption of these substances".

- Provisional Measure no. 2.134–30 of 24 May 2001, laying down that the materials destined for advertising and packages of tobacco products, except those destined for exportation, contain warnings and images which illustrate their meaning.
- Resolution from the National Sanitary Surveillance Agency no. 104 of 31 May 2001, that deals with the insertion of warnings, followed by images, on the packages and advertising materials for tobacco derived smoking products and the inclusion of the phone number of the "Stop Smoking Phone Service" on the packages and advertising materials of the tobacco derived smoking products and which forbids the use of any device that avoids or limits the visibility of the warnings.
- Interministerial Administrative Rule no. 1.498 of 22 August 2002, which gives rewarding certificates to the health care and educational institutions engaging in campaigns on tobacco control.
- Resolution from the National Sanitary Surveillance Agency no. 14 of 17 January 2003, altering resolution no. 104/01, concerning the substitution of the warnings and related images on the packages and advertising materials and which forbids the diffusion of the levels of nicotine, tar and carbon monoxide of the tobacco brand.

(h) Related to control and inspection of tobacco derived products:
- Law no. 9.782 of 26 January 1999, which establishes a National Sanitary Surveillance System and creates the National Sanitary Surveillance Agency (NSASA), responsible for the regulation, control and inspection of cigarettes, cigars and any other smoking product, derived or not from tobacco.
- Law no. 10.167 of 27 December 2000, altering Law no. 9.294/96 determining the fine to be paid in case of violation of the Law and determining the competent inspection services.
- Resolution from the National Sanitary Surveillance Agency no. 46 of 28 March 2001, which established the maximum levels allowed of tar, nicotine and carbon monoxide present in the primary current of the smoke of the cigarettes commercialised in the country, to a maximum of ten mg/cig, one mg/cig and ten mg/cig and also forbids to mention in publicity or on packages descriptions, such as classes, ultra low levels, low levels, smooth, light, soft, moderate levels, high levels, and others that may induce the customer to a misleading interpretation about the levels contained in the cigarettes.
- Resolution of the National Sanitary Surveillance Agency no. 105 of 31 May 2001, concerning the reporting about the tobacco products, their composition, sales and production by tobacco companies.
- Normative Instructions from the Secretary of the Federal Reserve no. 194 of 29 August 2002, regarding tax collection on tobacco products.
- Ordinance no. 2.637 of 25 June 1998, fixing the content of cigarette packages to twenty units.

(i) About financing the growing of tobacco:
   – Resolution of Brazil's Central Bank no. 2.833 of 25 April 2001, forbidding the granting of public credit related to tobacco production.

3. SMOKING AND THE WORKING ENVIRONMENT

(a) The right to a healthy working environment

This right is protected by the Constitution

Article seven of "Chapter II, Social rights of the Constitution provides:

"The following are rights of urban and rural workers, among others that aim to improve their social conditions:

...

XXII – reduction of employment related risks by means of health, hygiene and safety rules".

Article 170 reads as follows:

"The economic order, founded on the appreciation of the value of human work and on free enterprise, is intended to ensure everyone a life with dignity, in accordance with the dictates of social justice, with due regard for the following principles:

...

VI – environment protection"

Section II on Health provides in Article 196:

"Health is a right of all and a duty of the State and shall be guaranteed by means of social and economic policies aimed at reducing the risk of illness and other hazards and at the universal and equal access to actions and services for its promotion, protection and recovery".

And Article 200:

"It is incumbent upon the unified health system, in addition to other duties, as set forth by the law:

I – to supervise and control proceedings, products and substances of interest to health and to participate in the production of drugs, equipments, immunobiological products, blood products and other inputs;
II – to carry out actions of sanitary and epidemiological vigilance as well as those relating to the health of workers;

...

VIII – to cooperate in the preservation of the environment, including that of the workplace".

Finally, Article 225 of Chapter VI on the Environment states:

"All have the right to an ecologically balanced environment, which is an asset of common use and essential to a healthy quality of life, and both the Government and the community shall have the duty to defend and preserve it for present and future generations.

Paragraph 1 – In order to ensure the effectiveness of this right, it is incumbent upon the Government to:

...

V – control the production, sale and use of techniques, methods or substances which represent a risk to life, the quality of life and the environment".

These constitutional guarantees underline the concern of the Brazilian legislators to see to it that that the constitutional environmental law principles are integrally applied to the working environment.

(b) The right of the employer to establish restrictive smoking policies

It is the duty of every company to protect its workers against tobacco smoke in the working environment and to establish specific policies to that end.

Beyond this, the responsibility lies with the Labour and Health Ministry, by means of the Inter-ministerial Administrative Rule MTb/MS no. 3.257, of 22 September 1988, which contains the duty to guard the health and welfare of the workers, including protection against tobacco smoking. This rule:

"– recommends that in all the workplaces, restrictive measures regarding smoking be adopted, especially where the environment is a closed one;
– entitles companies to reserve restricted areas for smokers;
– it is up to the internal commissions of prevention of accidents to promote educational programmes demonstrating the harmful effects of smoking; and
– the ministers of labour and health, together, shall give rewarding certificates to companies that excel in anti-smoking campaigns".

This amply underlines that in Brazil the employer must not only install restrictive policies regarding smoking, but also submit himself/herself to the inspection by the Ministry of Work.

It must, at the same time be underlined that there is no prohibition of the right to smoke and that a worker cannot be discriminated against for reason of smoking.

(c) No-smoking as a condition for employment.

Given the harm caused by smoking in the scope of the working relations, some companies do not hire employees, who are smokers and that they prefer to dismiss the smokers in case of redundancies.

From the analysis of a study, involving 128 large and medium sized Brazilian enterprises, undertaken by Huggard-Caine, a consulting company specialized in human resources, it follows that 70% of companies, when hiring workers, prefer non-smokers above smokers.

Such a preference, however, would violate the Constitutional right of equal treatment. The Constitution, indeed, guarantees the promotion of "the welfare of all, without the prejudices of origin, sex, race, colour, age and any other forms of discrimination", where "all are equal before the law, without distinction of any nature, assuring the Brazilians and the foreigners residing in the country the inviolability of the right to life, to freedom, to equality, to safety and to property". "Any form of discrimination attempted against the fundamental rights and liberties", based on Article five XLI of the Constitution will be punished".

Besides that, Law no. 9.029 of 13 April 1995 prohibits any discrimination regarding access to the employment relationship or towards the employment and maintenance thereof, based on sex, origin, race, colour, civil state, family situation or age, excluded, in this case, the protection of minors".

It follows, as a general rule, that the refusal to hire someone or to dismiss him for the reason of being a smoker or not, is a discriminative act, forbidden by the Brazilian law.

(d) Smoking directed policies.

Brazil has been developing numerous programmes, projects and partnerships together with companies and non governmental organizations, aiming at the control of smoking.

Notwithstanding the "lobbying" especially by the tobacco companies, which see in these prevention measures a threat to the tobacco commerce, good results have been obtained. One of the main actors promoting the control of smoking is NICA (National Institute of Cancer), which is an organ of the government, linked to the Health Ministry and which is developing numerous projects, the main one being the NATIONAL PROGRAMME OF CONTROL OF SMOKING AND OTHER RISK FACTORS.

Brazil also plays an important role at international level and has been a driving force behind the WHO's efforts to conclude a framework agreement on Tobacco.

A National Commission for the Control of the Usage of Tobacco (1999) was established.

This Commission was composed of representatives of various Ministries.

August 2003, the National Commission of Implementation of the Convention – International Frame for Tobacco Control (NCCIFTC) was created, replacing the National Commission for the Control of the Tobacco Using.

The new commission's main goal is to elaborate the organization and implementation of a governmental agenda for the implementation of the obligations of the Frame Convention for the Control of Tobacco.

A National Programme of Smoking Control was established.

This programme addresses four groups: The first one is the public at large, children and teenagers; the second one, involves actions to stimulate smokers to stop smoking; a third group aims at protecting the health of non smokers from the exposure to the tobacco smoke, including the working environment; and finally there are measures that regulate the making of tobacco products and their commercialisation.

With these objectives, the programme creates a context which:

- reduces the social acceptance to smoking;
- reduces the stimulations of young people beginning to smoke and encourages the smokers to stop smoking;
- protect the population from the risks of the exposure to the environmental smoking pollution, and to reduce the access to tobacco derivatives;
- raises the smokers' access to tobacco by helping them to stop smoking;
- allows for controls and inspection of all the aspects related to commercialised tobacco products.

(e) Sanctions and litigation

Brazil has enacted legislation to diminish tobacco consumption like addressing the publicity of tobacco and by raising taxes.

Mention should be made of:

- Inter-ministerial Administrative Rule no. 3.257 of 22 September 1988, which promotes prohibition of smoking at the work place. The award of certificates to the companies which distinguished themselves in anti-tobacco campaigns should be underlined.
- article 220 of the Constitution of the Brazil Federative Republic of 1988, in the chapter referring to social communication, this allows for legal restraints on the commercial advertising of tobacco.
- the Law 8069/90, concerning the Child and the Adolescent Statute, prohibiting the selling of tobacco products to children.
- the Law no. 10.167 of December 2000, according to which it is forbidden to smoke in all Brazilian aircrafts.

Mention should also be made of the judicial decisions relating to the compensatory actions for moral damages (pain and suffering) for the benefit of the families of ex-smokers, who passed away as a consequence of diseases related to consuming cigarettes or other tobacco derivatives.

In this sense, the Court of Justice of Rio Grande do Sul condemned, unanimously, Souza Cruz to pay compensation for moral damages of R$ 408,000 to the widow and the four children of an ex-smoker, who died of lung cancer.

(f) Smoking at the workplace.

Every company must protect its workers from tobacco smoke in the work place.

For this, it must establish specific policies, as well as rules and provide information, enlightening people about the harms caused by smoking and second-hand smoking.

The policies of restriction to smoke in work places have resulted in rates of abandoning the addiction around ten to 20% in one year, according to research made about the theme.

Conscious of these facts, according to a report published by the Journal "Valor Econômico", the Brazilian companies are starting to evaluate the cost to maintain smoking employees.

The pause for a coffee break and smoking, the level of absenteeism and the increase in the price of the health insurance are being measured and questioned. Many companies that had already been making educational campaigns related to smoking are adopting programmes to help their employees to abandon the addiction. The actions involve alternative therapies to the medical treatments based on anti-depressives and chewing gum.

For the president of the Brazilian Life Quality Association (BLQA), Cecília Shibuya, a change is happening in the way that Brazilian companies are acting about smokers. "Before, they were more concerned with the theory, offering broadcasts, informative bulletins, but today there is the enlightening realization that they need to strive more to help the employees to get rid of smoke", she says.

According to her, only providing for restricted smoking areas, no longer seems to be sufficient. "Some programmes now, even involve the smokers family", she says.

Of the 114 companies that participated of the BLQA's II National Journey at the end of 2003 and that possess life quality programmes, 59 developed anti smoking actions.

A company's anti smoking programme of electro-electronics, for example, besides offering information about the harms caused by cigarettes, makes doctors available, who evaluate the cases and indicate treatments.

Companies like Brazil's Philips, Natura and Avon develop internal smoking prevention control programmes, giving a larger emphasis to the preventive health programmes instead of just concentrating on assisting medicine.

CONCLUSION

There is no doubt that Brazil needs to continue to address tobacco smoking through such measures as price and fiscal policies, illegal market control and address the smoking culture, sales control for younger people and the consolidation and centralization of a public smoking control policy.

Smoking in the workplace concerns especially the effects of passive smoking, causing workers to involuntarily expose themselves to cigarette smoke.

The greatest are the non-smoking workers in bars and other places where there is a greater concentration of smokers and where legislation that prohibits smoking in public places is not respected.

It is evident that the separation of the smokers and non smokers in the same (hospitality) space is worthless, since as the tobacco is being used, its smoke is diffused in an approximately uniform manner in the overall environment.

In Brazil, even though the adoption of restrictive measures against smoking is increasing in most of the Brazilian enterprises, bars and restaurants are not, or only partly, living up to the legal requirements regarding smoking.

But, no doubt, personal health stands paramount and further efforts have to be undertaken to protect everyone, including workers at the workplace, against the harmful effects of the use of tobacco.

BIBLIOGRAPHY

Brazilian Association of the Smoking Industry, 2001. Smoking Industry's profile.

Brazil Health Ministry, 2002. Research of the Smoker's Profile – 2001 – Municipality of Rio de Janeiro.

Brazilian Center Of Information About Psychotropic Drugs, 1997. IV Filing About the Usage of Drugs Among 1st and 2nd degree Students in ten Brazilian Capitals.

Brazilian Information Center About Psychtropic Drugs, 1999. I National Domestic Filing about the Usage of Psychotropic Drugs, Fapesp.

Etges, V.E., Ferreira, M., Camargo, M.E. *et al* (2002). The Impact of the Tobacco Culture on the Ecosystem and on Human Health in the Region of Santa Cruz do Sul/RS. – Preliminary report.

Health Ministry, 1998. Speaking about Smoking. National Secretary of Health Assistance. National Institute of Cancer. National Coordination of Smoking Control and Primary Prevention of Cancer (Sconpp). Rio de Janeiro, 3 ed.: 33.

Health Ministry, 2000, *Brazilian Cigarette. Analysis and Suggestions for Consuming Reduction.* Rio de Janeiro.

Rpsemberg, J. 2002. *Smoking Pandemic – Historical and Actual Scopes.* Health Secretary of São Paulo. Epidemiological Surveillance Centre. São Paulo/SP. Rio de Janeiro.

Brazil. Administrative Rule GM/MS No. 1.575, 29 August 2002. Consolidates the National Programe of Smoking Control, and Provides other attitudes. Union's Official Diary, Brasília, DF, Set. 3 2002. Section 1, p. 42–47.

Gigliiotti, A. P. Habits, attitudes and beliefs of Smokers in four Brazilian capitals: A comparison with 17 European countries. São Paulo, 2002.

Health Ministry, 2002. National Institute of Cancer, Preventing and Surveillance Coordination. National Programe of Control of Smoking and Other Cancer Risk Factors – Logical Model and Judgement. Rio de Janeiro.

8. Ireland

Michael Ohle

On 29 March 2004, Ireland became the first European country to implement legislation creating smoke-free enclosed workplaces. The ban was introduced under the Public Health (Tobacco) Act 2002 (the 2002 Act) and forms part of the Irish Governments overall strategy to reduce the number of people who smoke in the Republic.

ORIGINS OF THE BAN

The genesis of the ban on passive smoking in Ireland can be traced back five years or more when a group of Irish non-governmental organisations (NGOs) got together to lobby for legislative intervention. The Irish Cancer Society, the Irish Heart Foundation and ASH Ireland were responding to scientific research indicating that passive smoke damaged people's health. For many years, doctors had strong anecdotal evidence that people with respiratory problems such as asthma, who lived with a smoker, had more attacks than those who were not exposed to passive smoke. Now the solid evidence was there, as was a reliable method of measuring exposure to second-hand smoke.

As well as the international research and national political impetus, studies in the Republic were instrumental in reinforcing the case for a workplace ban.

The publication of the Report on the Health Effects of Environmental Tobacco Smoke in the Workplace gave the Minister for Health the authority with which to proceed with a ban. Put together by a range of specialists from Trinity College Dublin and University College Dublin and the Health and Safety Authority, it declared unequivocally that exposure to second-hand smoke in the environment caused cancer. It also found a link with heart disease. Significantly the expert report said that current ventilation technology is ineffective at removing the harmful effects of second-hand smoke.

Furthermore, Maurice Mulcahy, senior environmental health officer with the Western Health Board (WHB) and Dr David Evans of the Department of Public Health, WHB, examined 123 children from three schools in the Galway area.

They took saliva samples from the children in order to measure the level of cotinine – a breakdown product of nicotine – and a widely accepted method of assessing exposure to passive smoking. The researchers assessed the level of home smoking by parents by means of a questionnaire.

Children from smoking households had more than three times the cotinine concentration level than children from "smoke-free homes". Households where only a mother smoked accounted for twice the levels of those in children

R. Blanpain (ed.), Smoking and the Workplace, 113–118
© 2005 *Kluwer Law International. Printed in The Netherlands.*

where only the father smoked. The most common location for exposure to environmental tobacco smoke was the children's homes (27%) and other people's homes at 13%. Ten percent of children were exposed to smoke in restaurants and 9% in cars.

Referring to the fact that less than half of those questioned could recall a specific exposure to smoke, even though every child showed some level of cotinine in their bodies, Mulcahy says the research indicated that passive smoking is widespread among children.

GENERAL STATISTICS

Statistics and estimates of tobacco associated health problems in Ireland have been well documented and include:

- 7,000 people die from smoking related disease in Ireland every year. These deaths are preventable.
- 90% of lung cancers are caused by smoking.
- 50% of all smokers will die from smoking related diseases.
- Smokers have an increased risk of cancers, heart disease, strokes, low birth weight and many other diseases.
- Smokers lose an average of 10–15 years from their life expectancy.
- A non-smoker living with a smoker has a 25% increased risk of lung cancer and a 30% increased risk of heart disease.
- Passive smoke exposure increases the risk of stroke by 82%.
- Exposure to passive smoking in the workplace increases the risk of lung cancer by up to 40%.
- Exposure to passive smoking in the workplace increases the risk of heart disease, absenteeism, the rate of consultation with doctors and the rate of prescription usage.
- Standing in the path of a smoker or their cigarette or being in a room in which there are smokers' means being exposed to at least 50 agents known to cause cancer and other chemicals that increase blood pressure, damage the lungs and cause abnormal kidney function.
- Tentative estimates of the hospital costs to the state from smoking related illnesses indicate a figure of approximately EUR 100 to EUR 150 million per annum in current terms.
- Most recent figures for Cork and Kerry show that 210 deaths and 205 cases of lung cancer occur annually.
- 20% of all deaths annually in Ireland are smoking related – about 7,000 deaths. 1,000 deaths each year approximately in Cork and Kerry are smoking related.

The available data from published and unpublished surveys concur. Almost a third of Irelands population smoke and young adults and disadvantaged groups are over-represented. The findings in Cork and Kerry are in line with those of the rest of the country.

It was on foot of such research and statistics that the Health Minister Michael Martin proposed the necessary ministerial order to bring a ban into effect.

PUBLIC HEALTH (TOBACCO) ACT 2002 AND OTHER GOVERNMENT INITIATIVES

The Government has put in place several initiatives to combat smoking in Ireland.

In line with the current international trend, the Irish Government has placed an outright ban on the advertising of tobacco products along with tobacco company sponsorship of sporting and other events.

All tobacco retailers must be registered to sell tobacco products under the terms of the 2002 Act. If a retailer is convicted of an offence under the terms of the 2002 Act then he will lose his licence for the period of his conviction. It is also an offence to sell tobacco products to persons less than 18 years of age.

Ireland has recently ratified the world's first health treaty, the World Health Organisations Framework Convention on Tobacco Control. The EU is in the process of doing likewise. The Convention sets an international floor for tobacco control with provisions on several issues such as advertising and sponsorship, tax and price increases, labelling, illicit trade and second-hand smoke.

Section 47 of the 2002 Act as amended by the Public Health (Tobacco) (Amendment) Act 2004 (2004 Act) states the areas where the ban applies. The most significant of which is the ban on smoking in the workplace, in pubs, restaurants and night clubs. The onus is placed on the manager, occupier, or any other person for the time being in charge, to insure compliance with the legislation. Persons found in breach of section 47 are liable on summary conviction to a fine not exceeding EUR 3,000 and/or three months imprisonment and on indictment to a fine not exceeding EUR 125,000 and/or a term of imprisonment not exceeding two years. In proceedings for an offence under this section, it is a defence for a person to show that he made all reasonable efforts to ensure compliance with the provisions under this section. Certain premises are exempt from the ban and these premises are defined in the 2004 Act. They include: prisons, dwellings, bedrooms in hotels and B&B's, nursing homes, hospices, psychiatric hospitals and the Central Mental Hospital.

In practice most licensed premises have provided an outdoor area in which smokers can enjoy a cigarette. Under the 2004 Act a fixed or moveable roof can cover this "outdoor area", provided that not more than 50% of the perimeter is surrounded by one or more walls (inclusive of windows, doors, gates or other means of access).

The Office of Tobacco Control (OTC), the Health and Safety Authority, and the Public Health Boards through the appointment of authorised officers are responsible for policing the ban. The OTC and the Health Boards have the power to bring prosecutions under the 2002 Act. Both the OTC and their officers derive their powers under the 2002 Act (as amended). These officers carry out spot checks on licensed premises and places of work to insure compliance with the ban. In practice, a warning is usually issued to the owner/manager of the premises for a first offence. However, for any subsequent offence proceedings are normally issued. The main function of the OTC is to advise the Minister for Health in relation to the formulation and implementation of policies and objectives of the government concerning the control and regulation of the man-ufacturing sale, marketing and smoking of tobacco products. The OTC's remit may be extended or amended as the Minister sees fit.

The Health and Safety Authority enforces the ban across enclosed workplaces excluding the hospitality industry and health sectors, which are covered by the Regional Health Boards.

SUCCESS OF THE BAN

The ban has now been in force for the last five months. Early goodwill towards the ban by members of the public has continued with support for the ban remaining consistently strong since its introduction.

Professor Paul Redmond, on behalf of the National Cancer Forum has wel-comed the introduction of the smoking ban in enclosed areas of work as the most important public health measure introduced in recent years. Pointing out that the measure will protect Irish people from the dangerous health effects of second-hand smoke; Professor Redmond commented, "this ban is a proportion-ate and balanced measure in tackling the devastating effects of tobacco in our society. It is very much supported by the Forum. The ban also reflects the anti-tobacco stance in Irish society generally".

The Health and Safety Authority announced at the end of May 2004 an average compliance rate of 90% with the workplace-smoking ban, since its introduction at the end of March. The Authority has received a total of 60 complaints and has carried out over 800 inspections for Environmental Tobacco Smoke compli-ance in relevant workplaces. The Authority has also fielded hundreds of calls on its health and safety help line – Infotel – from employers and employees seeking information on the ban in the run up to and during the initial stage of the ban.

Chief Executive Tom Beegan commented, "The first two months of the ban have been a resounding success. Employers have responded extremely well in build-ing compliance and they have shown a great willingness to achieve smoke-free workplaces. We are seeing very high levels of co-operation on our inspections. The relatively low level of complaints from the public also reflects the goodwill and sensible approach that employers and employees have taken to the ban".

A new survey commissioned by the Department of Health found 82% public support for the ban on smoking in the workplace (August 2004). The survey of 1,000 people was carried out recently by Lansdowne Market Research (a Dublin based market research company).

The figures, released on the 11 August, show that of those surveyed:
- 82% support the Smoke-Free at Work measure;
- 90% agreed that going smoke-free is of benefit to workers;
- 82% agreed that it benefits everyone in public places;
- 95% agreed that the legislation is a positive health measure.

The survey reported a positive response in relation to socialising in smoke-free hospitality venues with a majority of people confirming that the new smoke-free legislation improved their experience in pubs (70%) and restaurants (78%).

Over half of respondents (53%) indicated that they would be more inclined to eat in a pub since 29 March.

The Minister for Health welcoming the results said; "despite well-publicised stories on some venues and individuals failing to comply with the measure, the figures confirm the continued strong public support for working and socialising in smoke-free environments". The Minister continued; "There are still those who are trying to discredit what is commonly known as the smoking ban, but this negative approach has not affected the positive views of most people on this important public health issue. This measure is primarily about the health and safety of workers and the public. People recognise passive smoking as a signifi- cant health and safety issue. The facts on smoking and the damage caused by second-hand smoke are well established".

The Office of Tobacco Control also welcomed the finding in this research that 95% of the Irish public agree that the smoke-free workplace legislation is a positive health measure and highlights the fact that second-hand smoke causes fatal diseases. Recently published research in the British Medical Journal found that the increased risks of coronary heart disease from second-hand smoke (at 50–60%) had previously been greatly underestimated.

The OTC also confirmed that the 82% support level for the legislation itself largely coincides with the outcomes of the Office's own research.

The Minister for Health has recently received international recognition for his pioneering initiative. At a recent conference in Dublin as part of Irelands hosting of the EU presidency, Minister Martin was presented with the World Health Organisation's Special Director-General's award, for his leadership in Global Tobacco Control 2004. Minister Martin is only one of two recipients of this prestigious award in 2004 and the only awardee from Europe.

It is still too early to say with any degree of certainty what the effect will be on publican's profits. Some commentators predict doomsday scenarios with thou- sands of people in the hospitality sector being made redundant due to the lack of business as a result of the ban. While it is quite possible that publican's profits may take a knock, a walk around Dublin's famous watering holes on any given night confirms that people are embracing the ban and still going to pubs to socialise.

However a small number of publicans have been prosecuted under the ban, with a publican in Galway receiving the first fine under the Act. The District Court heard that an environmental officer inspecting the premises found customers smoking, ashtrays on the counter and discarded cigarette ends in the bar on 14 May this year.

The District Court heard an environmental health officer had previously warned the publican in April when cigarette butts were found on the floor. Three customers were found smoking when he returned to carry out a second check in May, which resulted in today's prosecution. A statement by the Office of Tobacco Control said: "Enforcement will be vigorously pursued against per- sistent offenders to ensure that the law is complied with". Professor Clancy, a respiratory consultant at St James Hospital, Dublin, added: "I hope this acts as a deterrent, but it is important that people recognise that the law has some force and they will be penalised for non-compliance".

However resistance to the ban does still exist. At the time of writing a West of Ireland publican is seeking to challenge the constitutionality of the ban on smoking in public places. However as can be seen from the recent research on public opinion, support is high and compliance strong with the general public.

The Government has justified its intervention in this area on the grounds of its responsibility for health and safety issues. It is to be commended for taking this bold step. This important public health initiative will ultimately reduce the burden that this disease places on Irish society and the positive benefits of this measure will become apparent over time.

9. Italy

Michele Colucci

INTRODUCTION

"An Italian without a cigarette or a mobile phone in hand just looks strange"

These are the words I am used to hear from my friends when they are on holiday in my beloved country. I explain to them that the government has banned smoking in private businesses serving the public and ordered government agencies to enforce the prohibitions. Still, banks put up "No Smoking" signs just a few feet from ashtrays. Ditto for some hospital waiting rooms.

This chapter provides an update on Italian legislation regarding smoking in general and the prohibition to smoking particularly in the workplaces. Some statistics will help to understand how serious this phenomenon is.

STATISTICS

Current smokers

Over the last few decades, self-reported smoking prevalence has tended steadily to decline among Italian men, whereas it has remained approximately stable among women.[1] Moreover, a systematic tendency towards increasing under-reporting of cigarettes smoked over time has been shown. There have also been fluctuating trends in smoking for young adults (15 to 24 years), with a rise in the mid 1990s and a subsequent decline.[2]

Age and sex

The percentage prevalence of current smokers in strata of age and sex is: At age 25 to 44, the difference of smoking prevalence according to gender was only 7% (41% in males and 34% in females), whereas at age 15 to 24 and 45 to 64, the male excess was around 12%. At age 65 and over, 20·8% of men but only 8·9% of women described themselves as current smokers.[3]

---

[1]   Gallus S, Colombo P, Scarpino V, Zuccaro P, Apolone G, La Vecchia C: Smoking in Italy, 2002, Smoking in Italy 2003, with a focus on the young, Tumori, 90: 171–174, 2004.

[2]   Gallus S, Colombo P, Scarpino V, Zuccaro P, Apolone G, La Vecchia C: Smoking in Italy, 2002. Tumori, 88: 453–456, 2002.

[3]   Gallus S, Colombo P, Scarpino V, Zuccaro P, Apolone G, La Vecchia C: Smoking in Italy, 2002, Smoking in Italy 2003, with a focus on the young, Tumori, 90: 171–174, 2004.

R. Blanpain (ed.), Smoking and the Workplace, 119–126
© 2005 *Kluwer Law International. Printed in The Netherlands.*

Level of education

For both men and women the greatest prevalence of smokers was found among individuals with a high or intermediate level of education: 34–36% of men with a senior high school diploma or university degree are smokers (vs. 24·4% of men with a poorer educational background) while the percentages obtained for women are 26–27% vs. 12·5% respectively. All the same, it has to be admitted that these results are strongly influenced by the fact that level of education is significantly related to age and the prevalence of smoking, as we have already seen, is much higher among individuals in the 25–44 age group, who are also the best educated.[4]

Age of starting/stopping smoking

The average age when people start smoking is just under 18. Males seem to be slightly younger than females when they take up the smoking habit (16·8 is the average age at which men starting smoking, versus 19.1 for women). More than half of the smokers or former smokers in our sample (57·0% of the total – 62·7% of males and 48·1% of females) began smoking before the age of 18. According to former smokers, the age when they quit smoking was – on average – 41·3 (42·3 for men and 39·6 for women).[5]

Average cigarette consumption

The average number of cigarettes smoked a day is 16·1 (18·6 among the men; 12·2 among the women). It is interesting to note that the average number of cigarettes smoked a day is fairly significantly lower if respondents consider how many they smoked on the day before the interview: the sample as a whole say they smoked an average of 13·8 cigarettes (15·6 for the men, 11·4 for the women), i.e. more than two less than stated in reply to the question on average daily consumption. Versus 2002 there is a very slight decrease in the average number of cigarettes smoked a day: for men, the number falls from 19·2 to 18·6 cigarettes a day; for women, from 13·1 to 12·2 cigarettes a day.[6]

Smoking and youth

The most interesting aspect of the present survey related to the young, showing in Italy is an apparent and appreciable decline in smoking prevalence both in men and in women. With an over-sampling of over 400 subjects aged 15 to 24 years, we had the possibility to obtain more precise estimates of smoking prevalence in this age group. The decrease could be related to the recent legislation towards smoking restriction,[7] to prevention campaigns against smoking, particularly addressed to the young, as well as to increases in the price of cigarettes

---

[4]   Gallus S. and others, *Ibidem.*
[5]   Gallus S, and others, *Ibidem.*
[6]   Gallus S, and others, *Ibidem.*
[7]   *See infra.*

over the last decade. Economic aspects have indeed shown to have an important role on tobacco control in Italy, especially in less dependent smokers, like the young. The apparent fall in the young is reassuring, although the 26·8% smoking prevalence in this age group remains unacceptably high, indicating the scope and urgency for further reduction. Although pharmacological support was more frequently reported in 2003 compared to the previous year, the limited utilization of any support for treating tobacco dependence emphasizes the importance of extending information on the availability of effective cessation support among Italian smokers, as well as of adopting a comprehensive legislation towards tobacco control.[8]

The legal framework

The Italian constitution

Section 32 of the Italian Constitution states that: "The Republic safeguards health as a fundamental right of the individual and the interests of the community, and guarantees free assistance to the poor".

The Constitution also provides for the right to a healthy environment. This fundamental right obviously also applies within enterprises. Employees have the right to a healthy environment, and this means the right to a "non-smoking" workplace.

Law No. 584 of 11 November 1975

Section 1 of Law No. 584 of 11 November 1975 lists the places where smoking is prohibited:

hospital wards,[9] classrooms in schools,[10]motor vehicles belonging to the State, to public institutions, and to individuals licensed to provide public transport services, underground railways, waiting-rooms in railway stations, bus, tram and trolley bus stations, harbours and airports, train compartments reserved for non-smokers (such compartments must be provided in all State railway carriages and passenger carriages on railways leased to private individuals), couchette and sleeping-car compartments on trains occupied by more than one person during night service.

Smoking is also prohibited in closed premises intended for public meetings, closed cinema or theatre auditoriums, closed dance halls, lobbies, college meeting rooms, museums, libraries and lecture rooms open to the public, art and picture galleries that are public or open to the public.

---

[8]   Gray N, Boyle P: The regulation of tobacco and tobacco smoke. Ann Oncol, 11: 909–914, 2000.

[9]   In the Circular No. 69 of 5 October 1976 for the application of the Law No. 584 of 1 November 1975 prohibiting smoking in specified premises and on public transport and related matters, the Minister for Health seizes the opportunity to define the following terms more precisely:
      "hospital wards": rooms intended for the accommodation of patients, thus excluding waiting rooms, corridors, *etc.*

[10] Circular 69 of 1975 defines classrooms in schools as those premises specifically intended for teaching activities, thus excluding corridors, toilets, stairways, halls, *etc.*

Managers of the latter premises may obtain an exemption from the provisions of that section provided that they install air-conditioning or ventilation system meeting the prescribed conditions.

Such exemptions are to be delivered by the competent mayor in consultation with the Medical Officer of Health. However they can be suspended or withdrawn should the installation be found not to be functioning or not functioning properly.

Law No. 584 of 11 November 1975 also requires the railway authorities to display, in a visible position in all carriages not reserved for smokers, notices prohibiting smoking. The same prohibition must be included in the instructions to passengers.

Any transgression of these provisions shall be punishable by a fine of EUR 5.164.

Government acts

During the last twenty years Law No. 584 of 11 November 1975 has been complemented by some other government acts regulating smoking in specific sectors. The most important acts are:

Ministerial Decree of 18 May 1976[11] lays down technical conditions for air-conditioning or ventilation systems. Failure of such systems to function or to keep air temperature and humidity within the prescribed limits must cause illuminated no smoking signs to switch on automatically at clearly visible points. Decree No. 753 of the President of the Republic of 11 July 1980[12] prohibits smoking in train compartments, tram and trolley bus, as well as in the waiting-rooms in closed stations. Any transgression shall be punishable by a fine of EURO 2.58 to 7.74.

Directive of the President of the Council of Ministers of 14 December 1995 refers to the prohibition of smoking on certain premises of the public administration and of public services.

Its provisions apply to all premises used by the public administration and public bodies as well as by persons in the private sector providing public services, if in either case, the premises are open to the public by reason of the functions involved.

The prohibition also concerns the premises listed in section 1 of Law No. 584 of 11 November 1975, even if the premises concerned are not "open to the public" (premises to which citizens and users have access without formality or special authorisation, during fixed hours).

Premises subject to such prohibition are to display a notice to this effect, indicating the regulation and the sanctions incurred as well as the authorities empowered to assure compliance with the prohibition and record infringements.

In 1998 the Italian government also approved a Nationwide solidarity

---

[11]   Ministerial Decree of 18 May 1976 laying down provisions governing air-conditioning or ventilation systems was drawn up by the Minister for Health in pursuance of *Section 3* of the Law No. 584 of 11 November 1975 prohibiting smoking in specified premises and on public transport.

[12]   Decree No. 753 of the President of the Republic of 11 July 1980 concerning new regulations on the railways and other means of transport.

agreement[13] in order to reduce the number of smokers as well as the daily consumption of cigarettes by taking a number of on-going actions will be stepped up entailing national, regional and local interventions focusing on: more strict enforcing of the smoking ban in public places and at work; monitoring the enforcement of the advertising ban of tobacco products (including indirect advertising); more clear visible warnings on individual cigarette packets; verifying the tar yield in cigarettes; curbing the availability of low-cost tobacco products; educating and informing the general public on smoking-related dangers; launching prevention campaigns among young people under 16 years of age and women during pregnancy; promoting 'stop smoking' programmes, with the participation of general practitioners.

Health and safety in the workplace

Legislative Decree 626/94: Employer Obligations

Italian law provides two principal pieces of legislation regulating safety issues in the workplace: Legislative Decree of 19 September 1994, no. 626 (Decree 626/94) and the Legislative Decree of 14 August 1996, no. 494 (Decree 494/96). Although closely related, the application of this legislation differs slightly depending on the context of the work environment. While Decree 626/94 sets out the general principles of safety standards for employees in Italy, Decree 494/96 provides additional duties for the employer in relation to construction or similar "on-site" activities.

Under the terms of Decree 626/94, an employer is subject to both general and specific duties concerning safety conditions in the workplace. From a general perspective, the employer must act in accordance with the basic principles and measures of health and safety listed in article three of Decree 626/94.

These principles include amongst others:

- the identification of risks connected with the employer's business activities;
- undertaking appropriate measures to reduce those risks;
- the creation of prevention programmes and health inspections in relation with specific risks;
- informing the employees on any issues regarding health and safety in the workplace
- protecting the workers from passive smoking (Title VII).

As for the specific duties of the employer, under the provisions of Decree 626/94, the employer must appoint an individual within the company to be responsible for prevention and protection, as well as a company doctor to handle any health problems arising in the company.

The employer is also responsible for the preparation of a prevention programme, including a list of interventions and measures to be implemented in order to improve safety standards.

The need to create increasingly satisfactory work conditions in terms of

---

[13]   The complete text of the agreement is available on http://www.ricercaesanita.it/medicinaesanita/rel4.pdf.

safety entailed the recognition of the need of a controlled workplace, biological monitoring and sanitary surveillance.

According to article 16 of the Legislative Decree 626/94, sanitary surveillance includes preventive controls (clinical, biological examinations and instrumental surveys) carried out in order to determine the absence of contraindications to work for workers, and ultimately to ascertain their health conditions with respect to the risks they may incur. Article 17 of the same legislative decree vests physicians with some particular functions:

– carrying out an updated risk health record for every worker submitted to sanitary surveillance to be kept by the employer, with the protection of the professional secrecy;
– carrying out medical examinations asked by the worker (besides those laid down by article 16) in case such request is linked to professional risks;
– co-operating with the employer and with the prevention and protection services to develop and carry out measures to protect the workers' health and psychophysical safety;
– co-operating to the training and information activities of the workers;
– visiting the workplaces at least twice a year and participating in planning the controls of the workers' contact with particular agents, whose results must be communicated timely in order to take the proper measures;
– co-operating with the worker to set up a first-aid service;
– informing the workers about the sanitary controls they underwent and, in case of contact with agents having long-term effects, about the need to carry out controls even when they stop doing the work which entailed the contact to such agents;
– informing workers who want to know about the results of their sanitary controls and, upon request, giving them a copy of the sanitary documents;

The Legislative Decree 626/94 shocked the work environment that had often paid little attention to the development and the evolution of the regulations – both medical and otherwise – whose goals were safer workplaces and the protection of the workers' health.

In particular this Decree finally implemented European Directives 89/391/CEE, 89/654/CEE, 89/655/CEE, 89/656/CEE, 90/270/CEE, 90/394/CEE and 90/679/CEE concerning the amelioration of the working place in safety and health, and could be used as a valid legal base by those who wanted to ban smoking from the workplace because of its chemical and carcinogen nature.

Case law on smoking

Two important decisions by the Italian Constitutional Court (sentences no. 202/91 and 399/96) established the principle of subordination requiring that freedom to smoke must be subject to compliance with the right to health of a third party, as established by the Constitution (section 32) and the Civil Law (section 2043).

On 7 May 1999, in its decision, the Constitutional Court ruled that: "The compensation for damages caused by exposure to environmental tobacco smoke, considered to be damage of the right to good health, finds its basis in the link between section 32 of the Constitution and section 2043 of the Civil Law".

On 11 December 1996 it was ruled that: "The preventive protection of non-smokers at work may be considered as sufficient when, by a series of measures adopted according to different cases, the risk related to exposure to environmental tobacco smoke, if not removed, is reduced to such a low level that it can be excluded". This case began with the request of 300 employees of the Turin Bank Company who appealed to a court in order to obtain a measure of protection from second-hand smoke exposure. The Constitutional Court emphasised that the constitutional right of health protection prevails over the freedom to smoke. It also underlined the responsibility of the employer for reducing its employees' exposure to health risks.

Two managers of the Paribas Bank in Milan, Italy have been convicted of criminal manslaughter in the death of a female bank employee who suffered a fatal asthma attack triggered by workplace exposure to second-hand smoke. They were sentenced to three months in jail and fined EUR 50,000 (GBP 32,000).This criminal court decision opens the door for a civil wrongful death lawsuit by the employee's family to recover damages for causing her death. Monica C. was 35-years-old, married, and had a 10-year-old child. She had asked to be relocated and had supported her request with medical certificates that proved her gradual health deterioration. Her requests were ignored.

In the Sposetti case, an employee of the Ministry of Education was diagnosed with lung cancer thought to be caused by her exposure to second-hand smoke at the workplace. She inhaled her colleagues' smoke for almost seven years. Her request for her infirmity to be recognised as due to her occupation was rejected. The rejection was contested before the Regional Administrative Court of Law of Lazio, which on 3 June 1996 stated that: "It is well known (...) that exposure to environmental tobacco smoke represents a possible cause of lung cancer". Thus, infirmity "due to work" was accorded to the petitioner.

The latest developments

In 2003 the Italian Parliament passed a milestone piece of legislation, Law no. 3 of 16 January 2003,[14] that bans smoking almost anywhere indoors except for private homes and specially designated smoking areas. All enclosed spaces, including cafes and bars, would be affected.

Italians who ignore smoking bans in places like cinemas, hospitals, offices, schools, museums, buses and airports risk fines ranging from EUR 25 to 250. The fine is doubled if the violation takes place in the presence of pregnant women or children up to 12 years old.

In order to have the ban respected, the health ministry has asked for police help. In case of a violation, any citizen will be entitled to call the local police, who will fine the transgressor.

Failure to enforce smoking bans results in even stiffer fines, ranging from 200 to 2,000 euros. Public places would have a year to adopt the measure after

---

[14]   Published in the Official Journal n. 15 of 20 January 2003.

the law goes into effect. Smoking areas will also have to be created in places such as prisons.

On 23 December 2003, the Council of Ministers' President implemented section 51 of the Law no. 3, dated 16 January 2003 aimed at protecting non-smokers' health.

The respective Decree establishes that:

- places of public premises reserved to smokers must be bounded on all sides by high walls; the entering doors must be provided with an automatic lock and those places may not constitute the only access, which non-smokers cannot avoid to use, – areas reserved to smokers must be provided with apposite mechanic means of forced ventilation, apt to grant a supplementary air change capacity,
- apposite warning disclaimers, properly evident and featuring an explicit "NO SMOKING" alert, must be displayed in areas where smoking is not allowed,
- such disclaimer must also contain clear indications as to prescriptions set by law, as to sanctions applicable to infringements and as to the subjects entitled to control the compliance with the smoking ban and in charge of delivering fines for infringement,
- places, where smoking is allowed, must be clearly indicated through apposite luminous signs displaying the disclaimer "AREA RESERVED TO SMOKERS".

The decree entered into force on 13 January 2004, but there is a one-year moratory period for complying with the prescribed requirements. In January 2005, at least there is hope, smokers will face hard times in Italy.

The Difficult transition from law to practice

Italian law bans or curbs' smoking in public places but enforcement is sloppy and violations are still rampant. Italians are simply not bothered by anti-smoking rules, and complaints from non-smokers are often treated with disdain. The question whether smoking bans reduce smoking, still remains open. Perhaps Italians should listen more to the Vatican when in 1997 approved a list of "indulgences" to be applied particularly to those who refrain from smoking in public places such as an office.[15] In other words, those who give up smoking stand a better chance of going to Heaven.

---

[15]   This list of indulgences, officially entitled the Enchiridion Indulgentiarum, updates guidelines laid down by Pope Paul VI in 1968. *The Times, 17 September 1999.*

10. Japan

Fumiko Obata

GENERAL INTRODUCTION

0-1. History of tobacco use in Japan

Up to the end of Edo period, the slender, thimble-bowled kiseru pipe was the sole means of smoking known in Japan. After the revival of large-scale contact with the outside world in the late nineteenth century, other styles of tobacco consumption such as cigars and cigarettes were introduced.[1]

The Meiji-era government was quick to realize the value of tobacco as a potential source of revenue. In 1904, all stages of tobacco leaf processing and sale were brought under government control as a national monopoly, which remained in effect until 1985.[2]

The marked increase in the urban population of Japan during the 1920s was reflected in the steadily growing popularity of cigarettes.

During World War II, countless shortages occurred, goods and raw materials of all sorts were requisitioned for military use, and austerities programmes became increasingly strict.

Immediately after the end of the war, tobacco consumption was one of the few small luxuries that remained available to people of all economic levels. Its unending popularity made it important as a source of government income, for the tobacco tax rate exceeded 20% of the retail price. Due, however, to wartime decimation of personnel and equipment, rates of production plummeted, and, like other consumer goods, tobacco products were rationed, with the daily consumer quota cigarettes per person. As a result, black-market sales flourished.

The period of economic growth following the Tokyo Olympics of 1964 gave increased purchasing power to ordinary consumers, and tobacco brands were diversified and increased.[3]

According to the survey by Ministry of Health, Labour and Welfare in 2002, 45·9% of men and 9·9% of women have the custom to smoke in Japan.[4]

0.2. History of response to tobacco's health hazards

Japanese government prohibited the sale of tobacco products to children. The minimum age for lawful purchases was set at the age of 20.

---

[1] Tobacco & Salt Museum, http://www.jti.co.jp/culture/museum/english/tobacco/japan/newforms.html.

[2] *Id.*

[3] Tobacco & Salt Museum, *supra.*

[4] Safety and Health Division, Ministry of Health, Labour and Welfare, Shokuba no Kitsuentaisaku no Susume (2004, Central Labour Accident Prevention Association) 42.

R. Blanpain (ed.), Smoking and the Workplace, 127–140
© 2005 *Kluwer Law International. Printed in The Netherlands.*

Although continuing to issue statements denying that there was reliable proof that smoking is hazardous to health, Japanese tobacco industry under government control placed on cigarette packs a message cautioning the purchaser that "Be careful not to smoke too much. Cigarette smoking may be hazardous to your health".[5]

In 1976, National Railways divided the cars of the bullet trains (Kodama Shinkansen) into non-smoking and smoking cars. In 1978, airline companies started to divide the airplane seats into non-smoking and smoking seats and national hospitals started to divide their rooms into non-smoking and smoking areas. In 1980, one of the passengers of Shinkansen brought a suit against National Railways insisting that half of the cars of Shinkansen should be non-smoking cars.[6]

In 1981, Dr. Hirayama published his thesis in which he showed the relation between passive smoking and lung cancer. In 1987, Ministry of Health and Welfare published the report about smoking and health hazards. In 1990, Tokyo Metropolitan Government and Fukuoka District and High Courts started to use their new buildings that had established smoking areas. The Ministry of Finance asked the tobacco shop association to stop selling tobacco with vending machines in night time. In 1996, the Ministry of Labour published the report on smoking in the workplace and "the Guideline for Measures of Protection from Tobacco Smoke in the Workplace".[7]

In Japan, the transport industry was the pioneer to deal with the tobacco problem. The Government started to directly respond to tobacco health hazards in the 1980s.

1. THE RIGHT TO THE PROTECTION OF HEALTH

1.1 Constitutional law

The fundamental rights of Japanese citizens are stated in the Japanese Constitutional Law. This law does not specify the right to a healthy environment.

However, the Basic Environment Law was adopted in 1993 in order to comprehensively and systematically promote policies for environmental conservation to ensure healthy and cultivated living for both the present and future generations of the nation as well as to contribute to the welfare of mankind, through articulating the basic principles, clarifying the responsibilities of the State, local governments, corporations and citizens, and prescribing the basic policy considerations for environmental conservation.[8]

This law provides that the State is responsible for formulating and

---

[5]   Tobacco Industry Law since 1972, Article 39.

[6]   Ministry of Health, Labour and Welfare, http://www.health-net.or.jp/tobacco/history/hist04.html.

[7]   Ministry of Health, Labour and Welfare, http://www.health-net.or.jp/tobacco/history/hist03.html.

[8]   Basic Environment Law (Law No. 91 of 1993. Effective on November 13, 1993), Article 1.

implementing fundamental and comprehensive policies with regard to environ-mental conservation, pursuant to the basic principles on environmental conservation.[9]

And the Law provides that citizens shall make efforts to reduce the environmental damage associated with their daily lives so as to prevent interfer-ence with environmental conservation, pursuant to the basic principles.[10]

But there are few discussions about whether this Law can directly protect citizens from tobacco's health hazards.

1.2 Jurisprudence

The Supreme Court declared that Japanese citizens have the sanctity of person-ality.[11] The right to keep a healthy condition can be understood as belonging to the sanctity of personality.[12]

Japanese jurisprudence includes the right to remedies for injuries from intentional or careless molestation – the right not to be harmed by others.[13]

A suit was brought seeking damages from tobacco manufacturer for the injury that smoking caused to individual. The individual also asserted that tobacco manufacturers should place on cigarette packs a message caution-ing the purchasers that "Smoking Causes Lung Cancer, Heart Disease, Emphysema. It Harms Your Surroundings, too".[14]

The tobacco manufacturer successfully defended against the suit. The suit was unsuccessful due to lack of clear proof that smoking, rather than other health risks caused the particular illness or death.[15]

2.   SMOKING BANS IN GENERAL

2.1   Situation at various public places before 2002

a.   Health Facilities[16]

A 1965 survey found that 68% of male physicians and 19% of female physicians smoked. In 1987, this had fallen to 30% of male physicians and 4% of female physicians. A 1993 survey of 713 medical facilities nationwide found that 73% had placed some restrictions on smoking. Smoking restriction is being per-formed in all national public hospitals and medical care centres, and in all Tokyo public hospitals and health centres.

---

9   Basic Environment Law, Article 6.
10   Basic Environment Law, Article 9.
11   Supr. Ct., June 11, 1986 Civil Cases 40–4–872.
12   JR Higashi Nihon, Sendai High Ct., Akita Branch, Dec. 25, 1990, Labour Judgment 690–13.
13   *Id. See* Civil Code, Article 709.
14   Nagoya Dist. Ct., Jan. 31, 2002, http://courtdomino2.courts.go.jp/kshanrei.nsf/ Listview01/ B295099828959017492.
15   *Id.*
16   Committee on Guideline for Smoking Restriction in Public Places, March 1996, (Reference Materials 1 Present Situation of Smoking Restriction), Ministry of Health, Labour and Welfare, http://www.health-net.or.jp/tobacco/more/mr280105.html.

b.   Educational facilities[17]

Smoking was prohibited in school buildings in nine percent of elementary schools, nine percent of junior high schools, and eight percent of high schools. Smoking areas had been established in 36% of elementary schools, 30% of junior high schools, and 24% of high schools. According to a 1996 survey of 40 high schools in Tokyo, 58% had restrictions on smoking in staff rooms, and 88% had restrictions on smoking during meetings.

c.   Governmental office[18]

The lobby at the Ministry of Health and Welfare has a smoking area with air cleaning equipment, and smoking is prohibited in other areas of the lobby. Smoking is also prohibited in all meeting rooms.

In 1995, the Health Promotion and Nutrition Division of the Health Service Bureau, Ministry of Health and Welfare surveyed 90 offices of all the prefectures, cities designated by government ordinance, and so on. It found that one percent of these offices prohibited any smoking in lobbies and the like, while 28% were conducting smoking restriction. Complete smoking restriction was in place in the offices of the Tokyo Metropolitan Government, Minato Ward, and other local governments.

d.   Public transport[19]

JR East Railways Co. is moving ahead with smoking restriction based on the needs of passengers. In bullet trains (Shinkansen) with 12 cars, four of the cars with reserved seats are non-smoking and three are smoking. Two of the cars without reserved seats are non-smoking, and two are smoking. Half of the first-class ("Green") cars are non-smoking, and the other half is smoking. Smoking restriction is being performed at all 376 stations within the wards and suburbs of Tokyo, and smoking is prohibited in all ordinary trains. In addition, smoking restriction is in place at 133 stations further removed from the centre of Tokyo. First-class cars using a smoking restriction device developed jointly with JT (Japan Tobacco Co.), which prevents smoke from flowing way from the passengers on these routes, evaluates these cars positively.

Among airline companies, about 40% of JAL (Japan Airlines) passengers prefer to smoke. However, JAL prohibits smoking on all of its domestic flights which are two hours or less in duration (about 80% of all domestic flights). ANA (All Nippon Airlines) and JAS (Japan Air System) divide the airplane cabins into non-smoking and smoking seats. On international flights, all airplanes divide their cabins into non-smoking and smoking seats. JAL has established seats for smoking which are back-to-back with the last row of seats in the B747 model, and is developing an air regulation system jointly with JT to further prevent smoke from flowing out into the surrounding area. It intends to apply this system in the future.

---

[17]   Id.
[18]   Committee on Guideline for Smoking Restriction in Public Places, supra.
[19]   Committee on Guideline for Smoking Restriction in Public Places, supra.

e. Financial institutions[20]

In 1995, the Health Promotion and Nutrition Division of the Health Service Bureau, Ministry of Health and Welfare conducted a questionnaire survey of 21 banks by way of the Federation of Bankers Associations of Japan. The responses showed a variety of measures among different banks, with 62% of the banks having established smoking areas and performing smoking restriction, while ten percent of the banks had branches with partitions and so on for smoking areas.

f. Restaurants[21]

At the end of 1994, there were about 1.45 million food and drink establishments in Japan. More than 80% of these had at least five employees, and 81% were run by individual entrepreneurs, a high proportion. The responses to the questionnaire survey of 213 establishments showed that 85% of the establishments kept ashtrays available for use. Although just six percent had facilities with separated non-smoking and smoking seats, 60% considered that non-smoking and smoking seats should be separated in the future.

The most popular reason for opinions against smoking restriction, at 37%, was that the establishment is too small or that there are not many seats for patrons. In 22% of restaurants in Tokyo, air purification devices were in place. Several chains, such as family restaurants, provided non-smoking seats.

g. Lodging facilities[22]

Nationwide, there are 80,000 to 100,000 lodging facilities, 6,633 of which are hotels. In 1995, the Health Promotion and Nutrition Division of the Health Service Bureau, Ministry of Health and Welfare conducted a questionnaire survey of 12 hotel companies by way of the Japan Hotel Association. It found that 54% of the hotel companies provided non-smoking rooms, non-smoking floors, or the like, and that 27% had smoking areas and conducted smoking restriction in lobbies, 73% in restaurants, and 36% in lounges.

According to a questionnaire survey of 20,000 lodging facilities performed by JTB (Japan Travel Bureau) in 1995, about three percent provide non-smoking rooms, including 0·2% of traditional inns. Some lodging establishments had improved sales by making their entire facilities non-smoking. Problems related to smoking in guest rooms include the remaining odour of tobacco smoke, in addition to the prevention of fires started by cigarettes.

h. Sales[23]

In 1995, the Health Promotion and Nutrition Division of the Health Service Bureau, Ministry of Health and Welfare conducted a questionnaire survey of eight department stores in Tokyo by way of the Japan Department Stores

---

[20] Committee on Guideline for Smoking Restriction in Public Places, *supra.*
[21] Committee on Guideline for Smoking Restriction in Public Places, *supra.*
[22] Committee on Guideline for Smoking Restriction in Public Places, *supra.*
[23] Committee on Guideline for Smoking Restriction in Public Places, *supra.*

Association. Since smoking is prohibited in sales areas by a fire prevention ordinance, all of the stores have smoking restriction. However, the survey found that half of them lack partitions and the like in their smoking areas.

2.2   Health Promotion Law adopted in 2002

Laws that totally prohibit smoking in places such as restaurants and enclosed workplaces have not been adopted by Japanese government, even though there is a law that attempts to separate smokers from non smokers in many public places and most government buildings.

Article 25 of the Health Promotion Law provides that "A person who manages public places which are used by large numbers of people like schools, auditoriums, hospitals, theatres, galleries, public halls, markets, department stores, offices, governmental offices, restaurants etc. shall endeavour to take necessary measures for preventing passive smoking".[24]

"Public places" include railroad stations, bus terminals, airplane terminals, ship terminals, financial institutions, museums, social welfare facilities, shops, hotels, inns, stadiums, recreation facilities, and passenger cars of public transport.[25]

There are two smoking restriction methods, one of which is prohibiting smoking completely and the other is providing a completely separating space as a smoking area. Since public places have many different characteristics, including the scale and structure of facilities and usage situations, appropriate smoking restriction measures should be actively promoted in accordance with the facility conditions and the needs of visitors. The social roles of the facilities should also be considered carefully in selecting smoking restriction methods.[26]

Chiyoda ward of Tokyo has prohibited smoking in the busy street since 2002.[27] Those who break this regulation must pay 2,000 yen as penalty. Smoking in the busy street has been forbidden in the regulations of Fukuoka city,[28] Suginami ward of Tokyo,[29] and so forth since 2002 or 2003. More cities plan to make regulations on smoking in the busy street.

2.3   New suits

On 22 July 2004, 26 taxi drivers and taxi users brought a suit seeking damages from the Japanese Government for the discomfort and injuries caused because of passive smoke in taxis. They insisted that the government should have prohibited smoking in taxis.[30]

On 11 June 2004, a citizen who had visited the National Sumo Stadium to see sumo-wrestling brought a suit seeking damages from Japan Sumo

---

[24]   Health Promotion Law (2002, Law No. 103), Article 25.
[25]   Ministry of Health, Labour and Welfare, Kenpatsu No. 043001 and Shokuhatsu No. 043001 of April 30, 2003.
[26]   Id.
[27]   Chiyoda ward regulation No. 53 of June 25, 2002.
[28]   Fukuoka city regulation No. 59 of Dec. 19, 2003.
[29]   Suginami ward regulation No. 15 of Oct. 1, 2003.
[30]   Kyoudou Tsushin Newspaper, July 22, 2004.

Association for the discomfort because of passive smoking. He insisted that Japan Sumo Association does not follow article 25 of the Health Promotion Law.[31]

3.   SMOKING AND THE WORKPLACE

3.1   Industrial safety and health law

In "Chapter 5 – Health and Safety", the Labour Standards Law provided that an employer had a duty to take necessary measures to ensure that its workers not be subjected to danger and health impairment from work-related machinery or other equipment, dust or other harmful substances, temperatures or other aspects of the work environment.[32]

With the increase in large, high speed, complicated machinery and equipment, the growing intensity of work, and the use of new dangerous and harmful raw materials during the high economic growth in the early 60s, the possibility of industrial accidents increased, and the number of accident victims grew dramatically. To deal with this situation, an intention was formed to drastically amplify the simple provisions of the Labour Standards Act. The Industrial Safety and Health Law was enacted for this purpose. Through repeated revisions, the content of that law was subsequently filled out and broadened.[33]

The purpose of the Industrial Safety and Health Law is to secure the safety and health of workers in workplaces by, among other things, establishing standards for the prevention of injury due to industrial accidents, strengthening the safety management system, and adopting measures to promote voluntary initiatives. At the same time, along with ensuring worker health and safety at workplace, it has the goal of facilitating the establishment of comfortable working environments.[34]

The Law intends to attain these goals by promoting comprehensive and systematic measures for accidents prevention. Thus, the Industrial Safety and Health Law, supplementing the Labour Standards Law, not only set minimum standards for safety and health. To implement workplace safety and health, it also imposes a duty, backed up by penal sanction, upon persons involved in the manufacture and circulation of dangerous machinery and harmful materials, and upon general contractors and their clients with regard to hazardous construction. In addition, to ensure worker health and safety at the workplace and to advance workers' health and facilitate the goal of establishing comfortable working environments, it imposes upon employers various type of "duties to endeavour", which are established by guidelines and administrative guidance. To achieve these goals, the Law establishes administrative measures such as the

---

[31]   Kyoudou Tsushin Newspaper, June 11, 2004.

[32]   Labour Standards Law (Law No. 49 of 1947) Chapter 5.

[33]   Kazuo Sugeno, Japanese Employment and Labour Law (2002, Carolina Academic Press & University of Tokyo Press) 338; Nobuo Hatanaka, The Occupational Safety and Health Law of Japan (2003, Japan Institute of Labour) 9, 15.

[34]   Industrial Safety and Health Law (Law No. 57 of June 8, 1972) (Latest Amendments: Law No. 91 of May 31, 2000), Article 1.
       Sugeno, *supra* note 33, at 338, Hatanaka, *supra* note 33, at 9 and 19.

Welfare and Labour Minister's formulation of policies aimed at preventing industrial accidents, and of supportive measures for employers.[35]

In these respects, the Law carries out an even broader, diverse and higher regulation than the Labour Standards Law. At the same time, in light of its diverse regulatory content, unlike the Labour Standards Law and the Minimum Wages Law, it does not stipulate a direct effect on labour contract. The Industrial Safety and Health Law, does not create any private-law rights. Its character is purely that of a public-law.[36]

There are no definitional provisions for "safety" and "health". It is said that "safety" refers to the elimination of any danger of injury to a worker's body or health that would be caused by an unusual event in the course of the worker's employment. "Health" refers to the creation of a situation in which there is no danger to a worker's health emanating from the normal materials handled by the worker, or by the manner or environment in which the work is performed.[37] As tobacco smoke in workplace can be a danger to a workers' health, the Industrial Safety and Health Law can be used in order to protect workers from tobacco's health hazards.

3.1.1   General provision

The Industrial Safety and Health Law sets out the obligations of persons who are affected by it.

At first, the employer must not only comply with the minimum standards for preventing industrial accidents, but also endeavour to ensure the safety and health of workers in workplaces through the materialization of a comfortable working environment and the improvement of working conditions. The employer must also endeavour to co-operate in the measures for the prevention of industrial accidents to be taken by the State.[38]

Besides observing matters necessary for preventing industrial accidents, the worker must endeavour to cooperate with employers and other interested persons with respect to measures implemented by such persons relating to the prevention of industrial accidents.[39]

3.1.2   Measures for preventing the hazards to or health impairment of workers

As an important regulation of safety and health, the Industrial Safety and Health Law, requires employers and other persons to take measures for preventing hazards and health impairment of workers.

The employer is required to take necessary measures to deal with the following types of health impairment: (a) health impairment due to raw materials, gases, vapours, dusts, insufficient oxygen in air, pathogens, etc.; (b) health

---

[35]   Sugeno, *supra* note 33, at 339.

[36]   Sugeno, *supra* note 33, at 339. Fumiko Obata, "Rodo Anzen Eisei Hoki no Hoteki Seishitsu (Legal Character of Industrial Safety and Health Law)" 112 Hogaku Kyokai Zasshi No. 2, p. 212, No. 3, p. 355, No. 5, p. 613.

[37]   Sugeno, *supra* note 33, at 339.

[38]   Industrial Safety and Health Law, Article 3. *See,* Hatanaka *supra* note 33, at 19.

[39]   Industrial Safety and Health Law, Article 4.

impairment due to radiation, high temperatures, low temperatures, ultrasonic waves, noises, vibration, abnormal atmospheric pressure, etc.; (c) health impairment due to operations such as gauge monitoring, precision work, etc.; and (d) health impairment due to exhaust fumes, waste fluid or solid wastes (Article 22).[40] With respect to the buildings and other places of operation where workers are engaged, the employer must also take necessary measures for the maintenance of passages, floor and stairs, and also for ventilation, lighting, illumination, heating, prevention of moisture, and take provisions for rest, evacuation and sanitation, and also measures required for maintaining the health, morale and life of workers (Article 23).[41]

Under these articles, the Ordinance on Health Standards in the Office clarifies the content of the measures.[42]

3.1.3 Measures for maintaining and promoting health

In order to improve the level of safety and health in the workplace, the employer must endeavour to create comfortable working environment by taking continuous and systematic measures as follows: (1) measures to manage the maintenance of comfortable working environment; (2) measures to improve work practices engaged in by workers; (3) establishment or maintenance of facilities or equipment to refresh workers' fatigue suffered in the course of work; (4) other measures than mentioned in the preceding three items, necessary to create comfortable working environment.[43]

The Minister of Health, Labour and Welfare publishes guidelines for the appropriate and effective implementation of the measures to be taken by employers for the creation of comfortable working environment.[44] The employer's efforts are assisted by grants of government credits and technology.[45]

The Ministry of Health, Labour and Welfare has been promoting the creation of comfortable working environment with dissemination and establishment of the "Guidance for Measures Implemented by Employers to Create a Comfortable Working Environment". It also authorizes comfortable working environment promotion plans prepared at workplaces so that the safety and health standards can be enhanced, including measures of protection from exposure to tobacco smoke. Consequently the number of authorized plans has been increasing year after year to reach 2,407 in FY 2002. At workplaces with comfortable working environment promotion plans, about 70% to 90% of total establishments acknowledge that the image, atmosphere and cleanness of the workplace have improved.[46]

As for measures against exposure to tobacco smoke, implemented as part of the comfortable office environmental promotion, the "Guideline for Measures of Protection from Exposure to Tobacco Smoke in Workplaces" was formulated

---

[40]   Industrial Safety and Health Law, Article 22.
[41]   Industrial Safety and Health Law, Article 23. See, Hatanaka, *supra* note 33, at 68.
[42]   Ordinance on Health Standards in the Office, Article 5.
[43]   Industrial Safety and Health Law, Article 71–2. *See*, Hatanaka, *supra* note 33, at 104.
[44]   Industrial Safety and Health Law, Article 71–3.
[45]   Industrial Safety and Health Law, Article 71–4. *See*, Hatanaka, *supra* note 33, at 104.
[46]   Ministry of Health, Labour and Welfare, Annual Report on Health, Labour and Welfare 2002–2003 (2004) 183.

to enhance organizational efforts at the workplace for the protection from exposure to tobacco smoke in 2003.[47] The Guideline recommends employers to make use of the health committee in order to select the smoking restriction methods in the workplace. It also requires workers to endeavour to state their opinion about the measures for preventing passive smoke. Assuming that employers select to provide a completely separating space as a smoking area, the Guideline recommends employers to provide smoking rooms with the facilities for the discharge of tobacco smoke and to keep the quantity of air borne dust 0·15 milligram or less. The old guideline of 1996 recommended employers to provide smoking rooms or smoking areas with facilities for the discharge of tobacco smoke or air purifiers.[48] The guideline requires employers to take necessary measures to make the air flowing from non-smoking areas into smoking rooms 0·2 m per second or more.

Only about half of workplaces address this problem, although the number is on the rise. This guideline must be followed more seriously because workers feeling annoyed at smoking in the workplace account for as much as 50% or more of all the workers.[49]

3.1.4   Organization for safety and health management

One of the important objectives of the Industrial Safety and Health Law is the establishment and maintenance of a safety and health management system at the workplace.

Toward this end, the Law requires the employer to establish a health committee at each workplace of the scale defined by Cabinet Order, in order to have it investigate and deliberate on the following matters and state its opinion to the employer: (1) matters pertaining to countermeasures which are to form the base for preventing the impairment of workers' health; (2) matters pertaining to the basic measures for maintaining and improving the health of workers; (3) matters pertaining to health among the matters relating to the measures for eliminating the causes and the recurrence of industrial accidents; and, (4) in addition to the matters set forth in the preceding three subparagraphs, matters important for preventing the impairment of workers' health, as well as maintaining and improving the health of workers. (Article 18)[50]

Section 2 of the article provides that the health committee shall be composed of the members stated below, and the number of members under item one shall be only one: (1) the general safety and health manager, or one nominated by the employer from among those who are other than the general safety and health manager and exercise overall control over the execution of the undertaking at the workplace concerned or those similar to the above; (2) one whom the employer nominated from among health officers; and (3) one nominated by the employer from among industrial physicians; (4) one nominated by the employer from among the workers at the workplace concerned who are experienced in health control. Section 3 of the article provides that the employer may

---

[47]   Ministry of Health, Labour and Welfare, Kihatsu No. 0509001 of May 9, 2003.
[48]   Ministry of Health, Labour and Welfare, Kihatsu No. 75 of Feb. 21, 1996.
[49]   Ministry of Health, Labour and Welfare, *supra* note 46, 183.
[50]   Industrial Safety and Health Law, Article 18. *See*, Hatanaka, *supra* note 33, at 58.

nominate a member of the health committee from among the working environment measurement experts in charge of working environment measurement at
the workplace concerned.[51]

The employer and workers can make use of a health committee in order
to discuss smoking restriction in workplace. Workers can state their opinion on
smoking restriction to their employer in the committee.

3.2 Damages action for injury caused by exposure to environmental smoke and injunction

3.2.1 Workers' accident insurance system and damages-providing system

When a Japanese worker has a job related illness or injury caused by his or her
employer or by fellow employees, the workers claim for damages is not limited
to recovering worker's compensation insurance benefits.

If an employer has paid compensation for a workers accident under the
Labour Standards Law, the employer will be exempt, up to the amount of such
payments, from responsibility for damages under the Civil Code based on the
same grounds (i.e., for the same employment accident). If payments equivalent
to accident compensation under the labour Standards Law are to be made
under the Workers' Accident Insurance Law, the employer will also be exempt
from responsibility for making compensation under the Labour Standards Law.
As a result, payments received under the Workers' Accident Insurance Law are
similarly interpreted as limiting the amount of civil damages recovered by a
worker accident-victim or that worker's survivors.[52]

On the other hand, an employer is not exempt from responsibility for
that portion of a loss that exceeds the amount of workers' accident compensation or workers' accident insurance benefits. This means that the worker accident-victim or that worker's survivors may claim damages under the Civil Code
against the employer. This can be referred to as the concurrent operation of the
Workers' Accident Insurance system (including the Workers' Accident
Compensation system) and the damages-providing system.[53]

3.2.2 The doctrine of employers' duty to care for employee safety and health

There are three legal contexts in which an employer's responsibility for damages
can be pursued. First is the ordinary exploration of responsibility in tort under
the Civil Code.[54] Second is the exploration of the responsibility of an owner or
occupier[55] for defects in the construction or maintenance of a structure on land.
The third context is an exploration of liability for non-performance of an obligation in a contract relationship.[56]

Until about 1971, the majority of damage claims were made in the first or

---

[51] Industrial Safety and Health Law, Article 18 (2). *See*, Hatanaka, *supra* note 33, at 59.

[52] Sugeno, *supra* note 33, at 400.

[53] *Id.* Takashi Araki, Labour and Employment Law in Japan (2002, Japan Institute of Labour)
130.

[54] Civil Code, Article 709 & 715.

[55] Civil Code, Article 717.

[56] Civil Code, Article 415. Sugeno, *supra* note 33, at 400.

the second context, and were upheld. In many of those cases, the employer had violated the safety and health provisions of the Labour Standards Law or the Labour Standards Law Safety and Health Ordinances. The courts construed these violations as negligent torts and as defective construction in assessing responsibility for using such materials.[57]

However, the Industrial Safety and Health Law was enacted and promulgated in 1972. In response to those events, the courts declared at the end of that year that an employer had a duty under a labour contract to ensure (i.e., guarantee) safety, and held that responsibility for a worker's accident resulting from defects in safety facilities and protective equipment which violated that duty was cognisable as a non-performance of a contract obligation.[58]

After the concept of this general obligation to ensure safety was supported in conformity with legal scholarship, it was established in a 1975 judicial decision. That decision declared a direct "duty to care for safety" on the part of the government towards civil servants (members of a self-defence unit), but held more generally that "on the basis of certain legal relations, the aforesaid duty to care for safety when the parties have entered into relations involving special social contracts will also be generally recognized as devolving on one or both parties toward the other based on the good-faith principle".[59]

Pursuant to this judgment, the concept of "an employer's duty to care for safety" in a labour contract relationship became firmly embedded in case law. Thereafter, on the basis of this concept, the third legal context became the main vehicle for asserting damage claims against an employer.[60]

3.2.3 The actual content of the duty to care for safety

An important practical factor in suits involving a violation of the duty to care for safety is who should assert and prove the facts that constitute such a violation. On this point, a Supreme Court decision has held that "it is the plaintiff's responsibility to specify the content of the violation of the duty (to care for safety) and to allege and prove the relevant facts".[61] Under this rationale, it is not enough for a plaintiff to assert only the existence of the previously discussed abstract duty to care for safety. The plaintiff must specify the specific content of the duty to care for safety in applying that abstract duty to the particular circumstances of the accident (e.g., the duty to install certain types of safety equipment, the duty to carry out a proper inspection of the machinery, the duty to conduct sufficient safety training with respect to certain matters), and must allege and prove the non-performance of that duty. The employer must then prove that the non-performance of such a concrete duty is not attributable to him or her.[62]

---

[57] Sugeno, *supra* note 33, at 400.

[58] *Id.* Moji Koun, Fukuoka Dist. Ct., Nov. 24, 1972, 696 Labour Judgment 235; Ban Chuzosho, Tokyo Dist. Ct. Nov. 30, 1972, 701 Labour Judgment 109.

[59] Sugeno, *supra* note 33, at 402. Jieitai Sharyo Seibi Kojo, Supr. Ct., 3 Petty Bench, Feb. 25, 1975, 29 Civ. Cases 143.

[60] Sugeno, *supra* note 33, at 403. Kawayoshi, Supr. Ct., Apr. 10, 1984, 38 Civ. Cases, No. 6, p. 557.

[61] Sugeno, *supra* note 33, at 402. Koku Jieitai Ashiya Bunkentai, Supr. Ct., 2 Petty Bench, Feb. 16, 1981, 35 Civ. Cases 56.

[62] Sugeno, *supra* note 33, at 402.

In a suit seeking damages from an employer in connection with a worker's accident for violating its duty to care for safety or for tortuous conduct (i.e., a worker's accident civil suit), it is proper to establish first that the injury, illness or death resulted from work performed by the worker. Stated differently, an appropriate cause-and-effect relationship must be shown between the performance of the work and the injury, illness or death.

3.2.4   Judicial orders protecting workers from environmental smoke

In one case a junior high school of Nagoya-city refused to provide a smoke-free environment for a teacher who suffered discomfort and injury because of passive smoke. The teacher requested Nagoya-city to prohibit smoking in workplace. As the committee of personal administration of Nagoya-city refused the teacher's request, the teacher sued Nagoya-city to recover the teacher's damages resulting from its violation of the duty to care for safety and health. In 1998, The Nagoya District Court has held that the teacher was not entitled to recover damages because it was not common for employers to prohibit smoking in workplace at that time.[63]

The employees of National Social Insurance Centre in Kyoto also requested the State to prohibit smoking in the office building. They sued the State to recover their damages resulting from its violation of the duty to care for safety and health or its infringement of the sanctity of their personality. The Kyoto District Court has held that they were not entitled to recover damages because the Centre had taken enough measures for preventing passive smoke hazards at that time in the light of the social situation concerning smoking regulation in Japan.[64] It pointed out that the Centre had already divided rooms into non-smoking and smoking area in workplace and the employees failed to show the cause-and-effect relationship between the passive smoke in workplace and their injury. The Court has also held that they were not entitled to relief in the form of an injunction prohibiting their employer from exposing them to tobacco smoke in the workplace because environmental tobacco smoke does not always cause particular illness and the Centre had taken enough measures in the social situation at that time. Though the Court referred to the content of the Health Promotion Law (Article 25), it pointed out that the employer does not need to prohibit smoking in workplace definitely. The Kyoto High Court has also held that the employees were not entitled to recover damages and relief in the form of injunction.[65]

In 2004, Tokyo District Court has held that the employee of the Edogawa ward was entitled to recover damages upon proving that his employer failed to take measures to prevent passive smoke and worsened his illness.[66] Though he had told his injury to the employer and requested to divide rooms into non-smoking and smoking area in the workplace, the employer did not take adequate measures. This is the first case for workers suffering from passive smoke in the workplace to be entitled to recover damages by the courts. It may be the beginning of the new stage about suits concerning passive smoke.

---

[63]   Nagoya-shi Jinjiiinkai, Nagoya Dist.Ct., March 22, 1990, Labour Judgment 594–20.
[64]   Kyoto Kanihoken Jimu Centre, Kyoto Dist.Ct., Jan. 21, 2003, Labour Judgment 852–38.
[65]   Kyoto Kanihoken Jimu Centre, Osaka High Ct., Sep. 24, 2003, Labour Judgment 872–88.
[66]   Japan Economic Newspaper, July 13, 2004. Asahi Newspaper, July 13, 2004.

3.3   Present situation of smoking policy in workplace

According to the survey by Ministry of Health, Labour and Welfare in 2002[67] (78·3% of 12,000 offices which employ more than ten workers answered to the questionnaire and 72·8% of 16,000 workers who are employed by the offices answered to the questionnaire.), 59·1% (100% of the offices which employ more than 5,000 workers, more than 90% of the offices which employ 300–4,999 workers) of all the offices take some measures to improve the working environment by reducing the health effect caused by smoking and passive smoking. 75·1% of these offices prepare a room for smoking and 42·7% prepare a room for non-smoking.

34% of the offices that do not take measures about smoking, point out that the reason why they can not take measures is the opposition of workers in workplace.

78% of the workers are under a passive smoking situation and 37·2% feel the discomfort caused by passive smoking.

90·7% of the workers want the employers to take measures about smoking.

According to the survey by Central Labour Accident Prevention Association,[68] 64% (574 offices) have a smoking policy in workplace. In 82% (469 offices) of which workers observe the policy. The main reason why workers do not observe the policy is a lack of information.

CONCLUSION

Laws that totally prohibit smoking have not been adopted by Japanese Government. The Health Promotion Law adopted in 2002 requires a person who manages public places which are used by large numbers of people to endeavour to take necessary measures for preventing passive smoking.

According to the survey by Ministry of Health, Labour and Welfare, 90·7% of all the workers want their employers to take some measures to improve the working environment by reducing the health effect caused by smoking and passive smoking. The employers must endeavour to create comfortable working environment in order to improve the level of safety and health in workplace under the Industrial Safety and Health Law. The Guideline formulated by the Ministry of Health, Labour and Welfare under the Industrial Safety and Health Law enhances organizational efforts at the workplace for the protection of workers from exposure to tobacco smoke. The employers and workers should make use of a health committee in order to discuss smoking restriction in the workplace.

As the Industrial Safety and Health Law does not provide for a direct effect on labour contract, courts would not held that employers who do not follow the Guideline violate their duty under a labour contract to care for employee safety and health. But if the employers fail to take adequate measures to prevent passive smoke which causes employees' illness, the suffered employee may be entitled to recover damages, as Tokyo District Court held in 2004.

---

[67]   Ministry of Health, Labour and Welfare, *supra* note 4, at 43–47.
[68]   Ministry of Health, Labour and Welfare, *supra* note 4, at 71–72.

11.   The Netherlands

Yvonne Waterman[1]

I.   INTRODUCTION

1.   A rich history

The Netherlands have a rich and continuing history when it comes to tobacco. From the sixteenth century onwards, Dutch traders travelled the world, making vast profits in providing most of Europe with this fashionable weed. Together with the trade in spices and slaves, tobacco formed the financial foundation for many of the grand houses which line the Amsterdam canals and are so admired for their beauty by tourists today. Even in the twenty-first century, the Netherlands are the worlds' largest exporter of cigarettes after the United States. The riches provided by tobacco and tobacco products are not only generated by export but also by the EUR 1200 million of generated taxes accrued by the national consumption of cigarettes, for one in three Dutch persons is a habitual smoker.[2] This makes the Netherlands, together with Belgium and Ireland, one of the smokiest countries in the European Union. Perhaps this also goes a little towards explaining why the Dutch generally do not much care to be reminded of these economic facts that put both the global population as well as their own population at risk.

However, the lure of lucre is becoming increasingly hard to reconcile with the evermore generally recognised and undeniable fact that the inhalation of tobacco smoke is seriously injurious to the health of both the active as well as the passive smoker. This understanding has initiated parliamentary response in the form of new laws which aim to reduce smoking in general and protect the health of particularly the passive smokers. Though in some regards – as will be explained later – these laws still leave something to be desired, the mere fact that they actually have been enacted may be considered to be a very positive sign. Also, due to the increasing availability of health information and the efforts of the anti-smoke lobby, the Dutch public is becoming more aware of the dangers of smoking and less tolerant towards smoking.

2.   'New' knowledge on the dangers of passive smoking

The recognition of the fact that smoking and being exposed to smoke actually is dangerous – seriously dangerous – to one's health has come quite belatedly to

---

[1]   Personal injury lawyer in Amersfoort, The Netherlands. Miss Waterman is presently undertaking the first Dutch court case against the tobacco industry and finishing a Ph.D. on the comparative employer's liability for occupational accidents and diseases at Tilburg University, the Netherlands. Comments and questions are welcomed at yvonnewaterman@hotmail.com.

[2]   Netherlands School of Public Health, Gezondheidseffectenrapportage, 1998.

R. Blanpain (ed.), Smoking and the Workplace, 141–167
© 2005 *Kluwer Law International. Printed in The Netherlands.*

141

The Netherlands. For decades this well-documented and researched danger has been pointedly ignored in this country almost to the point of stubborn obstinacy. It is sad to realise in hindsight that, while in the 80s and 90s the Surgeon General in America was already shouting from the rooftops about the health dangers of passive smoking ('environmental tobacco smoke'), in the Netherlands the little information that filtered through on this subject was hardly available to Dutch consumers, not taken very seriously by Dutch physicians and politicians, and openly derided and refuted by the many cigarette manufacturers.[3] Lung cancer isn't caused by tobacco, which is a natural product after all, but by asphalt dust and automobile fumes, it would be said. If tobacco was dangerous, why, our own tobacco industry would be the first to tell us so, and if not, then certainly the government, many consumers thought. Don't be so difficult, colleagues would say to a worker who complained of the literally breathtaking blue fog in the office. With the exception of a vague and little publicised report in 1975, even the Dutch Health Council ('Gezondheidsraad'), the official body to advise the government on health issues, remained silent on the subject of tobacco related diseases.

It was not until 1990 that the abundance of international scientific literature on the health dangers of passive smoking finally prompted the Health Council to publish a first report on this subject.[4] The Council very carefully concluded that passive smoking could possibly lead to an increased chance of lung cancer, but it was hesitant to underwrite other conclusions with regard to passive smoking-related diseases, stating that there was as yet too little evidence available to prove any causal relationship. Also, it considered that non-smokers who stay for any prolonged period of time in a smoky environment may experience irritation of the eyes and the mucous membranes of the mouth, nose, pharynx and lower airway passages. This could be worse for asthmatics and people with a preposition to allergies and cause them to avoid such environments. The report had little national impact.

---

[3]   Some early research on passive smoking: US Department of Health and Human Services, The health consequences of involuntary smoking. A report of the Surgeon General. Rockville (MD), Department of Health and Human Services, Public Health Service, Centers for Disease Control, Center for Health Promotion and Education, Office on Smoking and Health, 1986; Independent Scientific Committee on Smoking and Health: third report. London, HSMO, 1983; Independent Scientific Committee on Smoking and Health: fourth report. London, HSMO, 1988; US Environmental Protection Agency, Respiratory health effects of passive smoking: lung cancers and other disorders: US Environmental Protection Agency. Washington: Office of Air and Radiation, 1992; Effects of passive smoking on health. Report of the NHMRC Working Party on the effects of passive smoking on health. Canberra: Australia Government Publishing Service, 1987; Hackshaw AK, Law M and Wald NJ, The accumulated evidence on lung cancer and environmental tobacco smoke, in: British Medical Journal 1997, 315:980–8.

[4]   Gezondheidsraad, Passief roken. Den Haag: Gezondheidsraad 1990, publication no. 1990/18. Compare this hesitance with the following quote from the secretary of the US Department of Health and Human Services to the president of the American Senate (George Bush) in his introductory letter to the Surgeon General's report on unvoluntary smoking of 1986: 'Based on the current report, the judgment can now be made that exposure to environmental tobacco smoke can cause disease, including lung cancer, in nonsmokers. It is also clear that simple separation of smokers and nonsmokers within the same airspace may reduce but cannot eliminate nonsmoker exposure to environmental tobacco smoke'. And: 'Based on the evidence presented in this report, the choice to smoke should not interfere with the nonsmoker's choice for an environment free of tobacco smoke'.

Slowly though, as international publications found their way to the Netherlands in the 90s, it became undeniable that passive smoking is a very real health hazard to a great part of the national population. This changed matters, for it was generally assumed that if smoking was dangerous to health, then this was the personal choice of the smoker – he smoked at his own risk; but the same could hardly be said of a person who must inhale another's tobacco smoke involuntarily and may become ill as the result of this other person's choice to smoke.

In 2003, the Health Council published a second report on the health dangers of passive smoking.[5] It found that, with regard to adults, there is now enough evidence available to prove that passive smoking may cause lung cancer and that passive smoking in fact increases this potentially lethal risk by 20%.[6] However, in its considered opinion there is still insufficient evidence to prove that exposure to tobacco smoke can cause any other sort of cancer.[7] Also, it stated that the chance of heart disease is increased by passive smoking by an extra 20 to 30%.[8] Adapting American statistics on passive smoking to the size of the Dutch population, the Health Council estimated that passive smoking, yearly, is responsible for several hundreds of deaths as a result of lung cancer and several thousands of deaths as a result of various forms of heart disease.[9] It concluded its report by advising that these great numbers of premature deaths can be reduced relatively easily and quickly by one single measure: reducing the passive exposure to tobacco smoke.

3. The Tobacco Act

This new understanding also made passive smoking a constitutional matter, for, as the Dutch Constitution explicitly states in article 22, the government has a duty of care regarding the public health. Eventually, the understanding that

---

[5] Gezondheidsraad, Volksgezondheidsschade door passief roken. Den Haag: Gezondheidsraad, 2003; publication no. 2003/21.

[6] Gezondheidsraad, Volksgezondheidsschade door passief roken. Den Haag: Gezondheidsraad, 2003; publication no. 2003/21, p. 22.

[7] Gezondheidsraad, Volksgezondheidsschade door passief roken. Den Haag: Gezondheidsraad, 2003; publication no. 2003/21, p. 22. Compare this to the Surgeon General on passive smoking.

[8] Gezondheidsraad, Volksgezondheidsschade door passief roken. Den Haag: Gezondheidsraad, 2003; publication no. 2003/21, p. 23. It is positively remarkable how often the Dutch Health Council states that it cannot arrive at any conclusion with regard to the causal relationship between (passive) smoking and nearly every disease other than lung cancer or heart disease, as such conclusions prove to be no problem at all to the American Surgeon General, who in his annual Reports to the American Senate frequently mentions the existence of *tens of thousands* of studies which have been published on these very matters ... These Reports consist of a survey of all available knowledge on tobacco related health dangers together with recommendations to the Senate; as such they are an accessible way for scientists world-wide to dip into the global knowledge on this subject.

[9] The adjustment was merely with regard to the size of the Dutch population; as the incidence of smokers in the Netherlands is quite high in comparison with other European states and perhaps also in comparison with the United States, the possibility should be considered that perhaps the Health Council's estimations are very conservative when applied to the Netherlands. Also, please note that these figures give no information with regard to the death toll caused by *other* tobacco related diseases.

passive smoking is a matter of public health lead to the Tobacco Act 1988 ('Tabakswet'), that became effective as of 1 January 1990. The introduction of the Tobacco Act specifically states that its main purpose is to protect persons from passive smoking. In 2002 the Tobacco Act was revised and some important new regulations were added: as of 1 January 2004, all workplaces and all public transport must be smoke-free, though there are some notable exceptions to this rule.[10]

The achievement of the Tobacco Act is largely due to the unceasing efforts of The Queen Wilhelmina Fund ('Koningin Wilhelmina Fonds'), which focuses on cancer prevention and research, the Dutch Heart Foundation ('Nederlandse Hartstichting') and the Dutch Asthma Fund ('Nederlands Astma Fonds'). In 1974, these three organisations together founded STIVORO, which aims to provide the Dutch nation with information about the health risks of smoking. It does so by conducting and publishing research on smoking, by organising national 'quitting campaigns (particularly near the annual New Year's Day, to encourage new and healthy intentions), by providing information on methods on how to quit smoking, and by generally keeping the importance of quitting smoking on the national political agenda[11] and in the media. It is funded by its parent organisations and the government. Another similarly oriented organisation but with a more 'grass roots' background is CAN ('Clear Air Now'), which is of a more strident nature and more focused on protecting the rights of non-smokers to clean air, for instance by campaigning for smoke-free work places, restaurants and children's amusement parks. CAN is mostly funded by private donations.

4. The ambivalent attitude of the government

Yet even now that its own health advisory body has advised against exposure to tobacco smoke and, in its wake, the Tobacco Act explicitly prohibits smoking in the workplace, the ambivalent attitude of the Dutch parliament towards passive smoking shows itself by its refusal to apply the Tobacco Act to the hospitality industry, which is exempted from this Act. It would purportedly suffer too great a loss of employment if customers were forbidden to enjoy smoking cigarettes along with their beer or dinner. One can only presume that either the Dutch legislative power ascribes a stronger health to bartenders, barmaids, waiters and waitresses than it does with regard to workers in other workplaces (so that the first have no practical need of this legal protection), or that their right to health is considered subject to the interest of the national economy.

II. THE RIGHT TO HEALTH

Though Dutch law certainly recognises *de facto* the right of any person to enjoy good health, it is not stated anywhere specifically *de iure*. The closest in this

---

[10] Stb. 2002, 201.

[11] *See* for instance KWF, Nederlandse Hartstichting, Nederlands Astmafonds and STIVORO, Intensiveren en diversifiëren. Dossier over de gevolgen van roken en de effecten van niet-roken activiteiten ten behoeve van de kabinetsformatie 2002. Aangeboden aan het Ministerie van Volksgezondheid, Welzijn en Sport, The Hague, 15 April 2002.

context which may be found is Article 11 of the Constitution, which states that every person has a right to the inviolability of his body, excepting only such constrictions of this right as are based on enacted law. Though this article is usually interpreted in a criminal law context (meaning that no person shall be tortured), it may also be interpreted as a personal right to health or an implicit prohibition to infringe on a person's health, as indeed tobacco control lobbyists insist it is.

The Constitution also places a duty of care with regard to the public health on the government. Article 22 states that the government must undertake such measures as are conducive to the public health. This implies a duty to act where the state of the public health is threatened, as is definitely the case by passive smoking, which leads to a grand-scale loss of health and life. However, this article is meant to serve as an instruction to the government; it does not offer a personal right to health.

III. BANNING OF SMOKING AND LIABILITY

The Tobacco Act is an amalgam of regulations which, as its full title states, are all intended to curb the consumption of tobacco, with special regard to the protection of the non-smoker. As such, it is very much a work in progress with a varied content on many aspects of passive smoking. For instance, regulations concerning tobacco advertising and sponsoring may be found here, but also a compulsory obligation of tobacco manufacturers to co-operate with the government with regard to research aimed at discovering the content of tar, nicotine, carbon monoxide and other chemicals and materials in their products.

The inspection of the observance of the Tobacco Act is carried out by the Food and Goods Authority ('Voedsel en Waren Autoriteit', VWA). It hands out warnings and fines where it finds this not to be the case.

In the following paragraphs, I will outline the regulations and liability concerning the workplace, transport, public places, restaurants and bars and other places with regard to passive smoking. As not only the Tobacco Act, but also the Working Conditions Act and the Civil Code play an important role with regard to civil liability of the employer, I have chosen to discuss these a bit more extensively in the first following paragraph. However, it should be held in mind that they apply equally to any sort of (civil) work environment.

1. Smoking and the workplace

There are several regulations which provide an employee an opening to claim his right to a non-smoking workplace. Ranging from a general to a more specific nature, these are:

- the Working Conditions Act 1998, specifically Article 3.1a, b and c; this Act is of a general and instructive nature;
- the Civil Code ('Burgerlijk Wetboek' or customarily abbreviated as 'BW'), specifically Article 7:658; this article forms the basis for civil liability of the employer for occupational injuries and diseases;
- the Tobacco Act 1988, specifically Article 11a, section 1, which places a duty

of care on the employer to ensure a smoke-free workplace. This article has only become current since 1 January 2004.

I will discuss these regulations here below.

1.1   The Working Conditions Act 1998

Article 3.1a, b and c of the Working Conditions Act 1998 ('Arbeidsom standighedenwet', also known popularly as the 'Arbo-wet') instructs the employer to organise labour and production processes in such a manner that the employee will suffer no ill effect either with regard to his safety or his health, unless this cannot be reasonably required from the employer (a). To this end, the dangers and risks to the safety and health of the employee must be prevented as much as possible at their source; only if this cannot reasonably be required from the employer should he apply effective, preventative measures of a collective nature. Preventative measures on an individual basis are only permissible as a last resort; and even more so with regard to preventative measures for any specific individual (b). Also, the work place itself, the working methods, the tools and equipment and even the labour itself must be designed or organised in such a way as to be as much as possible adapted to the individual needs and characteristics of every individual employee (c).

Article 4, section 9 instructs the employer to take such measures as are necessary and effective in preventing employees from being exposed to unhealthy substances in the course of their work. As, according to any definition, tobacco smoke consists of many unhealthy elements, some of which are even carcinogenic, this article can easily be interpreted as an instruction to the employer not to expose the employee to passive smoking.

Article 5 of the Working Conditions Act 1998 places a duty on the employer to inventory and evaluate in writing the risks which the employee will or might face during the course of his labour; this risk inventory and evaluation will be reviewed as often as the working experience with it, changed working methods or labour conditions or the state of the art and professional services give cause to do so.

What this amounts to, in the context of this contribution, is that the employer must:

– undertake research into the possible health risks that his employees (may) face in the course of their employment; this research must include, as a result, the knowledge that passive smoking constitutes such a health risk (for this is certainly nowadays general knowledge);
– act on this knowledge by taking such measures with regard to the workplace and the required labour, et cetera, to ascertain to the extend as may reasonably be required of him that his employees are not exposed to inhalation of tobacco smoke;[12]
– prevent the danger of passive smoking at its source;

---

[12]   When Dutch labour law states that the employer is required to do something to the extend as may reasonably be expected of him, the employer will find that in practice this is very much indeed. Dutch judges are demanding where it concerns the health and safety protection of the employee.

– take heed of any special needs of particular employees, such as asthmatic or tobacco allergic employees.

Put briefly: the Working Conditions Act may be interpreted to place a duty of care on the employer to ensure that his employees are not exposed to passive smoking. This is, however, not an absolute liability. The Labour Inspector may fine the employer who broaches the Working Conditions Act regulations (though this will normally only be after several warnings have been issued and ignored).

1.2   Article 7:658 CC

The Civil Code contains an article which may be interpreted as placing a similar duty of care on the employer. This is Article 7:658 CC, which states that (as far as is relevant here):

Article 7:658 CC:
1. *The employer shall equip the premises on which and provide and maintain the tools and implements with which he requires the work to be performed in such a way and make such arrangements and issue such instructions in respect of the performance of the work as may reasonably be expected in view of the nature of the work to prevent the employee from occurring damage while in the performance of his work.*
2. *The employer is liable towards the employee for the damage which the employee may incur in the performance of his work, unless the employer is able to prove that the obligations mentioned in section 1 have been met or that the damage is largely due to the intent or the intentional recklessness of the employee.*
3. *[...]*
4. *[...]*

This article imposes a duty on the employer to organise his workplace, his production processes, et cetera, in such a manner and to such an extent as may reasonably be expected of him to ensure the safety and health of his employees. Though this duty does not, strictly speaking, lead to absolute liability, in practice however it goes very far indeed.

In order to properly organise and ensure his workplace as is required of him, the employer must thoroughly research whether his working conditions pose any health or safety danger to his employees. To do so, he may even need to look beyond the national borders for information, publications, conferences, and so on. Any occupational disease of which the employer knows of or ought to have known of, and against which he should have reasonably taken adequate protective measures but failed to do so, could lead to his liability ex Article 7:658 CC.

Only very rarely will an employer be able to escape civil liability to his employee on the ground that he did not know, nor could reasonably have known, of the health danger which has caused the employee harm and therefore was not failing in his duty of care towards the employee. It has not yet been established in Dutch law just when exactly the employer could and should have known of the health dangers of passive smoking. Taking a look over the national borders, it may be considered that in the United States and England, this knowledge was widely published by the late Eighties, so I carefully assume that the presumption of the Dutch employer's knowledge should not be off by more than a few years at most. Certainly over the past decade, it may be taken that the Dutch employer could or should have known – it being common knowledge and therefore easily available to him – that passive smoking is injurious to health. This directly implies that he is liable for damages if he has failed to protect his employee from passive smoking and the employee has suffered damage because of this. This is naturally even more so now that the Tobacco Act explicitly requires him to provide a smoke-free workplace as of 1 January 2004. An employer cannot defend his lack of preventive measures by professing a lack of knowledge concerning the law.

According to accepted case law, the employee need not provide proof of the employers blame for his damages; he may suffice by offering proof of his injury or disease and making a plausible case of a causal relationship between his injury or disease and his employment. It is then up to the employer to defend himself by disputing the nature or existence of the injury or disease or the causal relationship with the employment. If he cannot prove that he has fully met his duty of care and it is deemed plausible that his failure to do so has led to, or significantly contributed to, the employee's injury or disease, the judge will assume the existence of a causal relationship; liability is then nearly inescapable.

Three other escapes from employer's liability remain. Firstly, the employer may also try to prove that the damage has been caused by the employee's own fault, wilfully and intentionally; this is exceptionally hard to prove in a court of law and therefore only very rarely successful. Another way of achieving the same is by proving that the damage is or even might be caused by circumstances in the private life of the employee. Secondly, the employer must provide plausible arguments that the injury or disease of the employee would have occurred anyway, regardless of the manner in which he has fulfilled the duty of care owing to his employee. This, too, is almost never successful. The third way is to invoke Article 3:310 CC by proving that the employee's right to claim damages is proscribed. Considering that many tobacco related diseases may have 'long tails', i.e. can occur a long time after (prolonged) exposure to tobacco smoke (whether this be of an active or a passive nature), it could well be that Article 3:310 CC will become more important in this regard in the future, as has been the case with asbestos-related diseases.

There is a clear interaction between this employer's liability article and the aforementioned Working Conditions Act. An employee who has suffered a work related injury or disease will base his claim on Article 7:658 CC and often refer in his arguments to the Working Conditions Act, which gives more explicit details as to how an employer should ensure the safety and health of his working conditions, thereby showing in which particular manner the employer has failed in his duty towards him. This will now undoubtedly also be the case with regard to the Tobacco Act.

Perhaps it is well to point out that the Dutch employer's liability law has a somewhat old-fashioned origin: though it is meant to cover occupational accidents as well as occupational diseases, the (historical) fact is that it has grown mostly out of case law concerning occupational accidents which, due to their nature, usually have a time, a space and a cause which may all be quite exactly pinpointed. This has greatly influenced the development and nature of the rules regarding the burden of proof. However, over the past decade, the wave of 'new' claims, such as Repetitive Strain Injury, chronic neurotoxicity of organic solvents and mesothelioma – all occupational diseases – has shown that the Dutch employer's liability law is not quite geared to the legal problems which typically beset occupational diseases. To name but a few which might apply to employees who have become ill as a result of passive smoking at the workplace:

- a long incubation period ('long tail'), which will make it difficult later on to provide proof of what the working conditions were in the past, particularly with regard to causality; also, this may mean that the liable employer has disappeared or gone bankrupt;
- the possibility of limitation where an action is already proscribed before a claimant could even know he had a claim for compensation;
- a pluricausal origin of the disease; lung cancer for instance could be caused by passive smoking at work but also by passive smoking at the bar of the local sports club or even at home, by a former smoking addiction, by living near a speedway or even by bad genes. An employer could point out any number of possible causes for such a disease, while it is up to the employee to prove or at least make highly plausible that a *particular* causal relationship with the workplace exists.

Particularly a pluricausal origin of a tobacco-related disease could prove to be a very difficult obstacle in the course to prove the causal relationship between the disease and the working conditions. It is yet to be seen how the Dutch judiciary will cope with this. However, considering how it has been handling uncertain causality of diseases so far, my best guess is that in the case of uncertain causality of pluricausal diseases, such as lung cancer, it will *proportion* liability between the claimant and the defendant according to the chance that either one is responsible for the disease.[13] This is a clear break with standard case law, which stands for 'all or nothing'.

Once a causal relationship between the disease and the failure of the employer in his duty of care towards the employee *has* been established, it does not avail the employer held liable to point the finger towards another (previous or later) employer of the employee, even if this other employer had also failed similarly or perhaps even worse in his duty of care.[14] So it will presumably not help an employer to argue that the employee was also, or even worse, exposed to tobacco smoke at another employer's workplace.

Worthy of particular mention is the Dutch postal office worker Adriana 'Nanny' Nooijen, who suffered health problems as a result of the continual exposure to tobacco smoke at her work.[15] Her employer, the Dutch postal service PTT scoffed at her complaints and requests, particularly with regard to a smoking ban in the sorting area where she spent most of her time and in the

---

[13]   Middelburg District Court, 1 February 1999, NJkort 1999, 35 (Schaier v. De Schelde); also, Amsterdam Cantonal Court, 4 October 2001, JAR 2001, 223 (Van Hulst v. Y).

[14]   Cf. Supreme Court 2 October 1998, NJ 1999, 683 (Cijsouw II) and Supreme Court 2 October 1998 (C97/115HR), NJ 1999, 682 (Wijkhuisen); both cases concern asbestos claims.

[15]   Breda District Court in summary proceedings, 25 April 2000, KG 2000, 119 (Nooijen v. Koninklijke PTT Post BV).

corridors and the staff canteen. After six years of exhausting every possibility of negotiation without success, she took her employer to court on the ground that he had failed in his duty of care imposed by Article 7:658 CC and the Working Conditions Act – the first Dutch employee to do so.[16]

The President of the Breda District Court was most explicit in its ruling against the employer, stating that not only was he obliged to provide a smoke-free workplace on the grounds of Article 7:658 CC and Articles 3 and 4, section 9 of the Working Conditions Act, but, as his failure to do so had aggravated his employee's health complaints, this was even a matter of great urgency. Nanny Nooijen's efforts to achieve the smoke-free workplace to which she was entitled by law were received with great rejoicing by the Ministry of Health, Welfare and Sports, which was at the time drafting the article discussed here below: Article 11a, section 1 of the Tobacco Act.

1.3. Article 11a, section 1 Tobacco Act

Article 11a, section 1 of the Tobacco Act[17] is the most recent as well as the most specific of legal sources to establish an employee's right to a smoke-free workplace.

In the early Nineties, the Ministries of Health, Welfare & Sports and Social Affairs & Employment had come to an understanding with the Dutch employers' organisations that the last would ensure smoke-free workplaces by means of self-regulation, having professed to acknowledge the health dangers of passive smoking.[18] As a result, this kept any non-governmental workplace related article out of the original Tobacco Act. The understanding came naturally in a time when 'self-regulation' was very popular politically and socially. Reflecting the times, the then current media campaign of the tobacco industry even was 'We can work it out' ('we komen er samen wel uit') with regard to the relation between the smoker and the non-smoker. But instead of taking such measures, employers preferred that employees hash out the whole smoking business between themselves. Not surprisingly, many smokers ignored the implication to ask their colleagues whether they objected to their smoking; those who did would often hear 'of course not' while their colleagues actually were indeed bothered by the smoke but preferred to keep the work relationship with their smoking colleagues amicable.

However, after some ten years of watching the employers' procrastination, the Ministries arrived at the conclusion that too little had been achieved at too slow a pace towards a general smoke-free workplace. In particular, it was the Member of Parliament Hermann (Groen Links) who pointed out that at the rate things were progressing in this field, this achievement would take forever, if left up to the employers. It was high time for the legislative to step in and act.

---

[16] And, regrettably, to the best of my knowledge also the last; but by providing a precedence, Nanny Nooijen has done Dutch employees an immeasurable service.

[17] Stb. 2002, 201.

[18] The principle of a smoke-free workplace had been fully accepted by the employers' organisations, together forming the Foundation of Labour ('Stichting van de Arbeid), which published two recommendations on a smoke-free workplace. Cf. Stichting van de Arbeid, 'Aanbeveling over de bescherming van de niet-roker op het werk' (1992) and 'De lucht geklaard: een aanbeveling over rookbeleid van ondernemingen' (2001).

During the parliamentary debates on the desired revision of the Tobacco Act, he therefore introduced an amendment which clearly stated the direct right of the employee to a smoke-free workplace and the duty of the employer to provide this.[19] It was accepted.

I give the current text here below:

Article 11a, section 1, Tobacco Act:
    'Employers shall make such arrangements that employees will be enabled to perform their work without experiencing any nuisance or discomfort from the [tobacco] smoke of others'.

As of 1 January 2002, employers have a duty to ensure that employees are not exposed to passive smoking in their workplace. Though the section is directed to employers, it is also meant to indicate an enforceable right of employees to a smoke-free workplace.

The meaning of 'workplace' is not restricted to the actual location or precise spot where an employee habitually works; it also encompasses any rooms, hallways, toilets, canteens (even if exploited by a third party), waiting rooms, recreation areas, staircases, elevators, facilities or indeed any sort of inside space that is within the power of the employer.[20]

Another aspect concerns the employee himself: Article 11a, section 1 is not limited to the employees who have a labour contract with the employer. Rather from a reverse point of view, the employer has a duty of care to provide a smoke-free workplace for *all* employees, regardless whether these are his own employees or someone else's. His duty therefore also extends towards other persons, such as workers from temporary employment agencies, inspectors, representatives, etc.

The official commentary on the Decree Exceptions to the Smoke-free Workplace notes that this duty of care is, quite literally, not without bounds: it extends only as far as the employer's power to control 'his' workplace. This means that, for instance, the employer who hires a worker from a temporary employment agency is responsible for providing this person with a smoke-free workplace but the worker's formal employer, i.e. the temporary employment agency, is not.[21] The VWA, the Authority which inspects the observance of the

---

[19] TK 2000–2001, 26472, no. 13.

[20] Besluit uitzonderingen rookvrije werkplek, Stb. 2003, 561.

[21] I wonder whether this exception will uphold if it is contested in a court of law. The reason for this doubt lies in the fact that the first sentence of section 4 of Article 7:658 CC clearly states: 'He, who in the course of his profession or business would let anyone, with whom he has no labour contract, work for him, is liable in accordance with sections 1, 2 and 3 towards this person for any damage which he [this person, YW] may incur in the course of his work'. This is commonly held to mean that an employer who employs an employee whom he has hired or borrowed in one way or another off another employer, has a duty of care towards the safety and health of this employee which is exactly the same as it is with regard to his regular, contractual employees. And visa versa, too: the formal employer is just as liable for any damages, even if he had no employer's power at the place where his contractual employee was stationed. The (hired) employee may choose whether he will claim damages from the material employer, the formal employer or even both at the same time. The parliamentary reasoning behind this is – apart from the obvious, that hired employees have rights too – that the formal and material employers are in a position to agree between themselves beforehand who is formally and materially responsible for the employer's liability for occupational accidents and diseases, while the employee in question must in practice accept whatever working environment

Tobacco Act, may fine the material employer for failing to provide a smoke-free workplace but not the formal employer.

In practice, there are several ways to ensure that employees have a smoke-free workplace. Basically, these can be divided into three methods. The first is to ban smoking outright on the grounds of the employer. The effectiveness of this is evident but, as approximately one out of every three Dutch persons smoke, this had led to a great deal of unrest and has proved to be highly unpopular. The second is to allow the employees who smoke so-called stub-breaks ('peukenpauzes'); this, too, has led to a great deal of discussion. Many non-smoking workers feel that they are at a (financial) disadvantage as they have to work while others 'goof off' many times a day, while their smoking counterparts feel that they are being criticised unfairly for what they experience as a bodily need, much akin to being thirsty and going to the office kitchen for a drink of water frequently, or like having a small bladder and needing to visit the bathroom more often than others. This second method is often combined with the institution of an entirely enclosed and ventilated smoke-area. This is acceptable in terms of the Tobacco Act, as long as the contaminated air does not in any way mingle with the air which is breathed in the workplace to the extend that the workers there experience any nuisance or discomfort. Here, too, the same sort of discussion arises, perhaps even more so as smokers on average are a walking distance of 2·5 minutes away from the designated smoke area. Some employers just instruct their employees to have their smoke outside; though this too is in compliance with the Tobacco Act, it has proved to be a great annoyance to the smokers, as they feel they are thus treated as pariah's who are literally put out into the wet and windy cold. The third method is a policy of acquiescence: simply ignoring both the employees who smoke in the workplace and the employees who complain of this. This is the case in seven percent of all workplaces, as researched by the large trades-union FNV Bondgenoten.[22]

The study by the FNV Bondgenoten, which was published in April 2004, showed some other interesting aspects of the observance of the Tobacco Act with respect to the smoke-free workplace as well. It found that a third of all employers had no smoking policy *at all*, despite the fact that the health dangers of passive smoking in the workplace have been generally recognised by the Dutch employers for nearly fifteen years. Nearly 60% of all businesses provided their employees with a specific enclosed and ventilated space for smoking, while about ten percent sent their employees outside to smoke. All in all, a score of 70% clear smoke-free workplaces had been achieved.

2. Transport

Article 11a, section 2 states that all operators of passenger transport are obliged to undertake such measures as will ensure that passengers may complete their

---

he encounters. This means that *both* employers are responsible and liable to see that the requirements of the Working Conditions Act, the Civil Code and the Tobacco Act are met. It will be interesting to see whether this Decree will supersede art. 7:658 CC or the other way round – I'm betting on art. 7:658 CC, which has been revised relatively recently and is based on long standing case law.

[22]   FNV Bondgenoten, Peuken-pauze. De nieuwe Tabakswet in bedrijf. Problemen met de peuken-pauze, Utrecht, April 2004. Similarly revealing studies have been conducted by STIVORO, such

journey without experiencing any nuisance or discomfort by the smoking of others. As of 1 January 2004, this has led to a full prohibition to smoke in taxis, busses, trams, subways and railway carriages. This prohibition is very well observed by the passengers, who appear to consider this prohibition suddenly more a matter of mutual consideration than of enforcement – truly a double-turn in attitude!

The Dutch national railway operator, NS, has used this opportunity to also prohibit smoking in the railway buildings and on the platforms, save for a one meter-area around 'smoker's columns' (narrow, 1·5 meter high ashtrays, essentially), of which every station has at least one (right) in front of every entrance to the station and on every platform. In practice, this means that one will find the main station hall to be usually smoke-free, but before one gets there one has to make one's way through the throng of smokers who, standing around the smoker's column, inadvertently bar the entrance to enjoy a last smoke. As for smoking in the designated 'smokers column' areas on the platforms, though it is generally accepted (with a broad interpretation of what constitutes a meter's perimeter around the smokers column) in practice some smokers will ignore this.

The fine for smoking in public transport is EUR 25; throwing the stub on the ground will set the fined smoker back by EUR 40.[23] However, in the past ten months, in which I have passed through railway stations on a nearly daily basis, I have never actually seen a bus or train conductor or policeman admonish or fine anyone who smoked where it was not allowed, though I have seen plenty of conductors and policemen walk right past 'illegal' smokers.[24] I can only conclude from this that the enforcement of the Tobacco Act is not very stringent in this respect.

Any public transport operator who is found to be negligent in upholding the prohibition for passengers to smoke, risks a fine of EUR 300 for a first offence to a maximum of EUR 2,400 for repeat offences.

With regard to air travel, Article 11a, section 3 requires Dutch civilian airlines to undertake such measures as will ensure that passengers may complete their journey without experiencing any nuisance or discomfort by the smoking of others, in so far as these airlines are flying either to or from any Dutch airport. The official prohibition to smoke in aeroplanes is active as of 17 July 2002.

However, the Tobacco Act is provided with a loophole to allow some exceptions to the general rule of smoke-free passenger transport by means of an administrative order, in this case the 'Exceptions to Smoke-free Passengers Transport Act ('Besluit uitzonderingen rookvrij personenvervoer').[25] This administrative order has come into effect on 1 January 2004 and allows the

---

as 'Tabaksrook in de werkomgeving. Resultaten van het PARA-meter onderzoek onder wer-knemers', The Hague, 2003 and 'Tabaksrook in de werkomgeving. Resultaten van het PARA-meter onderzoek onder werkgevers', The Hague, 2003.

[23] Remarkably, any fines for smoking in public transport or public stations are not defined by the Tobacco Act but by the Passengers Transport Act ('Wet Personenvervoer').

[24] The newspaper 'De Telegraaf' reported on September 2, 2004, that between January 1 (when smoking in the railway stations, platforms and trains became prohibited), and the end of August, 357 train passengers were fined for smoking in a railway carriage, as were 76 persons for smoking on the railway platforms. More than a million Dutch commute by train each day.

[25] Stb. 2002 201, art. 11a-2,3 Stb. 2003 550 art. 11a-5.

following operators to be exempted from the duty to provide smoke-free public transport in case of:

– international trains (such as the Thalys and ICE) and ferries which cross Dutch borders and are operated by foreign operators or by international co-operating operators;
– open air transport.

3. Public places

Article 10 of the Tobacco Act states that all public places, such as institutions, services and organisations run by the State or a public body, are obliged to undertake such measures as will ensure that the public may make use of the services offered there in a smoke-free atmosphere. This was also stated by the original Tobacco Act of 1988, which became effective in 1990, so basically this has been active law for almost fifteen years now.

The same article also requires that all work in any public building must be done without the workers experiencing any nuisance or discomfort from the tobacco smoke of others, regardless of whether these workers are civil servants, employees, volunteers or hired labourers from a temporary employment agency or any other sort of worker's category.

In practice, it is not always clear what constitutes a public place. Government buildings, hospitals, schools, youth facilities, sewers, subsidised sports facilities, public swimming pools and libraries, these and many more are all public places as understood by the Tobacco Act. So are offices, sanitary facilities, hallways, canteens, coffee corners, dressing rooms, class rooms, staircases, any sort of communal or shared space in a public building. Even a privately exploited bar in a public building is considered to be a public place, as the Tobacco Act offers no exemption with regard to public buildings.[26]

However, any public place which offers a minimum of two waiting-rooms, canteens, et cetera, may allow smoking in the smallest of these, provided that the smoke causes no nuisance outside of this area. A designated, enclosed and ventilated smoking room is also permitted.

One would think that a period as lengthy as fifteen years would have ironed out any remaining kinks in this piece of legislation, but such is not the case. The cure- and care sector (psychiatric hospitals, nursing-homes, rest homes and homes for the elderly, et cetera) for instance is notorious for blithely ignoring this aspect of the Tobacco Act, which it feels is unpractical, unsociable and unfair on elderly persons who have a lifetime of tobacco addiction and wish to continue to smoke in a communal surrounding. By the same token, this means that for instance old age-pensioners in a nursing home 'enjoy' a right to a smoke-free environment which they cannot realise and are thus forced to suffer passive smoking.

It is only in the past year (2004) that the Minister for Health, Welfare and Sports, Hoogervorst, has cracked down and instigated stiff fines on such institutions. This has finally prompted them to make an effort to comply to the Tobacco Act. However, in practice this means that some of these institutions

---

[26] Stb. 2002, 201 art. 11a-4.

will literally have to adapt themselves to the point of actually rebuilding – so the Minister has granted them an exemption until 1 January 2005. In other words, the inhabitants of nursing-homes and other, comparable institutions will have waited fifteen years for their recognised right to a smoke-free environment to be enforced.

Minister Hoogervorst has yet to concentrate on schools ... Nearly a third of Dutch school children in the ages of 10–19 years smoke, often in school corridors, which means that the rest, as well as teachers, caretakers, cleaners, etc., are exposed to passive smoking. There are nowadays many serious efforts to discourage children from starting or continuing smoking. This has come relatively late: in the period of 1990–1996, next to nothing was done to effect Article 10 in schools.

Any public institution which fails to comply to the Tobacco Act in enforcing a smoking prohibition may be fined from EUR 300 for a first offence to a maximum of EUR 2,400 for repeat offences.

4.   The hospitality industry (hotels, restaurants, bars, etc.)

Over the past few years, as it seemed that the Dutch hospitality industry would be included in the revised Tobacco Act 2002 (specifically Article 11a, section 1), the same industry has put up a formidable and effective lobby against any sort of imposed passive smoking measure. It claimed that such measures would exact a tremendous toll in employment as well as be intolerably inhospitable towards the guests and diners who enjoy a smoke at their premises.[27]

This is a remarkable point of view for several reasons. Firstly, the industry has offered no arguments as to why such measures would cost so many jobs in the sector, so the validity of this argument is doubtful (as New York and Irish experiences would already appear to confirm). Secondly, knowingly risking and sacrificing the health of its own employees for the sake of customers' unwholesome pleasure seems rather callous. Thirdly, almost six million Dutch out of a national population of 16 million – which makes well over 70% of all restaurant goers – think that a mandatory smoking prohibition in restaurants would actually be a sensible idea – how does that reconcile with the notion that such a measure would be 'inhospitable'?[28] One cannot but wonder whether perhaps the attitude of the Dutch hospitality industry is at least a decade obsolete and quite out of touch with reality, as represented by the very customers it wishes to attract.

While all workplaces in all sectors of industry have had to comply with passive smoking regulations as of 1 January 2004, the hospitality industry has managed to stave this off by continuing negotiations with the Ministry of Health, Welfare and Sports. At first, this lead to a reprise until 1 January 2005 and in September of 2004, in a final showdown with the industry's representative organisation, the Koninklijke Horeca Nederland (KHN), Minister Hoogervorst backed down from his original plans to enforce a complete smoke-free workplace in hotels, restaurants and bars. Instead, he has allowed the hospitality

---

[27]   One wonders whether diners who prefer to enjoy their dinner without an unhealthy and distasteful blue haze hanging over them would classify such a surrounding as 'hospitable'.

[28]   Cf. TNS NIPO, Continu onderzoek rookgewoontes, August 2004.

industry until the end of 2008 to gradually self-regulate the instigation of smoke-free 'zones'.[29] This means that, until that time, the government has lost all say and all control on this industry; there is no enforcement of any regulation on passive smoking in hotels, restaurants, cafés and bars possible in the areas which are open to the public because there is no regulation at all to be enforced. It is all left up to the industry itself.

It is astonishing to compare how very determined the Minister of Health, Welfare and Sports has been to introduce legislation to prevent passive smoking in all workplaces, while completely ignoring the health risks which are faced daily by the 500.000 workers in the hospitality industry. Hoogervorst defended his about-face on the matter by referring to the heavy criticism and lack of back-up he received in parliament for his original plans. However, the Minister continues to maintain that employees in the hospitality industry do have a right to a healthy work environment, but has repeatedly declined to answer the question when this right will come into effect.

Even from the most neutral of viewpoints, the agreement between the Minister and the KHN leaves much to be desired. For instance, the agreement contains no definition at all of what constitutes 'smoke-free', nor what is meant by a 'zone'. This could mean two completely separated areas – one for smokers, one for non-smokers – but also no physical separation of any sort between the two at all. It could mean that the non-smoking zone consists of two tables in the draughtiest area of a restaurant. It could mean absolutely nothing until the end of 2008. It is up to every entrepreneur, regardless of whether he is a member of the KHN or not, to decide for himself what he will or will not make of this agreement, without any obligation or sanction whatsoever.

However, the agreement does explain what the gradual self-regulation is intended to lead to. By the end of 2008, 75% of all cafés and discotheques must have opted for a smoke-free zone. All restaurants must have a smoke-free area, while 95% of all hotels must offer a smoke-free breakfast; all hotels must offer smoke-free rooms. All ice-cream salons must be completely smoke-free, as should be 50% of all snack bars and cafés. All these percentages include the enterprises which are not represented by the KHN.

An administrative order, based on Article 11a, section 5 of the Tobacco Act, will replace the agreement by a formal exemption. At this point in time, however, this procedure is still in the stage where the Minister has informed the Second Chamber of his intention to issue such an administrative order.[30]

Both Stivoro and Can, who have continually opposed these develop-ments as well as the final agreement, have announced their intentions to strive towards smoke-free workplaces in this industry, if need be even going to court to achieve this.

In December of 2003, Can has in fact already done so in a test-case against the children's amusement park Duinrell, claiming that the Duinrell employees were tortuously exposed to passive smoking in their workplace.[31] However, the summary proceedings judge denied the claim, attaching great

---

[29]   TK, 29200 XVI, no. 278.
[30]   TK, 29200 XVI, no. 278.
[31]   The Hague District Court in summary proceedings, 17 December 2003, docket no. KG 03/1337 (Nederlandse Nietrokersvereniging CAN (Club Actieve Nietrokers) v. Attractiepark en Camping Duinrell BV).

importance to two facts. Firstly, that there has been long and still ongoing discussion in Dutch society with regard to the recognition of the fact that passive smoking is injurious to health, which has led to official measures to protect the health of employees from this danger. Secondly, that the legislative power has chosen, after extensive consultation with the main representative of the hotel and catering industry, to opt for a gradual, self-regulatory means of protecting the workers in this industry. Under these circumstances neither the exclusion from this legislation of these employees nor the absence of smoke-free workplaces at Duinrell could be held to be tortuous.

So far, no employee in the hospitality industry who is exposed to passive smoking and willing to go to court against his employer has come forward. I can therefore offer no case law on this subject.

5. Other places

The law concerning passive smoking in certain non-public places is much the same as regards public places, which has already been discussed. Article 11 of the Tobacco Act states that by administrative decree, controllers of premises which are used (either wholly or partially) for health care, welfare, social services, the arts, culture or sports, social-cultural work or education must undertake such measures as will ensure that the public may make use of the services offered there in a smoke-free atmosphere in accordance with Article 10 of the Tobacco Act. However, this only applies to such categories of buildings and institutions as are meant in the Decree exceptions smoke-free workplace, which first became effective as of 1 January 1990 and has recently been revised.[32] In practice, this means that any building or part of a building which is in any way, even partially, financially supported or subsidised by the State or is under the (partial) authority of the government and is used, even partially, for any of the uses which have been enumerated before, must be *fully* smoke-free.[33]

To give a practical example: supposing that Mr. X privately exploits a building by renting it out to several tenants, one of which is the local municipality Y. This particular tenant uses the ground floor as a sports accommodation for the Y citizens and has sub-rented part of it to be exploited as a bar to a commercial company, Z. Even though bars are, in general, exempt from the obligation to provide a smoke-free workplace, this particular bar will have to comply to the Tobacco Act, as it is located in a building which is (partially) used for a purpose (sports) which is subsidised by the (local) government. Mr. X., being the controller of premises, is required to ensure that every part of the building – every entrance, every hallway, every staircase, every bathroom facility and in this case, every bar, too – which is accessible to the public is in compliance with the Tobacco Act, regardless of the fact that the bar is exploited by someone else (Z).

---

[32] Besluit uitzonderingen rookvrije werkplek, Stb. 2003, 561.

[33] CAN successfully argued this point in the case against the municipality of Spijkenisse, which lifted a smoking ban in a parish-centre after many of its visitors had complained that they were no longer allowed to enjoy their billiard games with a smoke. Cf. Rotterdam District Court in summary proceedings, 20 April 2000, docket no. 135831/KG ZA 00–519 (Nederlandse Niet-rokersvereniging CAN v. Municipality of Spijkenisse).

In the combined campaign 'Agreements on smoking, a matter of good sport' (Rookafspraken, dat is wel zo sportief'), the Ministry for Health, Welfare and Sports and the NOC*NSF (the Dutch overall sports organisation) are endeavouring to have all sports accommodations completely smoke-free on a voluntary basis by 1 January 2006.

The Decree exemptions of the smoke-free workplace, lists a number of exemptions from Article 11a of the Tobacco Act.[34] Some of these have already been discussed, but for the sake of survey I have listed them briefly all here below:

- the parts of hotels, bars and restaurants (including snack bars) which are open to the public;[35]
- catering areas which are open to the public in concert buildings, music halls and theatres;[36]
- gaming halls;
- international and foreign passenger transport (under specific circumstances);
- spaces over which the employer has no say or control;
- private spaces;
- designated, enclosed smoking areas;
- open air, which includes outdoors sports, festivities, markets, music festivals, amusement parks et cetera.

As we have seen, the hospitality industry is exempted from the duty to provide smoke-free workplaces. However, it is not always clear whether a particular sort of catering service falls under the general meaning of 'catering industry'. Such is the case with regard to cinemas. Though formally there is now a negotiation going on between the cinema industry and the Ministry of Health, Welfare and Sports regarding the applicability of the Tobacco Act to this industry, in some cinemas full measures have already been undertaken to ensure smoke-free workplaces for their personnel on health grounds. Controllers of premises in other cinemas prefer to take the long view and wish for a similar reprieve as has been given to the regular hospitality industry, stating (in a truly hospitable way) that smoking is part of an evening out and any cinema visitor who feels that he would not care to buy drinks or popcorn in a smoky cinema lobby does not need to do so.[37]

For principal and practical reasons, the Tobacco Act is not targeted at

---

[34] Besluit uitzonderingen rookvrije werkplek, Stb. 2003, 561.

[35] The reference 'open to the public' is meant to indicate that any parts of such buildings which are *not* open to the public, such as kitchens, storerooms, connecting hallways, recreational rooms and bathrooms for staff, etc, are not exempted and must therefore be smoke-free. Employers' canteens must in all cases be smoke-free, even if they are exploited by third parties.

[36] Though most concert buildings, music halls and theatres provide catering services, this does not necessarily officially make them part of the catering industry. This exempts them not only from the Tobacco Act but also from the agreement which has been made between the Ministry of Health, Welfare and Sports and the KHN. However, as these organisations have pleaded a great dependency on bar intakes similar to that in the catering industry, it may be assumed that at some point the Minister will come round to either including them in the agreement which has been made with the KHN or ending the indefinite exemption.

[37] Cf. the newspaper article of Rob Musters, Roken taboe in Bredase bioscopen, in: BN/De Stem, 19 March 2004.

passive smoking in private surroundings, such as in the home.[38] As employers cannot control the non-smoking conditions which occur in the homes of their customers and clients, their employees will in practice have to accept whichever conditions they find. From a legal point of view however, there is nothing to stand in the way of an employer arranging a smoke-free workplace for his employee at the house of a client, or deciding not to serve him if the client refuses this request. It is a matter of choice: mostly the employer's choice.

Though it is difficult to put a number to the size of this group of employees who are in this position, it should not be regarded lightly: when one considers it, there are a great many professions in which a great deal of time is spent in private surroundings. Just think of the washing machine repairman, the plumber, the indoor painter, the district-nurse, the cleaning-lady, the door-to-door salesman, the remover, et cetera. The exemption of private homes in the Tobacco Act means that they are *de facto* denied the right to a healthy work environment. This is completely at odds with the Working Conditions Act, Article 7:658 CC and the Nanny Nooijen case, which all clearly establish a right of the employee not to be exposed to health dangers. It is only a matter of time before this is put to the question in court.

'Private surroundings' does not necessarily mean a space in someone's home. 'Living-room areas' in homes for the elderly, in jails, psychiatric wards, etc are also exempt. Though it is within the powers of the employer or the controller of premises to ban smoking in these places if he would care to, it is felt by the legislative power that doing so would be an unwarranted intrusion into a personal sphere of life that is, under such circumstances, often already painfully restricted.

The Tobacco Act does apply to the communal spaces of sites which contain more than one home, such as a block of apartments. It is up to the (legal) person who is legally responsible for such a building to ensure that for instance maintenance personnel can do its job in the smoke-free surrounding which is required by the Tobacco Act. To accomplish this, he will need to instate rules concerning smoking by his tenants or inhabitants in the corridors, staircases, elevators, hallways, basements et cetera. These can be incorporated into the general conditions of the tenancy or apartment sale agreement. Without a more formal legal basis, it is difficult to see how he may prevent smoking by visitors. There is as yet no case law on this available, to the best of my knowledge.

Not surprisingly, designated smoking areas are also exempted from the rigors of the Tobacco Act. These include not only smoking areas in office's and factories, but also for instance in tobacco factories where products are tested, and in tobacco shops which offer a trial smoke to 'taste'. It is not quite clear though what this means with regard to the staff who have to clean these designated smoking areas – naturally, they too have a right to a smoke-free workplace but this is hard to reconcile with work which must by its very nature be done in a smoky atmosphere! Again, this would seem to be in direct violation of the Working Conditions Act and Article 7:658 CC. As yet, there is no published case law available on this point.

The Minister for Health, Welfare and Sports recognises that it is also possible to experience passive smoking in the open air. However, he feels that it

---

[38]   Cf. art. 11a, section 1 Tobacco Act 2002.

would be overdoing things to also extend the duties of Article 11a to work outdoors, as any nuisance or discomfort as a result of passive smoking can, in his opinion, easily be avoided by removing oneself a few paces from the source of irritation. By reason of this exemption, all work at for instance outdoors festivities, markets, music festivals, amusement parks et cetera are exempted from the Tobacco Act.

IV. CONCLUSION

The Nanny Nooijen case accomplished three important things for Dutch employees. Firstly, it established that in the year 2000 existing labour law, that is to say the Working Conditions Act and Article 7:658 CC, clearly provided employees with the enforceable right to a smoke-free workplace. As these regulations have a decades-old history, it may be held that the ensuing duty of care of employers to provide a smoke-free workplace actually goes back to the time when they were first obliged to know of the dangers of passive smoking. Though an exact date for this has not been pinpointed in Dutch case law, considering the avalanche of documentation on this subject which has been internationally available to Dutch employers since the Eighties, this obligation may be assumed to go back as far as well. It just has been blithely ignored by many employers all that time.

Secondly, the necessity of her legal battle to establish her right not to be exposed to passive smoking with all its health hazards showed up the ambivalent and basically unwilling attitude of her employer to provide her with the smoke-free workplace to which she was entitled. This attitude was and is although to a decreasing extent, still typical of many Dutch employers. Her case made clear that even more explicit legislation was needed to protect employees' health, while its verdict made certain that the right of employees to a smoke-free workplace was included in the revised Tobacco Act. Yet few lessons seem to have been learned by this court case as the same events appear to repeat themselves all over again in the hospitality industry, which even nowadays still shows a decidedly ambivalent attitude, too.

It is, to put it as bluntly as it deserves, completely beyond comprehension why the Ministry for Health, Welfare and Sports has agreed to exempt the hospitality industry, which employs half a million workers, from the obligation to provide smoke-free workplaces for yet another five years. Like any other industry, this one has seen the drive and the need for smoke-free workplaces coming for years. Also, the experiences with the original Tobacco Act of 1988 have already shown that self-regulating of tobacco smoke exposure by employers does not work. Particularly in a society where the equality of all is rated so highly that it forms the first article in the Constitution, it is unjustifiable to treat the workers in this industry as if their health is less important than that of workers elsewhere.

Also, from a legal point of view, it is doubtful whether such an exemption *can* be enforced and upheld if it is contested in court. The fact that the Minister made a deal with the hospitality industry does not negate the existence of the Working Conditions Act and Article 7:658 CC. Neither does it either wholly or partially negate the duty of care of the employer towards his employees, nor does such an agreement make them any less vulnerable against an untimely and unnecessary death by lung cancer, heart disease, vascular disease, chronic bronchitis or emphysema. I am therefore eagerly awaiting a second Nanny Nooijen in waitress costume to come forward and prove in litigation that she, too, has a right to enjoy good health and not have it exposed to toxic and carcinogenic chemicals in the air where she must work for her living.

Thirdly, the decided lack of follow-up of the Nanny Nooijen case by other court cases has proven how particularly difficult it can be for employees to take their employer to court over their right to a smoke-free workplace. It puts the labour relationship, in which the employee is the weaker party, under tremendous stress. It aggravates the relationship with the fellow (smoking) employees, many of whom still see smoking as socially acceptable and think of complainers as overly fussy. Some employees may choose to accept the fact that they are unwillingly exposed to passive smoking; other may prefer to leave their present employer to seek employment in healthier workplaces; but not all employees have such options available to them.

It is up to the legislative power and the government to ensure that *all* employers ban smoking in the workplace. It can only be achieved by explicit legislation and strict enforcement of this legislation. This, in turn, will only come about by a change in attitude of society in its view of passive smoking as being socially acceptable when in fact it is quite unhealthy and therefore by definition antisocial. Such a change in perception can only be fuelled by mass education on the health dangers of passive smoking. At the end of the day, people must *understand* that passive smoking is a lethal danger, that it may kill them in any number of horrible and untimely ways. They must *choose* not to smoke passively; they must wish to instigate and enforce passive smoking measures. In the past ten years, much has been accomplished on this score; but there is still a long way to go.

When I think of it, I find I often compare in my mind the endeavour for smoke-free workplaces with the fight against tuberculosis, which took place a century ago. This fight was won by educating society about the health dangers of spitting in public and on the streets (at the time a normal way of behaviour), thereby exposing passers-by to the tubercle germ. In a similar way, the present-day society must be educated that, though perhaps smoking may be a personal choice, it is not acceptable behaviour to expose others to tobacco smoke with all its ensuing health risks. If such a grand-scale viewpoint can be achieved, perhaps, in time, ashtrays in the workplace will be considered as obsolete as spittoons. That would certainly mean a great deal to public health.

APPENDIX. THE ADRIANA NOOIJEN CASE

82307/KG ZA 00–150

PRESIDENT OF THE DISTRICT COURT, BREDA

25 April 2000   JUDGMENT IN SUMMARY PROCEEDINGS

in the case of:

ADRIANA JOHANNA NOOIJEN,
resident of Breda,
plaintiff in an application
for an injunction of 27 March 2000,counsel: R. A. H. Post,
solicitor: J. F. Roth,

v

The public limited company KONINKLIJKE
PPT POST B.V., with registered headquarters
in The Hague, and its branch office in Breda,
defendant,
counsel: M. C. de Regt,
solicitor: R. A. A. Duk of the Hague.

1. The conduct of the proceedings

This is apparent from the following documents deposited by the parties to influence the judgment:

– the application for an injunction;
– the memorandum of an oral pleading by J. F. Roth;
– the submission from the side of the plaintiff, hereinafter referred to as Nooijen, including documents produced as exhibits;
– the memorandum of an oral pleading by R. A. A. Duk and the documents produced as exhibits in the proceedings by the defendant, hereinafter referred to as PTT [the Belgian Post Office].

2. The dispute

Nooijen is seeking an immediately enforceable injunction ordering PTT:

Primarily:

To introduce, within fourteen days of being served with notice of the judgment, a complete ban on smoking in the PTT premises at Slingerweg 7, Breda, except for a designated smokers' room that causes no nuisance from tobacco smoke to non-smokers;

Alternatively:

To introduce in the PTT premises at Slingerweg 7, Breda, within fourteen days of being served with notice of the judgment, a ban on smoking in the room (sorting area) in which she works, the corridors in the building and the canteen that is provided for members of staff;

All this on pain of a penalty payment of 1000 Belgian francs for each day, or part of a day, for which PTT fails to comply with the order being requested.

PTT has contested the application.

3. The provisional order and its grounds

3.1

On the basis of the absence or inadequacy of evidence to the contrary and the documents produced, the following facts have been taken as a starting-point:

— Nooijen has been employed by PTT since 1 February 1988. She occupies a post as a (full-time) mail handler in the mail-sorting centre at Slingerweg seven in Breda.
— Nooijen's duties consist, *inter alia*, in the sorting and processing of mail, including registered letters and packages. The time she spends on this part of her duties amounts on average to some five hours each working day.
— The vast majority of these tasks are performed in a large sorting area in the company of a number of fellow mail handlers, a not inconsiderable proportion of who smoke tobacco products.
— Nooijen has since January 1993 regularly complained to her employer about her colleagues' smoking and asked for adequate measures to be taken to protect her from tobacco smoke in her work environment.
— efforts have been made in, *inter alia,* (work) consultation meetings to reach agreement on the issue of (non-) smoking with fellow-employees who smoke.
— Since 24 February 1997 Nooijen has been working at a special workstation created for her by erecting makeshift partitions in the above-mentioned large sorting area. There is still a large distance left open between these partitions and the ceiling. A ban on smoking has been imposed by PTT for this partitioned-off section of the large sorting area.
— Elsewhere in the mail-sorting centre there is also a ban on smoking in the ladies' toilet. In the canteen there is a ban on smoking between 11.30 and 13.30 hrs.
— In her letter of 9 February 2000 to PTT Nooijen asked for the formulation of an effective policy on smoking by making all work areas "non-smoking" with the exception of a dedicated smokers' room where smoke causes no nuisance to non-smokers.
— In its letter of 24 February 2000 PTT gave a negative response to this request.

3.2

Nooijen asserts that, quite aside from her personal hypersensitivity to tobacco smoke, far-reaching measures on the shop floor are to be expected from PTT as

163

a good employer, primarily in the form of an absolutely smoke-free work environment, such as to fulfil its obligations under labour law and the Health and Safety At Work Act to ensure a safe work situation and a workplace where she, and other non-smoking colleagues, can perform their work activities without danger to their own health.

As concerns the health risks of so-called passive smoking by non-smokers Nooijen has referred to the Tobacco Act and to the findings of scientific research.

3.3

PTT has argued that with the aforementioned action it has already taken it has gone far enough towards meeting Nooijen's wishes and that, for reasons to be discussed in detail below, the present claim should be dismissed.

3.4

That smoking is damaging to health and that non-smokers are also caused harmful health effects or nuisance by others smoking around them, especially if they suffer from disorders of the respiratory passages, is a generally accepted presumption and likewise the basis for the legislation on the protection of non-smokers in the 1989 Tobacco Act.

3.5

In 1999 the government introduced the Bill to amend the Tobacco Act (Parliamentary Papers Second Chamber, session 1998–1999, 26472), which is under debate in the Second Chamber. In it, the government takes as a starting-point for more detailed legislation the fact that in the case of tobacco smoke, unlike many other toxic substances in the air, no values have been specified for a maximum acceptable concentration. This means that the conclusion reached in the report by the National Health Council as cited by the plaintiff, to the effect that no safe lower limit can be set for exposure to a carcinogenic substance such as tobacco smoke, is adopted by the government. The same conclusion is also followed and taken as a starting-point in the present summary proceedings.

It was this that prompted the government to tighten the provisions of the Tobacco Act in the aforementioned Bill, which establishes the possibility of imposing an obligation on employers, via an implementing order (AmvB), "to take such measures as are necessary to enable employees to perform their work activities without thereby being subjected to nuisance and inconvenience caused by their colleagues' smoking".

3.6

The right to protection of physical well-being, or health, is a fundamental right enshrined in the Belgian Constitution. It naturally also takes effect in labour law. Article 7:658, paragraph 1 of the Belgian Civil Code imposes an obligation on employers to arrange areas in which work is performed on their behalf in such a manner as to, and to take all such measures and issue all such instructions as are reasonably necessary in order to, prevent employees from suffering injury in the performance of their work duties. Article three of the Working Conditions Act imposes an obligation on employers to organize the work in a manner, and arrange workstations in a manner, such that there is no resultant harmful influence on the health of the employee.

3.7

Article 4.9 of the Decree on Working Conditions prescribes that effective measures must be taken to prevent employees from being exposed to substances in the course of their work to a degree such that damage may be caused to their health or nuisance may be caused to employees. Paragraphs two and three of this Article lay down detailed rules on the order of priority according to which employers must take measures. They must begin with, *inter alia*, organizational measures that eliminate the danger at source. Only if this is not effective can other possible measures, such as the extraction of polluted air, be considered.

Given the above-mentioned hazard to health posed by tobacco smoke these statutory provisions mean that employers are under an obligation to ensure that both while they are working and during their breaks non-smoking employees are in an environment that is totally free from tobacco smoke. This is because there is no safe lower limit. The danger must, in the first instance, be tackled at source by means of an organizational measure. A total ban on smoking is appropriate to this purpose and is generally the indicated solution inside office buildings. Employers cannot counter this by invoking the wishes of other employees who want to smoke, since it is incumbent on these smokers to respect the health of non-smokers.

3.8

PTT is not fulfilling this obligation in its Slingerweg mail-sorting centre. Nooijen's workstation in the large sorting area is not really separated from her smoking colleagues who work in the same area. The argument that the ventilation system removes the risk of her being exposed to others' tobacco smoke does not release PTT from its obligation, and is in any case implausible. No technical reports to prove it have been submitted by PTT. Lastly, Nooijen is also exposed to colleagues' tobacco smoke in virtually all the other rooms in the sorting centre for virtually all the time.

3.9

Health protection is an issue that is by its very nature of urgent importance. This is true for everyone in general. In Nooijen's case there is the additional consideration that, on the basis of the statements produced, it is sufficiently likely that she belongs to the extra-vulnerable category of people who experience unusual health disorders and nuisance as a result of tobacco smoke. This case is therefore one in which the need for an arrangement to enforce the employer's obligation is a matter of urgency.

3.10

The primary claim concerns a complete ban on smoking in the PTT premises at Slingerweg 7, Breda, except for a designated smokers' room that causes no nuisance to non-smokers.

PTT has argued in its defence that a policy on smoking in a form such as this goes too far. It has, however, failed to give any indication whatever of which other specifically targeted organizational measures are feasible with respect to the sorting area in the Slingerweg premises that properly reflect the aforementioned starting principle of protection for non-smokers.

3.11

It is clear from the photographs of the large sorting area that have been deposited, and the floor plan of the building, that the premises in question consist of a normal office building of more or less average size. It is likely that in the course of her work Nooijen has occasion to be in all parts of the building, in some of them frequently and perhaps in others less so, but this frequency is of no importance. The same is true of all her fellow non-smokers among the workforce. This gives sufficient justification for treating the primary measure she requests as a matter of proportionality and reasonableness. PTT must take the health interests of all its non-smoking employees into consideration even though the present case concerns only an application for an injunction lodged by the plaintiff.

3.12

PTT has argued that the grant of this application would oblige it to act in contravention of Article 27, paragraph 1 of the Works Council Act: that if it is seen as being under any obligation at all this has to be confined to making a proposal for a rule on a smoking ban to the works council concerned.

This argument is not correct. The Works Council Act does not impinge upon the competence of the civil courts to impose an Order such as this on an employer. This Order is not subject to a requirement for endorsement by the works council.

Up till now PTT and the competent works council have failed for a long time to fulfil their responsibilities as regards their policy on smoking in the Slingerweg premises. Nooijen cannot reasonably be expected to wait any longer for appropriate initiatives from that quarter.

3.13

Contrary to what PTT has argued orally before the court, the fact that the employer is now reconsidering how far to go in protecting non-smokers as a result of the provisions of the Tobacco Act being made more rigorous does not constitute a reason for dismissing the application for an injunction. The fundamental right to health can be guaranteed via the private-law route irrespective of the possible advent (the Bill has not yet been made law) of a potential (the

Bill establishes only the possibility of imposing a ban on smoking via an implementing order) guarantee under public law.

3.14

On the grounds of these considerations the primary claim is allowable. The penalty is to be awarded as claimed, up to a maximum sum of 100 000 Belgian francs.

PTT is to be ordered to pay the costs as the party found to be at fault.

4.   Judgment in summary proceedings

The President of the Court

orders the defendant to introduce, within fourteen (14) days of the pronouncement of this decision, a total ban on smoking in the defendant's premises at Slingerweg seven in Breda, except for a designated smokers' room that causes no nuisance to non-smokers;

prescribes that the defendant shall pay the plaintiff a penalty payment of 1000 Belgian francs for each day of failure by the defendant to comply with this Order, subject to the payment of a maximum total penalty payment of 100 000 Belgian francs;

prescribes that the penalty payment specified in this Order is susceptible to subsequent adjustment by the court hearing the main proceedings in so far as it is found unacceptable by the standards of reasonableness and fairness to uphold the penalty payment chosen for the purpose, in view of the extent to which the obligation has been fulfilled, the gravity of the infringement and the degree of culpability of the infringement;

awards legal costs against the defendant and orders the latter to pay the costs incurred by the plaintiff estimated to date at 2022.56 Belgian francs; pronounces this Order immediately enforceable.

This judgment has been pronounced by J. P. Leijten, officiating President, and delivered in open-court summary proceedings of Tuesday, 25 April 2000, in the presence of W. J. M. de Haan, acting Registrar.

W. J. M. de Haan
J. P. Leijten

12. New Zealand

Gordon Anderson

GENERAL INTRODUCTION

In New Zealand, as in most developed countries, smoking is a major public health issue and a major cause of preventable deaths. By world standards New Zealanders, on average, are not heavy smokers. The level of daily smoking in New Zealand, about one adult in four, appears to be in the mid-range of smoking rates reported for OECD countries (OECD, 2003). Nevertheless, given the identified health and social costs of smoking it is unsurprising that Governments of all persuasions, along with community organisations, have taken a strong policy stance aimed at reducing smoking and tobacco use. In a review of tobacco control programmes from 1985 to 1998 Laugesen and Swinburn (1999) note that prior to the mid-1980s there was relatively little general community activity aimed at reducing tobacco use although the medical profession had been in the forefront of efforts to reduce smoking since the 1960s.

The 1980s saw two major initiatives. The first was the formation of ASH (Action on Smoking and Health) by major public health groups as a voluntary organisation having the objective of publicising and politicising tobacco issues.

The second was the development of a government Tobacco Control Programme beginning in 1985. These initiatives resulted in a strong and ongoing political, community and bureaucratic commitment to the reduction of tobacco use. Political opposition to some measures has come from the conservative parties but this has been confined to specific measures, most notably sponsorship by tobacco companies and prohibitions on smoking in bars and restaurants. Once such measures have been adopted this opposition tends to evaporate. In part the control initiatives consisted of public education programmes aimed at increasing information on the dangers of tobacco use but with focussed programmes aimed at adults (quit programmes) and adolescents ("why start'). The most important intervention, however, was the enactment of the Smoke-free Environments Act 1990 which, among other initiatives, implemented a number of provisions specifically aimed at workplace smoking.

The stated objectives of that Act were:

(a) To reduce the exposure of people who do not themselves smoke to any detrimental effect on their health caused by smoking by others; and
(b) To regulate the marketing, advertising, and promotion of tobacco products, whether directly or through the sponsoring of other products, services, or events; and
(c) To monitor and regulate the presence of harmful constituents in tobacco products and tobacco smoke; and
(d) To establish a Health Sponsorship Council

R. Blanpain (ed.), Smoking and the Workplace, 169–178
© 2005 *Kluwer Law International. Printed in The Netherlands.*

The reach of this Act has subsequently been extended by a variety of amending Acts most importantly the 2003 amendment. When the amendment to the Act comes into full force in late 2004 New Zealand will have one of the most restrictive regimes in the world prohibiting smoking in all workplaces, and enclosed spaces including bars and restaurants to which the public have access.

1. THE PROFILE OF TOBACCO USE IN NEW ZEALAND

The most recent figures on tobacco use indicate that 24% of New Zealanders smoke at least once a day (Ministry of Health, 2003). This figure represents a significant decline in smoking since the development of active tobacco control policies in 1985 when the rate of smoking was 32%. The rate of decline has, however, slowed significantly since the 1990s. In 1992 27% of adults smoked but by 2002 (the latest available figures) the rate had dropped only to 24%.

More worrying is the detailed picture contained in the overall figures. The most disturbing statistics are those that indicate that smoking is increasingly and most persistently an issue closely linked to poverty and ethnicity. Rates of smoking are significantly higher for those on lower incomes and for beneficiaries and blue collar workers, in reality primarily the same person. For example the rate of tobacco use drops rapidly for males (although less so for females) once household income exceeds NZ$ 30,000. Adult smoking rates by ethnicity are Maori 46%; Pacific Islanders 27%; Europeans 23%; and Other ethnic groups 10%.

For the longer term the concern from the figures is that the decline of tobacco use has slowed (or less optimistically stalled) and that tobacco use in the high use groups seems remarkably stubborn. The only groups evidencing sustained decreases are Europeans and older age groups although youth smoking (14–15 year olds) has decreased for all gender and ethnic groups except Maori females and Asian males.

2. PROTECTION OF HEALTH AND PUBLIC POLICY
   IMPLICATIONS

The International Covenant on Economic, Social and Cultural Rights (Article 12(1)) provides for the right to obtain the highest obtainable standard of health. Although New Zealand ratified this Covenant in 1978 the right to health was not specifically provided for in the New Zealand Bill of Rights Act 1990. Tobacco use is, however, an issue of considerable public and political importance in New Zealand. As noted, successive governments have adopted and supported programmes to reduce tobacco use, the most recent being the Tobacco Action Plan 2000. This Plan reflects the growing awareness of the dangers of passive smoking and places a particular emphasis on the prevention of harm as the result of such smoking. Woodward and Laugesen (2000 and 2001) in two reports on second-hand smoke attempted to identify the health consequences of passive smoking. They estimate that some 388 deaths per annum are attributable to passive smoking. In their report on non-fatal illness associated with passive smoking they make the point that children are particularly at risk but that workplaces are also an area of concern. Their figures suggest that 33% of children of secondary age are exposed to smoke at home and 39% of indoor workers are exposed during working hours. The 2003 amendments to the Smoke-free Environments Act are one tangible outcome of this increased awareness.

The major driver for tobacco control is, as might be expected, the cost to the health system and the economy generally of tobacco use. While estimates of the costs of smoking must be regarded with some scepticism, the Ministry of Health (1999) estimates that one in five deaths in New Zealand are linked to smoking and conservatively costs the health system an additional NZ$ 185 million per year. Another study estimates the social cost of smoking in New Zealand as 3·2% of total human capital and 1·7% of GDP (Easton, 1997). Tobacco use is the major public health issue in New Zealand, although as in many countries obesity is becoming to assume equal importance. Interestingly, the figures for obesity and smoking are approximately equal. A recent survey (Ministry of Health, 2003a) reports one in five adults smoke and the same number are obese. Unfortunately the preliminary data does not identify those who are both smokers and obese.

The ethnic dimension is of particular political significance in New Zealand because of the high rate of tobacco use among the indigenous Maori people. Over recent decades New Zealand governments have placed considerable importance on the relationship with Maori as a result of the recognition of the obligations owed under the Treaty of Waitangi 1840. This Treaty between the Crown and Maori ceded sovereignty over New Zealand to the British Crown but also made provision for the protection of the rights of Maori people. Over recent decades governments have taken significant steps to redefine the political relationship with Maori including measures to attempt to redress both historic grievances and modern economic deprivation. Smoking rates among Maori at 46% are double that of Europeans at 23%. The rate is particularly high among Maori women (48% overall but 60% for Maori women aged between 15 and 44). The combined effect of primary and secondary smoking is therefore one of the most important factors in the marked gaps in health status between Maori and non-Maori.

The Health Funding Authority (1999) makes the point that tobacco control is of particular relevance to Maori. The high rate of smoking not only has negative health impacts for both smokers and non-smokers (lung cancer, heart disease, sudden infant death syndrome, respiratory infections otitis media or glue ear, and diabetes) with children at particular risk. Smoking also contributes significantly to poor economic outcomes as the result of premature deaths, potential education disadvantages for children and the like. The current Government regards the reduction of Maori and non-Maori economic and social inequalities as a major social goal and clearly the reduction of rates of tobacco use must be central to the achievement of this goal.

3.   MEASURE TO REDUCE TOBACCO USE

Since a coordinated tobacco control strategy was initiated in 1985 governments have adopted a range of actions to reduce tobacco use. A number of such strategies focussed on publicity and information on the consequences of smoking together with targeted programmes to discourage starting tobacco use and to support smokers who wished to reduce or give up smoking. In addition, however, there have been a number of legislative measures designed to prevent or reduce smoking. These measures began in the late 1980s and have steadily increased in both scope and depth since that time. The most important legislative initiative was the Smoke-free Environments Act 1990 which has since been amended several times. The discussion in this section will focus on the broader legislative strategy although clearly this will overlap with the later discussion on smoking in the workplace.

1. Taxation

One major strategy to deter tobacco use has been to increase the cost of smoking. The affordability of smoking was halved between 1985 and 1998 with tax rates being raised in real terms on five occasions in addition to the inflation adjusted tax increases that have been in place since 1990. In 1998 the combination of excise tax and GST accounted for 70% of the price of a packet of cigarettes. The cost of a packet of cigarettes is now approximately NZ\$ 12, one and a half times the legal minimum hourly wage.

2. Age restrictions on sale

The Smoke-free Environments Act prohibits the sale of tobacco products to persons under 18, a prohibition recently extended to herbal cigarettes. Reinforcing attempts to prevent youth starting smoking are a number of other provisions including a prohibition on the sale of small quantities of tobacco products, restrictions on the display of tobacco products in close proximity to 'children's products' (products aimed primarily at children including confectionary and ice-cream), and a prohibition of free gifts of tobacco products including the giving of such products in conjunction with non-tobacco products.. The Ministry of Health has taken the enforcement of these provisions seriously and spends in the order of NZ\$ 1 million per year on enforcement. This policy appears to have resulted in a substantial decline in self-purchases by those under 18. The 2003 amendments have reinforced these provisions by allowing a three month ban on selling tobacco products to be imposed on repeat offenders.

3. Warnings

As with most countries New Zealand requires tobacco products to be clearly labelled with health warnings. The intensity of these warnings has been gradually increased.

4 Advertising

Of the various forms of tobacco promotion used by tobacco companies advertising is the most difficult to control. This is especially so in a small country such as New Zealand where the majority of films, magazines, television programmes and the like tend to be imported. In particular this makes the use of 'placement' techniques very hard to regulate. As direct advertising controls have come into effect tobacco companies have sought to avoid them by such techniques as having actors smoke in television and films. The Smoke-free Environments Act provides that 'no person shall publish, or arrange for any other person to publish, any tobacco advertisement in New Zealand' but then introduces a number of exemptions to the general rule. These exemptions are largely a pragmatic recognition of the fact that much advertising material is produced outside New Zealand and included in media not intended primarily for distribution, viewing or transmission outside New Zealand. The Act imposes strong controls over the use of tobacco trademarks in sporting or similar events.

While the display of tobacco products is not prohibited there are significant restrictions on the content of displays and the quantity of product that can be displayed.

5. The Health Sponsorship Council

The Council was created by the Smoke-free Environments Act with the objective of promoting a healthy lifestyle including by sponsoring sporting, artistic and recreational activity. The Council has a number of programmes including programmes focussed on Maori. It is perhaps best known for its "Smokefree Sport" brand which sponsors, among other sports netball which is the predominant competitive female sport in New Zealand.

4. PROHIBITIONS ON SMOKING IN PUBLIC PLACES

The Smoke-free Environments Act 1990 introduced a number of prohibitions on smoking in indoor environments including both workplaces and public areas. These prohibitions were significantly extended by the 2003 amendment to the Act. The discussion below states the position under current law but it should be noted that some of the prohibitions, particularly those relating to hospitality venues, do not come into force until the end of 2004.

1. Transport

Smoking has been prohibited on most forms of public transport since 1990 and has now been extended to cover taxis. The prohibition covers aircraft, passenger service vehicles, ships and trains as well as service areas associated with transport operations such as passenger terminals, lounges, waiting rooms and booking areas.

2. Educational premises, hospitals and prisons

While smoking has been prohibited in most indoor areas of a school since 1990 (schools being workplaces) from early 2004 smoking will be totally prohibited on the premises of any school or early childhood centre in both enclosed and open areas (including school grounds) at all times. Smoking in hospitals is permitted by patients or residents (but not other persons) as long as it occurs in a dedicated smoking room with its own ventilation system. An adequate equivalent non-smoking area must be available for each smoking room. A number of hospitals have, however, taken the prohibition further. Twenty-one district health boards (which run public hospitals) have agreed to move to a totally smoke-free policy by World Smoke-free day 2004. New Zealand's largest district health board, Auckland, has now banned smoking on its grounds and in its buildings and vehicles, for patients, visitors, volunteers and staff.[1] The regime on smoking in prison cells is somewhat less rigorous. A written policy on smoking is required but is based on the principle that where 'reasonably practicable' non-smokers should be separated from smokers.

3. Hospitality venues

Prior to the 2003 amendment licensed premises such as bars and restaurants were subject to relatively few controls. The most important was that restaurants and the food service area of bars should be half smoke-free and so far as 'reasonably practicable' be separated from smoking areas. This position changes dramatically with the amending Act. From late 2004 smoking will be banned in all internal areas of licensed premises, restaurants and casinos. In the absence of firm evidence on the potential effect of such a ban opinions are mixed and predictable as to the potential effect. Bar and restaurant owners are concerned that the ban will adversely affect their business and there is concern that smoking patrons will go elsewhere, causing lost profits.[2] In comparison, in 2003 anti-smoking group ASH claims such fears are unfounded. A review of studies in other countries indicated that a ban would have no effect on sales, and in some cases could increase them.[3]

4. Other places

The Smoke-free Environments Act requires all 'workplaces' to have a smoking policy and this part of the Act is likely to cover all other enclosed areas where smoking may be an issue. The law in relation to workplaces is discussed below. With the exception of schools noted above there are no statutory prohibitions on smoking in open spaces.

5. SMOKING AND THE WORKPLACE

Most New Zealand workers (with the exception of the hospitability industry) have now enjoyed smoke-free workplaces for over a decade.

---

[1]   *New Zealand Herald* September 22 2003.
[2]   For example, David Eames "Publicans Split Over No-Smoking Proposal" [sic] (9 December 2002) *The Evening Standard.*
[3]   ASH "Smoke-free bars don't lose business: new study confirms scare campaign unfounded" (3 March 2003) Media Release.

One of the major objectives of the Smoke-free Environments Act 1990 was

"to prevent, so far as is reasonably practicable, the detrimental effects of smoking on the health of any person who does not smoke, or who does not wish to smoke, inside any workplace or in certain public enclosed areas".

It is indicative of the changed attitudes over the intervening decade that this objective as re-enacted in 2003 now reads

"to prevent the detrimental effect of other people's smoking on the health of people in workplaces, or in certain public enclosed areas, who do not smoke or do not wish to smoke there".

At the same time the obligation on the employer has changed from that of preparing a written policy on workplace smoking to a more robust obligation to 'take all reasonably practicable steps to ensure that no person smokes at any time in a workplace'. While this change represents a stronger legislative approach the smoking policies required by the 1990 Act had considerable mandatory content including that smoking must be prohibited in any shared workspace, any part of the workplace to which the public had access and at least half of any cafeteria or lunchroom.

The Act now provides that no employee may smoke in a workplace and while employees are not subject to any statutory sanction, they could be subjected to disciplinary action from the employer.

This hardening of approach reflects partly a greater awareness of the dangers of smoking and public acceptance of the need for smoke-free workplaces but also increasing recognition of the costs of both active and passive smoking in the workplace. The Health Funding Authority (1999) summarises some of the costs to both the workforce and the economy which include lost productivity as the result of higher rates of absenteeism and premature death, illness rates among smokers attending work (respiratory problems) as well as both the nuisance and health effects of passive smoking. The report also notes the increased costs of cleaning, computer malfunctions, insurance costs, ventilation costs and the like associated with smoking.

While no figures are available reports indicate that some employers, especially major employers, do make quit smoking programmes available to employees. For example one of the hospital boards that have recently banned smoking completely on its grounds has initiated a quit smoking programme in conjunction with this move.

1. The employers' obligations

All employers are now required to take all take all reasonably practicable steps to ensure that no person smokes at any time in a workplace. A workplace is widely defined to include all internal areas (controlled by or occupied by the employer) usually frequented by employees or volunteers during the course of their employment including a cafeteria, corridor, lift, lobby, stairwell, toilet, washroom, or other common internal area and vehicles. The only exceptions relate to the accommodation areas of hotels, motels and passenger cabins and to accommodation assigned to a single employee and to designated smoking rooms in hospitals. It should be noted that there is no provision made for designated smoking rooms for the use of employees.

The Act also provides for a complaints procedure in respect of smoking in a workplace. This procedure allows 'any person' to complain to the employer of a workplace if that person believes on reasonable grounds that any other person has violated a provision of the Act. The employer is obliged to attempt to resolve the dispute but where a dispute cannot be resolved with 40 days it must be referred to the Director-General of Health who has power to appoint a person to investigate the complaint. While the emphasis of the procedure, both during the employer's investigation and that of the Director-General, is on an amicable resolution, enforcement proceedings may be taken. The preferred outcome stressed in the Act is the obtaining of an assurance, from either the employer of an employee who is breaching the Act, that the breach will not be repeated. The person representing employees in the workplace is entitled to be present at any meeting called by an employer to resolve the dispute.

While the Smoke-free Environments Act is the primary and most direct legislative control on workplace smoking it might be noted that legal obligations also arise under health and safety legislation and the contractual obligation to provide a safe workplace. The primary obligation on an employer under the Health and Safety in Employment Act is to identify and eliminate workplace hazards – a relatively easy obligation in the case of smoking.

2.   Sanctions

The enforcement policy of the Act is that the liability for policing the workplace falls on the employer or occupier of the space, not the smoker. Although the Act prohibits employees smoking in workplaces the only sanctions provided in the Act are imposed on employers or, in the case of schools, bars and restaurants and public transport, the occupier, licensee, manager, or operator as appropriate. No sanction is provided for employees or for patrons who smoke in a prohibited area. The only exception is that is an offence for a person to smoke on an aircraft. The maximum fine provided by the Act is NZ$ 4,000 for a body corporate and NZ$ 400 for an individual.

3.   Employment and dismissal of smokers

The issue of whether employers should be free to refuse to employ smokers has recently caused some controversy following the announcement by Crown Public Health (a subsidiary of several hospital boards) that it would not employ smokers in a programme aimed at helping Maori people quit smoking.[4] Although the issue has never been litigated a Human Rights Commission spokesperson issued a statement that discrimination against smokers was not contrary to the Human Rights Act 1993. Crown Public Health's decision has attracted considerable criticism from civil liberties groups, unions and others who argue that that the policy is likely to open the way to discrimination against persons who suffer from a variety of other 'lifestyle diseases' such as

---

4   *Sunday Star Times* 23 November 2003.

obesity. It might be noted that the Human Rights Act (section 21) does include disability (which includes physical illness) as one of the grounds on which discrimination is prohibited. It is at arguable that obesity is a disability as would be the health consequences of smoking and it is probable that the potential for lifestyle discrimination may be narrower than some commentators have suggested. Apart from this case it does not appear that smoking is a significant issue in relation to obtaining employment.

Smoking in the workplace may also constitute grounds for a justifiable dismissal although there have been few cases on this issue. In one case a radio announcer was held to have been justifiably dismissed for smoking in a non-smoking area. In that case the employee had received several warnings and staff in general had been continually advised of a no-smoking policy.[5] The grounds for dismissal were the employees' refusal to obey a reasonable and lawful order. It seems likely that a similar result would follow in any future case, especially as the employer's own legal obligations and liabilities have been significantly increased since the date of this case, as long as the employee involved had been given appropriate warnings.

4. Legal liability for the consequences of smoking

To date there has been very little litigation in New Zealand in respect of smoking generally and none in respect of workplace passive smoking. The question of an employer's liability is therefore still highly theoretical although a number of possibilities for obtaining redress are, in principle, available (Tokeley, 1993). The most likely form of action against an employer is likely to be an action based on a breach of the employer's common law and statutory obligations to provide a safe workplace.

In the particular case of health damage suffered as a consequence of passive smoking in the workplace it seems likely that the damage comes within the scope of New Zealand's accident compensation system although this point is likely to be clarified in a case due to come before the courts in the near future. The accident compensation scheme provides comprehensive cover for all injuries suffered as the result of an accident but at the same time precludes common law actions for injuries covered by the scheme. The definition of 'accident' in cases of the gradual accretion of harm is not fully clear. Passive smoking was excluded for some years but a change to the Injury Prevention, Rehabilitation and Compensation Act 2001 has meant that from April 2002 workers are technically able to receive compensation for illnesses caused by second-hand smoke in the workplace.

CONCLUSION

Since 1990 New Zealand law has prohibited smoking in most New Zealand workplaces. From the end of 2004 with the extension of this prohibition to bars and restaurants that prohibition will be total. New Zealand workers who wish to smoke will need to do so outside enclosed premises and in May workplaces

---

[5]   *Mitchell v Te Reo Irirangi O Ngati Raukawa HT 22/96* 14 November 1996 (not reported).

even that possibility is being closed. These prohibitions have generally, although the verdict on the ban in bars is still open, been widely supported by both smokers and non-smokers. New Zealand still has high levels of smoking but with the bans on smoking in public places the most vulnerable group of non-smokers are now children living with smokers. In terms of limiting the effect of the harm caused by smoking legislation has probably hit the edge of the point of political acceptability. The challenge for the future is largely educational.

REFERENCES

[The majority of these references are available for downloading from the New Zealand Ministry of Health's website: http://www.moh.govt.nz/moh.nsf]

Easton, B (1997) The Social Cost of Tobacco Use and Alcohol Misuse, Wellington, Dept. of Public Health, Wellington School of Medicine

Health Funding Authority (1999) *Toward a Tobacco-Free Plan for New Zealand: A Five Year Plan for HFA Funding for Tobacco Control (1999–2003)*. Wellington.

Tokeley, K (1993) *The Legal Protection of Non-Smokers From Exposure to Tobacco Smoke*. New Zealand Universities Law Review 15: 291.

Laugesen, M and Swinburn, B (1999) *New Zealand's Tobacco Control Programme 1985–1998*. Auckland. Health New Zealand

Ministry of Health (1999) *Taking the Pulse – the 1996/97 New Zealand Health Survey.*Wellington.

Ministry of Health (2003) *Tobacco Facts*. Public Health Intelligence Occasional Report No 20. Wellington.

Ministry of Health (2003a) *A Snapshot of Health: Provisional Results of the 2002/3 New Zealand Health Survey*. Wellington.

OECD (2003) *Health Data.*Paris.

Woodward, A and Laugeson, M (2000) *Deaths in New Zealand Attributable to Second-hand Cigarette Smoke*. Ministry of Health, Wellington.

Woodward, A and Laugeson, M (2001) *Morbidity Attributable to Second-hand Cigarette Smoke in New Zealand*. Ministry of Health, Wellington.

13.   Norway

Asbjørn Kjønstad

1.   INTRODUCTION

At the end of the 1960s Norwegian authorities prepared a comprehensive plan aimed at influencing smoking habits.

This was to be done through the following three measures:

(1) A systematic information programme on the harmful effects of smoking.
(2) Therapeutic measures; helping people to stop smoking.
(3) Restrictions of the sale of tobacco products.

Norway is a welfare state northernmost in Europe with a population of just over four million. It is a long and narrow country with more than 20 thousand kilometres of coastline. We have experienced four "waves" of legal measures in connection with tobacco-related diseases.

First, the Tobacco Act, which was passed in 1973 and came into force in 1975. The purpose of this Act is "to limit the health damage caused by the use of tobacco products". The Tobacco Act gives a clear signal of the authorities' deep concern with the health damage caused by smoking.

The Tobacco Act introduced a total ban on all advertising for tobacco related products, an order that tobacco products should be labelled with a warning concerning the health hazards of cigarette smoking; and a prohibition of the sale of tobacco products to persons under the age of 16 – from 1996 the age of 18. The purpose was to counteract the tobacco industry's increasing influence on smoking.

The second "wave" was the so-called "Smoking Act" of 1988. This was a welfare act, which had as its primary intent the protection of non-smokers from becoming passive smokers. While Norway was a pioneer of, and received international attention in connection with the advertising ban, our actions concerning smoke-free environments were not at the forefront internationally.

The third "wave" was a ban on all new tobacco and nicotine-containing products of 1989. It is prohibited to produce, import to Norway, sell or hand over to others new types of tobacco and nicotine-containing products. The same applies to tobacco and nicotine-containing products intended to be used in ways other than those normally practiced in Norway.

The fourth "wave" – tort law cases – stems from the US, which has otherwise played a leading role with regard to product liability and consumer protection. A combined active and passive smoker has won a case in the Norwegian Supreme Court,[1] while an active smoker has lost a case.[2]

---

[1]   Rt. 2000 p. 1614. *See* point 4 below.
[2]   Rt. 2003 p. 1546: Unni Lund v. Tiedemanns Tobakksfabrik A/S.

R. Blanpain (ed.), Smoking and the Workplace, 179–190
© 2005 *Kluwer Law International. Printed in The Netherlands.*

2.   THE DEBATE ON THE "SMOKING ACT" OF 1988

In the Norwegian media there was a massive attack on the provision providing the right to breathe smoke-free air. A trinity, consisting of the tobacco industry, some well-known persons and many journalists, fought a battle for the right to smoke anywhere and at any time.[3]

The tobacco industry and retailers had their business interests to protect. As much smoking as possible, in as many places as possible, gives the highest number of sales, and ensures the tradition of smoking. The tobacco industry is fighting to retain the market in industrialised countries and has intensified its marketing efforts to spread the smoking habit in developing countries.

A small group of well-known citizens – in particular some barristers – gained the limelight in the media which should have focused on the thousands of sufferers with allergies and asthma, children, and others affected by smoke. This group argued for the freedom of the individual, but the "freedom" to harm others cannot be permitted.

The journalists supported this group of pro-smokers. Newspaper offices and broadcasting houses have been renowned for heavy smoking. Journalists cynically used the power of the written word and the airwaves to promote their own interests.

Obviously there were some journalists who wanted to talk to those of us who had formulated the new "Smoking Act". In the course of a few months in 1988, I was interviewed some 20 times about the Act. But – with two exceptions – these interviews were never printed. They were "censored" by the smokers at the editorial desks. This has never happened to me before. Unfortunately, I am not the only one to have experienced this with regard to the "Smoking Act". Very few newspapers gave a balanced picture of the new Act, in spite of the fact that it was supported by 80 to 90% of the population – even among smokers.

A survey has shown that, by and large, the Act concerning smoke-free indoor air has been positively received, that the Act is respected at places of work, and that it has led to increased well-being. Since the Act was enforced, the situation has become more difficult for some smokers, but the majority of the population are better off. People, who react adversely to tobacco smoke, can now go to the theatre, to airports and, in many other respects, take part in social and cultural life in the same way as others.

3.   LEGAL PROTECTION AGAINST PASSIVE SMOKING IN THE "SMOKING ACT" OF 1988

3.1.   Introduction

The Tobacco Act of 1973 was aimed at smokers and potential smokers. Non-smokers had no legal protection. But in May 1988, the Tobacco Act was amended to include a new section, the so-called "Smoking Act".

---

[3]   *See* Asbjørn Kjønstad, Debatten om røykeloven, Lov og Rett 1988 pp. 453–454.

3.2.   The contents of the "Smoking Act" of 1988

The first sentence of the "Smoking Act" reads as follows:

"In premises and means of transport to which the public have access the air shall be smoke-free. The same applies in meeting rooms, work premises and institutions where two or more persons are gathered".

As can be seen, this provision is not formulated as a ban on smoking, but as a right to breathe smoke-free air.[4] When the Norwegian Council on Smoking and Health proposed the Bill, it was important to present it as an Act which gave people a right and not one which imposed a prohibition. There has been a tendency in Norway to oppose the introduction of prohibitive legislation.

The principle of smoke-free air is to apply to premises "to which the public have access". Such premises include all indoor rooms in houses, buildings and halls, for example:

(1) Post offices, social security offices, and other offices providing public services.
(2) Shops, travel agencies, banks and other premises for private services.
(3) Lobbies, lifts, staircases, toilets, and similar rooms which people use for short periods.
(4) Churches, cinemas, theatres, opera houses, teaching premises, waiting rooms and similar places frequented by the public for longer periods.
(5) Taxicabs, buses, trams, trains, ships, aircraft and other public conveyances engaged in domestic trade.

The "Smoking Act" does not guarantee smoke-free environments in private homes. This may appear inconsistent, since studies have shown that the people most exposed to the harmful effects of passive smoking are spouses, children and other family members. In spite of this, it has not been the wish to interfere in people's private lives. But when a smoke-free indoor environment has become the norm in society at large, this has also usually followed in the homes. The Children's ombudsman has argued for the extension of the Smoking Act to rooms in private homes where children sleep and stay for a longer time.

3.3.   Smoking at the workplace

The "Smoking Act" applies to conference rooms and other work premises. A person sitting alone in his or her office may still smoke, but when two or more persons work in the same room, smoking is not permitted.

Smokers have no right to have special areas reserved for them. However, if a company or building has several rooms of the same kind, then smoking may be permitted in one of these rooms. This applies, for example, to a company having two relaxation rooms. Another possibility is to split one relaxation room into two by a dividing wall. In such cases, the best and largest room has to be reserved for non-smokers.

Dividing a room into two by using a wall is very different from dividing a

---

4   Statens tobakksskaderåd, Lufta er for alle! Retten til å puste i røykfri luft, Oslo 1985.

room into a smoking and non-smoking zone. As a rule, unless there is excellent ventilation, smoke will pass into the zone where smoking is not permitted. A strict condition is imposed on permitting a room to be divided into smoking and smoke-free zones. It must be impossible for the smoke to pass into the smoke-free zone.

Some doubt may arise as to whether a room is to be regarded as an office or as a conference room. This question must be decided after assessing how many colleagues or visitors are received there, and for how long. If a so-called office is normally visited in the course of the day by more than two-three persons, and these visits last for a total of two-three hours, the room will take on the character of a conference room where smoking is not allowed.

3.4. Exceptions from the basic principle of smoke-free indoor air

The most important exception in the "Smoking Act" of 1988 was that smoking was permitted in restaurants and hotels. This exception was introduced after strong pressure from the hotel and restaurant sector. The Bill proposed that one third of the seats and the rooms should be reserved for non-smokers. The hotel and restaurant sector maintained that if this provision were adopted, the sector would lose customers and money, and would have to lay off staff. The authorities yielded to this pressure and concentrated their efforts on having the rest of the Bill passed.

However, a provision was adopted which required the gradual introduction of smoke-free environments, particularly in connection with new buildings, and the reconstruction of existing buildings. In the course of five years, at least one-third of the tables, seats and rooms should be reserved for non-smokers. In the course of the next five years, this was extended to one half of the seats and tables. Furthermore, reception areas, corridors and other public areas should be smoke-free.

In April 2003, the Norwegian Parliament extended the Smoking Act. From 1 June 2004 all restaurants, bars, pubs and other places serving food and drink shall be smoke-free. The purpose of this total ban is first and foremost to protect the health of the restaurant workers.

4. PASSIVE SMOKING AND TORT LIABILITY

A Norwegian tobacco case was ruled on in the Appeal Court in January 1999. A 41-year-old lady contracted lung cancer after having smoked for 20 years and having worked in a heavily smoke-filled discotheque for 15 years. She sued her employer's insurance company – the Workers Compensation Insurance.

Two medical experts appointed by the court assessed how much the passive smoking in the discotheque and how much her own active smoking could be seen as having contributed to her contracting lung cancer. They concluded that the contribution of passive smoking constituted a minimum of 40%, while her own active smoking, constituted a maximum of 60%.

The Court of Appeal could not disregard the passive smoking as insignificant. There was hereby a causal connection between the hazardous effects of the work environment and her health injuries. However the Court of Appeal came to the conclusion that the compensation had to be reduced by 25% because of her own contribution. This part of the case was appealed to the Supreme Court.

In October 2000, the Norwegian Supreme Court awarded this lady full compensation. One dissenting judge voted for half compensation.

In the US, the tobacco industry can be sued for both active and passive smoking. Suits on the basis of passive smoking are regularly filed against the tobacco industry in that country.

A decision by the Supreme Court is of course of great significance as a legal source. In principle it is very important that this court has found in favour of a person who has been injured by tobacco smoke. This seems to me like a nail in the coffin of the tobacco industry.

5.   SMOKE-FREE RESTAURANTS FROM 1 JUNE 2004

5.1.   Introductory remarks

On 1 June 2004, a total ban on smoking in restaurants was implemented in Norwegian legislation. This prohibition comprises work premises and rooms to which the public has access, though not open air restaurants.

The prevention of smoking aims at protecting three groups of people:

(1) Employees: Restaurant staff;
(2) Guests: People suffering, for instance, from asthma and allergies, as well as those affected by tobacco smoke;
(3) Young people who might be encouraged to start smoking in cafeterias and restaurants.

5.2.   The wording and the objectives of the Act

The object of the Tobacco Act is "to limit the health damage caused by the use of tobacco products". This also includes the detrimental effects on health resulting from passive smoking.

The Tobacco Act section 6, first and second paragraphs, states:

"In premises and means of transport to which the public have access the air shall be smoke-free. The same applies in meeting rooms, work premises and institutions where two or more persons are gathered. This does not apply in living rooms in institutions, but the institution is obliged to make smoke-free rooms available to those who request it.

If within a certain area, several premises are used for the same purpose, smoking may be permitted in half of these premises. The division of a premise or means of transportation into a smoke-free area and a smoking area is permitted only when it is impossible for the smoke to pass into the smoke-free area. The smoke-free premises and areas must not be smaller or of a lower standard than the premises and areas where smoking is permitted. There shall be a total ban on smoking in restaurants and other serving places".

In the first paragraph, the major areas to which the Act applies are: First, premises, means of transport, and institutions with public access such as, for instance, shops, waiting rooms, cinemas, and public transport. Second, work premises where two or more people are gathered, such as factory halls, offices, conference rooms, and cafeterias. I will underline that most restaurants, from the point of view of the guests, are considered rooms with public access. From the point of view of the staff, however, restaurants are considered working premises.

In second paragraph first sentence, there is an exception to the regulation on a smoke-free environment if, in the premises, there is more than one room intended for identical purposes. For instance, a company might have two staff rooms, in which case smoking might be permitted in one of these.

However, this exception does not apply to restaurants. A company having two cafeterias or a hotel with two restaurants is not allowed to permit smoking in one of these.

An important aspect of the new Act is that the previous arrangement where there were designated smoking areas in a room whereas other areas in the same room remained smoke-free is now abolished. It has proved almost impossible to prevent smoke drifting from a smoking area to a smoke-free area. Further, ventilation systems are both expensive and inadequate.

5.3. Regular serving places

The Tobacco Act section 6, second paragraph, fourth sentence states: "By serving places are meant rooms where the serving of food and/or drink takes place and where the conditions are suitable for consumption on the premises".

Included in this definition are restaurants, cafés, pubs, bars, and cafeterias. There is no requirement that guests should pay for the service, that they should be seated in chairs and/or that the room should be provided with tables.[5] A "beer hall" in which the patrons are standing while drinking is covered by the smoking prohibition.

Neither is there a requirement that serving be the major activity in the room.[6] A foyer or a hotel reception area where the serving of food is provided is also covered by the smoking prohibition. So are also tea/coffee shops and take-outs, where eating is possible.

5.4. Self-service

The *travaux préparatoires* to the Act emphasize that premises providing self-service are covered by the smoking prohibition.[7] Cafeterias and roadside inns are important examples of these.

A health economist has argued that the expression "self-service" has a restricted interpretation. According to his opinion a separate room which waiters only occasionally enter for the purpose of tidying it up, should not be

---

[5]   Ot.prp. no. 23 (2002–2003) p. 27; and Innst. O. no. 72 (2002–2003).
[6]   Ot.prp. no. 23 (2002–2003) p. 27.
[7]   Ot.prp. no. 23 (2002–2003) pp. 27 and 35.

considered a room in which work is carried out, and therefore should not be included, regardless of whether self-service implies "serving".

I disagree with him: A large self-service cafeteria of, for instance 200 tables, can manage with the same number of waiters as a small, exclusive restaurant with 20 tables. However, for those working in a cafeteria permitting smoking, and responsible for, say, 50 tables to be cleaned and ashtrays to be emptied, the pollution might be as severe as for those attending to five tables in an exclusive restaurant where smoking is permitted. In respect of those working in a self-service cafeteria, exposure to smoking is hardly occasional.

The mentioned health economist further claims that "at this point the proposal is misleading".[8] He has published a large number of articles – primarily in the press – criticising the Minister of Health and the medical experts who took part in the drafting of the proposition on which the Smoking Act is based.

Discussion of this issue in further detail is beyond the scope of this article. In my opinion, his criticism misses the point, and has been vehemently rejected by Norway's foremost experts on passive smoking, professors and toxicologists Tore Sanner (chemistry) and Erik Dybing (medicine).[9] In referring to 106 articles on passive smoking, they claim that as many as 63% of these show that passive smoking, is injurious to health, and that three-quarters of the remaining articles are written by authors associated with the tobacco industry. It is estimated that, on a yearly basis, approximately 500 Norwegians die from passive smoking.[10]

5.5. Living rooms in institutions and hotels

According to the Tobacco Act section 6, first paragraph, third sentence, the smoking prohibition does not apply to "living rooms in institutions". Residents of nursing homes and homes for the elderly should be regarded as being similar to those living in their own homes; hence, they should themselves determine whether they wish to smoke.

This would presumably apply even if the serving of food and beverages takes place in such a room. There, the serving of food is a less frequent activity compared with other activities performed by staff in the room. However, the employer cannot require that staff should work in smoke-filled rooms.[11]

The main principle of the Tobacco Act section 6 with respect to at least half the number of rooms being smoke-free applies to hotels and other overnight accommodation. As far as the guests are concerned, a hotel room is comparable to a private home. In rooms where smoking is allowed, there is no prohibition rule in respect to smoking even if food and drink is provided in the form of room service.

---

[8]   Erik Nord, Muligheter for røyking på serveringssteder etter 1. juni 2004, Lov og Rett 2003, p. 574.

[9]   Tore Sanner and Erik Dybing, "Risiko for lungekreft og hjertesyksom ved passiv røyking, Tidsskrift for Den norske lægeforening (Journal of the Norwegian Medical Association), 2004; 124, pp. 387–388.

[10]   NOU 2000: 16 (Tobakksindustriens erstatningsansvar (liability of the tobacco industry)) pp. 93, 95, and 103.

[11]   These problems are discussed in the letters referred to in footnote 16 below.

6. WORK PREMISES WHERE TWO OR MORE PEOPLE ARE GATHERED.

6.1. The concept of work premises

According to the Tobacco Act section 6, first paragraph, second sentence, the air "in meeting rooms, work premises, and institutions where two or more people are gathered" shall be smoke-free. In plain language: work premises are rooms in which work is carried out. However, other rooms in business organisations are also covered. According to the *travaux préparatoires* to the "Smoking Act" of 1988, these comprise "cafeterias, entrance halls, elevators, staircases, hallways, toilets, and similar rooms where staff is present for longer or shorter periods of time".[12]

The mentioned health economist has advocated that the concept of work premises should comprise only "areas which are intended for the carrying out of work". Not included are "areas primarily intended for the users, but where workers could also be present, such as cinemas, bowling halls, waiting rooms, hotel rooms, dwelling rooms in institutions, etc".[13]

In my opinion, these are – from the perspective of the user – areas intended for the general public. From the point of view of staff, they are considered work premises. Both are covered by the "Smoking Act", and in the *travaux préparatoires* to the Act of 1988, these examples were first listed in the category of areas with access for the general public. However, this does not imply that they are not also included in the concept of work premises.

6.2. Staff rooms

The no-smoking rule applies without exception when the work premises refer to a room where food is consumed. If it is not of such a nature, and the business has two rooms of this kind, smoking is permitted in one.

Important in this respect is a room in which staff would take a break but which would not be characterised as an eating-room. If a hotel has two staff rooms, smoking might be allowed in one of them. However, this is an area reserved for staff, and guests may not enter for the purpose of smoking.

The Right Wing Party in the Norwegian Parliament proposed to establish smoking rooms for employees and guests.[14] However, this proposal was voted down in Parliament. Both in the proposal and in the recommendation from the majority of the Social Committee, it is emphasized that a smoking room adjacent to rooms where food and drink are consumed is not permitted.[15]

6.3. Private homes

Questions have been raised as to whether community nurses, home helpers, personal assistants, and others working in private homes are protected by the

---

[12]   Ot.prp. no. 27 (1987–88) p. 25.
[13]   Erik Nord, *op. cit.* p. 571, cf. pp. 572–573.
[14]   Innst. O. no. 72 (2002–2003) pp. 14 and 15.
[15]   Ot.prp. no. 23 (2002–2003) pp. 2, and Innst. O. no. 72 (2002–2003).

Tobacco Act section 6. This is primarily a question of whether the home of a client could be considered working premises for those providing the assistance.

As the municipality is considered the employer of those providing services on behalf of the municipality, and the latter is not in charge of areas in private homes, these could hardly be covered by the Tobacco Act. However, according to the Working Environment Act, the employer is responsible for employees being provided with a fully satisfactory working environment, and for organising working conditions in such a way that employees are not affected by smoke.[16]

Further, one might ask whether parties in private homes employing a serving staff are covered by the new regulation. Here, the employer is in charge of the areas concerned. In such cases, there is reason to refer to the Working Environment Act sections. 7, 8, and 14: The employer is responsible for providing a fully satisfactory working environment. Staff who are having to work in a smoke-filled environment do not have a fully satisfactory working environment.

6.4. The proprietor carries out the work

Some small cafés do not employ staff. The question then arises if such premises are considered working areas.

The mentioned health economist has argued that areas not served by employed staff, but by the proprietor, cannot be considered working areas in the legal sense of the word. He particularly refers to the amendments of 2003 having as "their main objective the protecting of serving staff".[17]

In this respect, I wish to point out that this was one of the objectives of the Act. Another objective was to protect the guests, with the intention of providing a more accessible environment for those suffering from asthma and allergies, etc. Yet another objective was that of protecting youth from areas where they tended to take up smoking.

In respect to cafés open to all and sundry, it scarcely helps to conclude that these are not considered working areas. The smoking prohibition applies to all areas with public access.

7. AREAS WITH PUBLIC ACCESS

7.1. Outdoor restaurants

The term 'rooms' comprises of all indoor rooms in houses, buildings, tents, and cottages. Normally, a room is enclosed by walls, a ceiling, a roof, and a floor, as well as being provided with doors and windows which can be closed. In such a room, smoke would remain for a certain period of time.

The Act does not give the right to a smoke-free outdoor environment. In outdoor restaurants, smoking is still permitted after 1 June 2004.

---

[16] See Ministry of Local Government and Regional Development, letter of 29 August 1996; Directorate of Health and Social Welfare, letter of 14 November 2002; Ministry of Labour and Government Administration, letter of 19 February 2003; Labour Inspectorate, letter of 10 March 2003; Ministry of Labour and Government Administration, letter of 18 March 2003.

[17] Erik Nord, *op.cit*. pp. 573–574.

In the *travaux préparatoires*, a borderline case is mentioned: "If a restaurant provides outdoor services in connection to its indoor services, and smoke drifts in from the outside, smoking on the outdoor premises should take place in such a way that the indoor air remains smoke-free".[18] Consequently, some outdoor restaurants would be covered by the Tobacco Act section 6.

In the Ministry of Health and Social Affairs circular relating to the Tobacco Act, a similar situation is mentioned, namely, "restaurants that open up an entire glass wall during the summer months, allowing smoke to drift into the room inside".[19] In this case, the room would not be considered smoke-free.

Outdoor restaurants often have a roof or a cover. However, this does not make them rooms, as understood by the Act. This is also the case where protecting walls have been erected.[20] However, the combination of a wall bordering the outdoor restaurant and a ceiling in addition to the protecting walls might actually be considered a room. According to the *travaux préparatoires*, in such cases it is important that ventilation would provide conditions similar to an outdoor area.[21]

7.2.   Clubs and organisations

In the *travaux préparatoires* to the Act, it is stated:

> "In respect of so-called membership clubs etc. ... , an actual evaluation [must be made] as to whether the general public is considered as having access or not. However, if the premises are open to all on certain conditions such as, for instance, membership, such premises would be included under section 6".[22]

The mentioned health economist has interpreted this as not applying to social clubs, academic organisations, writers' associations, mountaineering groups, taxi drivers' organisations, student organisations, housing cooperatives, organisations for the elderly or infirm, political unions and the like.[23]

In my opinion, this is an untenable interpretation of a passage in the *travaux préparatoires*, where it is stated that the principle of a smoke-free environment is relevant in at least two situations, namely, where the "premises are open to all", and where the "premises are open on certain terms, for instance, conditions of membership". The latter is a matter of opinion, and so is the actual evaluation which is referred to, whereas nothing is mentioned in respect of smoking being permitted in membership clubs other than the categories referred to.

A large number of Norwegians are members of several societies. However, we have not automatically assumed that smoking should be allowed during the serving of food at these associations. The main principle of the law is smoke-free serving places.

---

[18]   Ot.prp. no 23 (2002–2003) p. 27.
[19]   The Ministry of Health and Social Affairs, Circular I-15/2003. Amendments to the Act relating to the prevention of the harmful effects of tobacco, 1 June 2004, p. 5.
[20]   Ot.prp. no 23 (2002–2003) p. 27.
[21]   Ot.prp. no 23 (2002–2003) p. 28.
[22]   Ot.prp. no 23(2002–2003) p. 28.
[23]   Erik Nord, *op.cit.* p. 569 at pp. 570–571.

Of considerable significance as a legal source is the basic view taken by the majority of the Parliamentary Committee for Social Affairs (all members but one representing the Right Wing Party) which states: "The majority do not wish the Act to lead to the establishment of so-called "membership clubs" in order to circumvent the intention of the Act".[24]

The mentioned health economist has maintained that the prohibition against smoking does not apply to a certain type of association where the conditions for membership are that

(1) one signs a petition against the total ban referred to in the Smoking Act, and
(2) becomes a member of a society promoting the abolition of this ban.[25]

He has prepared a draft of the by-laws for such a society, and, according to the press, he is a "vital force" in establishing this kind of society.[26]

Actually, such a society would be open to all. Adherence to the purpose of the society and payment of membership fees are the usual conditions for membership. Smoking in such a society is contrary to the intentions of the Act and of the Social Committee.

One might assume that some societies should be able to hold their meetings, to eat, drink, and smoke without being in contravention of the Tobacco Act section 6. This applies to already existing cigar clubs which have their own buildings and do not employ staff. Similarly, this is the case if these clubs are renting premises from which smoke cannot spread to rooms supposed to be smoke-free. In a club such as this, smoking is one of the main aims, which is permissible as long as one is not polluting the air inhaled by other people.

8. EXEMPTION

According to the Tobacco Act section 6, tenth paragraph, the supervisory authority may "in special cases" provide exemption from the regulations contained in or pursuant to this section.

The Labour Inspectorate in Oslo received some ten applications for exemption in the course of the first year (1988–89). In these cases, the Inspectorate requested more information on ventilation, the consequences of a total ban on smoking, the possibilities and cost of building special rooms for smokers, and whether any employees have allergies, etc. The Labour Inspectorate received no response to these questions, and therefore did not consider exemption.

In respect to restaurants and other areas where food and beverages are being served, it is emphasized in the *travaux préparatoires* to the new Act that the authority to provide exemption should only be exercised "in exceptional cases", when it would "seem most unreasonable to comply with the regulations of section 6" and when "special reasons apply".[27]

---

[24] Innst. O. no. 72 (2002–2003) p. 12.

[25] Erik Nord, *op. cit.* p. 571.

[26] Dagbladet, 30 December 2003.

[27] Ot.prp. no. 23 (2002–2003) p. 30.

9. ENFORCEMENT OF THE "SMOKING ACT"

One of the arguments used against the Act was that it would be difficult, or even impossible, to enforce. This argument holds no water. The Labour Inspectorate reported that, compared with certain other legislation, the "Smoking Act" was easy to enforce. It is clear and leaves little room for personal interpretation.

It is the owner, or the person who has the premises at his disposal, who bears the prime responsibility for ensuring that the smoking rules are observed. The means used are posting no-smoking signs, turning smokers away, supervising the premises, as well as inspection by the authorities and the imposition of penalties.

It should be clearly indicated by means of a notice at the entrance to all restaurants and other areas where food and beverages are being served that smoking is prohibited. It should be assumed that those in charge of restaurants and similar premises would display such signs and that most patrons would respect the prohibition. With a total prohibition, very few interpretation problems would emerge.

If a person in a restaurant or similar premises violates the prohibition, a representative of the enterprise should first give a warning. If the warning is ignored and the smoking continues, the person concerned should be expelled from the premises.

Those in charge of restaurants and other areas where food and beverages are being served should establish internal control systems, i.e. systematic means to ensure that the operation is carried out according to the requirements of the Act. Such internal control systems should be documented for inspection by the supervisory authority.

The Municipal Council (in effect, the municipal health services) and the Labour Inspectorate constitute the actual authority. The latter may make decisions in respect to investigations, give orders for altering procedures, and impose coercive fines in cases where orders have not been carried out within a given time-frame.

According to the Tobacco Act section 10, anyone who violates this prohibition or directive in or pursuant to the law, shall be fined. Both an intentional and a negligent violation are criminal offences.

14. Spain

Antonio Ojeda Avilés[1]

1. GENERAL INTRODUCTION

Up to about five years ago, levels of tobacco use were continuing to rise among the Spanish population, ignoring the anti-tobacco campaigns that had been gathering strength in the country. As a clear sign of the magnitude of the phenomenon, at every major set of traffic lights there was an unemployed person selling packets of cigarettes to the drivers temporarily halted there, despite protests from proprietors of the *estancos*, i.e. the retail outlets authorized by the state to sell tobacco products legally. The percentage of women smokers was increasing, as a symbol of their integration into the world of work, and there was no decline in the incidence of smoking-related illnesses. However, over the past five years large numbers of people, both men and women, have given up the addiction and the anti-tobacco campaigns are succeeding in reaching the individual consumer, to whom they offer ways and means of controlling consumption. The younger generation, for its part, has stopped taking up smoking since it is regarded as an older person's habit and also because the increase in the price of cigarettes has made them more difficult to afford. Divulgence of the practices engaged in by the tobacco companies to establish and maintain addiction to cigarettes, largely due to the 'Minnesota case' and to the emergence of numerous references to Spain in the many documents declassified by the tobacco companies,[2] which revealed subsidies and schemes to poison public opinion within the country, has had important repercussions in the matter. For example, the congratulation by R J Reynolds of Doctor Rafael Picó for having 'killed' a Bill in 1974 which was seeking to have health warnings of damaging effects included in cigarette packets, the part played by D. Francisco Braña Pino in a campaign involving books, articles and academic publications on the benefits of tobacco and the conspiracy led by Philip Morris in 1990 and 1992 to avoid the control of tobacco in Spain had a considerable effect on public opinion, already alerted as it was by having learned of the incorporation of ammonia in cigarettes as a way of keeping up consumption.[3]

---

[1] Translated by Rita Inston.

[2] During the 1970s the North American tobacco companies had acquired plantations in the Canary Islands and other areas of Spain for the cultivation of American blonde tobacco (Adler, *Canary Islands*, www.rjrtdocs.com) and during the 1980s they tried to have cultivation of the autochthonous 'black' tobacco switched to blonde by, among other things, financing Brazilian agronomists who advised the Spanish Government's Agrarian Extension Service on establishing cultural and curing practices suitable for blonde tobacco (Smeeton, *Agronomic Research Program – Spain 1984/85*, www.rjrtdocs.com).

[3] *See* the documentation in Sato Mas, Villalbi, Granero, Jacobson and Balcazar, 'Los documentos internos de la industria tabaquera y la prevención del tabaquismo en España', *Gaceta Sanitaria* 17 (2003), p. 9 ff.

R. Blanpain (ed.), Smoking and the Workplace, 191–207
© 2005 *Kluwer Law International. Printed in The Netherlands.*

This climate of more and better information has been accompanied by practical measures. For instance, the Ministry of Health and Consumer Affairs created a special department to co-ordinate the fight against tobacco, once it had been declared a *harmful substance* in the Royal Decree of 1988 which will be analysed here. A draft National Plan for the Prevention and Control of Tobacco Use is in the process of being approved by the Autonomous Communities with a view to imposing a ban on smoking in the workplace, establishing the right of workers not to breathe air contaminated with smoke. Other measures proposed in the Plan are to increase the price of tobacco and to raise the minimum age for smoking to 18. And since 31 May 2001 associations of laryngectomy patients have been bringing claims before the courts demanding that the tobacco companies should insert information in cigarette packets on the ingredients used in manufacturing the product, eliminate the harmful ingredients and accept liability for the cost of treatment and rehabilitation of the 30,000 people in Spain who have undergone laryngectomy. So far, the courts have rejected these claims. Lastly, on 21 February 2002 the Autonomous Community of Andalusia lodged a claim against six tobacco companies demanding that they should be held liable for the cost of hospital treatment for a group of 242 patients suffering from ischaemic heart disease, lung cancer and chronic obstructive pulmonary disease, as we shall see later. The other sixteen Autonomous Communities are watching this initiative closely without as yet taking any steps themselves, prompting a comment from experts that 'it is surprising that only one Autonomous Community has denounced the totally unethical practices of the tobacco companies, and paradoxical that it does not even have the backing of at least the consumer associations, when we are all of us as citizens paying (economically, as well as the health cost relating specifically to smokers) for the abuses committed by the industry'.[4]

It is necessary to bear in mind a particular circumstance that is of great importance in the case of Spain: the manufacture and sale of tobacco has always been a state monopoly, inasmuch as from the 18 century onwards there existed the Real Fábrica de Tabacos in Seville, a gigantic establishment with its own prison and church which provided the setting for a number of operas connected with the world of cigarette manufacturers and has nowadays been converted into a University. The 20th century saw the birth of the modern-day version of a public tobacco enterprise, Tabacalera Española, which was finally privatised towards the end of the 20th century as a result of its sale to the French tobacco company Altadis. The existence of a national enterprise as the axis and motive force of tobacco consumption in Spain significantly held back the attitude of the public authorities to addiction to the substance, and it may be said that it is only with the above-mentioned privatisation that an adequate public-health policy on the matter has gathered strength.

The National Health Survey of 1997 showed that the overall incidence of tobacco use among the Spanish population aged 16 and over was 35·7% at that time, with the percentage of habitual smokers being 42·1% for men and 24·7% for women. Already in the Survey it was revealed that the percentage for men had fallen by several points in the past ten years, whereas that for young women

---

[4]   Soto Mas *et al., op. cit.,* p. 13.

had increased. The segment of the population with the largest number of smokers, in this order of things, was that between the ages of 25 and 44 (52·3%), followed by the 16–24 age-group (39·7%).

In Royal Decree 1911/1999 of 17 December, which approves the National Strategy on Drugs 2000–2008, the average age of contact with this substance is 16·6 years in the population as a whole, with an appreciable percentage of young people under the age of 14 having already tried it. Certain authors state that 40% of 13-year-old children had already consumed tobacco at least once, and 15% admitted to smoking on an occasional basis.[5] These figures are important, as we shall see later, because they make it possible to refute the argument that smoking is a voluntary choice on the part of the individual concerned and cannot be blamed on the tobacco company, particularly in the case of companies which include additives like ammonia to establish and maintain addiction.

In Spain tobacco caused 621,678 deaths between 1978 and 1992, amounting to 14% of total mortality. A third of these tobacco-related deaths were premature, i.e. among the population aged 35–64, with an overwhelming predominance of men (93·4%), although there were annual increases of 6·7% for women in this age range. In the most recent study by Banegas in 2001, the number of deaths in Spain during 1998 attributed to tobacco was 55,613, accounting for 16% of all deaths among people aged over 35, with the majority specifically due to lung cancer, chronic obstructive pulmonary disease and ischaemic heart disease.

2. THE RIGHT TO HEALTH PROTECTION

Article 15 of the Spanish Constitution of 1978 proclaims as a fundamental right that 'everyone shall have the right to life and to physical and moral well-being and shall not, under any circumstances, be subjected to torture or to inhuman or degrading punishment or treatment'.

Article 40 of the Constitution requires the public authorities to be vigilant in ensuring health and safety at work. As a consequence of this constitutional mandate, the old General Ordinance on Health and Safety at Work of 1971 was replaced by a modern and progressive Prevention of Occupational Risks Act (Law 31/1995), which will be mentioned in more detail below.

Article 41 of the Constitution prescribes that the public authorities shall maintain a public social-security system for all citizens guaranteeing adequate social-welfare assistance and benefits in situations of need, especially in the event of unemployment, without restricting the freedom to set up voluntary schemes to supplement it. The General Social Security Act of 1974 regulates the basic principles of health-related assistance for employees in manufacturing industry and services, accompanied by Royal Decrees and Ministerial Orders complementing the most important aspects, such as Royal Decree 63/1995 on National Health System benefits. The most recent version of the General Social Security Act (Law 1/1994) also regulates other aspects relevant to health, connected with accidents at work and occupational diseases.

---

[5]   The study is a rather old one: Mendoza Berjano, Sagrera Perez and Batista Boquet, *Conductas de los escolares españolas relacionadas con la salud 1986–1990*, Madrid, CSIC, 1994, p. 181 ff.

Lastly, Article 43 of the Constitution recognizes the right to health protection, declaring that 'it shall be the duty of the public authorities to organize and protect public health through protective measures and the necessary benefits and services. The rights and obligations of everyone in this respect shall be laid down by law'. Fulfilment of this mandate led to the promulgation of the General Health Act (Law 14/1986) and Law 16/2003 on the Cohesion and Quality of the National Health System.

3.   BANNING SMOKING IN GENERAL

Royal Decree 192/1988 of 4 March (*BOE*, 9 March), as amended by Royal Decree 1293/1999, establishes restrictions on the sale and use of tobacco with a view to protecting the health of the population. Based on Article 25(2) of the General Health Act cited above,[6] its most important precept is contained in Article one, which classes tobacco as a *harmful substance*, signifying that in the event of any conflict between the right to health of non-smokers and the right of smokers to consume tobacco the former will always prevail in all places or circumstances where the right to health may be affected. There are two other precepts of a general nature: one stipulates that packets must carry a warning on the health risk and the nicotine and tar content of cigarettes, and the other imposes some upper limits on their content.

(a) The most sweeping ban applies to forms of public transport, both urban and intercity, in which standing passengers are allowed, i.e. forms of transport which are or potentially are very crowded. In those which carry only seated passengers, separate accommodation where smoking is permitted must be provided, amounting to less than half of the total and situated at the rear. In rail or maritime transport, accommodation reserved for smokers may be organized in the form of separate carriages or cabins, always provided that such accommodation does not exceed 36% of the total. However, there is a total ban on smoking in school buses and in forms of transport wholly or partially intended for those under the age of 16 or people who are ill. In the case of taxis, the Royal Decree leaves the question of a ban to be decided by the local authorities, but in the absence of any regulations the right of the non-smoker, whether driver or customer, must prevail.

(b) Public places are also subject to a general ban on smoking, which the Royal Decree breaks down into various divisions. Thus, smoking is not permitted in social care establishments intended for those under the age of 16; in health centres, departments or establishments; in educational establishments; in enclosed commercial premises where large numbers of people congregate; in rooms for general public use, reading and exhibitions; in theatres, cinemas and other *enclosed premises* used for public spectacles and sporting events; in lifts or elevators; and in premises where foodstuffs are manufactured, processed, prepared or sold. It can be seen from this that the ban applies to enclosed spaces frequented by the public, but not workers, with respect to whom the restrictions will be examined below. It is relevant to note that the

---

[6]   In accordance with this Article, bans and minimum requirements must be imposed on the use of and trafficking in goods where there is presumed to be a risk or damage to health.

ban in enclosed spaces is not absolute, since they must incorporate a defined area for smokers save where this is not feasible, in which case the ban will be total. Educational and health establishments must also provide such an area for smokers, although without mingling teaching staff with pupils or health-establishment personnel with users.

(c) There is no ban on smoking in premises intended mainly for the consumption of food, although within such premises a ban applies to personnel concerned with handling food (chefs and kitchen staff). The Royal Decree is ambiguous in its reference to premises 'intended mainly for the consumption of food', since it is obviously alluding to restaurants, cafés, bars and the like but would also appear to encompass places where there is multiple use – both sale and consumption, for example – if the latter is preponderant.

(d) The Public Administrations are classed as workplaces, but often have rooms where the public are attended to and the number of officials present is far smaller than the number of visitors. Areas of the offices of Public Adminstrations intended for directly serving the public are also subject to the ban on smoking. It should be noted that, unlike health and educational establishments, the rest of the area of such government offices is not subject to the ban, save in those cases similar to workplaces.

(e) Three types of activities possibly merit special mention in the list of establishments with a ban on smoking: social care establishments, the home help sector and fuel service stations. In the collective agreements relating to these activities corresponding bans feature for workers but, logically, not for users. The Royal Decree only makes express mention of social care establishments for those under the age of 16, although many of the establishments intended for those over that age fall within the definition of a health centre, service or establishment which, as we have seen, is covered by the ban. As regards, lastly, the home help sector, in a country where the social-security system does not envisage this activity as a matter of public provision for which it is responsible there are numerous people working in this field to whom the ban does not apply, although they are in contact with a wide sector of the public.

The ban is accompanied by a series of penalties that can be imposed on the owners of establishments covered by it, who are also required to display notices clearly stating the ban and to make a complaints book available to the public. The imposition of penalties is initiated via legal proceedings, and they are independent of other civil, criminal or other liabilities. Heavy penalties, involving a fine of 3,000–15,000 euros, are incurred by, *inter alia*, failure to comply with the above bans in cases where because of its duration, the people concerned or other concurrent facts or circumstances it implies a serious health risk although it is not deemed to constitute gross negligence. Minor penalties, involving a fine of up to EUR 3,000, are incurred by inadequate signing to indicate areas dedicated to smokers, the absence of a complaints book available to users or failure to comply with the regulations in cases where these are not deemed to constitute either negligence or gross negligence.

4.   BANNING SMOKING IN THE WORKPLACE

As we have just seen, there is no general ban on smoking in workplaces, although – as stated earlier – such a ban is envisaged by the National Plan for the Prevention and Control of Tobacco Use, if it is finally approved. As yet, the legislation imposes only a number of specific bans, based on general health and safety regulations, which will be analysed here.

The Prevention of Occupational Risks Act (Law 31/1995) is the normative instrument from which we can deduce the general rules applicable to the risks posed by tobacco use. It covers the practical aspects of occupational risk assessment within enterprises, planning risk prevention and the rights and obligations of the different parties involved, although it does not establish a formal right of the employee to a healthy atmosphere at work or, as the WHO proclaims in Article eight (2) of its Framework Convention on Tobacco Control of 21 May 2003, 'effective ... measures providing for protection from exposure to tobacco smoke in indoor workplaces'. The 1995 Act features an important general duty on employers, whether public or private, to protect workers against occupational risks, and this protection must be *effective* (Article 14) and must be provided *in all aspects connected with work, by adopting whatever measures are necessary for the protection of workers' health and safety (ibid.).*[7] It also provides for an obligation on workplace-level health and safety committees and safety representatives to collaborate with the National Health System and the health authorities (Articles 38 and 39). Likewise, the Workers' Statute (in its latest version Law 1/1995) does not go any farther than an ambiguous declaration of the right of workers to 'their physical well-being and to an adequate health and safety policy' (Article 4) and to 'effective protection in regard to health and safety' (Article 19).

The General Social Security Act of 1974 is no more specific, in stating that the objectives of health and safety at work are to 'eliminate or reduce the risks posed by particular establishments or jobs' and to 'achieve, individually or collectively, an optimum state of health' (Article 26). The same Act states that the purpose of health assistance for employees in manufacturing industry and services is to provide medical and pharmaceutical services that will preserve or restore the health of recipients and also their capacity to work (Article 98).

The most recent version of the General Social Security Act (Law 1/1994), in its turn, contains a provision that is important in dissuading employers from allowing a high level of tobacco use in their establishments that is harmful to health. Its Article 123 states that all financial benefits payable on the grounds of an accident at work or an occupational disease will be increased by 30–50% in cases where the harm suffered is caused by plant or machinery that lacks the necessary safeguards or results in their being unused or used in unsatisfactory conditions, or in cases of failure to observe general or specific measures for health and safety at work or *basic principles essential to health* or to ensuring adequate conditions for the individual in each type of work. Liability in this respect falls directly on the employer, who is unable to cover it through any insurance company. The case-law of the Spanish Supreme Court has interpreted this Article as signifying that mere compliance with what is specifically laid down by the regulations on safety at work does not release employers from this increased liability, but that they must also observe the legal provisions on the duty of care and of good faith in protecting the employee.

To conclude the general legislative provisions, the General Health Act

---

[7]   Among other monographs, *see* Igartua Miro, *La obligación general de seguridad*, Tirant, Valencia 2000.

(Law 14/1986) lays down in its Article 21 the duties of the health authorities with respect to occupational health, with relevant allusions to keeping a watch on working *and environmental* conditions that may be harmful or unhealthy during pregnancy and breastfeeding; identifying and preventing *factors of the work microclimate* that potentially have harmful effects for workers' health; and, lastly, monitoring workers' health in order to detect at an early stage the risk and impairment factors that may affect their health.

I.   General principle: the right to a healthy workplace and clean air

Above and beyond the general and abstract provisions there are, first, the rules on banning smoking in workplaces contained in Royal Decree 192/1988 and, second, the Royal Decrees on specific risks at work which derive both from the relevant specific Directives and from the Prevention of Occupational Risks Act (Law 31/1995), where detailed precepts are laid down on particular work environments.

Royal Decree 192/1988 says little on the subject of banning smoking in workplaces. It confines itself to establishing a ban in those premises where there is an increased risk to workers' health because the harmful effect of tobacco is combined with the damage to health caused by an industrial pollutant. Consequently, we may deduce that tobacco is not banned in its own right, but only where in the risk map it is accompanied by a product or element used in the manufacturing process or work activity that alters the normal risk level. Another isolated ban refers to areas where pregnant woman are working, which, in other words, presupposes a temporary ban that is lifted as soon as the female worker concerned gives birth, since no protection is provided during the post-confinement period in cases where a mother decides to breastfeed her newborn infant.

The following is a review of the prescriptions laid down in the various Royal Decrees on specific risks at work.

— Royal Decree 1389/1997 of 5 September, approving minimum arrangements intended to protect the health and safety of workers employed in mining activities (*BOE*, 7 October): In rest areas adequate measures must be adopted to protect non-smokers from the harmful effects due to tobacco smoke. When the working day is interrupted regularly and frequently and there are no rest areas, other areas must be made available where workers can stay during the interruption to work in cases where workers' health and safety so requires. In such areas adequate measures must be adopted to protect non-smokers from the nuisance and risks caused by tobacco smoke. A ban on smoking or on being in possession of tobacco or any other object used to light cigarettes is established by agreement. In areas that present special fire or explosion hazards smoking must be banned.
— Royal Decree 1216/1997 of 18 July, establishing minimum health and safety arrangements for work on board fishing vessels (*BOE*, 7 August): The siting, structure, acoustic and thermal insulation and arrangement of workers' living accommodation and service areas where these exist, as also the means of access to the above, must afford adequate protection against inclement weather and the sea, vibrations, noise and emanations issuing from other

areas that may cause nuisance to workers during their rest periods. Where the design, dimensions or purpose of the vessel so permit, workers' living accommodation must be situated so as to minimize the effects of heaving or pitching and acceleration. As far as is possible, adequate measures must be adopted to protect non-smokers from the nuisance caused by tobacco.

– Royal Decree 486/1997 of 14 April, establishing minimum health and safety arrangements in workplaces (*BOE*, 23 April): Without prejudice to what is laid down regarding the ventilation of certain premises in Royal Decree 1618/1980 of 4 July approving the Regulation on heating, air-conditioning and sanitary hot water, the minimum air-renewal rate in work premises must be 30 cubic metres of clean air per hour and per worker in the case of sedentary activities in environments that are neither hot nor contaminated by tobacco smoke, and 50 cubic metres of clean air per hour and per worker in other cases, in order to avoid a contaminated atmosphere and disagreeable odours.

The ventilation system used and, in particular, the distribution of the inlets for clean air and outlets for stale air must ensure an effective renewal of the air in the work premises concerned.

In workplaces which do not have dedicated rest areas but in which work is interrupted regularly and frequently, rooms must be made available where workers can spend the time during these interruptions if their continued presence in the work area for these periods entails a health and safety risk for them or for third parties.

Both in dedicated rest areas and in the rooms mentioned above adequate measures must be adopted to protect non-smokers from the nuisance caused by tobacco smoke.

– Royal Decree 1627/1997 of 24 October, establishing minimum health and safety arrangements for work on construction sites (*BOE*, 25 October): In dedicated rest areas or living accommodation provided for workers adequate measures must be taken to protect non-smokers from the nuisance caused by tobacco smoke.
– Royal Decree 665/1997 of 12th May on the protection of workers against the risks connected with exposure to carcinogenic agents during work (*BOE*, 24 May): This regulates the delimitation of risk areas, stipulating the use of adequate health and safety signs that include a ban on smoking in such areas and allow access only to personnel who need to work there, excluding workers who are especially vulnerable to these risks.

In accordance with Articles 18 and 19 of the Prevention of Occupational Risks Act, the employer must take adequate steps to ensure that workers and their representatives receive appropriate training and are kept informed on the measures that have been adopted in implementation of this Royal Decree.

Similarly, the employer must take appropriate measures to ensure that workers receive sufficient and adequate training and detailed information based on all available data, particularly in the form of instructions, regarding:

(a) the potential health risks, including the additional risks due to tobacco consumption;

(b) the precautions that must be taken to prevent exposure;

(c) arrangements concerning personal hygiene.

The employer must provide workers with information on types of plant and equipment and associated receptacles that contain carcinogenic or mutagenic agents.

- Royal Decree 2177/1996 of 4 October, approving the Basic Building Regulation 'nbe-cpi/1996: Fire Protection for Buildings' (*BOE*, 29 October): Residential Use. The term 'residential' refers to temporary accommodation in establishments classed as a hotel, inn, residential home, tourist apartments or the equivalent which are managed by an economic actor other than the combined occupants and are equipped with shared services such as cleaning, catering, laundry, rooms for meetings and events, sports and pastimes, etc.

    Under section 2.2, the areas of a residential-use establishment used for other activities that are subsidiary to the main activity, such as cafeterias, restaurants, function rooms, sports or event halls, etc., must comply with the requirements laid down for their use.

    n this type of establishment fire-prevention precautions must be complemented by the content of other regulatory provisions: a plan indicating the location of exits affixed to the door of each residential unit, a ban on smoking, etc.

- Royal Decree 150/1996 of 2 February, amending Article 109 of the General Regulation on basic safety rules in mining (*BOE*, 8 March): In rest areas adequate measures must be adopted to protect non-smokers from the nuisance caused by tobacco smoke.
- Royal Decree 863/1985 of 2 April, approving the General Regulation on basic safety rules in mining (*BOE*, 12th June): Article 85 stipulates that there is a total ban on taking cigarettes, lighters and smoking accessories into the mine. Express authorization from the relevant directorate is required to take in any object capable of producing sparks or flames or high temperatures that needs to be used exceptionally in work inside the mine. Lighting must be provided in all cases by officially authorized lamps or lights. Article 133 states that within the enclosed vicinity of a deposit there is a total ban on smoking and on taking in objects capable of producing a naked flame or high temperature and inflammable substances, and this ban must be indicated with clearly visible notices.

II. Employers' powers to introduce measures banning tobacco in their establishments

As a general principle, the Spanish legal system grants employers the authority to organize their entrepreneurial activity as they think best, always subject to observance of the relevant legal provisions and, in particular, workers' rights. Royal Decree 192/1988 prescribes, in this sense, that 'the owner of an establishment or set of premises which, whatever its purpose, is open to members of the public may impose bans on smoking therein, subject to the display of adequate notices informing users of the fact (additional provision). As regards whether an owner can do the same in establishments which are not open to members of the public but where there are workers employed by the owner, there is doubt as to whether the answer is no, in favour of workers who wish to smoke, or yes, by analogous application of what is prescribed for establishments open to the public. Article 20 of the Workers' Statute, which establishes the employer's managerial prerogative and the employee's duty of obedience, states that the employee must carry out the agreed work subject to the employer's authority, in compliance with the co-operation and due care required by the relevant legal provisions, collective agreements and *orders and instruction issued by the employer in the proper exercise of his managerial powers* and, if none such exist, custom and practice.

It might be supposed in principle that the employer can issue instructions which ban smoking in the workplace. However, the Spanish Constitution establishes the right of everyone to personal freedom (Article 17) and the free development of one's personality is one of the fundamental principles of the political system and social peace (Article ten), which means, according to the Constitutional Court, that any restrictions imposed on these fundamental rights and principles must be justified and observe the principle of proportionality, i.e. must not go beyond the strict minimum required to achieve the end in view. When these ideas are applied to the supposition under consideration here, the most appropriate answer seems to be that an employer can ban tobacco in workplaces that are not open to the public when this is done for health purposes (for example, the room or area in question is too small to allow smoking), is negotiated in a collective agreement, is appropriate for the particular type of work involved, or is a safety measure against a fire risk. However, a ban prohibiting an individual worker from smoking in a factory where there is no risk of any type would be deemed to lack justification and proportionality. At all events, the 'health purposes' argument is open to broad interpretation where there are a number of workers in a particular room or area, given that in the Spanish legal system tobacco has been declared a harmful substance, which signifies that the right of non-smokers must prevail over that of smokers. A single complaint from the former would enable an employer to ban tobacco in the room or area concerned as a justified and proportionate measure.

It seems useful to examine the extent to which a ban or smoking and tobacco use is negotiated in collective agreements. Among the agreements currently in force and applicable, at least 64 establish such a ban, mostly in sectors such as transport, the food industry, fuel service stations and the home help sector.

The following is a review of these latter collective agreements:

- Collective Agreement for Intercity Passenger Bus Transport in the Province of Seville (*BOP*, 15 October 2003). Article 48. 'The following shall not be deemed to constitute misconduct or punishable offences: [...] 3. Acts whose commission presupposes expression of the employee's private sphere (swearing, smoking, etc.) or is related to the employee's physical appearance or dress, always provided that [such acts] are not contrary to the general rules laid down by the employer or the public authorities in the exercise of their respective powers'.
- Collective Agreement for Service Stations in the Autonomous Community of Valencia, 2003–2005 (*DOGV*, 29 September 2003). Article 56. 'Serious misconduct [...] 11. Smoking by staff or lighting cigarettes, lighters or any other similar device within the area defined by the regulations as hazardous, or supplying products intended for the commission of any of these acts'.

- Collective Agreement for the Pyrotechnics Industry in the Community of Valencia (*DOGV*, 21 August 2003). 'Health at work. [...] Smoking is prohibited within the manufacturing site, and it is also prohibited to take into the manufacturing site any alcoholic beverages or personal belongings (without express authorization) that can be used to produce fire or sparks or are likely to affect safety in the workplace'.
- Collective Agreement for Private Residential Homes for the Elderly and the Home Help Service (Inter-province) (*BOE*, 30 July 2003). Article 55. 'Disciplinary rules: A) Misdemeanours. [...] 8. Smoking during the performance of work'.
- Collective Agreement for the Vegetable Canning Industry (Inter-province) (*BOE*, 12th February 2003). Article 55. 'Classification of gross misconduct. The following constitute gross misconduct: [...] 9. Smoking in areas where it is prohibited for health and safety reasons. This ban must be indicated very clearly in the areas concerned by means of stickers, notices or any other suitable system'.
- Collective Agreement for the Dietetic Products and Prepared Foodstuffs Industry in Catalonia, 2002 (*DOGC*, 4 April 2003). Article 63. 'By virtue of the strict technical and health regulations applicable to companies in the dietetic products and prepared foodstuffs industry, there is a total ban on smoking in the manufacturing areas of such companies. Failure to comply with this ban shall be penalized as gross misconduct'.
- Collective Agreement for Butane Gas Distributors in the Province of Vizcaya (*BOB*, 2 May 2002). Article 33. 'Disciplinary rules. [...] The following constitute serious misconduct: [...] 12. Smoking within the premises of the workplace'.
- Collective Agreement for the Pulp, Paper and Cardboard Industry (Inter-province) (*BOE*, 17 August 2001). Article three. 'Serious misconduct: [...] 21. Smoking in areas where this is prohibited'.
- Collective Agreement for the Anthracite Mining Industry in the Province of León (*BOP*, 13 August 2001). Article 39. 'Misconduct. c) The following shall constitute gross misconduct: [...] 10. Smoking within the mine or taking into it cigarettes, lighters and other implements used for producing flames or sparks. 11. The repetition or reoccurrence of serious misconduct, provided that it is committed within a period of 90 days and has been penalized'.
- Arbitration Award establishing the Regulations on the Grade Structure, Career and Financial Advancement of Workers, Pay Structure and Code of Conduct in the Coalmining Sector (Inter-province) (*BOE*, 24 April 1996). Article 30. 'Classification of misconduct. 1. The following constitute misdemeanours: [...] o) Taking cigarettes, lighters, flints or other implements that can be used for producing sparks or flames and other smoking accessories into mines classed as presenting firedamp'.

III.   Can a ban on smoking be a requirement laid down in the contract of employment?

In principle, the answer is yes, although some further qualification is needed. In an enterprise whose collective agreement establishes a ban on smoking, any new worker has to accept it and comply with the ban like the other workers. A sample has just been presented of the numerous agreements which impose

201

restrictions of this type. And before that a review was also given of numerous national rules, mainly in the form of Royal Decrees, which likewise make it impossible to smoke in the workplace, either for health reasons or in order to avoid causing nuisance to work colleagues. However, the question can be approached from the different, albeit related, perspective of whether the employer could unilaterally impose the obligation not to smoke as a contractual condition, meaning that any infringement of that obligation would justify penalizing the employee.

In this connection, Article 49 of the Workers' Statute prescribes that the contract of employment can be terminated 'for the reasons validly set out in the contract, unless the latter constitute an abuse of right by the employer'. This precept signifies, first, that resolutive conditions must be agreed between the parties; and, second, that they may not constitute an abuse of right by the employer. To dismiss a worker for the mere fact of smoking when it does not affect the health and safety of other workers or of the establishment probably constitutes an excessive measure that would not be deemed admissible in the Spanish legal system.

However, another hidden or implicit element of the precept is that it says nothing whatever on penalties short of dismissal. The fact of not being able to dismiss an employee does not, it might be thought, prevent a lesser penalty from being imposed. To resolve the issue we also have to refer to Article four of the Workers' Statute covering the rights of workers, since there are two among them which may suggest a different slant. Specifically, subparagraph 1(c) of the said Article alludes to the right not to be discriminated against for the purposes of employment on the grounds of sex, marital status, age, race, social status, religious or political ideas, membership or non-membership of a trade union, language within the Spanish state, or mental, physical or sensory disabilities that do not affect the capacity to work. As can be seen, the potential grounds classed as discriminatory do not include non-smoking. Article 17 of the Workers' Statute adds the possession of family ties with other employees in the company as another ground classed as discriminatory, but this again has no bearing on what we are considering here. The second provision in Article four that may be relevant to banning smoking, i.e. its paragraph 1(e), recognizes the right of workers to their personal privacy and to due consideration for their dignity, including protection against offensive verbal and physical behaviour of a sexual nature and against harassment on the ground of racial or ethnic origin, religion or beliefs, disability, age or sexual orientation. Although the answer in this case is more complex, it seems unlikely that a *contractual* ban on smoking constitutes an encroachment on the worker's personal privacy and dignity, since in the final analysis it is up to the individual to adapt to the work environment they are entering. As we have seen, numerous agreements establish such a ban and none has to date been contested on this ground.

IV. Health and safety legislation

A review has already been given in **Subsection 1** above of the Royal Decrees on specific health and safety measures at work and on the general ban on smoking wherever tobacco is combined with an industrial pollutant or where pregnant employees are working. One rule that can be singled out from all the specific measures is the obligation to renew the air at a rate of 50 cubic metres per hour and per worker, rather than 30 cubic metres, in cases where the environment is hot or contaminated by tobacco smoke. Another obligation that repeatedly features in these various Royal Decrees consists in protecting non-smokers from the nuisance caused by tobacco smoke. The reader is referred to what was said in that Subsection.

In Spain there are various workplace-level institutions responsible for overseeing health and safety: the employer must set up risk prevention services which draw up a risk map and a safety plan and monitor the latter's implementation (Article 30, Prevention of Occupational Risks Act of 1995); safety delegates, who are elected by and from among the members of the workers' committee, are similarly entrusted with the task of monitoring compliance with safety regulations and measures on behalf of the workforce (Article 35 of the same Act). Lastly, health and safety committees are joint bodies set up in all workplaces with 50 or more employees for consultation on risk prevention plans, accident and illness rates in the workplace concerned and the activities of the risk prevention services (Article 38 of the same Act). If a ban on smoking originates from the risk prevention plan or is connected with health and safety, these three institutions possess powers to enforce it with respect to the employer and the workforce, although the powers in question are somewhat indicative; only safety delegates are authorized by law to report omissions or offences committed by the employer to the workers' committee, which in its turn can then report this to the Labour Inspectorate or lodge a complaint before the labour courts demanding a penalty or ruling against the employer on these grounds. If, on the other hand, a ban on smoking is not related to a health and safety regulation and is not contained in the relevant collective agreement or individual contracts of employment, the powers of the above-mentioned institutions are non-existent, save where assessment shows there to be a connection with health and safety, which, in view of the numerous medical reports on the matter, does not present any logical or legal difficulties. In this respect Royal Decree 192/1988, which was examined in section 2 above, states ambiguously, that 'the co-operation' of health and safety committees and workers' committees 'shall be requested in implementing and overseeing these provisions'.

V.   Can smoking constitute a form of harassment?

The answer depends on the circumstances in each particular case, but is an unequivocal yes in those situations where the non-smoker is the victim of premeditated behaviour on the part of superiors or of fellow workers (i.e. bullying) designed to humiliate him. Law 63/2003 introduced moral harassment as a new ground for dismissal in the Workers' Statute, consisting in 'harassment for reasons of racial or ethnic origin, religion or beliefs, disability, age or sexual orientation directed against the employer or individuals who work in the enterprise'. One of the ways of harassing a person, obviously, can consist in creating an environment contaminated by tobacco smoke when the victim has made it clear that they dislike smoking. The employer must take adequate measures to prevent such tobacco-related harassment in cases where it is found to be premeditated and designed with a purpose in view, extending if necessary to dismissal of the author or authors of the psychological besiegement; if this is not done, the employer may be penalized by the labour authorities, on a proposal from the Labour Inspectorate, for failure to observe the rights of the worker concerned.

VI.   An example of anti-tobacco policies in public enterprises or bodies in Spain

The Andalusian Health Service (SAS), i.e. the network of hospitals and health services in the Autonomous Community of Andalusia employing a total of 80,000 workers, incorporates in all of its hospitals an Anti-Tobacco Unit which forms part of the Pneumology Department in each establishment. Each such Unit consists of a doctor specializing in lung disease and a psychologist, plus administrative staff. Every person employed at the hospital, and also every insured person within its catchment area, can ask for an appointment at the Unit with a view to receiving specialized assistance, which takes the form of a course designed to help them give up their addiction during which they talk to other patients and exchange experiences and are given free pharmaceutical treatment.

VII.   Penalties

These have been described in the analysis of Royal Decree 192/1988 given in section 2.

VIII.   Control

Responsibility for this lies with the Ministry of Health and Consumer Affairs, and in those Autonomous Communities possessing decentralized competence in health matters (which nowadays means all of them) with the relevant Executive Council. This administrative authority can impose the penalties described earlier, as well as having the actions of anti-tobacco policy entrusted to it.

IX.   Employer liability for damage to workers' health

This relates to Article 123 of the General Social Security Act, which prescribes a 30–50% increase in the cost of the pension for disability or death payable by employers who have been found guilty of negligence as regards healthy conditions and the work environment or safety measures in the workplace.

Spain's system of liability for damages entails considerable individual adjustment to the harm suffered and to the main actors, and as a result there are as yet no known instances of either legal proceedings or judgments against employers held liable for tobacco-related illnesses. Spanish courts demand conclusive proof of a direct relation between the alleged cause and the harm suffered (*relation of cause and effect*). Should an employee attempt to claim that tobacco smoke in the establishment where he works has caused the lung cancer from which he is suffering, he has to prove this with all the means at his disposal, yet the courts will still require that no other contributory cause exists that refutes liability, such as hereditary antecedents.

As one illustration of this, we can point to the case-law on the similar issue of exposure to asbestos dust, and specifically to the Supreme Court's judgment of 6 March 2002,[8] which analyses the industrial-action claim lodged by the combined workforce representation of a company manufacturing asbestos pipes to demand payment of a wage supplement recognizing the difficulty, toxicity and danger for workers brought into direct contact with the dust of this substance. It should be noted that what was being asked for was simply a wage supplement provided for by the relevant collective agreement, which the employer was refusing to pay, and that asbestos is an industrial substance recognized as causing occupational diseases (asbestosis, fibrosis and cancer of the lungs, larynx or pleura).[9] As it turned out, in the view of the Supreme Court 'the decisive factor is the diversity of assessment, which must be carried out not on a general basis but in an individualized manner for each particular job, signifying that it would in principle be possible to arrive at different conclusions for different jobs, depending on the concurrent danger factors inherent in them'.

Another example relating to claims for damages has already been mentioned earlier, i.e. the claim lodged by the Autonomous Community of Andalusia against six tobacco companies operating in Spain,[10] in which the health services of this regional government were demanding reimbursement of the hospital costs occasioned for a sample of 242 patients diagnosed as suffering from three tobacco-related illnesses: ischaemic heart disease, lung cancer and chronic obstructive pulmonary disease. The patients in question accounted for a total of 3,245 days of hospitalisation, at a proven cost of 1 769 964 euros. The claim, originally lodged with the Madrid courts, was referred on through successive instances up to the Civil Chamber of the Supreme Court, which has been inhibited by the fact that the judges believe a claim should also have been lodged against the State, the owner until recently of the public enterprise that was the predecessor of Altadis, in which case the competent jurisdiction would have been the administrative trial courts.

The legal basis of the claim is founded in Article 127 of the General Social Security Act (Law 1/1994) and Article 83 of the General Health Act (Law 14/1986). In accordance with the former, the public health system is entitled to claim back 'from the third party vicariously liable' the cost of health services it has provided, and can either take action for reimbursement through joinder as a plaintiff in criminal or civil proceedings that have been instituted to obtain compensation, or take direct legal action itself as an injured party. Article 83 of the General Health Act, for its part, states that Public Administrations which have provided health care to users on the assumption of compulsory insurance are entitled to claim back the cost of the services provided from the third party vicariously liable.

In the claim in question, the supporting evidence produced includes, numerous scientific articles by medical experts,[11] as well as various statistics,[12]

---

8   Application 437/2001.
9   Royal Decree 1995/1978 of 12 May, Social Security System Schedule of Occupational Diseases, section C.1(b).
10   Altadis SA, JT International SL, British American Tobacco España SA, Tabacos Canary Islands SA, Philip Morris Espain SA and CITA Tabacos de Canarias SL.
11   Especially that by Castillo Gómez et al., Tabaco y Salud (no date or source).
12   Drugs Commissioner, Los andaluces ante las drogas, Seville 2001; Ministry of Health and Consumer Affairs, Encuesta Nacional de Salud de España 1997, Madrid 1998; etc.

clinical histories of the patients concerned, their permission to use the medical data, a report on the presence of ammonia in five brands of cigarettes, and judgments from both a Provincial Court and a Court of First Instance.

It is in proving the relation of cause and effect between tobacco and the costs incurred that the claim, in our opinion, falls down, since it does not succeed in demonstrating *in each one of the alleged cases* that tobacco was the original cause of the illness that occasioned hospitalisation. It is affirmed from the outset that it is an indisputable fact that tobacco is damaging to health owing to the presence of vaso-constrictive substances, and that these forms of damage need to be treated medically. However, it does not go on to demonstrate that *these patients* have fallen ill due to tobacco; that is to say, the claim does not progress from the abstract level to the concrete cases involved, which, as we have seen, is a fundamental requirement if the court is to find in favour of its demands. The most that it succeeds in establishing is that 'all of the patients treated are smokers or ex-smokers', according to their clinical histories; that the tobacco companies have included ammonia as one of the ingredients in their cigarettes; and that in Spain the average age for starting to smoke is below the age of majority, meaning that the fact of having become addicted should not be attributed to the free will of the patients concerned.

X.   An example of anti-tobacco policy in Spanish enterprises.

Employers are extremely cautious in their approach to anti-smoking policy, and make efforts to adapt only to the legal bans that exist, without going any farther by adopting complementary measures. A typical example in this respect is the attitude of a major company where, given the type of personnel employed and the sector in which it operates (telecommunications), a more belligerent stance might be expected. I am referring to Telefónica de España. In its workplaces it goes no farther than applying the Royal Decree mentioned here so frequently, and makes this known to its staff through notices and information sheets of the following type:

	*Air-Conditioning Machinery Rooms	*Lift Machinery Rooms
	*Archives	*Lifts or Elevators
	*Automated Equipment Rooms	*Lubrication Pits
	*Battery Rooms	*Medical Departments
	*Boiler Rooms	*Offices open to the Public
	*Cable Conduits	*Operating Rooms
	*Cable Galleries	*Operations Centre
	*Classrooms and Lecture Halls Concentrator Rooms	
WARNING	*Cleaning Areas	*Paint Bays
	*Cleaning with Inflammable Fluids	*Passenger Transport Vehicles
	*Cloakrooms	*PC-32 Exchanges
NO	*Compartmented Equipment Rooms	*Photocopying Rooms
SMOKING	*Computer Rooms	*Photographic Studios
	*Connection Switchboard Rooms	*Power Rectifier and Switchboard
←	*Control Rooms	Rooms
	*Distributor Rooms	*Pressurizing-Set Rooms
	*Electric Meter Areas	*Radio Rooms
	*Fixed and/or Mobile Containers	*Refuse Areas
	*Garages	*Telephony Training Laboratories
	*Generating-Set Halls	*Transformer Rooms
	*Kitchens	*Transmission Rooms
	*Libraries	*Warehouses
		*Waste Dumps

5. CONCLUSIONS

Only large enterprises apply the smoking bans envisaged in the legislative rules and collective agreements analysed in the preceding pages. In Spain, however, the great majority of enterprises are small or medium-sized. Nonetheless, the general climate is beginning to be one of awareness of the dangers of tobacco and consideration for non-smokers. We have been silently witnessing a revolution in public opinion, which already nowadays is no longer indifferent to or in favour of a smoky atmosphere, but quite the opposite. Whereas, previously a room filled with tobacco smoke was seen as a familiar, comfortable or friendly environment in which people were able to express themselves freely and drank strong alcohol, today this scenario is exceptional, and could even be said to be regarded as unpleasant by the majority.

The legal battle is in its early stages, and the claim lodged by the Autonomous Community of Andalusia, as well as those lodged by the associations of laryngectomy patients, are starting to lay the foundations for more aggressive actions.

However, the citizens of Spain do not set about change in a drastic manner, and we do not find associations or individuals intent on martyrdom to the anti-tobacco cause, as has been seen at times in the United States and especially California. The dialogue between smokers and non-smokers in our country is usually courteous and good-humoured, and meanwhile the great majority of the population is coming out unequivocally in favour of a smoke-free environment.

15. Sweden

Birgitta Nyström

1. BACKGROUND

It took a long time until smoking was considered to be a problem and a hazard to public health in Sweden. In the period after the Second World War many men smoked, but the amount of smokers among men began to diminish in the beginning of the 1970s. Among women smoking the amount was rather rare before the 1960s, but then began to rise substantially, and did not start to decline until the end of the 1970s. In the beginning of the 1960s public measures to inform the people about smoking as a health problem started. In the 1970s restrictions regarding tobacco advertising were issued and it became obligatory to write a warning about the health risk on tobacco products. During the 1980s smoking was prohibited in a growing number of public places. In 1983 the National Work Environment Agency (*Arbetsmiljöverket*) and the Swedish National Board of Health and Welfare (*Socialstyrelsen*) together issued advisory rules about non-smoking in different kinds of premises. The Tobacco Law, which prohibits smoking in a number of different places, was issued in 1993. The Tobacco Law has since then been strengthened a couple of times (*see infra*).

The public opinion regarding smoking has changed rapidly during the last 15 years towards a much more reluctant view to smoking. Today 70% of the Swedes want a non-smoking environment according to studies undertaken by the Swedish National Institute of Public Health (*Folkhälsoinstitutet*). Twenty years ago one in three grown up Swedes were smoking daily, today it is one in five. Even in the beginning of the 1990s there were people smoking in other people's homes without asking for permission! Such behaviour, today, would be considered as very impolite. Today no one would dream of lighting a cigarette in for example an office, a shop or a library. Recent studies show that the public opinion is rather positive to smoke-free restaurants and a majority are annoyed by tobacco smoke when they visit cafés and restaurants.

Today, most employees are guaranteed the right not to be exposed to tobacco smoke at work against their will. When the 1993 Tobacco Law was issued it was judged that it was to go too far to totally ban smoking in work places. But even before the Tobacco Law there existed workplaces with a voluntary ban on smoking. The Tobacco Law lays down rules on a ban on tobacco smoking in some work premises and the provision of non-smoking areas in others. Many workplaces have introduced a total ban on smoking inside the buildings, even in rooms where the employee works alone, i.e. their own working room.

The Swedish National Institute of Public Health has been discussing the problem of smoking for a long time. They estimate, approximately, that at least

R. Blanpain (ed.), Smoking and the Workplace, 209–218
© 2005 *Kluwer Law International. Printed in The Netherlands.*

7,000 Swedes die every year because they are smokers. The institute also estimate that an employee who smokes costs his/her employer something between
27,000 and 36,000 Swedish crowns (approximately something between EUR
2,900 and 3,900) yearly compared to a non-smoking employee. This is because
the smoking employees use about 30 minutes a day of employer time to smoke
and are absent because of health problems about eight days more than their
non-smoking colleagues. According to the Institute 500 people die in Sweden
yearly due to passive smoking.

There will be a ban on smoking in restaurants and bars from June 2005.
The main reason for this is that smoking is a work environment problem for the
employees. Restaurant guests can choose to go to another place less filled with
smoke, but this is not an opportunity for the employees. Nevertheless, the ban
on smoking in restaurants and pubs etc. is also considered to be good for public
health. Restaurants etc. will be accessible to people who are allergic or have
asthma. Already before this legislation enters into force, there are pubs and
restaurants that voluntary ban smoking (*see infra* 4).

2.   BANNING OF SMOKING IN GENERAL

In the Government Bill from 2002 "Goals for Public Health"[1] it is settled that
the national goal for public health in Sweden is the creation of social conditions
to make equal rights to good health for all citizens. Eleven special goals for
public health are identified. One of these goals is to reduce the use of tobacco
and alcohol.

Questions related to smoking, such as restrictions on smoking in certain
places indoors and outdoors, a smoke-free workplace, warning texts on tobacco
products, restrictions in trade and marketing of tobacco products as well as
product control are regulated in the Tobacco Law from 1993 (SFS 1993:581).

2.1.   Public places, transport, hotels

Smoking is forbidden in rooms intended for childcare, schools and other premises for children's and young people's activities including schoolyards (the
Tobacco Law 2 section 1). Smoking is also forbidden in all kinds of health care
premises (2 section 2), in all jointly used rooms in housing accommodations
and in different kinds of institutions (2 section 3). Further, according to the
Tobacco Law (2 section 4) smoking is forbidden on all kinds of public transport
within Sweden, this ban includes all kinds of rooms and terminals intended for
the users of public transports.

In all kinds of buildings and rooms where the public has admittance,
except for restaurants cafés and so on, smoking is also forbidden (2 sections 5,6).

In hotels and other accommodations aimed at casual staying the owner
is obliged to have a certain number of rooms where smoking not is allowed
(section 4).

---

[1]   Prop. 2002/03:35 *Mål för folkhälsan.*

2.2. Restaurants, bars, cafés

The danger for non-smokers to be exposed to tobacco smoke, so-called passive smoking, has been paid attention to since the 1980s. Research shows that working in a smoky environment leads to poorer health. According to the Swedish National Institute of Public Health, 40–80 Swedes yearly suffer from lung cancer because of tobacco smoke in their environment. Non-smokers exposed to tobacco smoke in their work place have a 16–19% higher risk to get lung cancer according to the Institute.

When the Tobacco Law was issued in 1993 the owners of restaurants, bars etc. with more than 50 seats were obliged to arrange a non-smoking area with seats. From 1 January 2003 this rule was extended to all restaurants, bars, cafés etc.[2] When the Swedish Parliament accepted this new rule it was stated that all restaurants and so on, should be non-smoking before 1 January 2004, and if this was not possible by voluntary means, a proposal to legislate should be worked out.

Several surveys regarding restaurants and smoking have been conducted. One of them shows that nearly half of 600 restaurants questioned considered that a total ban on smoking was a good idea, and more than half of them did not think that a ban would reduce the profit. In another survey half of the employees were worried about passive smoking as a health hazard. More than half of the employees said that they had to work in a smoky environment and about one fifth of these employees consider themselves to have got poorer health. About half of all employees in hotels and restaurants want a work environment without smoke, and more than half of the employees do not think that a ban on smoking would affect the number of customers.[3] Surveys among restaurants and cafés, that are voluntary smoke-free, show that the main reason for the ban on smoking is the employees' health, but also to improve the environment for the guests. The result of the smoke-ban is that it has become easier to recruit employees and many guests – even smokers – are satisfied with the non-smoking environment. A third of the employers considered that the ban also has lead to better economy.[4]

In December 2003 the Swedish Government decided to make a proposal to the Parliament (*Riksdag*) that it should be forbidden to smoke in restaurants, pubs, cafés, nightclubs etc. from 1 June 2005.[5] Legislation about smoking in Norway, Ireland, the United States and Canada had been studied as patterns. The Swedish Government stated that international experience showed that voluntary steps towards non-smoking in restaurants and bars were not enough legislation was necessary. The proposal was accepted by the Parliament during spring 2004. The main purpose behind the new legislation is to protect the health of the employees, but also the protection of young peoples' health is specially mentioned as an important reason for banning smoking in cafés and bars. It was decided that it was too complicated and there was also a possibility that it could disturb competition if legislation tried to separate different kinds of establishments where food and drinks are served, therefore the ban comprises

---

[2]   Prop. 2001/02:64 *Vissa tobaksfrågor* (Some questions in relation to tobacco).
[3]   Prop. 2003/04:65 *Rökfria serveringsmiljöer* (Smoke-free restaurants etc.) p. 20.
[4]   Prop. 2003/04:65 pp. 20–21.
[5]   Prop. 2003/04:65.

all kinds of undertakings where serving of food and/or drinks are taking place. It is not necessary that food should be served, or that food or drinks are served at a table. It includes all premises in the establishment, including cloakrooms, dance floor, toilets, elevators etc. It also includes more temporary forms of restaurants, bars and so on, like in tents during summer and the like. Excluded from the ban are out of doors serving and if the establishment has been hired for a private party or dinner.

Exceptions from the ban on smoking in restaurants will be for separate smoking rooms. Such rooms are not allowed to be more than a small part of the restaurant, i.e. not more than 25% of the public premises. Smoking rooms should be situated where guests do not have to pass through them. The employees should not have to stay in the smoking rooms more than temporarily when people are smoking. It could, for example, be necessary for an employee to enter the smoking room to empty ashtrays or to intervene if there seems to be some trouble. Furthermore, it will not be allowed to serve food or drinks or to bring food or drinks into a smoking room. This also includes a ban on entertainment and gambling in the smoking room.

The Hotel & Restaurant Workers Union has been engaged in the question about smoking for years. They see legislation as the only possible solution to solve this work environment problem for their members. The employers in the sector, on the other hand, are negative to the ban on smoking. They are afraid of loosing customers. They see large problems with a construction where it is the employers' responsibility to avoid smoking from customers (*see* section 5), and they also point to the problem that there might be order problems outside the restaurants if guests are forced to go outdoors when they want to smoke. The employers also point to the risk of fires because people are hiding when they secretly smoke indoors.

2.3. Exceptions

It is possible to install smoking rooms for the staff in schools and in childcare establishments. In other places where smoking is forbidden it is allowed to smoke in separate places especially intended for smoking (the Tobacco Law 2 sections 2–6).

When the ban on smoking in restaurants etc. enters into force 1 June 2005 there will be an exception for separate smoking rooms (*see supra* 2.2.).

There are also possibilities for other kinds of exceptions if there are special circumstances. Examples of special circumstances could be related to the design of the room, if there is ample space, good ventilation etc. Also in small rooms there could be special circumstances, it could for example seem unreasonable to demand a special smoke-free area considering the total area to dispose over.

2.4. Control and sanctions

The owner, or other person who is in command of the premises, has the responsibility that the rules are acted upon. If a person – after being told not to – continues smoking, he/she could legally be removed off the premises (the Tobacco Law section 7).

3. SMOKING AND THE WORKPLACE

3.1. Employees' right to a healthy workplace

The general objectives of the 1977 Work Environment Act are for the work environment to be satisfactory with reference to the nature of work and social and technical developments in the community at large, for working conditions to be adapted to the physical and mental attitudes of human beings, and for work to be organised in such a way that the individual employee can influence their working situation. Under the Work Environment Act the employer is required to ensure that conditions associated with occupational hygiene, such as air quality, are satisfactory (the Work Environment Act Chapter 2 section 4). Tobacco smoke in the work place was discussed in the *travaux préparatoires*[6] to the rule in Chapter 2 section 4. The Work Environment Agency established a decision in 1994 that the possibilities to act against smoking in a work place within the work Environment Act were very limited. From the 1 July 1993 the new Tobacco Law regulates smoking more in detail, and in 1994 the Tobacco Law was extended with an obligation for the employer to ensure that an employee should not be exposed to tobacco smoke against his/her will (section 8). Restaurants etc. were an exception from this rule. The latter will be changed from 1 June 2005.

The rule in the Tobacco Law section eight means that it might be possible to smoke in a work place if every employee agrees upon it, or if it is possible to arrange ventilation so that no employee can feel the smoke. The possibility to smoke in one's own working room is dependant upon ventilation and so one can ensure that no smoke enters the premises where non smokers work or rest.

3.2. The employers' right to property

When the ban on smoking in restaurants, pubs and so on was proposed in the spring of 2004 it was questioned if the proposal could infringe with the Swedish Constitution.[7] According to the Constitution limitations in the right to pursue industrial activity is possible only in order to protect important public interests, and all citizens has a right to their property; a right which only could be circumscribed with reference to important public interests. Further, an owner has a right to economic remuneration if the state reduces the owners' possibility to use his property. Voices were raised that this should make it possible for the owners of restaurants, pubs and so on to urge compensation from the Swedish state if they loose money because of the ban on smoking. The Government and the Parliament rejected this argument and decided that restrictions in these rights motivated by public health do not constitute a right to compensation. This seems to be a very reasonable position.

---

[6] In Sweden when seeking the answer to questions regarding the content of the law considerable weight is traditionally attached to a statute's *travaux préparatoires*, i.e. what is said about the aim of the rule and details and examples discussed in connection with a certain rule by the Committee that prepared the legislation or in the Government Bill.

[7] Before a Government Bill is proposed to the Swedish Parliament a committee consisting of very high lawyers, the Council of Legislation (*lagrådet*), are supposed to overlook the proposal, and a.o the Council paid attention to this.

3.3. Recruitment and smoking

It is in principle possible for an employer to choose not to hire individuals who are smokers. This is within the employers' right to hire at will. There is no legislation that protects smokers against discrimination. A study carried out in 1998 reveals that some 20% of employers state that they are not willing to hire smokers.[8]

The above-mentioned right for the employer to hire at will is a basic presumption in the private sector. This means that a private employer does not need to apply objectively, justifiable reasons in choosing whom he/she will hire. The entire public administration, on the other hand, is subject to the requirement of objectivity and impartiality, which is laid down in the Swedish Constitution. In addition, the State as employer is under further requirement that the sole appointment must be justifiable according to the criteria, merit and competence, where merit refers to the length of experience and competence to the aptitude. Of course, all employers both in the private and in the public sectors are subject to legislation on discrimination.

It could be questioned if a public employer has the option to choose not to hire employees that are smokers. This might be against the requirement of objectivity and impartiality. On the other hand, it is possible to find cases where an employer's demand for a non-smoking employee could be judged as an objectively justifiable reason, e.g. employees working with allergy patients.

3.3. Disciplinary penalties, dismissal

The employer has as a basic principle the right to direct and organize work. This is a very old principle and many of the powers for the employer involved in this concept have undergone considerable restrictions. But it is possible for the employer to totally forbid smoking in his/her premises and refuse to arrange special smoking rooms. Such rules are normally elaborated in cooperation with the trade unions. It is under the employers' prerogative to transfer an employee to another working room in another part of the work place, if – for example – another employee has made complaints about the transferred employee smelling from smoke in a shared work room. The employer has the right to direct work, but if the transfer is permanent and means a major change in the employee's working conditions, the employer has to initiate co-operative negotiations with the local trade union with which he has a collective agreement according to the 1976 Co-Determination Act. The employer must postpone his decision until the negotiations have been pursued.

The employers' possibility to apply disciplinary measures against, for example, an employee deliberately breaking the rules on smoking in the work place is very limited. According to the Co-Determination Act the employer must be backed up by special rules about disciplinary action in law or collective agreement. In legislation there are only rules applying to state employees, for local government employees there are certain rules in the collective agreement

---

[8]   Fahlbeck, R./Sigeman, T., European Employment & Industrial Glossary: Sweden. Sweet & Maxwell. European Foundation for the Improvement of Living and Working Conditions, 2001, p. 330.

and for the private sector rules about discipline in collective agreements are very unusual.

According to the 1982 Employment Protection Act the employer must have a just cause for dismissal. The definition of a just cause has been left mainly to the courts and today there is a huge amount of case law on the matter. The employer has to demonstrate that in a particular case circumstance that constitute just causes actually exist. The just cause must be an objective reason of some weight and relevance to the employment relationship. If an employee, for example, intentionally many times overrides the rules about smoking at the work place, thereby exposing other employees/guests/customers to tobacco smoke and the employer clearly explains that this behaviour is unacceptable; the situation might constitute a just cause for dismissal. It has probably to be a rather extreme situation. Further, it is not possible to dismiss an employee if the employer can transfer him/her to alternative work within the company.

3.5. Health and safety rules

In Sweden much of the regulation of the work environment takes the form of non-statutory regulations issued by central authorities, in particular the Work Environment Agency. These regulations represent an important regulatory instrument in the field of work environment. In 1983 – before the Tobacco Law was issued – the Agency issued general advice on the restriction of tobacco smoking. Today, there are no general regulations from the Work Environment Agency about smoking and the workplace. Nevertheless, in the general rules about the shape of the work place[9] there are instructions about ventilation in rooms where tobacco smoke could be found and about ventilation in separate smoking rooms.

Regarding smoking rooms in restaurants, it is according to the new legislation that enters into force in July 2005 possible for the Government or an authority, which the Government directs to issue rules about the smoking room and its ventilation. Probably the Work Environment Agency will issue non-statutory regulations in this field.

According to the managerial prerogative the employer can formulate regulations and policies about the work place. Such rules could include health and safety matters, and also questions about smoking at the work place. Rules about tobacco smoke must be within the limits of the Tobacco Act, the Work Environment Act and the regulations from the Work Environment Agency. They must also pay attention to the rules about co-determination for the employees.

3.6. The role of employee representatives

There is a long tradition of employee participation in Sweden. There could be situations in relation to tobacco smoke at the work place when the employer has to initiate negotiations with the trade union, *see supra* 3.4. But the trade unions and their representatives also play an important role when it comes to

---

[9]   AFS 2000:42 *Arbetsplatsens utformning.*

the work environment as a matter of cooperation between all those at the workplace. It is important to understand though that the prime responsibility for the work environment rests with the employer.

A safety representative must be designated in all workplaces where five or more employees are regularly employed. The employee side in the light of the workplace, the nature of the work and other circumstances surrounding the work decide the number of representatives. They have time-off rights and entitled to undertake any necessary training on full pay. The safety representative represents the employees in all work environment related matters.

A safety committee must according to the Work Environment Act be formed in every workplace with 50 or more employees and in smaller workplaces if the employee side so request this. The committee's main function is to establish objectives for health and safety activities and to ensure that these objectives are attained. The committee's involvement in all work environment related matters must commence at the earliest possible stage in the planning and decision-making process. It is composed of representatives of both sides.

4. PRACTICE

The main rule is that an employee has a right not to be exposed to smoke at his/her work place. This will also be true for employees in bars, restaurants, nightclubs etc. from 1 June 2005.

The city of Lund is a town with about 100.000 inhabitants situated in the very south of Sweden. The University of Lund is the largest university in the Nordic countries and certainly this has left its mark on the town with many restaurants, cafés and so on. The municipality of Lund has, together with a committee against allergy, started a project in 2002 initiated by the Swedish National Institute of Public Health. The project is called the Golden Fork, and in the spring of 2004, 22 restaurants in Lund engaged in this project. The aim of the project is to have totally non-smoking restaurants. Members of the Golden Fork are not even allowed to have a smoking-room or the like. The 22 restaurants are very satisfied with the non-smoking policy. They have not lost any customers and they consider that their working environment has improved.

5. CONTROL AND SANCTIONS

It is the local municipality that has the immediate control regarding all smoke-free areas according to the Tobacco Law. The control usually takes form of inspections on the premises, control how smoking rooms, ventilation etc. are designed, control of the knowledge about the rules on smoking among employers and employees. The county administration has an overall control of all the local municipalities in its county, and the Swedish National institute of Public Health is the nationwide authority on this point. Regarding control of smoke rooms for employees and the employers' right to a smoke-free workplace according to the Tobacco Law section 8 (*see supra* 3.1.) as well as the rules in the Work Environment Act, it is the Work Environment Agency that is the responsible authority.

The Government is planning to give the Swedish National Institute of

Public Health the task to evaluate how the ban on smoking in restaurants is followed when the new legislation has been in force for some time.

When violations of the Tobacco Law take place the controlling authority can decide to give a prohibition or an improvement notice. This means that the owner can be ordered either to cease doing something or allowing it to be done or to do something or arrange for it to be done. The prohibition or the improvement notice could carry a penalty of fine in the event of non-compliance. Such a fine is unlimited, so they can be large and there is nothing to prevent a new and a larger fine from being imposed following a previous one.

There is a problem with places where there is an owner or a user that is responsible for how the premises are used, e.g. restaurants and bars. A guest who despite an order from the restaurant owner or the employees in the restaurant continues smoking can be put off the premises. If the Tobacco Law is violated several times in the same restaurant or bar it could result in the authorities withdrawing the permission to serve alcohol. The employers in the sector find it difficult to accept that it is the owner of the restaurant, bar, café etc. that in practice could be punished if the guests are smoking.

6. LEGAL LIABILITY FOR DAMAGES

An employee that has been injured by environmental tobacco smoke could receive compensation form the state according to the 1976 Industrial Injury Act. Most employees are also covered by a supplementary private scheme under a collective agreement. Both these compensation systems are financed from employer contributions.

Classification as industrial injury covers injuries resulting from an accident or other harmful effect occurring in the core of work. Employees alleging that they have been injured have to show the existence of a demonstrable connection between the injury sustained and the harmful factor. The interpretation of the concept injured has been different from time to time and in a period before 1993 the interpretation was so wide that the cost for the state rose enormously. In 1993 it became much more difficult to prove the connection between the injury and the harmful factor and today (after changes in 2002) the employee has to show that there are predominant reasons to believe that there is a connection.

In case law there are a few examples when the courts have found that passive smoking has caused lung cancer or other lung problems alone[10] or together with the exposition for other chemical substances in the work place.[11] There are also examples from case law on situations where it has been discussed if an employee's lung cancer or other serious lung problems have been caused by chemical agents in the work environment or by the employees own smoking habits.

---

[10] A noticeable case was decided 28 November 1985 by *Försäkringsöverdomstolen* (then the Swedish high court for the social insurance system). A non-smoking woman died of lung cancer. She has been exposed to passive smoking in the work place. Her family got compensation from the industrial injury insurance (case No 2722/83:8). In case 268/90 the Court did not find enough connection between passive smoking and the injury.

[11] Case No 1995/83 2 February 1988.

7. CONCLUDING REMARKS

The developments in Sweden have for a long time been towards a more reluctant view on smoking. Next year the last work environment – restaurants, bars etc. – will be non-smoking. The number of Swedes smoking has decreased considerably. Today, in most situations and environments indoors – except parties and in restaurants, pubs and the like – it is unusual to smoke and it is natural to ask if others permit smoking. But this is a very recent change of attitude and unfortunately there are signs today of a growing number of smokers among young Swedes. We can only hope that the ban on smoking in restaurants and other places will not only protect the employees but also prevent young people from starting to smoke.

16.   Turkey

Kadriye Bakirci

I.   GENERAL INTRODUCTION

In Turkey, cigarette smoking is a very common habit and a public health problem. The average age at which young people start the habit has been decreasing, and the smoking rate among youngsters and women is increasing steadily.

Surveys have revealed that nearly half (44%) of the population aged 15 years and over are regular smokers, and this rate could be as high as 65–75% among some of the male groups. Based on current estimates, some 70,000–100,000 people die due to smoking-related health problems each year, a figure which is 10–15 times that of the number dying in motor vehicle accidents.[1]

Smoking in the workplace is still as accepted a habit as drinking coffee. However, environmental tobacco smoke is a toxic indoor air pollutant, associated with a number of risk factors to those exposed. These include a greatly increased risk of heart disease, lung cancer resulting from prolonged exposure, aggravation of asthma, increased coughing, wheeze and phlegm, aggravation of existing respiratory complaints, and health threats to unborn children. Exposure to other people's tobacco smoke causes a range of impacts from the fatal or serious conditions mentioned above, to irritation, sore eyes and throat, distraction, and odiferous hair and clothes. Though the latter are 'minor' conditions, they may reduce productivity and create resentment among non-smokers.

Although tobacco control activities on the part of voluntary organizations date back to the 1970s in Turkey these activities have been officially undertaken by the Ministry of Health only since 1987. The National Committee on Tobacco or Health was established in 1995, with the participation of more than 20 voluntary organizations and some state departments. The Committee made advocacy while the draft Anti-Tobacco Bill was being discussed in The Parliament at the beginning of 1996. For the first time, the hazards of smoking and banning of smoking in public places was discussed in Parliament, and in November 1996 the "Act on the Prevention of the Harms of Tobacco Products (Anti-Tobacco Act)" came into force.

No lawsuit resulting from second-hand smoking in the workplace has ever arisen in Turkey.

---

[1]   (1996), Impact of the Ban on Smoking In Public Places in Turkey, International Development Research Centre (IDRC) Survey, Ankara.

R. Blanpain (ed.), Smoking and the Workplace, 219–226
© 2005 *Kluwer Law International. Printed in The Netherlands.*

II. THE OBLIGATIONS OF THE STATE AND THE ANTI-TOBACCO ACT

According to the Turkish Constitution the State is required:

- to ensure the welfare, peace, and happiness of the individual and society; ... and to provide the conditions required for the development of the individual's material and spiritual existence (Article five),
- to protect the right of the individual to be treated equally without any discrimination before the law, irrespective of language, race, colour, sex, political opinion, philosophical belief, religion and sect, or any other such considerations (Article ten),
- to protect the right of the individual to life and the right to protect and develop his/her material and spiritual entity (Article 17),
- to protect the right of the individual not to be subjected to ill-treatment (Article 17),
- to guarantee the right of the individual not to be required to perform work unsuited to his/her age, sex, and capacity (Article 50),
- to protect the right of the individual to live in a healthy balanced environment (Article 56), according to this provision "it is the duty of the state and citizens to improve the natural environment, and to prevent environmental pollution",
- to secure the freedom of the individual to work and conclude contracts in the field of his/her choice (Article 48),
- to provide special protection for minors, women and persons with physical or mental disabilities with regard to working conditions (Article 50),
- to take all necessary measures to protect youths from addiction to alcohol, drug addiction, crime, gambling and similar vices, and ignorance.

However, the Anti Tobacco Act prohibits smoking only in certain types of workplaces. It excludes from its scope most private-sector workers, and those public workers employed in governmental offices with less than 5 workers. As a result, smoking remains common in many offices. Since it does not cover all workers it can be considered discriminatory.

On the other hand, for some, such as those with asthma or respiratory illnesses or pregnant women, a smoky workplace may actually be a barrier to their employment. A total ban would uphold the employment rights of people who are particularly affected by smoke. Secondary smoking also constitutes ill treatment for children and young employees: there is an association between respiratory illnesses in children and the amounts of pollution in the areas where they live.

The limited nature of the protection provided by the Anti-Tobacco Act is in breach of the State's Constitutional obligations.

The Anti-Tobacco Act (No. 4207) bans all kinds of advertisements of tobacco products, sales of tobacco products to minors (less than 18 years of age), smoking in public transport and associated waiting rooms, and in health, education, and cultural establishments and all governmental offices (public institutions) where five or more people are working, and it requires that details of the format and content of public health messages and warnings be posted in public places and on cigarette packages. The Act also requires that all public and private TV channels assign a minimum of 90 minutes' worth of air-time per month to the broadcasting of education programmes on the health hazards of smoking and on methods of protection.

III. THE OBLIGATIONS OF EMPLOYERS AND EMPLOYEES

1. The obligation of employers to safeguard their employees

Under Turkish Law, employers have an obligation to safeguard their employees and provide an environment suitable for them to undertake their contractual duties. The legal basis of this obligation is either legislation or specific employment contracts. As a consequence of these obligations an employer can be held liable for damage to health resulting from his own actions, those of his representatives, and those of any co-workers or third parties under his control.[2]

It is therefore not only in the interests of non-smokers, but also in the interests of employers to provide an adequate no-smoking policy.

A. *Employers obligations under the Turkish Constitution*

According to the Turkish Constitution Article 11, the provisions of the Constitution are fundamental legal rules binding upon legislative, executive and judicial organs, and on administrative authorities and other institutions and individuals. Therefore, the provisions of the Constitution mentioned above are binding for employers as well as the State. Employers are legally bound to safeguard the right to equality (Article ten), the right to life and the right to protect and develop the employees' material and spiritual entity (Article 17), the right not to be subjected to ill treatment (Article 17), the right to work (Article 48), the right not to be required to perform work unsuited to the employees' age, sex, and capacity (Article 50), the right to special protection for minors, women and persons with physical or mental disabilities with regard to working conditions (Article 50), and the right to live in a healthy, balanced environment (Article 56).

B. *Employers' obligations under the Anti Tobacco Act*

Smoking is forbidden in public transport and its waiting rooms, in health, education, and cultural establishments, and in all governmental offices (public institutions) where five or more people are working (Anti Tobacco Act, Article two).

Employers are required to designate a smoking area in the workplace, to post signs warning that breaches of the no-smoking rule are subject to a fine, and to identify the designated smoking area(s) in the workplace. Smoking areas should be well ventilated so that smoke is not re-circulated into the rest of the building (Articles two and four).

The owner, manager or person in charge of the workplace is legally

---

[2] *See* Kadriye Bakirci (2001), "Remedies for Sexual Harassment of Employees Under Turkish Law", European Public law, Volume 7, Issue 3, September, pp. 473–483.

responsible for ensuring that the ban on smoking in the workplace is complied with (Article four). It is an offence for employers or their representatives not to implement the Act. Employers and any employees breaching the ban on smoking in the workplace may be subject to a fine. The fine can be doubled if the infraction is repeated (Articles five, six and seven).

There is no provision related to inspections to ensure that the ban on smoking in the workplace is being implemented. Labour inspectors from the Employment Ministry can only inspect general compliance with health and safety requirements by the Employment Act (Employment Act, Articles 91–97).

C. Employers' obligations under the Employment Act

According to both the Employment Act No. 4875, Article 77, and the Obligations Act, Article 352, an employer must take all the necessary measures to ensure occupational health and safety in his/her establishment(s). The provisions of the Employment and Obligations Acts and the related regulations as regards the employees' health and safety are of a mandatory nature.

However this duty does not cover the provision of a working environment free from tobacco smoke. Employers are only required to provide good working temperatures, adequate lighting, and so on. There is no general duty upon employers to regulate smoking in the workplace, except on grounds of risk relating to fire, explosion or hygiene. There are regulations under a variety of health and safety edicts that ensure workers should enjoy smoke-free rest rooms; employers also have a duty to provide a safe working environment and system of work, and must ensure that wherever possible employees are not exposed to hazardous substances

D. Employers' obligations under the Employment Contract

Under employment contracts, employers have an implied duty to safeguard/protect their employees. The concept of the duty needs to be established in good faith and it is a broad duty. In my opinion this duty also covers the protection of non-smokers' rights, thereby ensuring that their employees are not exposed to tobacco smoke. Forcing employees to work in smoky workplaces constitutes a workplace health hazard. Therefore, employers have a duty to provide a safe, healthy workplace, and an employer's failure to eliminate the hazardous condition caused by tobacco smoke can constitute a breach of the duty to provide a safe workplace.

With today's level of awareness on second-hand smoking it would be difficult for any employer to argue that they are not in breach of these duties by not prohibiting smoking at work in all areas except for specifically designated places where non-smokers have no reason to enter. There is no known safe level of exposure to second-hand smoke. A smoking room and ventilation system is not adequate protection for workers from the harmful effects of second-hand smoke. Therefore, healthy, smoke-free air in the workplaces is a right. This goes beyond an issue of inconvenience for smokers or a revenue issue for businesses. Protecting workers' health and preventing more smoking-related sicknesses and deaths is of paramount importance.

Employers, whether they have designated a smoking area or have chosen to prohibit smoking altogether in the workplace, are responsible for ensuring compliance in their workplace. In other words, they should, within reason, ensure that smoking is confined to the designated areas or, if smoking is prohibited completely, to ensure that no one smokes in that workplace

2. The obligations of employees

The employee is obliged to abide by the instructions and orders given by his/her employer. These instructions and orders are predicated on the employer's right to manage the enterprise. Employer's orders and instructions are limited by the mandatory provisions of the law, the collective agreement, the needs of the establishment and the requirement that the job be performed in accordance with prevailing custom. Here, three issues deserve special attention: namely, the control (search) of employees during access to and departure from the workplace; "no smoking" regulations; and restrictions on the alcoholic beverages.

According to Turkish attitudes, orders about not smoking are an invasion of the employees' right to privacy which is guaranteed by the Turkish Constitution. Article 20 provides that "Everyone has the right to demand respect for his or her private and family life. Privacy of an individual or family life cannot be violated". Therefore it is suggested that a non-smoking rule unilaterally imposed by the employer is enforceable only if established by law, the collective agreement, or the labour contract. In operations where there is a danger of fire, the employer can impose smoking restrictions based on the employee health and safety provisions of the Employment Act No. 4875, Article 77, which states that every employer shall take all the necessary measures and maintain all the needed means and tools in full; and employees are under the obligation to obey and observe all the measures taken in the field of occupational health and safety. According to this opinion the employer may also establish a no smoking restriction in situations where smoking on the job is bound to reduce output.[3]

There is a conflict between what some regard as a right to smoke, and what others regard as a right to clean air – or at least, air that is not unnecessarily polluted. However, where there is a conflict the right to clean air should come first. In my opinion the provision of clean air is a logical extension of any concern to improve working conditions. So it falls within the scope of the employer's right to manage the enterprise. Since smoking is a personal habit and not an implied contractual term, the employee cannot claim the right to smoke at work.

By developing the smoke-free workplace policy both employers and employees will enjoy an enhanced corporate image, a healthier workplace, more harmonious working relations among co-workers and improved staff morale.

---

[3]   *See* Toker Dereli (1998), Labour Law and Industrial Relations in Turkey, Kluwer Law International, The Hague, London, Boston, p. 96.

IV.   THE RIGHTS OF EMPLOYERS AND EMPLOYEES

1.   The rights of the employers

A.   The right to ban smoking

There is no law that prohibits the employer from banning smoking in the workplace; that is, the employer is free to do this. Even though certain places are exempt from the ban, all employers (even those who are exempt) still have the right to enforce the legislation. In other words, even though the above organisations and institutions are not obliged to enforce the ban, they are free to do so if they wish to minimise health risks. Every employer is obliged to protect the health of employees, customers, residents and visitors to their premises.

It is, however, important to note that the issue of a smoking ban should be handled as sympathetically as possible and with full consultation. Any policy must take into account the needs of all employees. In some situations a complete ban may be justified for safety reasons, but the imposition of such a ban else-where without proper consultation could lead to resentment and enforcement problems.

Therefore, employers should make provisions for smokers: separate smoking areas, rather than a complete ban which could alienate smokers and lead to activities such as smoking in toilets. It must be recognised that smoking is an addiction, and most smokers would find it very difficult to give up smoking at work.

B.   The right to discipline employees

Breaches of the policy will normally be dealt with through education and coun-selling. If counselling and negotiation fail, employees who refuse to observe the policy on smoking will be subject to normal disciplinary procedures

C.   The right to dismiss the employees

According to Employment Act No. 4875 Article 25/II, the employer may break the contract, whether for a definite or indefinite period, before its expiry or without having to comply with the prescribed notice periods in the event of immoral, dishonourable or malicious conduct or other similar behaviour if the employee refuses, after being warned, to perform his duties or if either wilfully or through gross negligence the employee imperils safety or damages machinery, equipment or other articles or materials in his care, whether these are the employer's property or not, and the damage cannot be offset by his thirty days' pay.

As a last resort, employees who regularly interrupt their work with unofficial breaks (whether or not for the purpose of smoking), or who refuse to observe the policy on smoking, can be dismissed if their employer has forbidden this practice and has carried out a full disciplinary procedure. In this event employees cannot claim severance pay.

2. The rights of the employees

A. The right to refrain from working

By interpreting Articles 90 and 325 of the Obligations Act, an employee who has been subjected to an unhealthy working environment would have the right to stay away from work and continue to claim his or her pay until the offence has been properly rectified.[4]

However, since there is no general ban on smoking in the workplace the employees' right is not being respected or supported. Therefore, employees might feel intimidated and fearful of exercising their right of refusing to work in the affected areas.

B. The right to terminate the employment contract

Employment Act No. 4875 provides a right to breaking the employment contract by the employee for the reasons of health. According to the Employment Act, article 24/1 (a) the employee is entitled to break the contract before its expiry, whether for a definite or an indefinite period and without having to observe the specified period of notice, if the performance of the work stipulated in the contract endangers the employee's health or life for a reason which it was impossible to foresee at the time the contract was concluded.

Employees who must leave their jobs due to an allergy or hypersensitivity to tobacco smoke may be entitled to unemployment insurance benefits. Employees who quit due to exposure to tobacco smoke have "good cause" to quit, and are therefore eligible for benefits.

C. The right to sue the employer

Non-smokers who live in workplaces where employers do not adequately protect them from second-hand smoke can utilize other legal recourses to find protection. These lawsuits may be enough to persuade employers and business owners to voluntarily adopt policies that protect non-smoking employees and customers.

By interpreting articles of the Civil Code[5] a non-smoking employee can ask the court to order that the employer provide a smoke-free environment (Civil Code, Article 24); and/or ask the court to grant compensation for both material (pecuniary) and non-material (moral) damages (Civil Code, Articles 24 and 24/a) for damages to health caused by exposure to second-hand smoke in the workplace.

An employee who is fired for seeking a smoke-free workplace may also be eligible to appeal against termination if s/he is engaged for an indefinite period, is employed in an establishment with thirty or more workers and meets a minimum seniority of six months. According to the Employment Act an employer who terminates the contract of an employee who meets these criteria must produce a valid reason for such termination connected with the capacity or conduct of the employee or based on the operational requirements of the establishment or service (Article 18). An employee who alleges that no reason

---

[4]   *See* Bakirci (2001), p. 482.
[5]   *See* Bakirci (2001), pp. 482–483.

was given for the termination of his employment contract or who considers that the reasons shown were not valid to justify the termination shall be entitled to lodge an appeal against that termination with the labour court within one month of receiving the notice of termination (Article 20). If the court concludes that the termination is unjustified because no valid reason has been given or the alleged reason is invalid, the employer must re-engage the employee in work within one month. If, upon the application of the employee, the employer does not re-engage him in work, compensation to be not less than four months wages and not more than eight months shall be paid to him by the employer. In its verdict ruling the termination invalid, the court shall also designate the amount of compensation to be paid to the employee in case he is not re-engaged in work. The employee shall be paid up to four months' total of his/her wages and other entitlements for the time s/he is not re-engaged in work until the finalization of the court's verdict (Article 21).[6]

In cases where the employment contracts of employees fall outside the scope of Articles 18, 19, 20 and 21 of the Employment Act (mentioned in the above paragraph), employees who are fired for seeking a smoke-free workplace may also be able make a claim against retaliatory (abusive) termination. According to Article 17 of the Employment Act, if the employee is abusively dismissed (for instance, as a result of his filing a grievance), the employee shall be paid compensation amounting to three times the wages for the term of notice.[7]

Persons whose livelihood has been regularly provided by the deceased employee can also file suit for damages caused by the death of the employee due to the employer's breach of the duty to safeguard his or her employee (Obligations Act, Article 45/2).

IV. CONCLUSION

On average, people spend about eight hours daily in their workplace. A non-smoking employee is exposed to second-hand smoking if s/he works with a smoker. Therefore, the government should approve a new regulation limiting smoking in the workplace so as to "significantly improve" the rights of non-smokers. The employers should be "required to take necessary measures to ensure that non-smoking employees are not exposed to health damaging tobacco smoke". And it should cover all the businesses and cover everyone: employees and management, visitors, clients and patients

It is important to recognise that 'workplaces' comprise a very diverse range of institutions – not only factories and offices, but also shops, public and government buildings, schools, bars, restaurants, prisons, hospitals and residential care, public transport, and many other environments. No single policy will accommodate all situations. In many cases a complete ban on smoking will be possible and preferred, in others an employer may choose to allow for a smoking room. In some circumstances, smoking may continue but measures will have to be taken to reduce employee exposure.

---

[6]   *See* Kadriye Bakirci (2004), "Unfair Dismissal in Turkish Employment Law", Employee Responsibilities and Rights Journal, Volume 16 (Issue: 2), June.
[7]   *See* Bakirci (2004).

17.   United States of America

*Alvin L. Goldman**

GENERAL INTRODUCTION

History of tobacco use in the United States

When European settlers first invaded North America, they discovered that the indigenous population consumed a variety of foods and medicines which were unknown in Europe. Many of these novel items, including their seeds and plants, were shipped back to the mother countries where eventually their use became part of European diet and customs. Among these exports to the Old World were the cured leaves and seeds of the tobacco plant, the genus *nicotiana tabacum*, a hearty weed, related to the chile pepper, potato, mandrake, eggplant and tomato, whose uses varied among Native American tribes.[1]

Most indigenous groups in the New World recognized tobacco as a mind altering drug that could stimulate visions. Many tribes held the plant in high esteem and accepted its affects as providing a medium between the world of humans and that of spirits. It was used in puberty rites to test internal strength, as a protector from evil spirits, and as a spiritual cleanser. In some instances the user inhaled the smoke from dried, burning tobacco leaves; on other occasions the user drank an infusion made with the leaves. A ceremonial use involved spreading smoke from burnings tobacco leaves over various parts of the body. Tobacco was also smoked by the indigenous people in a variety of ways. In addition to burning cured leaves in the bowl of a pipe, often the dried leaves were wrapped in corn husks or in the leaves of reeds. Most tribes included tobacco as a medicinal herb. For this purpose it variously was smoked, applied in a poultice or ingested in a tea. Additionally, many Native Americans consumed tobacco as a chewed supplement to increase endurance and suppress hunger.[2]

In time, the use of tobacco spread throughout the world. Settlers, as well as Europeans and, eventually, Asians and Africans, adopted their own methods of using this weed as a stimulant that was sniffed, smoked or chewed. They enhanced the ease of use and potency of its effects by identifying the special attributes (colour, flavour, aroma, nicotine concentration, malleability) of the 95 different known species of tobacco, and increased both its strength and productivity through careful cultivation and propagation, and by refining techniques for curing the leaf. By the mid-17th century, tobacco had become a crop of

---

*   The author wishes to thank Rebecca A. Novak for her very able help with various research tasks and Cheryl Culver for her always attentive administrative assistance.
[1]   J. Winter, *Tobacco Use by Native North Americans*, 2000, U. Okla. Press, at p. 4.
[2]   J. Winter, above, at pp. xv, 3, 11–83.

R. Blanpain (ed.), Smoking and the Workplace, 227–254
© 2005 *Kluwer Law International. Printed in The Netherlands.*

considerable commercial importance in North America both for domestic consumption and for exportation.[3]

Tobacco originally was smoked in the Western Hemisphere in forms similar to modern pipes and cigars. Although, the use of paper cigarette wrappers was introduced in Spain in the early 16th century, this less expensive, more convenient method of consumption did not become wide-spread until the late 17th century. The cost reduction was further accelerated in the late 19th century, when machinery was developed that automated cigarette rolling, pasting and cutting, a convenience that, coupled with changes in the methods of cultivation and processing which reduced the harshness of inhaled tobacco smoke, facilitated the addiction of persons at all income levels.[4]

By the mid-20th century, tobacco smoking in the US had become so common that the offer of a cigarette was a symbol of friendliness and hospitality. Among men, the gift of an expensive cigar had become the customary means of celebrating the birth of a child, a wedding, or an outstanding achievement, as well as the completion of a fine meal. At first, cultural mores largely confined tobacco use to adult men. Because of the harshness of the smoke and taste, the habit was considered too coarse for the delicacies of women – or, at least, women of higher social status. However, by the early 20th century, tobacco use had gained status as a symbol of independence and the habit became widely adopted among women seeking to declare their liberation from the stranglehold of a male dominated society. It also became a symbolic means by which children, especially those in the age range of puberty, attempted to demonstrate their maturity.

Motion pictures helped spread the image of cigarette smoking as a behavioural norm; it was an ever-present prop in American films and the prolonged inhale or exhale became a standard device for giving dramatic emphasis.[5]

The US military did its part to promote the use of tobacco by making cigarettes readily and cheaply available to troops. Thus, during World War II, millions of young men became hooked on the nicotine habit while puffing cigarettes to fill-in the long periods of confined idleness that are characteristic of military duty. Cigarette manufacturers took advantage of the situation by periodically offering free cigarettes to military personnel in a gesture they portrayed as corporate patriotism.

Additionally, tobacco companies were among the earliest, most aggressive and most innovative users of mass media for promoting their products.

Historic use of tobacco in the workplace

In the late 18th century, medical professionals had begun to recognize that nicotine, the primary chemically active substance in tobacco, is a powerful,

---

[3] *Encyclopedia Britannica* 2004, cd version, "Tobacco", "United States: History, Colonial to 1763, Settlement".

[4] *Encyclopedia Britannica* 2004, above, at "Cigarette".

[5] Random surveys of major American motion picture films reveals a decline in the frequency of depictions of smoking starting in 1951. That decline continued until the early 1980s. Thereafter, the frequency of scenes with someone smoking increased. That increase accelerated, has continued to climb and reached a new high of 10'9 incidents per film hour in 2002. Biotech Week, March 3, 2004, at p. 528.

addictive, toxic drug. They soon documented that, depending on how it is inhaled – whether in short or long puffs – it can either act as a stimulant or a tranquilliser.[6] These psychoactive qualities were a potential aid to productivity because they improved endurance, at least in the short run, and eased the burdens of job-related stress. In time, employers adopted a variety of practices that facilitated the worker – addict's access to this performance enhancing drug. Thus, by the early 20th century, cigarette vending machines and ashtrays were fixtures in most US workplaces and, where cigarette smoking posed too great a safety hazard or encumbered work performance, smoke breaks and smoking rooms or areas became an accepted part of the work schedule and environment.

History of responses to tobacco's health hazards

Early in the 20th century, state and local governments generally recognized three hazards of tobacco consumption. One was the fire risk created by burning or smouldering tobacco. In response, many laws and regulations were adopted prohibiting smoking in public places that were considered particularly suscepti-ble to massive injuries resulting from conflagrations ignited by lit tobacco pro-ducts. Similar regulations were adopted to keep these sources of ignition away from highly flammable chemicals or materials. However, such fire-safety regula-tions tended to be confined to those situations where the dangers were most evident.[7] Accordingly, although smoking might be prohibited in those parts of theatres that had upholstered chairs or draperies, it was permitted in other theatre sections. In like regard, although smoking was prohibited adjacent to a gasoline pump, it was permitted where the cashier was located inside the gaso-line station, a place where, typically, tobacco products were sold. Hence, these safety regulations did little to protect workers from exposure to tobacco smoke.

Tobacco use often increases the need to expectorate, especially if the tobacco is chewed. Therefore, a second recognized hazard of tobacco use was the spread of disease. Based on this danger, some restraint upon tobacco use resulted from the adoption of state and local laws that prohibited spitting on sidewalks and on the floors of public hallways or similar places.

Finally, both for cultural reasons and, undoubtedly as an implicit recognition of the apparent health hazard, many state and local governments prohibited the sale of tobacco products to children. The minimum age for lawful purchases often was set as low as 14, though sometimes it was high as 18. Enforcement was difficult, however, and generally not stringent. Merchants often were content to make the sale to a child who claimed that the purchase was for a parent or older sibling. With the spread of cigarette vending machines, enforcement became futile despite warnings on the machines prohibiting purchases by minors.[8]

In the 1950s, research was detecting clear links between smoking and the risks of coronary artery disease; chronic bronchitis; emphysema; and cancer of

---

[6]   *Encyclopedia Britannica* above, at "Nicotine".

[7]   For a modern example of such legislation, *see* Michigan Comp. Laws § 408.820 which bans smoking on elevators.

[8]   More recent laws have given special emphasis to banning smoking in schools. *See*, for example, Tex. Penal Code § 48.01.

the lungs, bladder, oral cavity, and oesophagus. In response, the leading companies in the tobacco industry created the Council for Tobacco Research which held itself out as an objective research entity. The Council's activities concentrated on questioning the link between tobacco use and disease. It asserted that leading research authorities had not found reliable proof that cigarette smoking is a cause of lung cancer. Based on the Council's reports, the tobacco industry insisted that the research which asserted that smoking was harmful was flawed science and at best inconclusive.

A decade later, associations of people opposed to smoking, supported by organized medical professionals and some federal government agencies, became more vocal in calling for government intervention to combat the epidemic of tobacco related illness and death. The tobacco industry continued to rebuff most efforts to curb smoking and succeeded in reducing the effectiveness of the few anti-smoking efforts which gained government support. The industry's ability to limit legislative efforts was based, in part, on the fact that it was an important source of political campaign contributions which had especially strong influence with legislative representatives from the several states in which tobacco was a key cash crop or where cigarette and cigar factories employed large numbers of workers.[9] In no small part, the industry was aided by the millions of nicotine addicts who regarded the reformers as alarmists and the proposed restrictions as an affront to their individual liberty.

In the mid-1960s, although continuing to issue statements denying that there was reliable proof that smoking is a health hazard, US cigarette manufacturers attempted to quiet the anti-smoking forces by placing on cigarette packs a message cautioning the purchaser that "cigarette smoking may be hazardous to your health". Congress was not satisfied with this voluntary approach and in the law known as the Federal Cigarette Labelling and Advertising Act (FCLAA),[10] soon authorized the Federal Trade Commission to adopt regulations requiring the inclusion of such a statement on cigarette packs. In 1970, the warning label regulations were strengthened to read: "The Surgeon General has determined that smoking is dangerous to your health". The next year, the Federal Communications Commission was given statutory authority to enforce a new Congressional ban on advertising cigarettes and little cigars by means of electronic communications.[11] Most importantly, this removed advertising from one of the most effective merchandizing methods in American culture – commercial television.

The mounting evidence of the toll smoking was taking on the health of Americans, and the evident persistence of nicotine addiction, was accompanied by increased professional and public voices calling for a more determined governmental effort to discourage or end tobacco consumption. In 1984 Congress

---

[9]   This influence was enhanced by the fact that many of these legislators came from states in which office holders tended to stay in office for long periods with the result that under the seniority system generally followed in Congress, many of the "tobacco state" legislators held very important committee and sub-committee chairs. Under House and Senate rules, these presiding positions provide considerable power because of the chair's direct or indirect ability to control the agenda, the selection of committee staff, and the determination of when the committee meets and adjourns.

[10] P.L. 89–92, adopted July 27, 1965, effective January 1, 1966.

[11] 5 USC § 1335. V.K. Viscusi, *Smoke-filled Rooms: A Postmortem on the Tobacco Deal*, Univ. Chicago Press, 2002, at p. 138. The statute carefully defined both items.

adopted a modified mandatory cigarette labelling law and specified the size and placement of new warning language not only for cigarette packs, but also for billboards and other advertisements. Under the new law, the required warning had to contain one of the following the statements: "SURGEON GENERAL'S WARNING: Smoking Causes Lung Cancer, Heart Disease, Emphysema, and May Complicate Pregnancy"; "SURGEON GENERAL'S WARNING: Quitting Smoking Now Greatly Reduces Serious Risks to Your Health"; "SURGEON GENERAL'S WARNING: Smoking By Pregnant Women May Result in Foetal Injury, Premature Birth, and Low Birth Weight"; or "SURGEON GENERAL'S WARNING: Cigarette Smoke Contains Carbon Monoxide". The legislation provided for these warning labels to be rotated under a regulated schedule.[12] Thus, these strengthened warnings, alerting the public to the health hazards of smoking, became the widespread accompaniment of cigarette ads on billboards and in newspapers and magazines.

On the other hand, the new legislation also included a provision pre-empting the states from imposing any further restrictions on the advertising or promotion of cigarettes.[13] The Supreme Court of the United States has ruled that this last provision prevents a state from adopting such laws as prohibiting billboards within 1,000 feet of a school. On the other hand, the Court noted that the federal law does not prevent a state or local government from enforcing zoning regulations that restrict the size and location of billboards that advertise tobacco products so long as the same restrictions apply to billboard advertisements of all other commercial products. In addition, the Court ruled that the pre-emptive effect of federal regulations does not prevent a state or local government from regulating conduct involving sale or use of cigarettes, such as prohibiting the sale of cigarettes to minors or requiring that tobacco products be placed outside the reach of customers so that sales personnel will be able to prevent minors from having access to them.[14] Although the Court observed that the federal law does not pre-empt state regulation or prohibition against advertising of other tobacco products such as cigars, pipe tobacco, or chewing tobacco, it ruled that the Constitutional protection of free expression prohibits a state from restricting the advertising of these lawful products in a manner that was too broad to be justified by the state's interest in protecting minors from being enticed to adopt the habit.[15]

Probably the first major success in directly curbing smoking was achieved in 1973 when, as is discussed in more detail in section 2, below, a federal regulation was adopted which required larger commercial passenger airplanes to provide a no-smoking section for each class of service. Six years later, this restriction was expanded to a requirement that no-smoking sections on airplanes be large enough to accommodate all passengers wishing to sit in that area. The same federal administrative order mandated additional separation of pipe and cigar smokers from the no-smoking area, and provided that smoking

---

[12] 15 US Code § 1333.
[13] 15 US Code § 1334.
[14] *Lorillard Tobacco Company v. Reilly*, 533 US 525, 550–51, 569(2001).
[15] *Lorillard Tobacco Company v. Reilly*, 533 US 525, 565 (2001). For example, because of the free speech protection, a state cannot prohibit billboards that advertise a brand of cigars within 1000 feet of a school if the advertisement is not specifically directed at children. Nor can a state prohibit a store from advertising the fact that it sells cigars.

was to be totally banned when ventilation systems did not adequately prevent smoke from reaching the no-smoking area. It is interesting that representatives of the airline industry challenged the adoption of these rules even though they would save the airlines the cost of providing and maintaining ash receptacles, reduce fire hazards, and eliminate damage to upholstery and occasional injury to flight attendants and passengers from stray glowing ashes.[16] Finally, as detailed in section 2, below, as a result of additional changes, since 1990 federal law prohibits all smoking during all phases of commercial passenger flights.

In recent years, many state legislatures, in an effort both to increase revenues and discourage smoking, especially by younger persons, have increased significantly the excise tax imposed on tobacco products and have pressed for better enforcement of age restrictions on purchasing such items. In 2000 the federal excise tax was US$ 0·39 per pack and the state excise tax per pack, was as high as US$ 1.00. In addition, cigarettes generally are subject to a state sales tax that, though varying by state and municipality, typically ranges somewhere between 5 and 8%.

Employer responses to new awareness of smoking hazards

By the 1970s a number of health oriented professional organizations, charities formed to combat particular diseases, and associations of persons opposed to the costs, discomforts, dirt and unsightliness caused by tobacco use, undertook efforts to educate the public concerning tobacco related health hazards, encourage smokers to free themselves from their addiction, and urge government officials to discourage, limit or eliminate tobacco use. Until well into the 1980s, these efforts to discourage smoking had little impact in the workplace. However, in the 1980s, the persistence of anti-smoking organizations and the expanding public dissemination by healthcare professional organizations of information concerning the ever more persuasive evidence of the health hazards of tobacco use began to have some impact on state and local legislatures and governmental executives. As detailed in section 2, below, these efforts resulted in some governmental bodies adopting laws or regulations prohibiting or restricting smoking in government buildings or, in some instances, in other public places. These prohibitions, of course, benefit those employed in such places by enabling them to avoid exposure to the hazards of tobacco smoke. Additionally, the inconveniences of maintaining the nicotine habit while employed in such places no doubt has encouraged many to take the necessary steps to overcome their addiction.

In addition to laws curbing smoking, as explained in section 3, below, by the 1990s increasing numbers of employers were discovering that there were significant cost savings to be gained from discouraging tobacco use. As a result, many adopted restrictions on smoking during work and some even attempted to prohibit all tobacco use by their employees.

---

[16] The history of the initial regulations was reviewed and the 1979 regulation was upheld in *Action on Smoking and Health v. Cab*, 699 F.2d 1209 (DC Cir. 1983).

Law suits challenging the tobacco industry

Another strategy adopted by individuals and anti-smoking organizations in the 1980s was to try to enlist judicial help in an effort to combat the health epidemic caused by tobacco consumption. Suits were brought seeking damages from cigarette manufacturers for the injuries and death that smoking caused to individuals. Key issues in such suits was whether the tobacco industry deceptively promoted nicotine addiction, whether smokers knowingly and voluntarily undertook the health risks, and whether smoking in fact caused the smoker's illness. Although dozens of suits had been brought against cigarette manufacturers, by the mid-1990s the industry had successfully defended against each of them.[17] The suits were unsuccessful due to lack of clear proof that tobacco companies took deliberate steps to addict people to smoking, the inability of smokers to credibly deny that they were aware of the health risks involved in tobacco use, and the inability of the smokers' lawyers to prove that smoking, rather than other health risks, including other sources of environmental pollution, caused the particular illness or death. The publicity of the suits, however, helped focus attention on the health hazards of tobacco use. Moreover, as detailed in section 1, below, starting in the last decade of the 20th century, state prosecutors and private attorneys gained important victories through the strategy of tort suits aimed at recovering damages for the harms smoking causes to non smokers as well as to smokers.

Current data on health and smoking in the US

According to the National Cancer Institute, a federal government agency, tobacco smoke has more than 3,000 chemicals.[18] At least 60 of those chemicals are carcinogens, including formaldehyde, nitrosamines, polycyclic aromatic hydrocarbons and benzopyrene. Tobacco smoke also has six toxins that affect cell health, including nicotine and carbon monoxide, and additional toxins that promote cell mutation or are tissue irritants. Not only are these chemicals inhaled by the smoker, about half of the generated smoke, containing much the same compounds, drifts into the air surrounding the smoker and any place where the smoke is circulated without the intervention of adequate filtration. The smoke that is not inhaled by the smoker is variously referred to as environmental tobacco smoke, sidestream smoke, second-hand smoke, secondary smoke, passive smoke, or involuntary smoke, and the compounds in that smoke are inhaled and absorbed by everyone in the affected environment.

The National Centre for Chronic Disease Prevention and Health Promotion, an agency of the federal government, issued a report in 2001[19]

---

[17] V.K. Viscusi, *Smoke-filled Rooms: A Postmortem on the Tobacco Deal*, Univ. Chicago Press, 2002, at p. 3.

[18] A report jointly issued by two federal agencies and two professional organizations, states that 4000 chemicals are found in the vapour and particle stages of tobacco smoke. American Lung Association, Environmental Protection Agency, Consumer Product Safety Commission, & American Medical Association, *Indoor Air Pollution: An Introduction for Health Professionals*, undated, at p. 5. The report is available at: http://www.epa.gov/iedweb00/pubs/images/indoor_-air_pollution.pdf.

[19] Report: "Cigarette Smoking Related Mortality".

estimating that in the US men who smoke are 22 times more likely to die from lung cancer than are male non smokers. For women who smoke the lung cancer death risk is nearly 12 times that of women who do not smoke. The risk of death from bronchitis and emphysema is almost ten times greater for male smokers and more than ten times greater for female smokers than for their non-smoking counterparts. In addition, the report states that in the US smoking increases threefold the likelihood that a middle-age man or woman will die from heart disease.

When the US Environmental Protection Agency examined this health issue in 1992 and, based on more than 30 epidemiologic studies, found that around 3,000 Americans die each year from lung cancer related to second-hand tobacco smoke. In addition it stated that environmental tobacco smoke increases childhood risks of serious lower respiratory tract infections, such as pneumonia and bronchitis; increases the on-set, frequency, and severity of symptoms in asthmatic children; and is related to higher incidence of childhood middle ear disease. The Agency concluded that "the widespread exposure to environmental tobacco smoke in the US presents a serious and substantial public health risk".[20]

The efforts to reduce smoking in the US have had some notable success. Information gathered by World Health Organization reports that the average annual per capita cigarette consumption in the United States in 2000 was 58% of the average rate thirty years earlier. (That is, 42% fewer cigarettes were consumed per capita.) The portion of adults who smoked was 23 3% in 2000 (men – 25·7%, women – 21%). In comparison, in 1970, 40·2% of the adult US population were cigarette smokers. The portion of youths estimated to have been cigarette smokers in 2000 was 23·1% (males – 26%, females – 20·1%).[21] Assuming, that most smokers begin as youths and many 'kick-the-habit' as adults, further significant declines in the ratio of adult cigarette smokers can be anticipated in the next couple of decades.

The number of deaths attributed to smoking peaked for males in the mid-1970s at 157 per thousand; for females the peak was twenty years later at 75 per thousand. Among other things, the data reflects the changing cultural patterns between the conduct of men and women in American society. In earlier generations there was a significantly higher frequency than today of men smoking than of women smoking, and male smokers typically consumed more cigarettes per day than female smokers.[22]

1.   THE RIGHT TO THE PROTECTION OF HEALTH

The fundamental rights of Americans are stated in the federal and state constitutions. These express principles do not specify the right to a healthy life or a healthy environment.

---

[20]   Environmental Protection Agency, Report: "Respiratory Health Effects of Passive Smoking: Lung Cancer and Other Disorders", 1992, Document 600–6–90–006F.

[21]   The National Cancer Centre reports a 1999 multi-state survey of students under age 18, which indicated that this figure may be low. That study found a high of 36% of high school students reporting cigarette smoking in Tennessee and a low of 25'2% reporting cigarette smoking in Florida. Much, of course, depends on what is asked and how cigarette smoking is defined. "Have you ever smoked a cigarette?" will no doubt give a higher figure than "Have you smoked two or more cigarettes during the past seven days?".

[22]   World Health Organization, Report: "Tobacco Control Country Profiles 2003, 2d Ed.".

Legislatures, however, have the responsibility to adopt laws promoting the general welfare. With the health risks of water, air, and food pollution becoming more pronounced and more evident, as discussed in sections 2 and 3, below, in recent years federal, state, and local legislatures have adopted laws designed to reduce exposure to contaminants including those created by tobacco use. Similar steps have been taken by some governmental executives, such as state Governors and municipal Mayors, under their authority to regulate the use and operation of public property.

In addition, American jurisprudence includes the right to remedies for injuries from intentional or careless molestation – the right to not be harmed by others. As previously noted, initially lawyers were unsuccessful in their efforts to get courts to award damages for illness caused to smokers or to non-smokers' who have had to live, work or visit smoke-filled environments. However, in the early 1990s, a new legal strategy was undertaken by a group of state attorneys-general[23] who brought a series of suits to recover from the tobacco industry the increased costs to the states of providing medical assistance to the elderly and indigent due to the higher overall medical expenses of caring for smokers. Since the states had not undertaken the risks of smoking[24] and it was not necessary to prove that smoking was the causal factor in any particular individual's illness, the central issue in making these suits factually credible was establishing that the industry was both aware of the health hazards of its product and had adopted strategies to promote and perpetuate nicotine addiction. The effort to recover against the tobacco companies was greatly aided when a high ranking tobacco company researcher revealed that in fact these were conscious policies of his company and others in the industry. He identified corporate documents that corroborated this assertion and showed that the tobacco companies had pursued these policies for at least thirty years.[25]

The tobacco companies sought to exclude this new evidence on the ground that the documents were illegally taken in violation of the researcher's confidentiality agreement with his employer. However, a Congressional Committee required the production of the documents for its own investigation of the issue of the health hazards of smoking and to demonstrate that the top executives of the tobacco companies had lied in earlier testimony to the Committee. Whether the courts would bar the documents obtained from the researcher in breach of his confidentiality agreement no longer posed a serious barrier to the proof needed in the suits by the states; the documents were now available as a result of Congress' investigation.[26]

---

[23] The Attorney General is an elected state official charged with representing the state's legal interests including prosecuting crimes.

[24] A potential defence that remained, however, was the fact that the states had not outlawed smoking. Arguably, the states had thereby undertaken the known risks of higher healthcare costs for nicotine addicts who became partially or wholly dependant on government paid medical care.

[25] S. Glantz, J. Slade, L. Bero, *et al.*, *The Cigarette Papers*, 1996, Univ. of California Press, at pp, 6–14.

[26] Even if the tobacco company would have been permitted to protect its internal secrets from such a "misuse", an assertion that would not necessarily have been honoured by most courts, the tobacco company could not, through its confidentiality agreement, prevent a legislative committee from conducting an investigation of its records to ascertain whether prior testimony by corporate officers was perjured.

In time, the tobacco industry settled the law suits brought by the states. Separate settlements were reached with four states after which a Master Settlement Agreement involving the tobacco companies and the remaining states was negotiated and signed in 1998. Together with the earlier settlements, the tobacco companies agreed to pay almost US$ 243,000,000,000. The payments were spread over 25 years with each of the tobacco companies being required to contribute a specified amount per pack of cigarettes sold by it – in effect, a tax on current smokers. In addition, the tobacco companies agreed to no longer use advertisements targeted at children, eliminate the use of cartoon characters in their advertisements, not use billboard advertisements, cease engaging in political lobbying designed to resist legislation aimed at reducing youth smoking, not allow tobacco brand names to be used on other merchandise, and not provide youths with free samples of their products.[27]

The settlement appears to have given encouragement for a new wave of individual suits by alleged victims of smoking and these suits have had more success than those decided prior to the Master Settlement Agreement.[28] In addition, still pending against the tobacco industry is a suit brought by the federal government in 1999 seeking $289,000,000,000 in damages. This suit is based on the premise that, in violation of a federal anti-racketeering statute, the industry schemed to defraud children by undertaking marketing campaigns designed to entice them into becoming smokers even though they were too young to legally purchase or use tobacco products.[29]

2. SMOKING BANS IN GENERAL – ENFORCEMENT AND COMPLIANCE

Nicotine as an addictive but unregulated drug

In the US most known addictive drugs are either illegal or their use is regulated. The federal Food and Drug Administration (FDA) has the authority to regulate drugs and devices for administering drugs. The governing statute defines drugs as including non food articles intended to affect the body's structure or function. In 1995, the FDA, for the first time, announced its intention to regulate tobacco use. Its subsequent ruling, in 1996, explained that tobacco use is addictive, is

---

[27] V.K. Viscusi, *Smoke-filled Rooms: A Postmortem on the Tobacco Deal*, Univ. Chicago Press, 2002, at p. 33, 38. The Settlement also required the three major tobacco companies to annually provide US$ 300,000,000 to finance a non profit organization's campaign to educate children against smoking. The obligation was conditioned on these companies maintaining at least 99.05% of the market share. In 2003 they reported that because their share had declined to less than 93%, they would cease providing those funds. *Denver Post*, March 17, 2004, at p. 4A.

[28] V.K. Viscusi, above, at pp. 45–58. *See*, for example, *Broin v. Philip Morris Companies Inc.*, 641 So2d 888 (Fla. App., 3d Dist. 1994), a damages suit by flight attendants, which was settled for a US$ 300,000,000 payment to establish a research foundation to study the effects of second-hand smoke, plus US$ 49,000,000 reimbursement of expenses and payment of lawyers' fees. In addition, an undisclosed amount, described only as several hundred thousand dollars, was paid to a few flight attendants who had objected to the lack of individual damages being included in the settlement. J. Oliphant, "Lawyers Net US$ 50 Million in Florida Flight Attendants' Second-Hand Smoke Class Action," *The Legal Intelligencer*, September 22, 1999, at p. 4.

[29] *US v. Philip Morris Inc* 2004 US Dist. *Lexis* 2663 (D. DC 2004).

very dangerous to human health, and that over 80% of smokers had their first cigarette prior to age 18 and over half were regular smokers by that age. It then adopted a series of regulations designed to combat smoking by youths. These included prohibiting sale of cigarettes or smokeless tobacco to persons under age 18, requiring a photo identification from purchasers younger than 27, prohibit the sale of cigarettes in quantities smaller than 20, prohibit the distribution of free samples, and prohibit sales through self-service displays and vending machines except in adult-only locations. There were also restrictions on the manner in which these products could be advertised and promoted. Tobacco product manufacturers and retailers challenged the FDA's statutory authority to regulate tobacco distribution and persuaded a 5–4 majority of the Supreme Court that the regulations were beyond the scope of the FDA's authority. The prevailing opinion of the Court was that the authority of the FDA was always understood to be aimed at dealing with drugs that make therapeutic claims and that Congress did not intend to regulate tobacco through the same mechanisms used to regulate distribution and use of other drugs.[30]

No smoking rules on commercial aircraft

The previously noted decision of the Civil Aeronautics Board[31] to adopt a regulation requiring larger commercial passenger airplanes to provide a no-smoking section for each class of service did not come at the initiative of health conscious government officers; rather, it came at the initiative of an anti-smoking group, Action on Smoking and Health (ASH). ASH was not content with that opening victory. It pressed for the total elimination of smoking on air carriers and for measures to ensure rigorous enforcement of all smoking restrictions. The Department of Transportation adopted regulations in 1990 that prohibit all smoking on all scheduled commercial passenger flights, and also require that a lighted "no smoking" sign be visible to every passenger during every segment of a flight, that passengers be orally briefed at the beginning of the flight regarding the prohibition against smoking, and that passengers be warned that it is a federal offence punishable by a fine of up to US$ 2000 to tamper with airplane lavatory smoke detectors.[32] These regulations, of course,

---

[30]   *Food and Drug Administration v. Brown & Williamson Tobacco Co.*, 529 US 120 (2000). In its conclusion, the Court's opinion explained: "Owing to its unique place in American history and society, tobacco has its own unique political history. Congress, for better or for worse, has created a distinct regulatory scheme for tobacco products, squarely rejected proposals to give the FDA jurisdiction over tobacco, and repeatedly acted to preclude any agency from exercising significant policymaking authority in the area. Given this history and the breadth of the authority that the FDA has asserted, we are obliged to defer not to the agency's expansive construction of the statute, but to Congress' consistent judgment to deny the FDA this power." 529 US at 159–60.

[31]   The responsibilities of the Civil Aeronautics Board were transferred to the Department of Transportation on January 1, 1985.

[32]   Congress implicitly ratified these regulations in 1994 when it passed a law prohibiting smoking on all scheduled air passenger flights except those of more than six hours' duration. An amendment adopted in 2000 eliminated the six hour exception and provided for negotiated limitations on smoking aboard foreign carriers flying passengers to or from the US if the foreign government objects to the total ban. 49 US Code 41706.

are even more protective of the flight crews' health, than they are of passenger health inasmuch as the crews otherwise are constantly exposed to tobacco smoke hazards during their working hours.

However, the federal air transportation regulations do not eliminate all flight crew smoking. Exceptions allow the captain of an airplane to authorize smoking in the flight-crew compartment if it is separated from the passenger compartment and either the plane is not in motion on the ground, is not in the process of taking-off or landing, and passengers are not aboard. Similarly, except during take-off or landing, the captain may authorize smoking in a separated flight-crew compartment of an airplane that is not turbojet powered, holds fewer than 30 passengers, and is flying solely within a single state.[33] The airline or the charter, of course, can prohibit its captains from exercising this option.

It is rare to encounter a passenger who tries to violate the no smoking rules aboard an airplane and airline personnel (and many fellow passengers) vigorously enforce these rules when there is a violation.

American airports have joined in the effort to protect non smokers from involuntary exposure to tobacco smoke. Typically smoking is confined to specified areas (often bars) or smoking rooms. However, not all such areas have sufficiently separated ventilation to provide a total protection against such exposure.

Other public transportation

Interestingly, passenger railroads in the US traditionally confined smokers to special cars, thus protecting non smokers from sidestream pollutants. Railroad workers, nevertheless, did not have such protection unless they were assigned solely to cars in which smoking was prohibited. Since 1991 smoking has been prohibited on buses carrying passengers between states. However, the federal regulations do not extend to the bus terminals.[34] In many states, nevertheless, state or local laws restricting smoking in public buildings or places of public accommodation (see below) prohibit smoking or segregate smokers from non smokers.[35]

Federal buildings

Through its regulatory power in operating and controlling property owned by the federal government, in the 1980s the General Services Administration (GSA), an agency of the Executive Branch charged with operating and maintaining government buildings, adopted a regulation requiring agencies using government buildings for non residential purposes to establish smoking areas

---

[33]   14 Code of Fed. Reg. §§ 23.791, 23.853, 129.29, 121.317, 135.117, 135.127, 252.3. On flights that are chartered to fly "on-demand", as contrasted with scheduled flights, there are additional minor exceptions to the general prohibition against smoking on commercial flights. The regulation does not provide a justification for the exceptions.

[34]   49 Code of Fed. Reg. §§ 374.201, 374.309.

[35]   Although separation of passengers is prohibited based on race, colour, creed, or national origin, there is no prohibition against separation based on smoking. 49 Code of Fed. Reg. § 374.113.

so as to protect non smokers from unwanted exposure to tobacco smoke. In the 1997, pursuant to Executive Order 13058, the GSA broadened the restriction to prohibit smoking in interior spaces owned or rented by executive agencies of the federal government or in outdoor areas in front of building air intakes. Indoor smoking is to be allowed in designated areas from which air is exhausted directly to the outside, and away from air intake ducts, and in which negative air pressure is maintained so that indoor air drifts into rather than out of that area. In addition, workers cannot be required to enter such designated areas during business hours while anyone is smoking.[36]

State and local no smoking laws

State, county, and municipal governments have been leaders in adopting laws prohibiting smoking, especially in government owned or leased buildings. In some localities the restrictions involve a total prohibition on indoor smoking, in others the regulations confine smoking to designated places set aside for smokers. Total bans on smoking often are accompanied by prohibitions against smoking within a designated distance of building entrances. Typically these laws apply to buildings that house government employees, provide government services, and to government operated public facilities such as concert halls, auditoriums, libraries, schools, and local transportation vehicles and terminals.[37]

In addition, states, county, and municipal governments have imposed similar regulations on privately operated places of public accommodation. Such laws have particularly targeted restaurants and bars. Although the political campaigns leading to the adoption of such laws have mainly focused on public health, protecting the health of employees who work in these businesses is among the arguments posed in support of such measures.

Owners of restaurants and bars often are actively opposed to restrictions on smoking. Often their employees, especially those who are smokers, voluntarily join in that opposition. A key argument is that smokers will cease patronizing their businesses. Many in the restaurant and liquor sales industry believe that smokers drink more alcohol and are better tippers than non smokers, so that loss of their patronage will significantly hurt the industry. The counter-argument is that there are more non smokers than smokers, that many non smokers will patronize these businesses more frequently if no longer subjected to sidestream tobacco smoke, that non smokers are not less generous in their tipping or less active in their drinking. Two studies of the revenues of restaurants and bars before and after a total ban was imposed on smoking in their locations found that revenues, as reflected in sales taxes paid by such establishments, continued to grow after the smoking ban was imposed.[38] Since tipping in the US normally is a customary percentage of the patron's bill, apparently neither the owners nor service personnel would have lost income as a result of the change.

---

[36]   41 Code of Fed. Reg. §§ 102.74.320 to 102.74.345.
[37]   For example, *see* Kan. Stat. § 72–53,107; Mass. Gen. Laws 272:§ 43A; Michigan Comp. Laws §§ 333.12601, 333.12905, 750.473, Exec. Order 1992–3; Ohio Rev. Code § 3791.031; Wash. Rev. Code § 70.160.010, Wash. Admin. Code § 296–62–12000.
[38]   *Denver Post* February 13, 2004 at p. 19A.

The American Non-smokers' Rights Foundation advocates, in favour of total bans on smoking, in enclosed workplaces, restaurants and bars. It maintains a survey of localities that have adopted such total bans and reports that as of the beginning of 2004, three states (Delaware,[39] New York[40] and Florida[41]) and over 90 cities or counties in the US had adopted such bans. Most of the latter were in California and Massachusetts but several were in Arizona, Colorado, Oregon, Texas and West Virginia. Perhaps most notable of the local bans was in Honolulu, Hawaii. Four states (California,[42] Connecticut,[43] Maine[44] and Utah[45]), and over 50 cities or counties in other states, were listed as having total bans on smoking in restaurants. (The California and Maine laws prohibit smoking in bars as well as restaurants.) Boston and Dallas are the two largest cities on the list of localities that ban restaurant smoking, but the most interesting city on the list is Lexington, Kentucky, since Lexington is a major centre for marketing and warehousing tobacco. The Foundation also listed the state of South Dakota as prohibiting smoking in enclosed workplaces.[46]

Additionally, some states impose partial restrictions on smoking in places of public accommodation, such as restaurants, or in enclosed workplaces, so as to ensure that non smokers are subject to reduced exposure to second-hand smoke.[47] Some of these laws, or the regulations adopted pursuant to the law, include detailed air quality standards to ensure that smoke-free areas are not polluted by smoke drifting from rooms or areas where smoking is permitted.[48]

The number of state and local governments adopting anti-smoking laws has grown rapidly since the mid-1990s and anti-smoking laws are currently under consideration in many jurisdictions.[49]

3.   SMOKING AND THE WORKPLACE

Occupational safety and health law

The federal Occupational Safety and Health Act (OSHA), adopted in 1970, was intended to "to assure so far as possible every working man and woman in the Nation safe and healthful working conditions".[50] OSHA requires an employer

---

[39]   Del. Code Title 16, § 2901.

[40]   NY Pub. Health Law §§ 1399-n to 1399-s.

[41]   Fla. Stat. Ch. §§ 386.201–386.205.

[42]   Ca Labour Code § 6404.5.

[43]   Conn. Gen. Stat. § 19a-342.

[44]   Me Rev. Stat. Tit. 22, § 1541.

[45]   Utah Code § 26–38–1.

[46]   The Foundation regularly updates its lists which can be found on the internet at www.no-smoke.org/lists. A similar federal government operated web site can be found at: http://www2.cdc.gov/nccdphp/osh/state.

[47]   *See* for example, Conn. Gen. Stat. § 31–40q, Mich. Comp. Laws § 333.12905, Wash. Admin. Code § 296–62–12000, Wash. Rev. Code §§ 70.160.010.

[48]   *See* for example, Minnesota Rules §§ 4620.0400, .0750, .0955.

[49]   To illustrate, this last sentence was written on February 18, 2004 in Summit County, Colorado. A ban on restaurant smoking was adopted the previous evening by governing council of Dillon, Colorado, one of four townships in the county. Similar proposals were pending before the governing councils of the county and each of the county's other three townships.

[50]   29 US Code § 651(b).

to "furnish to each of his employees employment and a place of employment which are free from recognized hazards that are causing or are likely to cause death or serious physical harm to his employees". Additionally, it authorizes the Secretary of Labour to adopt Occupational Safety and Health Standards which require conditions "reasonably necessary or appropriate to provide safe or healthful employment and places of employment". Both employers and employees are required by OSHA to comply with those Standards.[51] Importantly, the Department of Labour's Occupational Safety and Health Administration has sole authority to enforce the federal Act. Individual suits may not be brought to enforce the rights declared by the federal Act or to enforce the Standards established under the Act. Thus, there is no remedy for violations unless the Occupational Safety and Health Administration decide to treat a particular working condition as a violation of the Act.

Based on the above statutory language, there are two possible types of OSHA violations. The first, referred to as a General Duty Clause violation, is failure to furnish a place of employment free from "recognized hazards that are causing or are likely to cause death or serious physical harm". The second type of violation is failure to abide by a safety or health Standard that was adopted by the Secretary of Labour.

Case law holds that to prove a violation of the General Duty Clause, the Occupational Safety and Health Administration must show that the condition or activity in question is known by the employer or is generally known in the industry to pose a danger of serious harm.[52] It would seem obvious that the pronouncements by federal public health officials, such as the Surgeon General and the US Environmental Protection Agency, regarding the link between serious diseases and smoking or exposure to sidestream smoke would be a sufficient basis for concluding that the dangers of smoking, both to the smoker and to those exposed to the sidestream smoke, pose a recognized danger of serious harm and, therefore, an employer that permits smoking in the workplace is in violation of the General Duty Clause. Nevertheless, the Occupational Safety and Health Administration, does not cite employers for allowing smoking at work sites unless the smoking poses a hazard of fire or explosion. A justification for not treating tolerance of workplace smoking as a violation of the General Duty Clause is that the when OSHA was adopted, the health hazards of sidestream smoke were not clearly established and Congress was still being very cautious in advising the public regarding the health hazards of smoking. Accordingly, Congress probably did not intend OSHA to suddenly become an instrument for banning workplace smoking.

On the other hand, what may not have been sufficiently clear in 1970, when OSHA was adopted, is no longer in serious doubt. A decade or two later, with the greatly increased agreement within the medical and public health professions that there is a proven link between sidestream smoke and various serious illnesses, the standard created by the General Duty Clause – removal of

---

[51] 29 US Code §§ 652(8), 654. Enforcement against employer violations involves both orders to abate the violation and civil penalties. In some instances, criminal penalties can be imposed. The Act assumes that employers will discipline employees who commit safety or health violations. No government penalties are imposed on employees for violations.

[52] *Pratt & Whitney Aircraft v. Secretary of Labor*, 649 F.2d 96 (2d Cir. 1981).

recognized hazards of serious physical harm – would appear to require administrative enforcement of the provision as a mandate that smoking no longer be tolerated in the workplace. Additionally, the fact that employers of an estimated 70% of the US workforce now impose restrictions on indoor smoking[53] further demonstrates that the hazards of smoking are known generally in all industries and, therefore, tolerance of such conduct falls within the prohibition of OSHA's General Duty Clause. Therefore, failure to pursue such enforcement can only be ascribed to lack of political courage on the part of those who have occupied the office of Secretary of Labour and subordinate policy-making positions in the Department of Labour during the past couple of decades. Their apparent fear is that a significant portion of the roughly 25% of voters who are nicotine addicts will take political retribution against the President's party should it put such direct muscle into the health campaign against smoking.

The alternative means of using OSHA to combat the workplace health hazard of exposure to the toxic fumes produced by smoking, would be to adopt an OSHA Health Standard, banning or confining workplace smoking based on a finding by the Secretary of Labour that such a ban is reasonably necessary or appropriate to provide healthful employment and places of employment. In the early 1990s, the National Institute for Occupational Safety and Health, a federal research agency established by the Occupational Safety and Health Act to advise the Secretary of Labour respecting work safety and health standards, recommended that environmental tobacco smoke is a potential occupational carcinogen and that standards should be adopted to reduce exposures to such sidestream smoke to the lowest possible levels. Anti-smoking groups similarly urged adoption of Health Standards to protect employees from sidestream tobacco smoke.

In 1994 the Department of Labour began the public hearing process to determine what Health Standards, if any, would be recommended to the Secretary of Labour. However, rather than confine its inquiry to the issue of tobacco smoke, the single most pervasive workplace air quality pollutant, the Department of Labour directed the advisory committee's inquiry to the problems posed by all indoor air contaminants. The Action on Smoking and Health (ASH) organization condemned that strategy as unnecessarily complicating the issue and characterized the government's inquiry as "ranging from mold to chicken feathers". The resulting public hearings, at which over 400 witnesses testified, continued for over six months, and when it concluded the record consisted of more than 335,000 pages.

Although OSHA establishes time limits for the appointed advisory committee to reach a recommendation in such proceedings, the deadlines passed without a recommendation being made. ASH sued to try to force a decision on the smoking issue by the agency but the federal court accepted the Department of Labour's argument that because various airborne contaminants potentially share the same or similar ventilation and control problems, it was reasonable for the government agency to examine these issues together. The court also ruled that the statutory time limits, which in their text appear to be mandatory, are mere goals and, therefore, the court would not order the Department to

---

[53] The Department of Labour, itself, has cited this figure. US Department of Labour News Release 01–476, Dec. 14, 2001.

make a prompt decision regarding a Health Standard respecting smoking in the workplace.[54]

Indeed, the Department of Labour never did adopt an OSHA Health Standard restricting workplace smoking.[55] The closest it has come to protecting workers from sidestream smoke is a regulation that prohibits smoking when parties are conducting a deposition in connection with an OSHA hearing.[56] The Department officially withdrew the prospective Indoor Air Quality Standard on 14 December 2001 over seven years after the process had been initiated. In doing so, the Department stated that its decision had the support of major anti-smoking groups, including the American Heart Association, the American Cancer Society, the American Lung Association, Americans for Non-smokers' Rights, and the Campaign for Tobacco-Free Kids. The announcement also asserted that the Health Standard no longer was needed because local law and voluntary employer actions were resolving the issue. In support of this contention, the Department's announcement cited the American Lung Association's estimate that almost 70% of Americans are now employed in businesses that have a smoke-free workplace policy.[57] That reasoning, of course, is a shallow cover for the previously noted fear of political retribution from voters who are addicted to nicotine. The fact that the employers of almost 70% of US workers act responsibly with respect to protecting their workers' health is no excuse for allowing the other 30% to act irresponsibly. For example, the fact that gas masks are voluntarily provided by the vast majority of employers whose workers are potentially exposed to toxic fumes surely would not be an acceptable explanation for the Department of Labour to decline to adopt a Standard requiring all employers to make such masks available for the protection of endangered workers.

Leaders of the anti-smoking groups that urged the Department of Labour to drop the procedure for adopting the Indoor Air Standard had a different explanation for their support of that action. They expressed fear that, under the Bush administration, the Department of Labour would adopt a weak standard which would be worse than no standard at all.[58] The expressed fear was that the

---

[54] *Action on Smoking and Health (ASH) v. Department of Labor*, 100 F. 3d 991 (DC Cir. 1996). *See*, also, the denial for reconsideration where Judge Wald expressed concern that the agency not treat the decision as excusing it from proceeding with deliberate speed to reach a decision. 107 F.3d 901, 903 (DC Cir. 1997). The willingness of the court to accede to the delay reflected far greater judicial deference to the Department than to Congress which, in setting a time limit for making recommendations specified that the advisory committee "shall submit to the Secretary its recommendations regarding the rule to be promulgated within ninety days from the date of its appointment or within such longer or shorter period as may be prescribed by the Secretary, but in no event for a period which is longer than two hundred and seventy days." 29 US Code 655(b)(1).

[55] It has adopted OSHA Safety Standards prohibiting smoking where there is a threat of fire or explosion. *See*, for example, Standard 1910.1029(i)(5)(i) concerning the operation of coke ovens. The Department of Labour also has adopted Standards respecting exposure to other toxins which reflect its recognition that tobacco smoke exposure increases the risk that those exposed to the particular toxin will get cancer or other serious illnesses. *See*, for example, OSHA Medical Surveillance Guidelines for Asbestos – Non-Mandatory – 1910.1001 App H.

[56] 29 Code of Fed. Reg. 2200.56(h)(5).

[57] US Department of Labour News Release 01–476, Dec. 14, 2001.

[58] L. Girion, "OSHA Drops Plan for Smoke-Free Workplace", *Los Angeles Times*, Pt. 3, p. 3, Dec. 19, 2001.

standard would only partially ban indoor smoking and would pre-empt local governments from adopting more stringent restrictions.

To appreciate the expressed concern that a federal OSHA Health Standard regarding smoking might do more harm than good, it is necessary to understand that the federal Safety and Health Act allows states to adopt their own system for regulating work safety and health so long as the state scheme includes specified procedural approaches and is at least as effective as the federal programmes protections of safe and healthful employment.[59] The Department of Labour must certify a state plan as meeting these requirements.[60] About half of the states have adopted such federally certified plans. States with a certified plan would be able to adopt a total ban on workplace smoking even if the Department of Labour had a less stringent Standard respecting workplace exposure to cigarette smoke. On the other hand, and crucial to the concern of anti-smoking groups that supported withdrawal of a proposed federal regula- tion of workplace air quality, if the federal programme had a Standard respect- ing smoking at work, states that do not have a federally certified occupational safety and health programme would be prevented from adopting a more strin- gent anti-smoking requirement for workplaces.[61] Because the Department of Labour has not adopted a Standard respecting sidestream smoke in the work- place, states with federally certified occupational safety and health protection plans of their own and states without such plans both are free to prohibit workplace smoking.

To illustrate, since 1994, California, which has a federally certified occu- pational safety and health programme, has had a law generally banning work- place smoking. It provides: "No employer shall knowingly or intentionally permit, and no person shall engage in, the smoking of tobacco products in an enclosed space at a place of employment".[62] However, the California law con- tains a number of exceptions, such as the cab of a vehicle if non-smoking workers are not present, a designated smoking area of a hotel lobby or residen- tial care facility if employees are not stationed in that area, and businesses that sell tobacco products. The California law also permits, but does not require, an employer to establish smoking rooms for employees taking a rest break so long as the air is exhausted to the outside the building. Employers with five or fewer employees may establish work areas in which smoking is permitted so long as the air is exhausted to the outside and all employees in the area consent to work in that area.[63] This California law would not be affected by adoption of a less stringent federal OSHA Health Standard governing smoking.

In contrast, in 2003, New York, which does not have a federally certified occupational safety and health programme, adopted a prohibition against indoor smoking at work.[64] Although this law, too, has some exceptions, they are more limited than those in the California law.[65] Because New York does not have a federally certified state occupational safety and health law, adoption of a

---

[59]   29 US Code § 667(c)(2).

[60]   29 US Code § 667.

[61]   29 US Code § 667(a); *United Steelworkers of America v. Auchter*, 763 F.2d 728 (3d Cir. 1985).

[62]   Calif. Lab. Code § 6404.5(b).

[63]   Calif. Lab. Code §§ 6404.5(d)-(f).

[64]   NY CLS Pub Health § 1399-o.

[65]   NY CLS Pub Health § 1399-q.

less stringent federal OSHA Health Standard governing smoking would invalidate the current New York prohibition.

It should be noted, at this point, that although a Health Standard adopted under the federal OSHA statute would prevent many states from adopting their own, more restrictive, regulations against exposure to tobacco smoke at work, state and local governments probably could accomplish much the same goal by passing a broader prohibition against smoking in all buildings used for commercial purposes. Because such a law would be aimed at protecting the health of the entire community, not just employees, it should not be within the pre-emptive scope of the federal OSHA law. As we have seen in section 2, above, many states and localities have already taken this broader approach to combating the tobacco caused health epidemic.

Protection from worker impairment caused by exposure to smoke

The Americans with Disabilities Act (ADA) entitles a worker to a reasonable accommodation if he or she suffers from an impairment which substantially limits a major life activity and that disability impairs the worker's ability to perform assigned work duties. So long as the employer can make reasonable accommodations that will enable the worker to perform the principal responsibilities of the job, the disabled worker is protected from dismissal or discrimination and is entitled to receive those accommodations.[66]

The Americans with Disabilities Act has a single reference to smoking in which it states that the Act shall not be construed to preclude the adoption of prohibitions or restrictions on smoking in places of employment or other places covered by the Act.[67] The purpose of this provision is to prevent the statute from being interpreted as pre-empting states and localities from adopting no-smoking regulations. This language was a precaution because under the doctrine of pre-emption, courts sometimes decide that the comprehensive nature of federal legislation was designed to "occupy the field" and, therefore, preclude any state or local legislation whether that legislation conflicts with or is consistent with the federal regulatory scheme.[68] It can be argued that the very fact that those who drafted and approved the ADA thought it necessary to include a provision reserving the right of states and local governments to prohibit or restrict smoking indicates that they assumed that needing protection from the adverse affects of sidestream smoke is a disability under the Act and that restrictions on smoking in the workplace is an appropriate accommodation for those workers. However, the alternative explanation for the express reservation of the employer's right to adopt smoking restrictions is to eliminate the possibility that smokers might otherwise claim that their addiction is a disability that must be accommodated by ensuring them the opportunity to smoke.

In some instances, employees have asserted that due to their medical

---

[66] For a detailed description of the protections provided by this statute, *see* United States monograph in the *International Encyclopedia for Labour Law and Industrial Relations*, Kluwer, at 356–58, 360.

[67] 42 US Code § 12201(b).

[68] *Motor Coach Employees v. Lockridge*, 403 US 274 (1971); *San Diego Building Trades Council v. Garmon*, 359 US 236 (1971).

condition, they cannot perform their work functions if exposed to environmental tobacco smoke. For example, in one case, an employee sued for damages under the Act because his employer allegedly did not enforce its smoke-free workplace policy. The employee suffered from asthma and claimed he was "disabled" within the meaning of the ADA because he had great difficulty breathing when exposed to sidestream tobacco smoke. He asserted that because the employer failed to enforce the no-smoking rule, despite the employee's complaints about the impact smoking had on him, and because he was harassed by fellow workers for complaining about their smoking, he was forced to quit his job. In response to the defendant's motion to dismiss the suit, a federal trial court ruled that the employee will be entitled to relief if he succeeds in proving the truth of his allegations.[69]

The requirement of demonstrating that one is "disabled" within the US Supreme Court's interpretation of the Americans with Disabilities Act has proven to be quite formidable inasmuch as an employee must show that the impairment not only interferes with the ability to perform the job, but also that it significantly interferes with activities that are of central importance to most people's daily lives. Moreover, according to the Supreme Court, the assessment of whether the impairment is substantially limiting on engaging in activities of central importance must take account of medications and devices that mitigate the disability.[70] For example, under the Supreme Court's rulings, if the asthma sufferer in the previously described suit can maintain a reasonable level of breathing by staying away from smoke-filled restaurants and social gatherings at which people smoke, or can overcome the attacks with strong medication, he is not likely to be found protected by the Act. Thus, even if the authors of the ADA anticipated that it would be used to protect workers from being incapacitated by having to work in an environment polluted by tobacco smoke, the Supreme Court's narrow interpretation of the Act's protections leaves few workers in a position to obtain a remedy under that statute.

Damages action for injury caused by exposure to environmental smoke

When an American worker has a job related illness or injury caused by his employer or by fellow employees, the worker's claim for damages generally is limited to recovering workers' compensation insurance benefits. These benefits provide medical care and a partial replacement of lost earnings. Because the employer pays the insurance premium, employers have a motivation to discourage conduct that will give rise to such claims. Thus, the desire to reduce the costs of claims of illness caused based by a smoke-filled work environment may play a role in encouraging employers to adopt rules protecting workers from sidestream smoke. Although some workers' compensation systems reject coverage for smoke related illnesses on the ground that the legislature did not anticipate such coverage when it adopted the statute, the result can be even greater liability for the employee's smoke related injuries and, therefore, an even greater employer incentive to ban smoking.

---

[69]   *Faircloth v. Duke University*, 267 F.Supp.2d 470 (M.D.N.C. 2003).
[70]   *Toyota Motor MFG., KY., Inc. v. Williams*, 534 US 184 (2002); *Sutton v. United Air Lines, Inc.*, 527 US 471 (1999).

For example, in one case a government agency (ironically, the state health agency) refused to provide a smoke-free environment for a worker who had developed a pulmonary disease that required her to avoid environmental smoke. She claimed she was forced to quit her job because of the agency's refusal to protect here from environmental smoke. When the former worker sought workers' compensation benefits because her disability prevented her from continuing to work at the agency, the benefits were denied on the ground that the worker's pulmonary disease was not the result of an industrial accident and was not within the scope of occupational diseases recognized by the state workers' compensation law. When she then sued the agency to recover her damages resulting from its failure to provide her with a safe work environment, the state's high court ruled that she was entitled to bring that suit.[71] Had she been granted the workers' compensation benefits, she would have received disability pay equal to about two-thirds of her normal earnings and been barred from any other recovery. In contrast, if she ultimately received a judgment on her damages suit, she would be entitled to recover the full amount of her lost earnings.

Job related injuries to seafarers and railroad workers are not covered by a workers' compensation insurance system but instead are protected by the Federal Employers' Liability Act (FELA). That statute gives workers who suffer a job related injury a right to sue to recover for pain, suffering, lost earnings and medical costs if the negligence or intentional misconduct of the employer or a fellow employee contributed to the injury. Accordingly, a federal appellate court has held that a locomotive engineer who suffered severe asthma was entitled to recover damages upon proving that his employer failed to enforce its no-smoking policy with the result that the engineer suffered asthma attacks after being in crew rooms in which other workers had been smoking.[72] Because recoveries in suits under the Federal Employers' Liability Act generally are much larger than those awarded under workers' compensation insurance, the FELA provides a greater incentive for maritime and rail employers to protect workers from such avoidable injury or illness.

Judicial orders protecting workers from environmental smoke

On occasion, courts have required employers to provide a smoke-free environment for a worker whose health is severely affected by exposure to sidestream smoke. In one case a worker alleged that the tobacco smoke at work caused him to have sore throats, nausea, dizziness, headache, blackouts, loss of memory, difficulty in concentration, aches and pains in joints, sensitivity to noise and light, cold sweat, gagging, choking sensations, and light-headedness. The state court ruled that if he proved his allegations, he would be entitled to relief in the form of an injunction prohibiting his employer from exposing him to tobacco smoke in the workplace and from adversely altering his pay or employment conditions.[73]

---

[71] *McCarthy v. Department of Social and Health Services*, 759 P.2d 351 (WA. 1988).

[72] *Wilhelm v. CSX Transp., Inc* 2003 US App. *Lexis* 10864 (6 Cir. 2003).

[73] *Smith v. Western Electric Co*, 643 s.w.2D 10 (Ct. App. MO. 1982).

Voluntary employer restrictions on tobacco use

A 1987 survey of employer policies respecting workplace smoking found that only 12% prohibited smoking and about half of the rest had no regulations respecting when and where workers could smoke.[74] However, toward the end of the 1980s, companies that provided health and life insurance began taking notice of the lower costs of health insurance for non smokers, especially those who live and work in smoke-free environments. Most health insurance in the US is provided by employers with the employer paying all or a substantial part of the cost of its employees' health care. Although, many employers do not give this benefit to their employees, those that do have learned that they can lower these costs by adopting a variety of measures to reduce or eliminate smoking, in their workplaces and among their workers. Information available through the American Lung Association's web site[75] calls attention to another self-interest reason for employers to establish smoke-free workplaces. It states that studies show that smokers have twice the on-job accident rate of non smokers. Possible explanations for this difference are the distractions of holding the burning cigarette, eye irritation and coughing. Another is that higher carbon monoxide levels in the smoker's system may lower alertness and reflex speed. In addition, the lit tobacco sometimes ignites flammable or explosive materials in the smoker's work area.

Whatever the reasons, the trend toward adopting anti-smoking measures in the workplace accelerated considerably in the 1990s and has continued as is demonstrated by the Department of Labour's previously noted estimate that almost 70% of American workers are now employed in smoke-free workplaces. Government agencies often have led the way by banning smoking from government workplaces or limiting smoking to areas where it will not be imposed on those seeking a clean air environment. Such protections have even been adopted in some states in which tobacco is an important crop.[76]

Nevertheless, the widespread addiction of the American population to nicotine still dissuades many employers from imposing an absolute ban on smokers in the work force. In addition, as explained below, supported by the tobacco industry's lobbying efforts, some states have adopted laws prohibiting discrimination based on a worker's use of a legal substance, such as tobacco, while away from the workplace. Accordingly, instead of trying to recruit or retain a work force of non smokers, many US employers offer assistance to help smokers overcome their addiction. This assistance often includes providing free clinics at which withdrawal techniques are taught; in some cases, the employer also subsidizes the cost of drugs that aid in such withdrawal efforts.[77] In addition, in an effort to dissuade workers from smoking, employers increasingly have removed cigarette vending machines from the work premises and allow

---

[74] Bureau of National Affairs, Inc., "Where There's Smoke: Problems and Policies Concerning Smoking in the Workplace, A Special Report, 2d Ed.", 1987.

[75] http://slati.lungusa.org.

[76] For example, *see* Tenn. Code § 4–4–121.

[77] One survey of employer sponsored smoking cessation programs found about a 20% success rate regardless of whether the employer offered a monetary incentive to stop smoking. 92 Amer. J. of Public Health 274 (2002).

smoking only during scheduled breaks and only in relatively isolated locations – often places that are outdoors and are unsheltered or only partially sheltered.

Even though there has been substantial progress toward eliminating tobacco smoke from American workplaces, many employers continue to accommodate employees who smoke. Among the possible explanations is a respect for self-determination or a sense of self-righteousness on the part of proprietors and corporate executives who themselves are nicotine addicts. Another is that some employers may not give adequate thought to assessing the costs to the employer resulting from smoking, especially if the employer does not provide health care insurance. Still another possibility is that some employers have made a cost-benefit assessment and conclude that the performance benefits of smoking outweigh the burdens. A rather cynical consideration in support of such a conclusion is the possibility that because smoking shortens an employee's expected lifespan some employers may calculate that the potential reduction in retirement benefits paid by the employer for retired smokers who die prematurely more than offsets the employer's increased medical insurance costs for such workers.

4. REGULATING SMOKING IN UNIONISED WORKPLACES

In those workplaces in which employees have a collective bargaining representative[78] employer initiatives to curb smoking are complicated both by the employer's duty to bargain concerning conditions of employment and the employer's duty to adhere to a collective agreement. Under the National Labour Relations Act, if a majority of employees in an appropriate bargaining unit have selected a bargaining agent, the employer is prohibited from unilaterally changing wages, hours or other terms and conditions of employment without first bargaining to impasse about the proposed change unless the change is required by law.[79] The National Labour Relations Board has held that amending a rule or current practice respecting employee smoking is a change in the conditions of work and, therefore, the change cannot be made without first bargaining to impasse with the employees' bargaining representative unless if the collective agreement specifies the scope of the employer's authority or the procedure for making changes to such rules or practices. An exception to that requirement is that an emergency ban on smoking may be imposed by an employer if there is substantial evidence that the smoking can cause a fire or explosion.[80]

The Federal Labour Relations Authority similarly has ruled that federal government agencies cannot make changes respecting smoking policies without first negotiating with the employees' designated bargaining agent.[81]

Often the more difficult question is whether the parties' collectively bargained agreement has specified the respective prerogatives of management and the employees respecting smoking. In the US there are two ways in which

---

[78] Less than ten percent of the private sector workforce and less than 14% of the total workforce.

[79] For a detailed discussion, see United States monograph in the *International Encyclopedia for Labour Law and Industrial Relations*, Kluwer, at 573–77. Bargaining units in the US normally are at the level of the work facility or the enterprise. Sometimes they are at the level of a craft or other subdivision of the work facility. For a detailed discussion, see *ibid* at 615–26.

[80] *NLRB v. Dynatron/Bondo Corp.*, 176 F.3d 1310, 1315 (11th Cir. 1999).

[81] *Dept. of Health and Human Services v. Federal Labor Relations Aauthority*, 920 F.2d 45 (D.C. Cir. 1990). This rule has been adopted as a formal regulation. 41 Code of Fed. Reg. 102–74.350.

disputes concerning rights and responsibilities established by a collective agreement are resolved. One is through a suit to enforce the agreement or remedy its breach. In the case of almost all private sector collective agreements, although such suits can be brought in federal or state court, federal law governs the substantive rules to be applied in enforcing the agreement.[82] Collective agreements covering most federal government employees are enforced through a special federal agency subject to review by the federal courts.[83] State law and state courts govern the enforcement of collective agreements with state and local workers, but federal courts can intervene in these latter matters when questions are raised under the US Constitution or federal laws or treaties.[84]

The other method of enforcing collective agreements is through the process of grievance arbitration. This is the prevalent enforcement method since most collective agreements, both in the private and government sectors provide that an arbitrator or arbitrators selected by the parties shall decide any disputes concerning the agreement's interpretation or application if the parties are unable to resolve them through grievance discussions. Disagreements as to whether a particular dispute is subject to arbitration can be decided by the courts. However, the courts apply a strong presumption in favour of construing the dispute as being within the scope of the collective agreement's arbitration procedure.[85] In addition, labour arbitration decisions under private sector collective agreements are subject to very limited judicial review. Courts are not to substitute their interpretation for that of the arbitrator regarding the facts or agreement;[86] they can reverse the arbitrator only if the decision was the product of corruption, fraud, lack of fundamental procedural fairness, ignored the parties' agreement, and went beyond the scope of the question submitted for decision or ordered someone to do something illegal.[87] Arbitration decisions involving collective agreements covering federal government workers are subject to somewhat broader review by an administrative agency.[88]

Arbitration is also the primary method for deciding disputes concerning the interpretation or application of collective agreements involving state or local government workers. State law governs the scope of judicial review of those

---

[82] *United Auto Workers v. Hoosier Cardinal Corp.*, 383 US 696 (1966); *Smith v. Evening News Ass'n.*, 371 US 195 (1962); *Charles Dowd Box Co. v. Courtney*, 368 US 502 (1962); *Local 174, Teamsters v. Lucas Flour Co.*, 369 US 95 (1962). Almost all private sector collective agreements are regulated either by the Labour Management Relations Act or the Railway Labour Act. *See* 29 US Code §§ 142, 152, 160, 185; 45 US Code §§ 151, 152, 181.

[83] United States monograph in the *International Encyclopedia for Labour Law and Industrial Relations*, Kluwer, at 605–09. However, as explained in the cited text, many aspects of federal postal worker collective relations are regulated under a separate statute which largely incorporates the provisions of the Labour Management Relations Act.

[84] See, for example, *Abood v. Detroit Board of Education*, 431 US 209 (1977).

[85] For a recent Supreme Court discussion of this doctrine, *see Wright v. Universal Maritime Service Corp.*, 525 US 70 (1998).

[86] Although parties can use multi-member arbitration tribunals, most often cases are submitted to a single arbitrator.

[87] *Eastern Associated Coal Corp. v. UMWA, Dist.*, 17, 531 US 57 (2000); *United Paperworkers International Union v. Misco Inc.*, 484 US 29 (1987).

[88] For a general description, *see* United States monograph in the *International Encyclopedia for Labour Law and Industrial Relations*, Kluwer, at ¶¶ 607, 907.

decisions. Generally, the standard of judicial review is the same as, or even more deferential than, the federal standard for private sector grievance arbitration.[89]

When labour arbitrators are presented with the issue of environmental tobacco smoke, the ultimate question is whether the parties' collective agreement requires or permits the employer to provide a smoke-free work environment.

Before examining the arbitral decisions on this issue, it is interesting to note that prior to the 1990s, a significant minority of labour arbitrators smoked and most (perhaps all) tolerated smoking during hearings even though smoking was not allowed in most courtrooms or legislative hearing rooms. In the latter situations, the prohibition reflected not health concerns or laws imposing such a ban, but rather the cultural attitude that smoking is an informal activity and, therefore, inappropriate to the formal nature of a trial or legislative hearing. In contrast, traditionally labour arbitration has been a relatively informal process under the ultimate joint control of the parties. Hence, labour arbitrators were reluctant to interfere with the parties' customary conduct at such hearings. Increased awareness of the health hazards of smoking, however, changed the attitudes of non-smoking hearing participants and, in time, a growing number of arbitrators (now probably a significant majority) decided to use their authority as presiding officer to ban smoking in the hearing room. Few report any resistance to this change.[90]

A labour arbitrator's responsibility is to enforce the lawful provisions of the collective agreement. Therefore, the first question the arbitrator must answer is what limits the collective agreement places on the employer's authority to regulate the workplace or workforce. That task is complicated by the fact that collective agreements often do not explicitly address the issue of tobacco use. In addition, it is complicated by the general willingness of arbitrators of union-management disputes to treat well-established customary workplace conduct as constituting an implied condition of employment unless the parties' collective agreement expressly provides that past practices have no contractual status.[91] Even if the parties implicitly or explicitly recognize past practices as binding, the parties often differ respecting: a) whether certain conduct was sufficiently

---

[89] *See* for example, *Township of Sugarloaf v. Bowling*, 759 A.2D 913 (PA. 2000); *Port Huron Area School Dist. v. Port Huron Education Ass'n*, 393 N.W.2d 811 (MI 1986); *Chief Administrative Justice v. SEIU*, 422 N.E.2d 776 (MA. 1981).

[90] These observations are personal impressions of the author, a part-time labour arbitrator. They are based on discussions with a large number of fellow arbitrators as well as on personal experience arbitrating in a region in which the smoking rate is higher than the national average. The issue has been explored at meetings of the National Academy of Arbitrators and anecdotes exchanged through the Academy's web-based discussion group and in conversations at professional meetings. The Academy's own conduct is illustrative of the American trend away from smoking. Prior to the late 1980s, the Academy, like most professional organizations, accommodated smoking at its conference sessions by providing ashtrays. With rising objections from non smokers, the Academy's arrangements committees shifted to a policy of asking smokers to sit in a separate section. In the early 1990s the policy changed again and smoking was banned in meeting rooms. A decade later, the customary expectations had become sufficiently established so that members and guests abide by the no-smoking rule regardless of whether it is posted or announced. ·

[91] Although such provisions often are found in collective agreements, other collectively bargained contracts expressly preserve rights established by past practices.

well established and known to both sides so as to constitute a past practice, b) what were the precise parameters of that past practice, and c) whether smoking is a personal activity not to be treated as a work practice or condition.[92] Assuming that smoking is treated as a "practice" of the shop, it is likely that the history of the workplace involved general toleration of smoking but some restrictions, that may have been changed from time-to-time, regarding when and where workers could smoke. Thus, the union is likely to argue that, based on past practice, there is an established right of employees to smoke. The employer, on the other hand, is likely to argue that, based on past practice, there is an established right of management to restrict smoking.

Often the collective agreement, though not explicitly addressing smoking, contains provisions specifying the employer's authority to establish "reasonable" workplace rules or to establish rules protecting employee health and safety. The task of the labour arbitrator, then, is to determine whether an employer imposed no-smoking policy is a reasonable approach to protecting workers from the hazards of environmental smoke. In such situations, arbitrators typically require the employer to allow smoking under circumstances in which non smokers will not be subjected to sidestream smoke and where there is no hazard of fire or explosion.[93] In upholding employer initiated smoking restrictions, arbitrators often find additional support for the reasonableness of the rule if it is accompanied by the employer's willingness to finance employee efforts to quit the habit.[94]

Unions often object to rules restricting smoking on the ground that the employer did not adequately consult with the union before adopting the rule. In such situations the labour arbitrator must first decide whether the collective agreement waived the duty to bargain about this subject. Arbitrators have found such a waiver based on contractual provisions regarding the employer's obligation to provide a safe and healthy workplace.[95] If there has not been a contractual waiver of the duty to bargain about the change, the arbitrator must then decide whether there was adequate consultation prior to the adoption of the new restriction. In some instances, the collective agreement establishes a safety and health committee and the arbitrator will set aside a restriction on smoking if the employer by-passed that committee.[96]

One situation in which labour arbitrators must decide about workplace smoking is when an employee grieves that he or she is being subjected to unwanted environmental smoke. In that type of case the worker's grievance is most likely to prevail if the collective agreement contains a provision promising the workers a healthy work environment. In the absence of such a provision, the arbitrator must decide either that the union and management have implicitly accepted the existence of a smoke-filled work environment as a condition of employment, or that a worker implicitly is entitled to work under tolerable conditions. There is no clear rule for guiding such decisions. However, the

---

[92]   Some arbitrators have characterized smoking as a privilege, not a right, and, therefore, not a vested benefit protected by past practices. For example, *Illinois American Water Co.*, 100 Lab. Arb. Rept. 836, 842 (D. Nielsen, Arb. 1993).

[93]   For example, *Cross Oil & Refining*, 104 Lab. Arb. Rept. 757 (M. Gordon, Arb. 1995).

[94]   For example, *Witco Corp.*, 96 Lab. Arb. Rept. 499 (W. Nelson, Arb. 1991).

[95]   For example, *Lincoln Brass Works*, 102 Lab. Arb. Rept. 872 (B. Haskew, Arb. 1994).

[96]   For example, *Lincoln Brass Works*, above.

strong trend to smoke-free work environments would appear to support the implicit entitlement of a worker to be free from tobacco smoke pollution.

Protection of privacy or autonomy as a limit on employer no-smoking rules

Because of the potential savings in medical insurance costs and reduction of absenteeism, some employers have insisted that not only must workers not smoke anywhere on the employer's premises or in the employer's vehicles, but also that they quit smoking altogether. In one case a city fire fighter challenged a regulation totally prohibiting first-year fire fighters from smoking. Citing the need for fire fighters to be in good health and physical condition, and noting the special risks of smoke inhalation to fire fighters, a federal appellate court rejected the employee's assertion that the regulation was arbitrary and, therefore, violated the fire fighter's right to due process of law. On the other hand, the court indicated that had the argument been raised, it may have been more sympathetic to an assertion that the unequal treatment between first year fire fighters and those with longer experience was a violation of the Constitutional principle of equal protection.[97]

The tobacco industry and its supporters have had some success in getting legislatures to resist efforts to control a worker's conduct when the worker is not engaged in work and is not on or in the employer's property. In response to urgings that privacy or autonomy interests are violated when employers try to intrude into employee conduct away from the workplace, roughly half of the states have adopted laws prohibiting discrimination based on a worker's use of a legal substance, such as tobacco, while away from the workplace and not engaged in work.[98] For example, an Illinois law makes it unlawful to refuse to hire, to dismiss or to disadvantage an employee with respect to compensation, terms, conditions or privileges of employment because the worker uses "lawful products" off the premises during nonworking time unless such use impairs the employee's ability to perform assigned duties. The statute has an exception for non-profit organizations dedicated to discouraging the use of such products. Additionally, it permits employers to have different insurance premiums or benefits for life, disability or health coverage based on the use or non-use of lawful products if the insurance cost is related to such use.[99]

5. THE FUTURE

Efforts to curb smoking have been supported both by Republican and Democratic political leaders and have been adopted by states and local governments in every region of the nation. Although laws that totally prohibit smoking in places such as restaurants and enclosed workplaces have not been yet adopted by any governmental units in the Central region of the nation,[100] even

---

[97] *Grusendorf v. City of Oklahoma City*, 816 F.2d 539 (10 Cir. 1987).

[98] Rothstein, *et al Employment Law*, 1994, at p. 69.

[99] 820 Ill. Comp. Stat. § 55/5.

[100] For example, Iowa, Missouri, Kansas, Nebraska. There is no apparent explanation for this regional gap.

in that part of the country there are state laws that attempt to separate smokers from non smokers in many public places and most government buildings.[101]

While those who resist these laws emphasize the claim that individual freedom of choice is at stake, adoption of restrictions on smoking in government facilities and places of public accommodation has occurred in parts of the country representing the full range of sub-cultural diversity including regions known for embracing the characteristic that Americans sometimes refer to as 'rugged individualism'.[102] Accordingly, there is good reason to expect that in the next five years many more state and local jurisdictions will adopt laws or regulations restricting smoking in enclosed places of public or employee access and will further expand the number of people who work in smoke-free environments. As a result, at some point in the next few years, anti-smoking advocates should no longer have need to fear that the Department of Labour, upon finally facing its clear responsibilities under the Occupational Safety and Health Act, will resort to a watered-down no-smoking rule. Therefore, when political changes place new leadership in the Department, it is to be expected that it will adopt a smoke-free standard for all enclosed workplaces.

---

[101] For an up-to-date list, *see* http://slati.lungusa.org/appendixa.asp.

[102] Examples of the latter include Arizona, Colorado, Texas, West Virginia, Maine and Utah, all of which have imposed such restrictions.